WELCOME TO BOSTON

Bursting with Yankee pride, Boston attracts visitors for its rich past and vibrant present. From Boston Common to Faneuil Hall to Fenway Park, the city is a hub of American history and culture. Buzzing neighborhoods such as the North End, Beacon Hill, and Back Bay mix venerable landmarks and lively street life. On the other side of the Charles River is bustling Cambridge, home of Harvard University and MIT. Wherever you choose to explore, Boston's locavore restaurants, chic galleries, and tempting shops are all easily accessible on satisfying strolls.

TOP REASONS TO GO

★ **Historic Icons:** The Freedom Trail links sites from the American Revolution's start.

★ **The Charles:** The river's bridges and esplanade reward exploration by foot or boat.

★ **Great Museums:** The Museum of Fine Arts and New England Aquarium satisfy curious minds.

★ **Stylish Shopping:** Newbury and Boylston Streets give shopaholics a boutique buzz.

★ **Cuisine:** Seafood restaurants and chef-led hot spots fuel a booming restaurant scene.

★ **Parks and Squares:** Boston Public Garden and Copley Square have prime people-watching.

15 ULTIMATE EXPERIENCES

Boston offers terrific experiences that should be on every traveler's list. Here are Fodor's top picks for a memorable trip.

1 The Swan Boats

No warm weather visit to Boston is complete without taking a spin on one of these iconic, foot-pedal powered Swan Boats. Astonishingly, they've plied this 4-acre pond in America's oldest botanical garden since 1877. *(Ch. 6)*

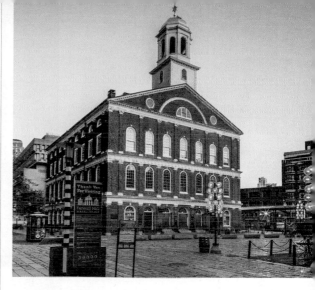

2 Faneuil Hall

Dedicated to the cause of liberty on the eve of the Revolution, Faneuil Hall has seen colonists protesting the Sugar Act and George Washington toasting the nation's birthday. *(Ch. 3)*

3 Fenway Park

The nation's oldest Major League Baseball ballpark, where the Red Sox have played since 1912 and Babe Ruth swung for the fences, is hallowed ground for most Bostonians. *(Ch. 7)*

4 Frog Pond

Ice-skating on the Boston Common Frog Pond is an iconic winter activity. With the golden dome of the State House as a backdrop, it's one for the memory books. *(Ch. 13)*

5 Isabella Stewart Gardner Museum

One of the city's most charming attractions is this small but lovely museum. It's a Venetian palazzo with an eclectic collection and gorgeous gardens. *(Ch. 7)*

6 Lobster Roll

Nothing says "New England" more than seafood, and nothing says it better—or tastier—than a lobster roll. Head to Boston's waterfront, where any number of restaurants beckons. *(Ch. 10)*

7 Samuel Adams Brewery

Tour and Taste Boston's iconic beverage and learn all about the history of brewing in the US. This is where R&D for entire Sam Adams beer line happens. *(Ch. 8)*

8 Museum Of Fine Arts

With almost half a million carefully curated objects spanning the centuries, this massive museum is one of the most highly regarded in the world. *(Ch. 7)*

9 Charles River

Take in a different perspective of the city as you canoe, kayak, or sail downriver on this watery landmark between Boston and Cambridge. *(Ch. 13)*

10 Freedom Trail

Walk back through history and explore our nation's founding on the iconic Freedom Trail, a 2.5-mile route that takes you past the city's most important historic sights. *(Ch. 1)*

11 Acorn Street

This charming one lane cobblestone street, complete with 19th-century row houses and gas lamps, is said to be the city's most photographed street. *(Ch. 2)*

12 Boston Tea Party Ships & Museum

This hands-on, family-friendly, interactive museum includes 3-D holograms, talking portraits, actors clad in Colonial period costumes, and two ship replicas. *(Ch. 5)*

13 Cannoli In "Little Italy"

The North End has an embarrassment of riches for Italian food lovers and cannoli (rolled fried pastry shells filled with sweet ricotta cheese) is a local favorite. *(Ch. 10)*

14 Newbury Street

Boston's version of New York's 5th Avenue is an eight-block-long street jam-packed with upscale shops, trendy cafés, quirky boutiques, and great people-watching. *(Ch. 6)*

15 Boston Public Library

This imposing 1895 Renaissance Revival building has magnificent murals and a Renaissance-style courtyard that's an exact copy of Rome's Palazzo della Cancelleria. *(Ch. 6)*

Fodor's BOSTON

Editorial: Douglas Stallings, *Editorial Director*; Salwa Jabado and Margaret Kelly, *Senior Editors*; Alexis Kelly, Jacinta O'Halloran, and Amanda Sadlowski, *Editors*; Teddy Minford, *Content Editor*; Rachael Roth, *Content Manager*

Design: Tina Malaney, *Art Director*

Photography: Jennifer Arnow, *Senior Photo Editor*

Maps: Rebecca Baer, *Senior Map Editor*; Mark Stroud and Harry Colomb (Moon Street Cartography), David Lindroth, *Cartographers*

Production: Jennifer DePrima, *Editorial Production Manager*; Carrie Parker, *Senior Production Editor*; Elyse Rozelle, *Production Editor*; David Satz, *Director of Content Production*

Business & Operations: Chuck Hoover, *Chief Marketing Officer*; Joy Lai, *Vice President and General Manager*; Stephen Horowitz, *Head of Business Development and Partnerships*

Public Relations: Joe Ewaskiw, *Manager*

Writers: Victoria Abbot Riccardi, Kim Foley MacKinnon, Megan Johnson

Editor: Margaret Kelly

Production Editor: Carrie Parker

Production Design: Liliana Guia

30th Edition

ISBN 978-1-64097-000-7

ISSN 0882–0074

All details in this book are based on information supplied to us at press time. Always confirm information when it matters, especially if you're making a detour to visit a specific place. Fodor's expressly disclaims any liability, loss, or risk, personal or otherwise, that is incurred as a consequence of the use of any of the contents of this book.

PRINTED IN THE UNITED STATES OF AMERICA

10 9 8 7 6 5 4 3 2 1

CONTENTS

1 **EXPERIENCE BOSTON** 15
   Boston Today 16
   What's Where...................... 10
   Boston Planner 22
   Great Itineraries 24
   Free or Almost Free 27
   Back Bay Art and
   Architecture Walk................. 28

2 **BEACON HILL,**
  BOSTON COMMON, AND
  THE OLD WEST END 37
   Beacon Hill and
   Boston Common.................. 40
   The Old West End 49

3 **GOVERNMENT CENTER**
  AND THE NORTH END 51
   Government Center............... 54
   The North End.................... 59

4 **CHARLESTOWN** 65
   Top Attractions 68
   Worth Noting..................... 71

5 **DOWNTOWN BOSTON** 73
   Top Attractions 77
   Worth Noting..................... 78

6 **BACK BAY AND**
  THE SOUTH END 85
   The Back Bay..................... 88
   The South End 97

7 **THE FENWAY** 99
   Top Attractions 103
   Worth Noting.................... 104

8 **BOSTON OUTSKIRTS** 105
   South Boston 109
   Dorchester....................... 109
   Jamaica Plain.................... 111
   Brookline 111

Fodor's Features

Follow the RedBrick Road:
Boston's Freedom Trail................ 30
A Whale of a Tale 272

9 **CAMBRIDGE** 113
   Harvard Square................... 116
   Brattle Street/Tory Row........... 122
   Kendall Square/MIT.............. 125

10 **WHERE TO EAT** 127
   Boston Dining Planner............ 129
   Restaurant Reviews.............. 130

11 **WHERE TO STAY**............. 163
   Boston Lodging Planner 165
   Hotel Reviews 167

12 **NIGHTLIFE AND**
   PERFORMING ARTS 179
   Nightlife Planner 181
   Nightlife 182
   Performing Arts.................. 202

13 **SPORTS AND**
   THE OUTDOORS............. 213
   Fenway Park...................... 214
   Planning......................... 216
   Sports 217
   The Outdoors.................... 223
   Parks 225

CONTENTS

14 SHOPPING............... 227

    Boston Shopping Planner......... 228

    Boston........................... 229

    Cambridge....................... 241

**15 SIDE TRIPS
FROM BOSTON**.............. 245

    Welcome to Side Trips
from Boston..................... 246

    Northwest of Boston 251

    The North Shore................. 259

    South of Boston 270

TRAVEL SMART BOSTON 279

INDEX 293

ABOUT OUR WRITERS....... 303

MAPS

Back Bay Art and
Architecture Walk................. 29

Beacon Hill, Boston Common,
and the Old West End............. 38

Government Center
and the North End................. 52

Charlestown....................... 66

Downtown Boston................. 74

Back Bay and the South End 86

The Fenway...................... 100

Boston Outskirts................. 106

Cambridge....................... 114

Harvard Square and
Brattle Street/Tory Row........... 120

Boston Dining
and Lodging Atlas 153–162

Northwest of Boston 251

Lexington........................ 253

Concord 256

The North Shore................. 260

Salem............................ 263

South of Boston 271

Boston MBTA 304

ABOUT THIS GUIDE

Fodor's Recommendations

Everything in this guide is worth doing—we don't cover what isn't—but exceptional sights, hotels, and restaurants are recognized with additional accolades. Fodor's Choice★ indicates our top recommendations. Care to nominate a new place? Visit Fodors.com/contact-us.

Trip Costs

We list prices wherever possible to help you budget well. Hotel and restaurant price categories from $ to $$$$ are noted alongside each recommendation. For hotels, we include the lowest cost of a standard double room in high season. For restaurants, we cite the average price of a main course at dinner or, if dinner isn't served, at lunch. For attractions, we always list adult admission fees; discounts are usually available for children, students, and senior citizens.

Hotels

Our local writers vet every hotel to recommend the best overnights in each price category, from budget to expensive. Unless otherwise specified, you can expect private bath, phone, and TV in your room. For expanded hotel reviews visit Fodors.com.

Top Picks	Hotels &
★ Fodor's Choice	Restaurants
	⌶ Hotel
Listings	⌷ Number of
✉ Address	rooms
✉ Branch address	⎮⎠⎮ Meal plans
☎ Telephone	✗ Restaurant
🖷 Fax	⌕ Reservations
⊕ Website	⌂ Dress code
✐ E-mail	▭ No credit cards
✇ Admission fee	⑀ Price
☉ Open/closed times	
Ⓜ Subway	**Other**
⊹ Directions or Map coordinates	⇨ See also
	☞ Take note
	⅄ Golf facilities

Restaurants

Unless we state otherwise, restaurants are open for lunch and dinner daily. We mention dress code only when there's a specific requirement and reservations only when they're essential or not accepted.

Credit Cards

The hotels and restaurants in this guide typically accept credit cards. If not, we'll say so.

EUGENE FODOR

Hungarian-born Eugene Fodor (1905–91) began his travel career as an interpreter on a French cruise ship. The experience inspired him to write *On the Continent* (1936), the first guidebook to receive annual updates and discuss a country's way of life as well as its sights. Fodor later joined the U.S. Army and worked for the OSS in World War II. After the war, he kept up his intelligence work while expanding his guidebook series. During the Cold War, many guides were written by fellow agents who understood the value of insider information. Today's guides continue Fodor's legacy by providing travelers with timely coverage, insider tips, and cultural context.

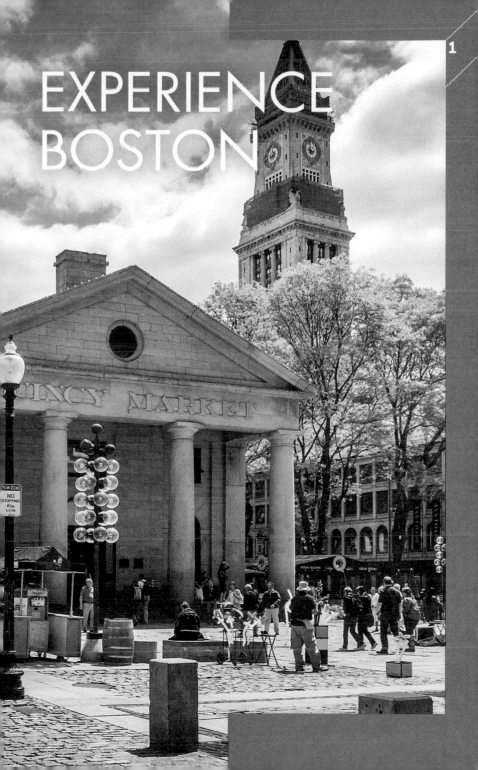

EXPERIENCE BOSTON

BOSTON TODAY

Boston is the undisputed birthplace of American history. It's home to a number of firsts: first public park (Boston Common), first botanical garden (the Public Garden), and even the first phone call (made by Alexander Graham Bell in 1876). Much of the political ferment that spawned the nation happened here, and visitors are often awed by the dense concentration of landmarks. Locals, on the other hand, take them in stride. This is a living city—not a museum—and, as such, its entrepreneurial spirit continues to evolve. Cambridge's Kendall Square, close to the Massachusetts Institute of Technology, is a hotbed of technological progress, while Boston's Innovation District in the Seaport area is home to a growing number of start-ups. Bostonians remain a proud, resilient bunch. This strength was apparent in the aftermath of the Boston Marathon bombings in April 2013, which happened near the Back Bay finish line. "Boston Strong" became the city's unofficial motto in the wake of the attacks, and the marathon continues to go on each year with an estimated 1 million spectators.

Enshrining Art

Although no one refers to Boston as "The Athens of America" anymore, appreciating art seems to be as characteristic of folks here as dropping "R's" and taking the "T." That explains why in recent years the Isabella Stewart Gardner Museum unveiled a stunning complex by architect Renzo Piano, who is also the genius behind Harvard Art Museums' $400-million reinvention. Now, three of the university's major museums—the Fogg, the Busch-Reisinger, and the Arthur M. Sackler—are under one roof.

Harboring Hope

This city has long been defined by its harbor: the first colonists were largely drawn here because of it, and local commerce has been inextricably bound to the water ever since. Over time, development obscured the view, and what was visible wasn't always pretty. Nevertheless, a decades-long, $3.8-billion clean-up effort has paid off. See for yourself on HarborWalk, a 45-mile-long path linking Columbus Park to the New England Aquarium, Seaport, and Fan Pier, with harborside sites, picturesque piers, parks, working wharves, hotel lounges, and urban beaches.

Communing with Kennedys

The year 2013 marked the 50th anniversary of the assassination of John F. Kennedy, and the memory of Boston's beloved native son lingers. Take a 90-minute walking tour covering sites associated with JFK or the inauguration of a 30,000-square-foot wing at the John F. Kennedy Presidential Library & Museum. The legacy of brother Ted is equally apparent next door at the Edward F. Kennedy Institute. The Rose Fitzgerald Kennedy Greenway, a mile-and-a-half string of parks, is named in her honor.

Exercising Options

There are lots of ways to get around Beantown: foot, cab, bus, ferry, subway, trolley, water taxi. But these days there's another eminently practical way for travelers to be transported: three-speed bicycle. The Hubway bike-sharing program makes it easy because pedal pushers can cheaply access one of 1,600 cycles from roughly 180 self-service "docks" citywide. (⇨ *Read how it works in the Travel Smart section.*)

Seeing Stars

Lights! Camera! Action! Those words are being heard a lot lately, because a state tax credit for film producers has translated into a moviemaking boom. As a result, playing "spot the star" is a popular pastime. Big-screen names like Leonardo DiCaprio, Johnny Depp, Jennifer Lawrence, Amy Adams, Denzel Washington, and homegrown celebs Ben Affleck and Mark Wahlberg have all worked here. Ditto for talents such as Jesse Eisenberg, Mila Kunis, and Anna Faris. Interested in an entirely different type of star? The Museum of Science is more stellar than ever thanks to Astronomy After Hours, the museum's free seasonal Friday night stargazing sessions in the Gilliland Observatory.

Changing the Channel

Revitalization of the Fort Point Channel neighborhood has been ongoing for a decade: the Boston Convention & Exhibition Center, the brazen Institute of Contemporary Art, the expanded Boston Children's Museum (by the monster Hood milk bottle), and the opening of Atlantic and Liberty wharves. The area's new high-water marks aren't beside the channel but rather in it: the Boston Tea Party Ships & Museum stand by the Congress Street Bridge, with guides in period garb. On-the-water recreational options allow tour boats, kayaks, and floating restaurants.

Eating Wicked Good Food

Sure, try traditional dishes like baked beans, codfish cakes, and slabs of roast beef at Yankee haunts like Durgin-Park and the Union Oyster House. But Boston lays claim to a long line of innovative chefs. M. Sanzian's invention of Boston cream pie in 1856 made quite a stir among Parker House patrons; a century later, Julia Child launched a culinary revolution from her Cambridge kitchen. Today, top chefs such as Jody Adams, Jamie Bissonnette, Joanne Chang, Tiffani Faison, Barbara Lynch, Ken Oringer, Michael Schlow, Ana Sortun, Lydia Shire, Ming Tsai, and Tony Maws make dining out a gastronomic adventure. These days, Fort Point houses several flashy new restaurants from locals like Lynch and Tsai plus celebrity chefs like Mario Batali, while the North End is an essential stop for mom-and-pop Italian food.

WHAT'S WHERE

The following numbers refer to chapters in the book.

2 Beacon Hill, Boston Common, and the Old West End. If you follow the Freedom Trail, you'll start up on Beacon Hill. The gas-lighted streets behind the gold-domed State House, lined with Federal townhomes, make this a great place to walk. Below Beacon Hill lies Boston Common; off to the north in the Old West End, the big draws are the Museum of Science and TD Garden, home to the Bruins and Celtics, Boston's pro hockey and basketball teams. The Boston Public Market, opened in July 2015, houses vendors selling dairy, fish, meats, and more.

3 Government Center and the North End. Architecture buffs may admire Government Center's brutalist structures, but most out-of-towners scurry past en route to Faneuil Hall and the trio of restored brick warehouses that share its name. Faneuil Hall Marketplace (Quincy Market) is chockablock with boutiques, bars, and a food court, while on the cobbled street, performers vie for attention. Just across the Greenway stands the North End, which

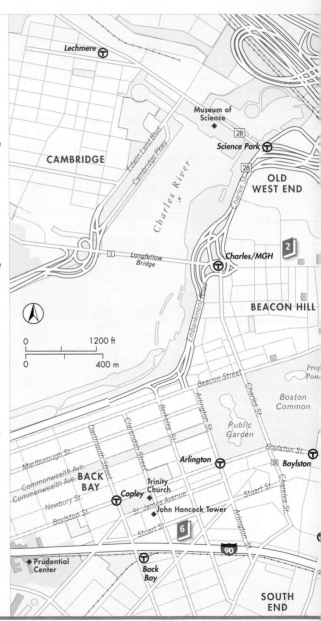

welcomed waves of 19th-century immigrants. Copp's Hill Burying Ground attests to a Puritan past, and Paul Revere House and Old North Church evoke the Revolutionary era.

4 Charlestown. Poised on the banks of Boston Harbor and the Mystic River, Charlestown's top sights can't be missed—literally. The Bunker Hill Monument is a towering tribute to one of the pivotal battles of 1775; the USS *Constitution*, America's Ship of State, flies a tangle of masts and rigging. Gentrification began here 40 years ago, when *Old Ironsides'* home was transformed from a navy yard into a National Historic Site.

5 Downtown. This mazelike section of central Boston scores points for diversity. Freedom Trail walkers come to see sights like the Old South Meeting House and Old State House. Families are drawn by the Aquarium and Children's Museum or enjoy strolling the Greenway. Playgoers flock to the Theater District. There is a mishmash of other districts, too, among them Downtown Crossing, Chinatown, and the loft-y Leather District.

WHAT'S WHERE

6 The Back Bay and South End. In Back Bay stand the city's skyscrapers (Prudential Center and John Hancock Tower) and arguably its most beautiful building, Trinity Church. Given the concentration of high-end shops around Newbury Street, you may want to emulate their couture. More shopping, as well as dining, await in the South End, beyond Huntington Avenue. Rebuilt bowfront houses earned the area a spot in the National Register of Historic Places. The neighborhood is home to the SoWa Open Market, a shopping district with indie artisans and food trucks.

7 The Fenway. Baseball fans, tourists, and intellectuals meet head on in the Fens: a meandering green space that serves as the first "jewel" in Boston's Emerald Necklace. Fenway Park, a veritable shrine to the Boston Red Sox, is just northwest of the Fens. To the south sit the Museum of Fine Arts and Isabella Stewart Gardner Museum. Nearby, the Longwood medical area houses most of the city's top hospitals.

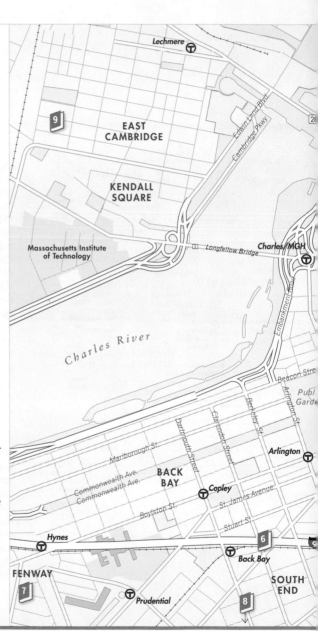

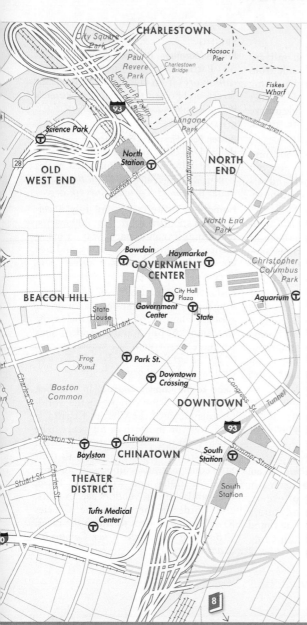

8 Boston Outskirts. South Boston (not the South End) was once a working-class Irish enclave. Its Seaport District is the poster child for waterfront revitalization, thanks to developments like the Boston Convention and Exhibition Center, the Institute of Contemporary Art, Fan Pier, and Liberty Wharf. The area is now rife with swank restaurants and hotels. South of "Southie" are the so-called Streetcar Suburbs, including Dorchester and Jamaica Plain. The former is home to the John F. Kennedy Presidential Library & Museum and University of Massachusetts. Jamaica Plain (J.P.) is home to the Arnold Arboretum, Jamaica Pond, and multicultural Centre Street.

9 Cambridge. The "People's Republic of Cambridge," a separate city across the Charles River, has long been a haven for writers, academics, and iconoclasts. Known for its largest landowners, Harvard University and MIT, Cambridge has gentrified in Harvard, Kendall, and Central squares, while maintaining its fair share of quirky cafés, independent bookstores, galleries, and shops.

BOSTON PLANNER

When to Go

Weather-wise, late spring and fall are the optimal times for a visit. Aside from mild temperatures, May offers blooming gardens throughout the city and October finds the surrounding countryside ablaze with colorful foliage. At both times, however, expect hordes of visitors.

More than 250,000 students flood into the area each September, then pull out again in May and June. So hotels and restaurants fill up especially fast on move-in, move-out, and graduation weekends.

The good news is that Boston is a four-season destination. Along with the most reliable sunshine, summer brings sailboats to Boston Harbor, concerts to the Esplanade, and café tables to sidewalks. Summer is prime time for a beach vacation, but advance planning is imperative.

Even winter has its pleasures. The cultural season heats up when it's cold, and Boston gets a holiday glow, thanks to the thousands of lights strung around the Common, Public Garden, and Commonwealth Avenue Mall. During the post-Christmas lull, temperatures fall, but lodging prices do, too. You're only two to three hours south of quality ski slopes in Maine, New Hampshire, and Vermont.

Mark Your Calendar

Greater Boston Convention & Visitors Bureau. There's *always* something happening in Boston. For a full selection of events, consult the Greater Boston Convention & Visitors Bureau. Kiosks can be found at Prudential Center and Boston Common. ☎ *888/733–2678* ⊕ *www.bostonusa.com.*

SPRING

Boston Marathon. Runners race 26.2 miles on Patriot's Day (⊕ *www.bostonmarathon.org*) from Hopkinton to Boylston Street, and horsemen reenact **Paul Revere's Ride** (⊕ *www.nationallancers.org*).

SUMMER

Boston Pops Fireworks Spectacular. Independence Day is capped off with pyrotechnics, real and musical, along the Charles River. ⊠ *DCR Hatch Shell on the Esplanade, Beacon Hill* ⊕ *www.July4th.org.*

Harborfest. Boston's six-day July 4 celebration sponsors more than 200 events, including Revolutionary War reenactments, special museum exhibits, and free concerts. ⊕ *www.bostonharborfest.com.*

FALL

Boston Film Festival. Get "reel" at the week-long fall Boston Film Festival, a forum for evolving filmmakers to express their artistic visions. At BFF, top independent films premiere, many with Massachusetts ties. ⊠ *200 Stuart St., Theater District* ⊕ *www.bostonfilmfestival.org.*

Head of the Charles Regatta. In October, sculling crew teams compete in the world-famous Head of the Charles Regatta, a tradition for more than 50 years. The world's largest two-day rowing event draws athletes from their teens to their 80s, collegians and clubbers, from England, Australia, and worldwide. Food, beer, and clothing vendors set up tents, and hordes gather atop the Charles River's many bridges to watch the races. ⊠ *Banks of the Charles River, Cambridge* ⊕ *www.hocr.org.*

FALL OUTSIDE THE CITY

Working Waterfront Festival. New Bedford's commercial anglers, celebrating America's oldest industry, cast their nets and strut their stuff at the Working Waterfront Festival, showcasing their skills (and fresh seafood) in fishing demos. There's also live entertainment; this festival is free and held the last weekend in September. ⊠ *State Pier, New Bedford* ⊕ *www.workingwaterfrontfestival.org.*

Essex County's **Topsfield Fair** (⊕ *www.topsfieldfair.org*) happens in October; Salem hosts witch trial reenactments and other **Haunted Happenings** (⊕ *www.hauntedhappenings.com*).

Celebrate turkey day at Plymouth's **Thanksgiving Parade** (⊕ *www.usathanksgiving.com*), or with dinner at **Plimoth Plantation** (⊕ *www.plimoth.org*).

Getting Around

"America's Walking City," with all its historic nooks and crannies, is best explored on foot. But when hoofing it around town seems too arduous, there are alternatives.

BY CAR

In a place where roads evolved from cow paths and colonial lanes, driving is no simple task. One-way streets, inconsistent signage, lack of parking, and aggressive local drivers add to the confusion. Nevertheless, having your own car is helpful, especially if you're taking side trips.

If you would rather leave the driving to someone else, you can call a cab or hail one on the street 24/7: they wait outside major hotels and line up near hot spots like Harvard Square, South Station, Faneuil Hall, Long Wharf, and the Theater District. Rides within the city cost $2.60 for the first 1/7 mile and 40¢ for each 1/7 mile thereafter (tolls, where applicable, are extra). Uber and Lyft are also popular options.

BY PUBLIC TRANSIT

The "T," as the subway system is affectionately nicknamed, is the cornerstone of a far-reaching public transit network that also includes aboveground trains, buses, and ferries. Its five color-coded lines will put you within a block of virtually anywhere. Subways operate from 5 am to 1 am (schedules vary by line). The same goes for buses, which crisscross the city and suburbia.

A standard adult subway fare is $2.25 with a CharlieCard or $2.75 with a ticket or cash. For buses it's $1.70 with a CharlieCard or $2 with a ticket or cash (more for an Inner or Outer Express bus). Commuter rail and ferry fares depend on the route. For details on schedules, routes, and rates, contact the **MBTA** (☏ *617/222–3200* or *800/392–6100* ⊕ *www.mbta.com*).

CHARLIEPASS AND THE CHARLIECARD

Retro music fans recall the 1959 Kingston Trio hit about a fellow named Charlie, who, unable to pay his fare, "never returned" from Boston's subway system. Charlie lives on as the mascot of the MBTA's ticketing scheme. There are two stored-value options: a plastic CharlieCard or paper CharlieTicket, both of which are reusable and reloadable with cash, or credit or debit cards. At a station, obtain a CharlieCard from an attendant or a CharlieTicket from a machine. CharlieCards can't yet be used on commuter rail, commuter boats, or Inner Harbor ferries. For most visitors, the best deal will be the unlimited one-day ($12) or one-week ($21.25) LinkPass.

GREAT ITINERARIES

BOSTON IN 1 DAY

Twenty-four hours isn't nearly enough time to absorb the city, but it's certainly worth a try. Start in the Back Bay, where you can stroll the shopping mecca that is Newbury Street before crossing over Boylston into Copley Square. Cross the Boston Marathon finish line, then head into the Boston Public Library, an architectural and literary wonder. Stroll through the Boston Public Garden and Boston Common before turning down Charles Street into historic Beacon Hill, where you can leisurely shop or grab a bite while wandering along the quaint cobblestone sidewalks. Head through Faneuil Hall on the way to the North End, Boston's beloved "Little Italy" neighborhood. Grab a cannoli at Modern Pastry (FYI, Mike's Pastries across the street is known for its hoards of tourists, but the locals go to Modern) and pick up the Freedom Trail in North Square, where you can also check out the Paul Revere House. You're just around the corner from the Old North Church and Copp's Hill Burying Ground, and within steps of a variety of delectable Italian restaurants along Hanover and Salem streets. Cap off your day with a heaping plate of pasta.

BOSTON IN 4 DAYS

Clearly every traveler moves at a different pace. One might be content to snap a pic of the Bunker Hill Monument and push on; another might insist on climbing the obelisk's 294 spiraling steps and studying the adjacent museum's military dioramas. Nevertheless, in four days you should be able to see the city highlights without feeling rushed. With more time, explore nearby communities.

Day 1: Hit the Trail

About 3 million visitors walk the Freedom Trail every year—and there's a good reason why: taken together, the route's 16 designated sites offer a crash course in colonial history. That makes the trail a must, so tackle it sooner rather than later. Linger wherever you like, leaving ample time to lunch amid magicians and mimes in Faneuil Hall Marketplace. Next, cross into the North End via the Rose F. Kennedy Greenway. Though hemmed in by water on three sides, this bustling neighborhood is crammed full of history. Don't miss Old North Church and Paul Revere's former home (Boston's oldest house, constructed almost 100 years prior to his arrival); then, after wandering the narrow Italianate streets, fortify yourself with espresso or gelato and cross the Charlestown Bridge. See the currently drydocked USS *Constitution* and climb the Bunker Hill Monument (a breathtaking site in more ways than one) before catching the MBTA water shuttle back to Downtown.

Day 2: Head for the Hill

Named for the signal light that topped it in the 1800s, Beacon Hill originally stood a bit taller until locals dug earth off its summit and used it as landfill nearby. Now its shady, gas-lighted streets, brick sidewalks, tidy mews, and stately Brahmin brownstones evoke a bygone Boston. (Lovely Mt. Vernon Street opens onto leafy Louisburg Square, where Louisa May Alcott once lived.) When soaking up the ambience, take in some of Beacon Hill's major sites from Boston's various theme trails: gold-domed Massachusetts State House, Boston Athenaeum, Granary Burying Ground, and the African Meeting House. Afterward, stroll to the Common and Public Garden. Both promise greenery and great people-watching. If shopping's your bag, cruise for antiques along Charles Street, the thoroughfare that separates them. In the evening, feast on dumplings or dim sum in pan-Asian Chinatown or go upscale at an ubertrendy restaurant (Ostra, Teatro) in the Theater District where restorations in recent years have been, well, dramatic.

Day 3: Take It All In

From the Back Bay you can cover a lot of Boston's attractions in a single day. Start at the top (literally) by ogling 360-degree views from the Prudential Center's Skywalk Observatory. (Or end with a drink at Top of the Hub upstairs.) Once you understand the lay of the land, plot a route based on your interests. Architecture aficionados can hit the ground running at the neoclassical Public Library (the nation's first) and Romanesque Trinity Church. Shoppers can opt for stores along Newbury Street and in Copley Place, a high-end mall anchored by Neiman Marcus. Farther west in the Fens, other choices await. Art connoisseurs might view the collections at the Museum of Fine Arts or Isabella Stewart Gardner Museum. Carnival-like Fenway Park beckons baseball fans to the other side of the Fens. Depending on your taste—and ticket availability—cap the day with a Symphony Hall concert or a Red Sox game.

Day 4: On the Waterfront

A spate of openings and reopenings in recent years has transformed the Seaport District into a magnet for museum hoppers. Begin your day artfully at the Institute of Contemporary Art (ICA) on Fan Pier. The mod museum's bold cantilevered design (computer printer?) makes the most of its waterside location. It makes the most of its art collection, too, by offering programs and exhibits that appeal to little tykes and hard-to-please teens. Keep

---

> **TIPS**
>
> Getting your mitts on Red Sox tickets may be tricky. Savvy spectators reserve online as soon as tickets become available. Procrastinators may get lucky at the ticket office next to Gate A, which opens at 10 am. If you strike out, a limited number are sold at Gate E two hours before game time. As a last resort, sidle up to that guy holding up tickets just after the opening pitch and haggle—or watch the action at Game On!, a sports bar attached to Fenway Park.
>
> Think you need a car to venture beyond Boston? Think again. Gray Line Sightseeing Tours (☎ 800/343-1328 or 781/986-6100 ⊕ www.graylineboston.com) offers coach excursions for Boston-based day-trippers to Lexington, Concord, Salem, and Plymouth. In autumn, foliage-themed tours are available, too.
>
> Diehard sightseers may want to buy a pass. The "Go Boston" Card (☎ 866/628-9027 ⊕ www.smartdestinations.com) covers more than 49 attractions, tours, and excursions and is sold in one-day to one-week increments from $56; CityPass (☎ 888/330-5008 ⊕ www.citypass.com) covers five key sites for $56.

tiny tots engaged with a run to the Children's Museum and its innovative exhibits; then relive a turning point in American history at the Boston Tea Party Ships & Museum's authentic-looking vessels and interpretive center. From there, continue on to that waterfront favorite, the New England Aquarium, where you can watch the sea lions and penguins frolic. On the wharf, sign up for a harbor cruise, whale-watch boat trip, or ferry ride to the beckoning Boston Harbor Islands.

BEYOND BOSTON PROPER

Day 1: Explore Cambridge

From pre-Revolutionary times, Boston was the region's commercial center and Cambridge was the burbs: a retreat more residential than mercantile, with plenty of room to build the nation's first English-style, redbrick university. The heart of the community—geographically and practically—is still Harvard Square. It's easy enough to while away a day here browsing the shops, lounging at a café, then wandering to the riverbank to watch crew teams practice. But Harvard Square is also the starting point for free student-led campus tours, as well as for strolls along Brattle Street's "Tory Row" (No. 105 was occupied by both Washington and Longfellow!). Fine museums include the family-friendly Harvard Museum of Natural History, loaded with dinosaur bones, gemstones, and 21 million stuffed critters. The newly remodeled Harvard Art Museum is another must. End your day in true Cantabrigian style by taking in a concert or lecture at Harvard's Sanders Theatre or with a show at the American Repertory Theater, helmed by noted artistic director Diane Paulus.

Day 2: Step Back in Time

You only have to travel a short distance to visit historic places you read about in grade school. For a side trip to the 17th century, head 35 miles southeast to Plymouth. The famed rock doesn't live up to its hype, but Plimoth Plantation (an open-air museum re-creating life among Pilgrims) and the *Mayflower II* are well worth the trip. A second option is to veer northwest to explore Revolutionary-era sites in handsome, suburban Lexington. Start at the National Heritage Museum for a recap of the events that kicked off the whole shebang; then proceed to Battle Green, where "the shot heard round the world" was fired. After stopping by Minute Man National Historical Park, continue to Concord to tour the homes of literary luminaries like Ralph Waldo Emerson, Louisa May Alcott, and Nathaniel Hawthorne. Conclude your novel excursion with a walk around Walden Pond, where transcendentalist Henry David Thoreau wrote one of the founding documents of the environmental movement, "Walden."

Day 3: A Shore Thing

Anyone eager to taste the salt air or feel the surge of the sea should take a day trip to the North Shore towns of Salem and Gloucester. The former has a Maritime National Historic Site—complete with vintage wharves and warehouses—that proves there is more to the notorious town than just witchcraft.

Prefer to just sun yourself? Year-round nature lovers flock to Crane Beach in Ipswich, about an hour north of Boston. Part of a 1,200-acre wildlife refuge, it includes 4 miles of sand rimmed by scenic dunes. For a quick sand-in-every-crevice experience, take either the MBTA's Harbor Express ferry south to Nantasket Beach in Hull or the commuter train north to Manchester-by-the-Sea's Singing Beach, where the sand has such a high silica content that it actually sings (or at least squeaks) when you walk on it.

FREE OR ALMOST FREE

Let Freebies Ring
Freedom may not be free, but the **Freedom Trail** is. So are 13 of the 16 attractions lining its route. The **Massachusetts State House**, for instance, schedules complimentary tours weekdays, 10 to 3:30. The **USS Constitution Museum**, meanwhile, is open daily from April through October from 9 to 6 and November through March 10 to 5. Mid-April through November, you're also welcome to join a free **National Park Service Tour** of the trail. Check with the Boston National Historical Park for details.

Try a Different Trail
The Freedom Trail's success has spawned other no-cost routes, including the **Black Heritage Trail** (⇨ *Box in the Beacon Hill, Boston Common, and Old West End chapter*) and the **Walk to the Sea**, which traces four centuries of civic development. The **Irish Heritage Trail** and **Boston Women's Heritage Trail** are other options. The former covers sites relating to Irish-Americans from John Hancock to John F. Kennedy as well as the 1840s Potato Famine. The latter pays tribute to ladies who gained fame as suffragettes and artists.

Artsy Alternatives
Symphony Hall (a Victorian showpiece with superb acoustics) and the historic **Boston Public Library** both run free tours. Moreover, the **Museum of Fine Arts** and **Institute of Contemporary Art** waive admission on Wednesday and Thursday evenings after 4 pm and 5 pm, respectively. It's worth noting as well that the **Isabella Stewart Gardner Museum** is always free for those under 18—and anyone named Isabella! Penny pinchers should also watch for events such as the Fenway Cultural District's **Opening Our Doors Day.** Held each Columbus Day, it sponsors concerts, lectures, and tours at some of Boston's finest arts institutions.

Enjoy Free Parking
When you're ready for a rest, remember that relaxing in Boston's parks doesn't cost a dime. If you have already visited the **Public Garden** and **Boston Common**, check out the **Emerald Necklace**. In 1878 landscape architect Frederick Law Olmsted began work on six pocket parks strung together by a greenway, resembling jewels on a necklace. Linked to the Common and Public Garden by the Commonwealth Avenue Mall, the Necklace extends over 7 miles from Downtown through Arnold Arboretum in Jamaica Plain to Franklin Park in Dorchester.

Feeling Indecisive?
HarborWalk (⊕ *www.bostonharborwalk. com*) offers visitors a bit of everything on its interconnected 45 miles of waterside trails and pathways. Aside from scenic viewpoints (some with free binoculars), amenities range from parks, public art installations, and interpretive panels to a pocket Maritime Museum at the Fairmont Battery Wharf Hotel. HarborWalk also provides a glimpse at paid attractions like the New England Aquarium's Marine Mammal Center. Traversing the trail could take days. Download a free audio guide from the website and enjoy a narrated stroll from Christopher Columbus Park to Fan Pier.

BACK BAY ART AND ARCHITECTURE WALK

In the folklore of American neighborhoods, Boston's Back Bay stands alongside New York's Park Avenue as a symbol of chic. In the 1850s, Boston's power brokers built Victorian mansions amidst lush green spaces and by the time the Great Depression hit, Back Bay was the city's poshest address.

Copley Square

Back Bay's hub embraces a range of architectural styles from Romanesque Revival to Bauhaus-inspired skyscrapers. The Fairmont Copley Plaza Hotel's Oak Long Bar + Kitchen, with its catbird seats, offers a perfect place to begin your walk. Designed in 1912 by Henry Hardenbergh, five years after his famed Plaza Hotel in Manhattan, the hotel underwent a $20-million centenary renovation. Boston Public Library, housing 9 million books, was conceived by architects Mead, McKim, and White, who opted for an Italian Renaissance palazzo. Modern architect Philip Johnson's 1972 wing respectfully reflects the original.

The Pru and Commonwealth Avenue

Heading up Boylston Street with the Library on your left, you'll find the 52-story Prudential Tower, built in the 1960s, and affectionately dubbed "The Pru." On a clear day from the top-floor Skywalk you'll see sweeping vistas of Boston. With the Pru behind you, take Gloucester Street across Newbury to Commonwealth Avenue, turn left, and cross Massachusetts Avenue to 395 Commonwealth, where you'll see Louis Comfort Tiffany's famous Ayer Mansion.

Boston Public Garden

At the bronze statue of George Washington at the foot of Commonwealth Avenue, enter Boston Public Garden, America's oldest botanical garden sheltering 24 acres of weeping willow, elm, spruce, and dawn redwood. The garden pond is spanned by a faux-suspension bridge while the garden itself abuts Boston Common. Exit with Washington behind you, walk one block to Newbury Street, turn right and head toward the Gothic Revival Church of the Covenant, on Newbury Street at Berkeley, built in 1867.

Trinity Church and Hancock Tower

Take Berkeley one block to Boylston Street then head back up Boylston to Copley Square to visit its crowning centerpiece, Trinity Church. This 1877 Romanesque Revival masterpiece conceived by Henry Hobson Richardson exhibits sumptuously carved interior woodwork, ornamented ceilings, and intricate stained glass. Another architectural award winner is the John Hancock Tower, behind Trinity Church on St. James Street. Architect Henry Cobb managed to construct this modernist 58-story building without disrupting the square's scale and proportion in part by having the glass panels mirror Trinity Church.

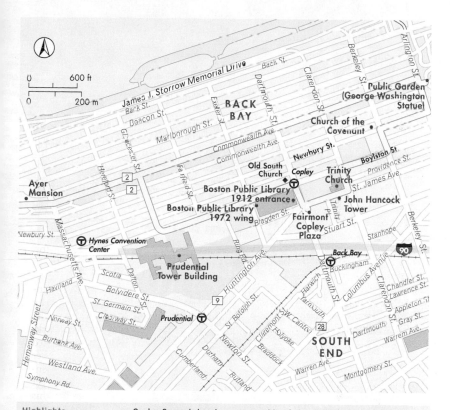

Highlights	Copley Square's handsome ensemble of church, park, library, and skyscraper; Boston Public Garden
Where to Start	Oak Bar in Fairmont Copley Square Hotel
Length	1.6 miles or about 1½ hours with brief stops
Where to End	Back where you started, people-watching from an Oak Bar settee or a bench facing the library or Trinity Church
Best Time to Go	Any time when you can see all the sights in daylight
Worst Time to Go	Rush hour or when it's raining or very cold
Editor's Choice	Strolling the mall in the snow, tiny cloister garden behind Trinity Church, George Washington with his attendant pigeons

FOLLOW THE REDBRICK ROAD

BOSTON'S FREEDOM TRAIL

by Mike Nalepa

Paul Revere

Paul Revere's ride

Benjamin Franklin

Samuel Adams

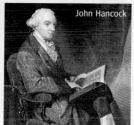
John Hancock

The Freedom Trail is more than a collection of historic sites related to the American Revolution or a suggested itinerary connecting Boston's unique neighborhoods. It's a chance to walk in the footsteps of our forefathers — literally, by following a crimson path on public sidewalks — and pay tribute to the figures all school kids know, like Paul Revere, John Hancock, and Ben Franklin. In history-proud Boston, past and present intersect before your eyes not as a re-creation but as living history accessible to all.

Boston played a key role in the dramatic events leading up to the American Revolution. Many of the founding fathers called the city home, and many of the initial meetings and actions that sparked the fight against the British took place here. In one day, you can visit Faneuil Hall—the "Cradle of Liberty"—where outraged colonial radicals met to oppose British authority; the site of the incendiary Boston Massacre; and the Old North Church, where lanterns hung to signal Paul Revere on his thrilling midnight ride. Colonists may have originally landed in Jamestown and Plymouth, but if you really want to see where America began, come to Boston.

Boston Common, Founder's Statue

⊕ www.nps.gov/bost
⊕ www.thefreedomtrail.org

☎ 617/242-5642

✉ Admission to the Freedom Trail itself is free. Several museum sites charge for admission. However, most attractions are free monuments, parks, and landmarks.

The 1729 Old South Meeting House, where many protesters gathered during the American Revolution.

PLANNING YOUR TRAIL TRIP

THE ROUTE

The 2½-mi Freedom Trail begins at Boston Common, winds through Downtown, Government Center, and the North End, and ends in Charlestown at the USS *Constitution*. The entire Freedom Trail is marked by a red line on the sidewalk; it's made of paint or brick at various points on the Trail. ⇨ *For more information on Freedom Trail sites, see listings in Neighborhood chapters.*

GETTING HERE AND BACK

The route starts near the Park Street T stop. When you've completed the Freedom Trail, head for the nearby Charlestown water shuttle, which goes directly to the downtown area. For schedules and maps, visit ⊕ *www.mbta.com.*

TIMING

If you're stopping at a few (or all) of the 16 sites, it takes a full day to complete the route comfortably. ■TIP➔ If you have children in tow, you may want to split the trail into two or more days.

VISITOR CENTERS

There are Freedom Trail information centers in Boston Common (Tremont Street), at 15 State Street (near the Old State House), and at the Charlestown Navy Yard Visitor Center (in Building 5).

TOURS

The National Park Service's free 90-minute Freedom Trail walking tours begin at the Boston National Historical Park Visitor Center at 15 State Street and cover sites from the Old South Meeting House to the Old North Church. Check online for times; it's a good idea to show up at least 30 minutes early, as the popular tours are limited to 30 people.

Half-hour tours of the USS *Constitution* are offered Tuesday through Sunday. Note that visitors to the ship must go through security screening.

FUEL UP

The trail winds through the heart of Downtown Boston, so finding a quick bite or a nice sit-down meal isn't difficult. Quincy Market, near Faneuil Hall, is packed with cafés and eateries. Another good lunch choice is one of the North End's wonderful Italian restaurants.

WHAT'S NEARBY

For a short break from revolutionary history, be sure to check out the major attractions nearby, including the Boston Public Garden, New England Aquarium, and Union Oyster House.

Above: In front of the Old State House a cobblestone circle marks the site of the Boston Massacre.

⚫ TOP SIGHTS

Benjamin Franklin Statue

Boston Common

The Granary Burial Grounds

Faneuil Hall

Park Street Church

Old North Church

Bunker Hill Monument

BOSTON COMMON TO FANEUIL HALL

Old State House

GOVERNMENT CENTER

Cambridge St.

0   100 yards
0   100 meters

Clinton St.

Hancock St.
Joy St.
Bowdoin St.
Somerset St.
Court St.

Boston National
Historic Park
Visitor Center

Faneuil Hall

Chatham St.

BEACON HILL
Mt. Vernon St.

State House

King's Chapel
and Burying
Ground

Old State
House

Boston
Massacre
Site

State St.

India S

Walnut St.
Beacon St.

School St.

Granary
Burying
Ground

Ben Franklin
Statue

Old Corner
Bookstore

Congress St.

Kilby St.

Milk St.

Broad St.

Franklin St.

Boston
Common

Park St.

Park Street
Church

PARK ST.

Old South
Meeting
House

Washington St.

Devonshire St.

Arch St.

Federal St.

KEY
--- Freedom Trail

Start: near the
Park Street T stop.

Freedom Trail
Foundation Center
Information

Many of the Freedom Trail sites between Boston Common and the North End are close together. Walking this 1-mile segment of the trail makes for a pleasant morning.

THE ROUTE

Begin at ★ **Boston Common,** then head for the **State House,** Boston's finest example of Federal architecture. Several blocks away is the **Park Street Church,** whose 217-foot steeple is considered to be the most beautiful in New England. The church was actually founded in 1809, and it played a key role in the movement to abolish slavery.

Reposing in the church's shadows is the ★ **Granary Burying Ground,** final resting place of Samuel Adams, John Hancock, and Paul Revere. A short stroll to Downtown brings you to **King's Chapel,** founded in 1686 by King James II for the Church of England.

Follow the trail past the **Benjamin Franklin statue** to the **Old Corner Bookstore** site, where Hawthorne, Emerson, and Longfellow were published. Nearby is the **Old South Meeting House,** where arguments in 1773 led to the Boston Tea Party. Overlooking the site of the Boston Massacre is the city's oldest public building, the **Old State House,** a Georgian beauty.

In 1770 the Boston Massacre occurred directly in front of here—look for the commemorative stone circle.

Cross the plaza to ★ **Faneuil Hall** and explore where Samuel Adams railed against "taxation without representation." ■**TIP→** A good mid-trail break is the shops and eateries of Faneuil Hall Marketplace, which includes Quincy Market.

Old Corner Book Store Site

★ = **Fodor's**Choice ★ = Highly Recommended ☾ = Family Friendly

NORTH END TO CHARLESTOWN

USS *Constitution*

Freedom Trail sites between Faneuil Hall and Charlestown are more spread out along 1½ miles. The sites here, though more difficult to reach, are certainly worth the walk.

THE ROUTE

When you depart Faneuil Hall, follow the red stripe to the North End, Boston's Little Italy.

The ☾ **Paul Revere House** takes you back 200 years—here are the hero's own saddlebags, a toddy warmer, and a pine cradle made from a molasses cask. It's also air-conditioned in the summer, so try to stop here in mid-afternoon to escape the heat. Next to the Paul Revere House is one of the city's oldest brick buildings, the **Pierce-Hichborn House**.

Next, peek inside a place guaranteed to trigger a wave of patriotism: the ★ **Old North Church** of "One If by land, two If by sea" fame. Then head toward **Copp's**

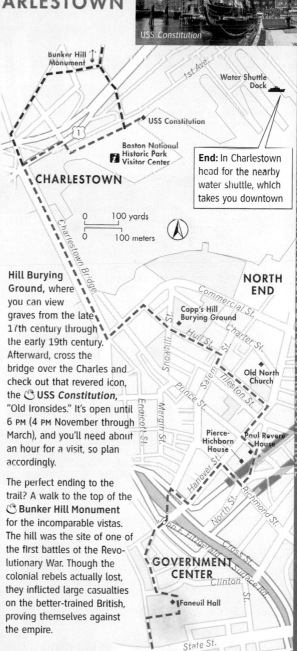

Bunker Hill Monument

1st Ave.

Water Shuttle Dock

USS Constitution

i Boston National Historic Park Visitor Center

CHARLESTOWN

End: In Charlestown head for the nearby water shuttle, which takes you downtown

Charlestown Bridge

0   100 yards
0   100 meters

NORTH END

Commercial St.

Copp's Hill Burying Ground

Charter St.

Snowhill St.

Hull St.

Salem St.

Tileston St.

Old North Church

Prince St.

Margin St.

Endicott St.

Hanover St.

Pierce-Hichborn House

Paul Revere House

North St.

Richmond St.

John F. Fitzgerald Surface Rd.

Cross St.

GOVERNMENT CENTER

Clinton St.

◆ Faneuil Hall

State St.

Paul Revere House

Hill Burying Ground, where you can view graves from the late 17th century through the early 19th century. Afterward, cross the bridge over the Charles and check out that revered icon, the ☾ **USS *Constitution*,** "Old Ironsides." It's open until 6 PM (4 PM November through March), and you'll need about an hour for a visit, so plan accordingly.

The perfect ending to the trail? A walk to the top of the ☾ **Bunker Hill Monument** for the incomparable vistas. The hill was the site of one of the first battles of the Revolutionary War. Though the colonial rebels actually lost, they inflicted large casualties on the better-trained British, proving themselves against the empire.

BEACON HILL, BOSTON COMMON, AND THE OLD WEST END

Getting Oriented

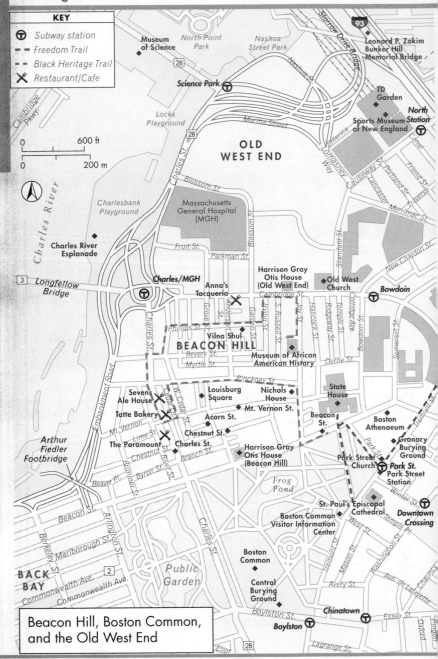

KEY

- **T** Subway station
- – – Freedom Trail
- – – Black Heritage Trail
- ✕ Restaurant/Cafe

Beacon Hill, Boston Common, and the Old West End

GETTING HERE AND AROUND

Bounded by Cambridge Street on the north, Beacon Street on the south, the Charles River Esplanade on the west, and Bowdoin Street on the east, the small neighborhood of Beacon Hill is best experienced on foot. Take the Green Line to the Park Street stop, and walk through the Common toward Beacon Street; the Red Line to the Charles/MGH stop and stroll past the shops on Charles Street; or the Blue Line to Bowdoin Street and head toward the State House.

The Old West End is accessible by T: jump off the Red Line at the Charles/MGH stop to reach the Esplanade; get off the Green Line at Science Park for the Museum of Science and a view of the Leonard P. Zakim Bunker Hill Bridge; and exit the Green Line at North Station for the Garden or for commuter trains to the northern suburbs.

TIMING AND SAFETY

Beacon Hill can be easily explored in an afternoon; add an extra few hours if you wish to linger on the Common and in the shops on Charles Street or tour the Black Heritage Trail. For the most part, the Old West End can be covered in a few hours. Extend your visit to a full day to take in the Museum of Science and an IMAX movie, check out the Sports Museum, and catch a game at the Garden.

At night, stay in well-lighted areas and avoid remote corners of the Common. Also be cautious walking late at night on Causeway Street—on nongame nights this area can be a bit deserted.

BEACON HILL QUICK BITES

Grab a sandwich at **The Paramount** (⌧ *44 Charles St., between Chestnut and Mt. Vernon Sts.*) or pub grub at **Sevens Ale House** (⌧ *77 Charles St., between Pinckney and Mt. Vernon Sts.*). Grab a cappuccino and croissant at **Tatte Bakery** (⌧ *70 Charles St., at Mt. Vernon St.*).

TOP REASONS TO GO

- Tour the State House and experience colonial history.

- Discover the history of Boston's African American community on the Black Heritage Trail.

- Explore the picture-perfect brownstones lining cobblestone streets.

- Meander through the Common and check out the Granary Burying Ground, the final resting place of Sam Adams, John Hancock, and Paul Revere.

- Window-shop for antiques on Charles Street.

- Enjoy the thrill of discovery at the Museum of Science.

- Catch a glimpse of the Leonard P. Zakim Bunker Hill Memorial Bridge at night awash in blue lights.

- Root for the home team (Celtics or Bruins) or check out the Sports Museum at the TD Garden.

FREEDOM TRAIL SIGHTS

- Boston Common
- The State House
- Park Street Church
- Granary Burying Ground

OLD WEST END QUICK BITES

In the Old West End follow the locals to **Anna's Taqueria** (⌧ *242 Cambridge St.*) for the yummiest Mexican takeout around.

Sightseeing
★★★★
Dining
★★★
Lodging
★★★
Shopping
★★★★
Nightlife
★★★

Past and present home of the old-money elite, contender for the "Most Beautiful" award among the city's neighborhoods, and hallowed address for many literary lights, Beacon Hill is Boston at its most Bostonian. The redbrick elegance of its narrow streets sends you back to the 19th century just as surely as if you had stumbled into a time machine. But Beacon Hill residents would never make the social faux pas of being out of date. The neighborhood is home to hip boutiques and trendy restaurants, frequented by young, affluent professionals rather than DAR (Daughters of the American Revolution) matrons.

BEACON HILL AND BOSTON COMMON

By Kim Foley
MacKinnon

Once the seat of the Commonwealth's government, Beacon Hill was called "Trimountain" and later "Tremont" by early colonists because of its three summits, Pemberton, Mt. Vernon Hill, and Beacon Hill, and named for the warning light set on its peak in 1634. In 1799 settlers leveled out the ground for residences, using it to create what is now Charles Street; by the early 19th century the crests of the other two hills were also lowered.

When the fashionable families decamped for the new development of the Back Bay starting in the 1850s, enough residents remained to ensure that the south slope of the Hill never lost its Brahmin character.

By the mid-20th century, most of the multistory single-family dwellings on Beacon Hill were converted to condominiums and apartments, which are today among the most expensive in the city.

A good place to begin an exploration of Beacon Hill is at the Boston Common Visitor Information Center *(below)*, where you can buy a map or a complete guide to the Freedom Trail.

TOP ATTRACTIONS

Acorn Street. Surely the most photographed street in the city, Acorn is Ye Olde Colonial Boston at its best. Leave the car behind, as the cobblestone street may be Boston's roughest ride (and so narrow that only one car can squeeze through at a time). Delicate row houses line one side, and on the other are the doors to Mt. Vernon's hidden gardens. Once the homes of 19th-century artisans and tradespeople, these little jewels are now every bit as prestigious as their larger neighbors on Chestnut and Mt. Vernon streets. ⊠ *Between West Cedar and Willow Sts., Beacon Hill* Ⓜ *Park.*

FAMILY

Fodor'sChoice

★

Boston Common. Nothing is more central to Boston than the Common, the oldest public park in the United States and undoubtedly the largest and most famous of the town commons around which New England settlements were traditionally arranged. Dating from 1634, Boston Common started as 50 acres where the freemen of Boston could graze their cattle. (Cows were banned in 1830.) Latin names are affixed to many of the Common's trees; it was once expected that proper Boston schoolchildren be able to translate them.

On Tremont Street near Boylston stands the 1888 **Boston Massacre Memorial**; the sculpted hand of one of the victims has a distinct shine from years of sightseers' caresses. The Common's highest ground, near the park's Parkman Bandstand, was once called Flagstaff Hill. It's now surmounted by the **Soldiers and Sailors Monument,** honoring Civil War troops. The Common's only body of water is the **Frog Pond,** a tame and frog-free concrete depression used as a children's wading pool and spray fountain during steamy summer days and for ice-skating in winter. It marks the original site of a natural pond that inspired Edgar Allan Poe to call Bostonians "Frogpondians." In 1848 a gushing fountain of piped-in water was created to inaugurate Boston's municipal water system.

On the Beacon Street side of the Common sits the splendidly restored **Robert Gould Shaw 54th Regiment Memorial,** executed in deep-relief bronze by Augustus Saint-Gaudens in 1897. It commemorates the 54th Massachusetts Regiment, the first Civil War unit made up of free black people, led by the young Brahmin Robert Gould Shaw. He and half of his troops died in an assault on South Carolina's Fort Wagner; their story inspired the 1989 movie *Glory.* The monument—first intended to depict only Shaw until his abolitionist family demanded it honor his regiment as well—figures in works by the poets John Berryman and Robert Lowell, both of whom lived on the north slope of Beacon Hill in the 1940s. This magnificent memorial makes a fitting first stop on the Black Heritage Trail. ⊠ *Bounded by Beacon, Charles, Tremont, and Park Sts., Beacon Hill* ⊕ *www.boston.gov/parks/boston-common* Ⓜ *Park St., Boylston.*

Boston Common Visitor Information Center. This center, run by the Greater Boston Convention and Visitors Bureau, is on the Tremont Street side of Boston Common. It's well supplied with stacks of free pamphlets about Boston, including a useful guide to the Freedom Trail, which begins in the Common. You can also book tours and pick up souvenirs here. ⊠ *139 Tremont St., Beacon Hill* ☎ *617/536–4100* ⊕ *www. bostonusa.com* Ⓜ *Park St.*

Several Founding Fathers rest at the Granary Burial Ground, a picturesque Freedom Trail stop.

Central Burying Ground. The Central Burying Ground may seem an odd feature for a public park, but remember that in 1756, when the land was set aside, this was a lonely corner of the Common. It's the final resting place of Tories and Patriots alike, as well as many British casualties of the Battle of Bunker Hill. The most famous person buried here is Gilbert Stuart, the portraitist best known for his likenesses of George and Martha Washington; he died a poor man in 1828. The Burying Ground is open daily 9 to 5. ⊠ *Boylston St. near Tremont, Beacon Hill* ⊕ *www.cityof-boston.gov/parks/hbgi/CentralBuryingCentral.asp* Ⓜ *Park St., Boylston.*

Granary Burying Ground. "It is a fine thing to die in Boston," A. C. Lyons, an essayist and old Boston wit, once remarked, alluding to the city's cemeteries, among the most picturesque and historic in America. If you found a resting place here at the Old Granary, as it's called, chances are your headstone would have been elaborately ornamented with skeletons and winged skulls. Your neighbors would have been impressive, too: among them are Samuel Adams, John Hancock, Paul Revere, and Benjamin Franklin's parents. Note the winged hourglasses carved into the stone gateway of the burial ground; they are a 19th-century addition, made more than 150 years after this small plot began receiving the earthly remains of colonial Bostonians. ⊠ *Entrance on Tremont St., Beacon Hill* ⊕ *www.thefreedom-trail.org/freedom-trail/granary-burying-ground.shtml* Ⓜ *Park St.*

Louisburg Square. One of Beacon Hill's most charming corners, Louisburg Square (proper Bostonians always pronounce the "s") was an 1840s model for a town-house development that was never built on the Hill because of space restrictions. Today, the grassy square, enclosed by a wrought-iron fence, belongs collectively to the owners of the houses facing it. The statue at the north end of the green is of Columbus, the one at the south end of Aristides the Just; both were donated in 1850 by a Greek merchant who lived on the square. The houses, most of which are now divided into apartments and condominiums, have seen their share of famous tenants, including author and critic William Dean Howells at Nos. 4 and 16, and the Alcotts at No. 10 (Louisa May not only lived but also died here, on the day of her father's funeral). In 1852 the singer Jenny Lind was married in the parlor of No. 20. Louisburg Square is also the current home of former U.S. Secretary of State John Kerry.

There's a legend that Louisburg Square was the location of the Rev. William Blaxton's spring, although there's no water there today. Blaxton, or Blackstone, was one of the first Bostonians, having come to the Shawmut Peninsula in the mid-1620s. When the Puritans, who had settled in Charlestown, found their water supply inadequate, Blaxton invited them to move across the river, where he assured them they would find an "excellent spring." Just a few years later, he sold them all but 6 acres of the peninsula he had bought from the Native Americans and decamped to Rhode Island, seeking greater seclusion; a plaque at 50 Beacon Street commemorates him. ⊠ *Between Mt. Vernon and Pickney Sts., Beacon Hill* Ⓜ *Park St.*

FAMILY **Museum of African American History.** Ever since runaway slave Crispus Attucks became one of the famous victims of the Boston Massacre of 1770, the African American community of Boston has played an important part in the city's history. Throughout the 19th century, abolition was the cause célèbre for Boston's intellectual elite, and during that time, blacks came to thrive in neighborhoods throughout the city. The Museum of African American History was established in 1964 to promote this history. The umbrella organization includes a trio of historic sites: the Abiel Smith School, the first public school in the nation built specifically for black children; the African Meeting House, where in 1832 the New England Anti-Slavery Society was formed under the leadership of William Lloyd Garrison; and the African Meeting House on the island of Nantucket, off the coast of Cape Cod. Park Service personnel lead tours of the **Black Heritage Trail**, starting from the Shaw Memorial on Boston Common. The museum is the site of activities, including lectures, children's storytelling, and concerts focusing on black composers. ⊠ *46 Joy St., Beacon Hill* ☎ *617/725-0022* ⊕ *maah. org* ☜ *$10* ☾ *Closed Sun.* Ⓜ *Park St.*

WORTH NOTING

Beacon Street. Some New Englanders believe that wealth is a burden to be borne with a minimum of display. Happily, the early residents of Beacon Street were not among them. They erected many fine architectural statements, from the magnificent State House to grand patrician mansions. Here are some of the most important buildings of Charles Bulfinch, the ultimate designer of the Federal style in America: dozens of bowfront row houses, the Somerset Club, and the glorious Harrison Gray Otis House. ⊠ *Beacon Hill* Ⓜ *Park St.*

Boston Athenaeum. It was William Tudor, one of the cofounders of the Boston Athenæum, who first compared Boston with Athens because of its many cultural and educational institutions; Bostonians still proudly guard the title "Athens of America." One of the oldest libraries in the country, the Athenæum was founded in 1807 from the seeds sown by the Anthology Club (headed by Ralph Waldo Emerson's father) and moved to its present imposing quarters—modeled after Palladio's Palazzo da Porta Festa in Vicenza, Italy—in 1849. Only 1,049 proprietary shares exist for membership in this cathedral of scholarship, and most have been passed down for generations; the Athenæum is, however, open for use by qualified scholars, and yearly memberships are open to all by application.

The first floor is open to the public and houses an art gallery with rotating exhibits, marble busts, porcelain vases, lush oil paintings, and books. The children's room is also open for the public to browse or read a story in secluded nooks overlooking the Granary Burying Ground. Take the guided tour to spy one of the most marvelous sights in the world of Boston academe, the fifth-floor Reading Room. With two levels of antique books, comfortable reading chairs, high windows, and assorted art, the room appears straight out of a period movie, rather than a modern scholarly institution. Only eight people can fit in the tiny elevator to the fifth floor, so call at least 24 hours in advance to reserve your spot on the tour. Among the Athenæum's holdings are most of George Washington's private library and the King's Chapel Library, sent from England by William III in 1698. With a nod to the Information Age, an online catalog contains records for more than 600,000 volumes. The Athenæum extends into 14 Beacon Street. ⊠ *10½ Beacon St., Beacon Hill* ☎ *617/227–0270* ⊕ *www.bostonathenaeum.org* ⊠ *Free* Ⓜ *Park St.*

Charles Street. Chockablock with antiques shops, clothing boutiques, small restaurants, and flower shops, Charles Street more than makes up for the general lack of commercial development on Beacon Hill. You won't see any glaring neon; in keeping with the historic character of the area, even the 7-Eleven has been made to conform to the prevailing aesthetic standards. Notice the old-fashioned signs hanging from storefronts—the bakery's loaf of bread, the florist's topiary, the tailor's spool of thread, and the chiropractor's human spine. Once the home of Oliver Wendell Holmes and the publisher James T. Fields (of the famed Bostonian firm of Ticknor and Fields), Charles Street sparkles at dusk from gas-fueled lamps, making it a romantic place for an evening stroll. ⊠ *Between Beacon and Cambridge Sts., Beacon Hill* Ⓜ *Charles/ MGH, Park St.*

Chestnut Street. Delicacy and grace characterize virtually every structure on this street, from the fanlights above the entryways to the wrought-iron boot scrapers on the steps. Author and explorer Francis Parkman lived here, as did the lawyer Richard Henry Dana (who wrote *Two Years Before the Mast*), and 19th-century actor Edwin Booth, brother of John Wilkes Booth. Edwin Booth's sometime residence, 29A, dates from 1800, and is the oldest house on the south slope of the hill. Also note the **Swan Houses,** at Nos. 13, 15, and 17,

The Black Heritage Trail

2

Until the end of the 19th century, the north side of opulent Beacon Hill contained a vibrant free black community—more than 8,000 at its peak—who built houses, schools, and churches that stand to this day. In the African Meeting House, once called the Black Faneuil Hall, orators rallied against slavery. The streets were lined with black-owned businesses. The black community has since shifted to other parts of Boston, but visitors can rediscover this 19th-century legacy on the Black Heritage Trail.

Established in the late 1960s, the self-guiding trail stitches together 14 sites along a 1½-mile walk. Park rangers give daily tours Monday through Saturday, Memorial Day through Labor Day, at 10 am, noon, and 2 pm, starting from the Shaw Memorial in Boston Common. To tour on your own, pick up brochures from the **Museum of African American History** (✉ 46 Joy St.) or download one online at ⊕ maah.org/trail.htm.

Start at the stirring **Robert Gould Shaw 54th Regiment Memorial** in Boston Common. Shaw, a young white officer from a prominent Boston abolitionist family, led the first black regiment to be recruited in the North during the Civil War. From here, walk up Joy Street to 5–7 Pinckney Street to see the 1797 **George Middleton House,** Beacon Hill's oldest existing home built by blacks. Nearby, the **Phillips School** at Anderson and Pinckney streets was one of Boston's first integrated schools. The **John J. Smith House,** at 86 Pinckney, was a rendezvous point for abolitionists and escaping slaves, and the **Charles Street Meeting**

House, at Mt. Vernon and Charles streets, was once a white Baptist church and later a black church and community center. In 1876 the building became the site of the **African Methodist Episcopal Church,** which was the last black institution to leave Beacon Hill, in 1939. The **Lewis and Harriet Hayden House** at 66 Phillips Street, the home of freed slaves turned abolitionists, was a stop on the Underground Railroad. Harriet Beecher Stowe, author of *Uncle Tom's Cabin,* visited here in 1853 for her first glimpse of fugitive slaves. The Haydens reportedly kept a barrel of gunpowder under the front step, saying they'd blow up the house before they'd surrender a single slave. At **2 Phillips Street,** John Coburn, cofounder of a black military company, ran a gaming house, described as a "private place for gentlemen."

The five residences on **Smith Court** are typical of African American Bostonian homes of the 1800s, including No. 3, the 1799 clapboard house where William C. Nell, America's first published black historian and a crusader for school integration, boarded from 1851 to 1865. At the corner of Joy Street and Smith Court is **Abiel Smith School,** the city's first public school for black children. The school's exhibits interpret the ongoing struggle started in the 1830s for equal school rights. Next door is the venerable **African Meeting House,** which was the community's center of social, educational, and political activity. The ground level houses a gallery; in the airy upstairs, you can imagine the fiery sermons that once rattled the upper pews.

commissioned from Charles Bulfinch by Hepzibah Swan as dowry gifts for her three daughters. Complete with Adam-style entrances, marble columns, and recessed arches, they are Chestnut Street at its most beautiful. ⊠ *Between Walnut and Charles Sts., Beacon Hill* Ⓜ *Charles/MGH, Park St.*

Harrison Gray Otis House. Harrison Gray Otis, a U.S. senator, Boston's third mayor, and one of the Mt. Vernon Proprietors (a group of prosperous Boston investors), built in rapid succession three of the city's most splendidly ostentatious Federal-era houses, all designed by Charles Bulfinch and all still standing. This, the third Harrison Gray Otis House, was the grandest. Now the headquarters of the American Meteorological Society, the house was once freestanding and surrounded by English-style gardens. The second Otis house, built in 1800 at 85 Mt. Vernon Street, is now a private home. The first Otis house, built in 1796 on Cambridge Street, is the only one open to the public. Otis moved into 45 Beacon Street in 1805, and stayed until his death in 1848. His tenure thus extended from the first days of Beacon Hill's residential development almost to the time when many of the Hill's prominent families decamped for the Back Bay, which was just beginning to be filled at the time of Otis's death. ⊠ *45 Beacon St., Beacon Hill* Ⓜ *Park St.*

Mt. Vernon Street. Mt. Vernon Street, along with Chestnut Street, has some of Beacon Hill's most distinguished addresses. Mt. Vernon is the grander of the two, however, with houses set back farther and rising taller; it even has a freestanding mansion, the second Harrison Gray Otis House, at No. 85. Henry James once wrote that Mt. Vernon Street was "the only respectable street in America," and he must have known, as he lived with his brother William at No. 131 in the 1860s. He was just one of many literary luminaries who resided here, including Julia Ward Howe, who composed "The Battle Hymn of the Republic" and lived at No. 32, and the poet Robert Frost, who lived at No. 88. ⊠ *Between Hancock and Charles Sts., Beacon Hill* Ⓜ *Charles/MGH, Park St.*

Nichols House. The only Mt. Vernon Street home open to the public, the Nichols House was built in 1804 and is attributed to Charles Bulfinch. It became the lifelong home of Rose Standish Nichols (1872–1960), Beacon Hill eccentric, philanthropist, peace advocate, and one of the first female landscape designers. Although Miss Nichols inherited the Victorian furnishings, she added a number of colonial-style pieces to the mix, such as an American Empire rosewood sideboard and a bonnet-top Chippendale highboy. The result is a delightful mélange of styles. Nichols made arrangements in her will for the house to become a museum, and knowledgeable volunteers from the neighborhood have been playing host since then. To see the house, you must take a tour (included in the price of admission). Check the website for special events and exhibits. ⊠ *55 Mt. Vernon St., Beacon Hill* ☎ *617/227–6993* ⊕ *www. nicholshousemuseum.org* 🎫 *$10* ☩ *Nov.–Mar., closed Sun.–Wed.; Apr.– Oct., closed Sun.* Ⓜ *Park St.*

Park Street Church. If this Congregationalist church at the corner of Tremont and Park streets could sing, what joyful noise it would be. Samuel Smith's hymn "America" was first sung inside the church, which was designed by Peter Banner and erected in 1809–10, on July 4, 1831. The country's oldest musical organization, the Handel & Haydn Society, was founded here in 1815. In 1829 William Lloyd Garrison began his long public campaign for the abolition of slavery here. The distinguished steeple is considered by many critics to be the most beautiful in New England. Just outside the church, at the intersection of Park and Tremont streets (and the main subway crossroads of the city), is **Brimstone Corner.** Whether the name refers to the fervent thunder of the church's preachers, the gunpowder that was once stored in the church's crypt, or the burning sulfur that preachers once scattered on the pavement to attract potential churchgoers, we'll never know—historians simply can't agree. ✉ *1 Park St., Beacon Hill* ☎ *617/523–3383* ⊕ *www.parkstreet.org* ✆ *Tours offered mid-June– Aug. only* Ⓜ *Park St.*

St. Paul's Episcopal Cathedral. Though it looks a bit like a bank, St. Paul's is actually the first Boston structure built in the Greek Revival style (1820). It was established by a group of wealthy and influential patriots who wanted a wholly American Episcopal parish—the two existing Episcopal churches, Christ Church (Old North) and Trinity, were both founded before the Revolution—that would contrast with the existing colonial and "gothick" structures around town. The building was to be topped with an entablature showing St. Paul preaching to the Corinthians—but the pediment remained uncarved for 190 years. Finally, in 2012, Philadelphia-based sculptor Donald Lipski, chosen out of a field of 150 artists, inscribed a nautilus shell into the pediment on a blue background, making for a contemporary and striking monument. ✉ *138 Tremont St., Beacon Hill* ☎ *617/482–5800* ⊕ *www. stpaulboston.org* Ⓜ *Park St.*

FAMILY
Fodor's Choice
★

State House. On July 4, 1795, the surviving fathers of the Revolution were on hand to enshrine the ideals of their new Commonwealth in a graceful seat of government designed by Charles Bulfinch. Governor Samuel Adams and Paul Revere laid the cornerstone; Revere would later roll the copper sheathing for the dome.

Bulfinch's neoclassical design is poised between Georgian and Federal; its finest features are the delicate Corinthian columns of the portico, the graceful pediment and window arches, and the vast yet visually weightless golden dome (gilded in 1874 and again in 1997). During World War II the dome was painted gray so that it would not reflect moonlight during blackouts and thereby offer a target to anticipated Axis bombers. It's capped with a pinecone, a symbol of the importance of pinewood, which was integral to the construction of Boston's early houses and churches; it also serves as a reminder of the state's early connection to Maine, once part of Massachusetts.

Inside the building are Doric Hall, with its statuary and portraits; the Hall of Flags, where an exhibit shows the battle flags from all the wars in which Massachusetts regiments have participated; the Great

Hall, an open space used for state functions that houses 351 flags from the cities and towns of Massachusetts; the governor's office; and the chambers of the House and Senate. The Great Hall contains a giant, modernistic clock designed by New York artist R. M. Fischer. Its installation in 1986 at a cost of $100,000 was roundly slammed as a symbol of legislative extravagance. There's also a wealth of statuary, including figures of Horace Mann, Daniel Webster, and a youthful-looking President John F. Kennedy in full stride. Just outside Doric Hall is *Hear Us*, a series of six bronze busts honoring the contributions of women to public life in Massachusetts. But perhaps the best-known piece of artwork in the building is the carved wooden *Sacred Cod*, mounted in the Old

> ## DUCK TOURS
>
> Boston Duck Tours is a Boston fixture, taking more than half a million people every year on unique amphibious tours: Boylston Street, Tremont Street, and the River Charles, all in one 80-minute trip. Tours depart from the Prudential Center and the Museum of Science, and run seven days a week, rain or shine, from late March to late November (all ducks are heated). Tickets are $39.50 for adults, $27 for kids ages 3–11, and $10.50 for kids ages 2 and under. Reserve tickets early. A seasonal tour is offered from the New England Aquarium (☎ 617/267–3825 ⊕ www.boston-ducktours.com).

State House in 1784 as a symbol of the commonwealth's maritime wealth. It was moved, with much fanfare, to Bulfinch's structure in 1798. By 1895, when it was hung in the new House chambers, the representatives had begun to consider the Cod their unofficial mascot—so much so that when *Harvard Lampoon* wags "codnapped" it in 1933, the House refused to meet in session until the fish was returned, three days later. You can take a guided tour or do a self-guided tour. ⊠ *Beacon St. between Hancock and Bowdoin Sts., Beacon Hill* ☎ *617/727–3676* ⊕ *www.sec.state.ma.us/trs/trsidx.htm* 🎟 *Free* ⊙ *Closed weekends* Ⓜ *Park St.*

FAMILY **Vilna Shul.** This historic treasure, one of the oldest synagogues in the region, is the focus of both ongoing renovation and research. The two-story brick building was completed in 1919 by Jews from Vilna (or Vilnius), the capital of present-day Lithuania. Modeled after the great synagogue of Vilna, it's the last remaining immigrant-era synagogue in Boston and stands in a neighborhood that was once deeply Jewish. The building, abandoned in 1985 after the congregation dropped to a single member, was bought by the Boston Center for Jewish Culture, which is overseeing its restoration. Above the doorway gleams renewed gilded Hebrew lettering; the hand-carved ark and the stained-glass Star of David are worth a peek; and murals depicting traditional themes are being uncovered from beneath seven layers of paint. Three skylights flood the space with natural light. Guided tours are available; call ahead to arrange. ⊠ *14–18 Phillips St., Beacon Hill* ☎ *617/523–2324* ⊕ *www.vilnashul.org* 🎟 *Donations accepted* ⊙ *Closed Sat.* Ⓜ *Charles/MGH.*

THE OLD WEST END

There are just a few reminders here of what was once the Old West End: a few brick tenements and a handful of monuments, including the first house built for Harrison Gray Otis. What once was a tangled web of streets housing myriad ethnic groups succumbed to a vast urban renewal project in the 1960s designed by I. M. Pei. The biggest surviving structures in the Old West End with any real history are two public institutions, Massachusetts General Hospital and the former Suffolk County Jail, which dates from 1849 and was designed by Gridley Bryant. The onetime prison is now part of the luxurious, and wryly named, Liberty Hotel.

Behind Massachusetts General and the sprawling Charles River Park apartment complex (famous among Storrow Drive commuters as the place with signs reading "If you lived here, you'd be home now") is a small grid of streets recalling an older Boston. Here are furniture and electric-supply stores, a discount camping-supply house (Hilton's Tent City), and many of the city's most popular watering holes. The main drag here is Causeway Street. North Station and the area around it, on Causeway between Haverhill and Canal streets, provide service to commuters from the northern suburbs and cheap brews to local barflies, and can be jammed when there's a game at the TD Garden, home of the Bruins and Celtics.

In addition to the Garden, the innovative Museum of Science is one of the more modern attractions of the Old West End. In the skyline, you'll see the Leonard P. Zakim Bunker Hill Bridge, which spans the Charles River just across from the TD Garden.

TOP ATTRACTIONS

FAMILY
Fodor's Choice
★

Museum of Science. With 15-foot lightning bolts in the Theater of Electricity and a 20-foot-long Tyrannosaurus rex model, this is just the place to ignite any child's scientific curiosity. More than 550 exhibits cover astronomy, astrophysics, anthropology, medical progress, computers, and the organic and inorganic earth sciences. Children learn the physics behind everyday play activities such as swinging and bumping up and down on a teeter-totter in the "Science in the Park" exhibit. The perennial favorite, "Dinosaurs: Modeling the Mesozoic," lets kids become paleontologists and examine dinosaur bones, fossils, and tracks. The Charles Hayden Planetarium produces exciting programs on astronomical discoveries. The museum also includes the Mugar Omni Theater, a five-story dome screen. The huge projection allows the audience to practically experience the action on-screen. Try to get tickets in advance online or by phone. ⊠ *Science Park at Charles River Dam, Old West End* ☎ *617/723–2500* ⊕ *www.mos.org* ⊠ *$25* Ⓜ *Science Park.*

WORTH NOTING

Leonard P. Zakim Bunker Hill Memorial Bridge. The crown jewel of the "Big Dig" construction project, the 1,432-foot-long Leonard P. Zakim Bunker Hill Memorial Bridge (or Zakim Bridge, for short), was designed by Swiss bridge architect Christian Menn and is one of the widest cable-stayed hybrid bridges ever built, and the first to use an asymmetrical design. The towers evoke the Bunker Hill Monument, and the distinctive fan shape of the cables gives the bridge a modern flair. The bridge was named for both Lenny Zakim, a local civil-rights activist who headed the New England Region of the Anti-Defamation League (and died of cancer in 1999) and the Battle of Bunker Hill, a defining moment in U.S. history. One of the best spots to view the bridge is from the Charlestown waterfront across the river. The best viewing is at night, when the illuminated bridge glows blue; sometimes other colors are used, like pink, to commemorate breast cancer awareness month. ⊠ *Old West End ⊕ www.leonardpzakimbunkerhillbridge.org.*

NEED A BREAK

✗ **Harvard Gardens. A Beacon Hill legend, this was the first bar in the city to get its liquor license after the repeal of Prohibition. Once considered a dive bar, it's much more upscale today, with a menu of tasty grilled fare, like gourmet burgers and steak tips and a scrumptious brunch, including a spectacular Bloody Mary. It opened in 1930, and was owned by the same family until the 1990s. Their classic Reuben provides a solid start to a day's exploring. The place is often packed with doctors and nurses enjoying postshift drinks. ⊠ 316 Cambridge St., Old West End ☎ 617/523–2727 ⊕ www.harvardgardens.com Ⓜ Charles/MGH.**

Old West Church. Built in 1806 using the design of builder and architect Asher Benjamin, this imposing United Methodist church stands, along with the Harrison Gray Otis House next door, as a reminder of the area's more fashionable days. The church was a stop on the Underground Railroad, and it was the first integrated congregation in the country, giving open seating to blacks and whites alike just before 1820. The building narrowly escaped demolition in the 1950s, when most of the West End was razed; thankfully it was saved and was named a historic landmark in 1971. ⊠ *131 Cambridge St., Old West End ☎ 617/227–5088 ⊕ www.oldwestchurch.org* ☾ *Closed Mon. and Sat.* Ⓜ *Bowdoin, Government Center.*

FAMILY **Sports Museum of New England.** The fifth and sixth levels of the TD Garden house the Sports Museum of New England, where displays of memorabilia and photographs showcase local sports history and legends. Take a tour of the locker and interview rooms (off-season only), test your sports knowledge with interactive games, and see how you stand up to life-size statues of heroes Carl Yastrzemski and Larry Bird. Call ahead to confirm open hours because it closes often for events. ⊠ *TD Garden, 100 Legends Way, Old West End ⊹ Use west premium seating entrance ☎ 617/624–1234 ⊕ www.sportsmuseum.org* ☜ *$12* Ⓜ *North Station.*

GOVERNMENT CENTER AND THE NORTH END

Getting Oriented

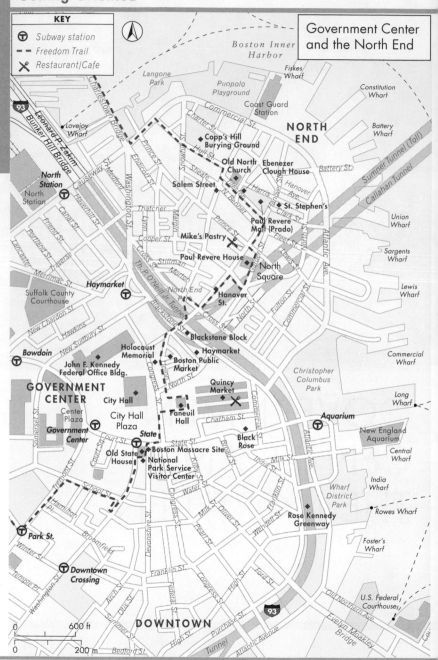

KEY
- Ⓣ Subway station
- – – Freedom Trail
- ✕ Restaurant/Cafe

Government Center and the North End

GETTING HERE AND AROUND

Government Center is best explored on foot. After a $113 million renovation, which closed the station for two years, the T reopened this modern station to great acclaim in 2016. Other nearby Green Line stops include Park Street and Haymarket. On the Blue Line, the nearest stations are State and Bowdoin. All of these stations are within a five-minute walk of Government Center Station. The T is your best bet for accessing the North End. Get off the Orange Line at Haymarket and walk southeast to Hanover Street; take a left there to enter the North End. Alternatively, exit the Blue Line at Aquarium and walk northeast on Atlantic Avenue, past Christopher Columbus Park, to access the North End.

TIMING AND SAFETY

You can easily spend several hours hitting the stores, boutiques, and historic sites of the Faneuil Hall and Quincy Market complex. On Friday and Saturday join crowds at the Haymarket farmers' market (wear good walking shoes, as the cobblestones get slippery with trampled produce).

Allow two hours for a walk through the North End, longer if you plan on dawdling in a café. This part of town is made for strolling, day or night. Many people like to spend part of a day at Quincy Market, then head over to the North End for dinner—the district has an impressive selection of traditional and contemporary Italian restaurants.

Be cautious in the Government Center area late at night. The North End is a relatively safe neighborhood; you'll have plenty of company day or night.

GOVERNMENT CENTER QUICK BITES

Quincy Market near Government Center is filled with stalls of every imaginable food, from lobster rolls to Indian to ice cream. Grab your grub and enjoy it outside on the benches between the North and South markets.

TOP REASONS TO GO

■ Shop 'til you drop at the North and South markets of Quincy Marketplace.

■ Imagine the debates of old during a tour of historic Faneuil Hall.

■ Grab a slice of Pizzeria Regina's cheesy best on the way through Quincy Market.

■ Enjoy a pint with a side of live Irish music at the Black Rose.

■ Come hungry, leave happy! Enjoy the delicious Italian fare in the North End, Boston's Little Italy.

■ Visit Old North Church and relive the night of Paul Revere's Ride.

■ Visit Paul Revere's house, the oldest standing home in Boston, to experience colonial life in Boston.

FREEDOM TRAIL SIGHTS

■ Boston Massacre Site

■ Copp's Hill Burying Ground

■ Faneuil Hall

■ Old North Church

■ The Old State House

■ Paul Revere House

NORTH END QUICK BITES

Head to **Mike's Pastry** (✉ *300 Hanover St.*) for cappuccino, cannoli, and people-watching in this bustling café.

Sightseeing
★★★★
Dining
★★★★★
Lodging
★★★★
Shopping
★★★★
Nightlife
★★★★★

Government Center is a section of town Bostonians love to hate. Not only does it house what they can't fight—City Hall—but it also contains some of the bleakest architecture since the advent of poured concrete; but hope is dawning for change. In 2016, the ugly and outdated Government Center T station was renovated and a stunning glass entrance now greets commuters. The plaza is home to feisty political rallies, free summer concerts, and occasional festivals, which transform the stark space into a block party. On the corner of Tremont and Court streets, look for the landmark Steaming Kettle, a gilded kettle cast in 1873 that once boiled around the clock. (It now marks a Starbucks.) More historic buildings are just a little farther on: 18th-century Faneuil Hall and the bustling Quincy Market.

GOVERNMENT CENTER

Updated by
Kim Foley
MacKinnon

The curving six-story Center Plaza building, across from the Government Center T stop and the broad brick desert of City Hall Plaza, echoes the much older Sears Crescent, a curved commercial block next to the Government Center T stop. The Center Plaza building separates Tremont Street from Pemberton Square and the old and "new" courthouses to the west.

The warren of small streets on the northeast side of Government Center is the North End. For visitors, Government Center is usually just a way station to get to Faneuil Hall, Quincy Market, and other downtown attractions, unless there happens to be a festival scheduled. Come during the annual Jimmy Fund Scooper Bowl ice cream event in June or during the city's July 4 festival, and you'll find bleak City Hall Plaza a bustling, jubilant spot.

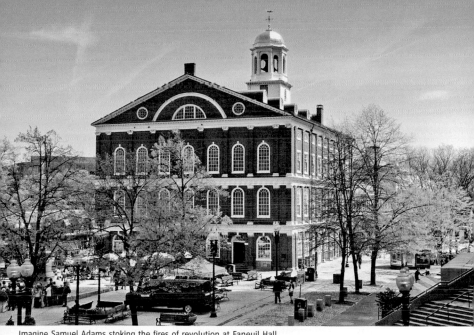
Imagine Samuel Adams stoking the fires of revolution at Faneuil Hall.

TOP ATTRACTIONS

Blackstone Block. Between North and Hanover streets, near the Haymarket, lies the Blackstone Block, now visited mostly for its culinary landmark the **Union Oyster House.** Named for one of Boston's first settlers, William Blaxton, or Blackstone, it's the city's oldest commercial block, for decades dominated by the butcher trade. As a tiny remnant of Old Boston, the Blackstone Block remains the city's "family attic"—to use the winning metaphor of critic Donlyn Lyndon: more than three centuries of architecture are on view, ranging from the 18th-century Capen House to the modern Bostonian Hotel. A colonial-period warren of winding lanes surrounds the block.

Facing the Blackstone Block, in tiny **Union Park,** framed by Congress Street and Dock Square, are two bronze figures, one seated on a bench and the other standing eye to eye with passersby. Both represent James Michael Curley, the quintessential Boston pol and a questionable role model for urban bosses. It's just as well that he has no pedestal. Also known as "the Rascal King" or "the Mayor of the Poor," and dramatized by Spencer Tracy in *The Last Hurrah* (1958), the charismatic Curley was beloved by the city's dominant working-class Irish for bringing them libraries, hospitals, bathhouses, and other public-works projects. His career got off to a promising start in 1903, when he ran—and won—a campaign for alderman from the Charles Street Jail, where he was serving time for taking someone else's civil-service exam.

Over the next 50 years he dominated Boston politics, serving four nonconsecutive terms as mayor, one term as governor, and four terms as congressman. No one seemed to mind the slight glitch created when his office moved, in 1946, to the federal penitentiary, where he served five months of a 6- to 18-month sentence for mail fraud: he was pardoned by President Truman and returned to his people a hero. ⊠ *Blackstone St., North End* Ⓜ *Haymarket.*

FAMILY
Fodor'sChoice
★

Faneuil Hall. Faneuil Hall has always sat in the middle of Boston's main marketplace and, to be clear, the single building facing Congress Street is the real Faneuil Hall, though locals often give that name to all five buildings in this shopping complex. Bostonians pronounce it *Fan-*yoo'uhl or *Fan-*yuhl. It was erected in 1742, the gift of wealthy merchant Peter Faneuil, who wanted the hall to serve as both a place for town meetings and a public market. It burned in 1761 and was immediately reconstructed according to the original plan of its designer, the Scottish portrait painter John Smibert (who lies in the Granary Burying Ground). In 1763 the political leader James Otis helped inaugurate the era that culminated in American independence when he dedicated the rebuilt hall to the cause of liberty.

In 1772 Samuel Adams stood here and first suggested that Massachusetts and the other colonies organize a Committee of Correspondence to maintain semiclandestine lines of communication in the face of hardening British repression. In later years the hall again lived up to Otis's dedication when the abolitionists Wendell Phillips and Charles Sumner pleaded for support from its podium. The tradition continues to this day: in presidential-election years the hall is the site of debates between contenders in the Massachusetts primary.

Faneuil Hall was substantially enlarged and remodeled in 1805 according to a Greek Revival design of the noted architect Charles Bulfinch; this is the building you see today. Its purposes remain the same: the balconied Great Hall is available to citizens' groups on presentation of a request signed by a required number of responsible parties; it also plays host to regular concerts.

Inside Faneuil Hall are dozens of paintings of famous Americans, including the mural *Webster's Reply to Hayne* and Gilbert Stuart's portrait of Washington at Dorchester Heights. Park rangers give informational talks about the history and importance of Faneuil Hall every half hour. There are interactive displays about Boston sights and National Park Service rangers at the visitor center on the first floor can provide maps and other information.

On the building's top floors are the headquarters and museum and library of the **Ancient & Honorable Artillery Company of Massachusetts,** which is free to visit. Founded in 1638, it's the oldest militia in the Western Hemisphere, and the third oldest in the world, after the Swiss Guard and the Honorable Artillery Company of London. The museum is open weekdays 9 to 3.

When such men as Andrew Jackson and Daniel Webster debated the future of the Republic here, the fragrances of bacon and snuff—sold by merchants in **Quincy Market** across the road—greeted their noses. Today the aroma of coffee wafts through the hall from a snack bar. The shops at ground level sell New England bric-a-brac. ⊠ *Faneuil Hall Sq., Government Center* ☎ *617/523–1300* ⊕ *www.nps.gov/bost/learn/ historyculture/fh.htm* 🎟 *Free* Ⓜ *Government Center, Aquarium, State.*

The haunting Holocaust Memorial sits at the north end of Union Park.

Holocaust Memorial. Located at the north end of Union Park, the Holocaust Memorial is the work of Stanley Saitowitz, whose design was selected through an international competition; the finished memorial was dedicated in 1995. During the day the six 50-foot-high glass-and-steel towers seem at odds with the 18th-century streetscape of Blackstone Square behind it; at night, they glow like ghosts while manufactured steam from grates in the granite base makes for a particularly haunting scene. Recollections by Holocaust survivors are set into the glass-and-granite walls; the upper levels of the towers are etched with 6 million numbers in random sequence, symbolizing the Jewish victims of the Nazi horror. ✉ *Union St. near Hanover St., Government Center* ☎ *617/457–8755* ⊕ *www.nehm.org* Ⓜ *Haymarket, Government Center, State.*

FAMILY
Fodor's Choice
★

Quincy Market. Quincy Market, also known as Faneuil Hall Marketplace, is not everyone's cup of tea; some people prefer grit to polish, and disdain the shiny cafés and boutiques. But there's no denying that this pioneer effort at urban recycling set the tone for many similar projects throughout the country, and that it has brought tremendous vitality to a once-tired corner of Boston. Quincy Market attracts huge crowds of tourists and locals throughout the year. In the early '70s, demolition was a distinct possibility for the decrepit buildings. Fortunately, with the participation of the Boston Redevelopment Authority, architect Benjamin Thompson planned a renovation of Quincy Market, and the Rouse Corporation of Baltimore undertook its restoration, which was completed in 1976. Try to look beyond the shop windows to the grand design of the market buildings themselves; they represent a vision of the market as urban centerpiece, an idea whose time has certainly come again.

The market consists of three block-long annexes: **Quincy Market, North Market,** and **South Market,** each 535 feet long and across a plaza from Faneuil Hall. The structures were designed in 1826 by Alexander Parris as part of a public-works project instituted by Boston's second mayor, Josiah Quincy, to alleviate the cramped conditions of Faneuil Hall and clean up the refuse that collected in Town Dock, the pond behind it. The central structure, made of granite, with a Doric colonnade at either end and topped by a classical dome and rotunda, has kept its traditional market-stall layout, but the stalls now purvey international and specialty foods: sushi, frozen yogurt, bagels, calzones, sausage-on-a-stick, Chinese noodles, barbecue, and baklava, plus all the boutique chocolate-chip cookies your heart desires.

Along the arcades on either side of the Central Market are vendors selling sweatshirts, photographs of Boston, and arts and crafts—some schlocky, some not—alongside a couple of patioed bars and restaurants. The North and South markets house a mixture of chain stores and specialty boutiques. Quintessential Boston remains here only in Durgin Park, opened in 1826 and known for its plain interior, brassy waitresses, and large portions of traditional New England fare.

A greenhouse flower market on the north side of Faneuil Hall provides a splash of color; during the winter holidays, trees along the cobblestone walks are strung with thousands of sparkling lights. In summer up to 50,000 people a day descend on the market; the outdoor cafés are an excellent spot to watch the hordes if you can find a seat. Year-round the pedestrian walkways draw street performers, and rings of strollers form around magicians and musicians. ⊠ *Bordered by Clinton, Commercial, and Chatham Sts., Government Center* ☎ *617/523–1300* ⊕ *www. faneuilhallmarketplace.com* Ⓜ *Government Center, Aquarium, State.*

■ NEED A BREAK ✕ **Black Rose.** If all that shopping and snacking has made you thirsty, you might want to stop for a pint at the Black Rose; take a right at the far end of the South Market. The bar-restaurant features traditional Irish fare and live music seven nights a week. ⊠ *160 State St., Government Center* ☎ *617/742–2286* ⊕ *www.blackroseboston.com* Ⓜ *Aquarium.*

WORTH NOTING

FAMILY **Boston Public Market.** Open year-round, the indoor Boston Public Market offers a great place to grab a sandwich, sample local foods, and even pick up a tasty souvenir. The New England-centric marketplace has more than three-dozen vendors, selling everything from produce to fresh fruit, as well as plenty of food stalls. Everything sold at the market is produced or originates in New England. There's also a food demonstration kitchen, where visitors might be able to catch a live cooking class (with samples). ⊠ *100 Hanover St., Government Center* ☎ *617/973–4909* Ⓜ *Haymarket.*

City Hall. Over the years, various plans—involving gardens, restaurants, music, and hotels—have been floated to make this a more people-friendly site. Possibly the only thing that would ameliorate Bostonians' collective distaste for the chilly Government Center is tearing it down. City Hall itself is an upside-down ziggurat design on a brutalist redbrick plaza. The design, by Kallman, McKinnell, and Knowles, confines administrative functions to the upper floors and places offices that deal with the public at street level. ⊠ *1 City Hall Sq., Government Center* Ⓜ *Government Center.*

Haymarket. Loud, self-promoting vendors pack this exuberant maze of a marketplace at Marshall and Blackstone streets on Friday and Saturday from dawn to dusk (most vendors are usually gone by 5). Pushcart vendors hawk fruits and vegetables against a backdrop of fish, meat, and cheese shops. The accumulation of debris left every evening has been celebrated in a whimsical 1976 public-arts project—Mags Harries's *Asaroton*, a Greek word meaning "unswept floors"—consisting of bronze fruit peels and other detritus smashed into pavement. Another Harries piece, a bronze depiction of a gathering of stray gloves, tumbles down between the escalators in the Porter Square T station in Cambridge. At Creek Square, near the Haymarket, is the **Boston Stone.** Set into a brick wall, this was allegedly a marker used as milepost zero in measuring distances from Boston. ⊠ *Marshall and Blackstone Sts., Government Center* ☉ *Closed Sun.–Thurs.* Ⓜ *Government Center.*

John F. Kennedy Federal Office Building. Looming at the northwest edge of City Hall Plaza, these twin towers are noted structures for architecture aficionados: they were designed by the founder of the Bauhaus movement, Walter Gropius, who taught at Harvard toward the end of his illustrious career. Gropius's house, designed by him in textbook Bauhaus style, is in nearby suburban Lincoln. ⊠ *15 New Sudbury St., Government Center* Ⓜ *Haymarket.*

THE NORTH END

On the northeast side of Government Center is the North End, Boston's Little Italy. In the 17th century the North End *was* Boston, as much of the rest of the peninsula was still under water or had yet to be cleared. Here the town bustled and grew rich for a century and a half before the birth of American independence. Now visitors can get a glimpse into Revolutionary times while filling up on some of the most scrumptious pastries and pastas to be found in modern Boston.

Today's North End is almost entirely a creation of the late 19th century, when brick tenements began to fill up with European immigrants—first the Irish, then Central European Jews, then the Portuguese, and finally the Italians. For more than 60 years, the North End attracted an Italian population base, so much so that one wonders whether wandering Puritan shades might scowl at the concentration of Mediterranean verve, volubility, and Roman Catholicism here. This is Boston's haven not only for Italian restaurants but also for Italian groceries, bakeries, boccie courts, churches, social clubs, cafés, and street-corner debates over home-team soccer games. ■TIP➔ July and August are highlighted by a series of street festivals, or feste, honoring various saints, and by local community events that draw people from all over the city. A statue of St. Agrippina di Mineo—which is covered with money when it's paraded through the streets—is a crowd favorite.

The statue of Paul Revere outside the Old North Church commemorates his famous ride.

Although hordes of visitors follow the redbrick ribbon of the Freedom Trail through the North End, the jumbled streets retain a neighborhood feeling, from the grandmothers gossiping on fire escapes to the laundry strung on back porches. Gentrification diluted the quarter's ethnic character some, but linger for a moment along Salem or Hanover street and you can still hear people speaking with Abruzzese accents. If you wish to study up on this fascinating district, head for the North End branch of the Boston Public Library on Parmenter Street, where a bust of Dante acknowledges local cultural pride.

TOP ATTRACTIONS

Copp's Hill Burying Ground. An ancient and melancholy air hovers like a fine mist over this Colonial-era burial ground. The North End graveyard incorporates four cemeteries established between 1660 and 1819. Near the Charter Street gate is the tomb of the Mather family, the dynasty of church divines (Cotton and Increase were the most famous sons) who held sway in Boston during the heyday of the old theocracy. Also buried here is Robert Newman, who crept into the steeple of the Old North Church to hang the lanterns warning of the British attack the night of Paul Revere's ride. Look for the tombstone of Captain Daniel Malcolm; it's pockmarked with musket-ball fire from British soldiers, who used the stones for target practice. Across the street at 44 Hull is the **narrowest house in Boston**—it's a mere 10 feet across. ⊠ *Intersection of Hull and Snowhill Sts., North End* ⊕ *www.cityofboston.gov/parks/hbgi/CoppsHill.asp* Ⓜ *North Station.*

FAMILY **Hanover Street.** This is the North End's main thoroughfare, along with the smaller and narrower Salem Street. It was named for the ruling dynasty of 18th- and 19th-century England; the label was retained after the Revolution, despite a flurry of patriotic renaming (King Street became State Street, for example). Hanover's business center is thick with restaurants, pastry shops, and Italian cafés; on weekends, Italian immigrants who have moved to the suburbs return to share an espresso with old friends and maybe catch a soccer game broadcast via satellite. Hanover is one of Boston's oldest public roads, once the site of the residences of the Rev. Cotton Mather and the Colonial-era patriot Dr. Joseph Warren, as well as a small dry-goods store run by Eben D. Jordan—who went on to launch the Jordan Marsh department stores. ⊠ *Between Commercial and Congress Sts., North End* Ⓜ *Haymarket, North Station.*

3

NEED A BREAK

✕ **Caffe Vittoria.** Caffe Vittoria is rightfully known as Boston's most traditional Italian café. Gleaming brass, marble tabletops, and one of the city's best selections of grappa keep the place packed with locals. ⊠ *290–296 Hanover St., North End* ☎ *617/227-7606* ⊕ *www.caffevittoria.com.*

Fodor's Choice
★ **Old North Church.** At one end of the **Paul Revere Mall** is a church famous not only for being the oldest standing church building in Boston (built in 1723) but for housing the two lanterns that glimmered from its steeple on the night of April 18, 1775. This is Christ, or Old North, Church, where Paul Revere and the young sexton Robert Newman managed that night to signal the departure by water of the British regulars to Lexington and Concord.

Although William Price designed the structure after studying Christopher Wren's London churches, Old North—which still has an active Episcopal congregation (including descendants of the Reveres)—is an impressive building in its own right. Inside, note the gallery and the graceful arrangement of pews; the bust of George Washington, pronounced by the Marquis de Lafayette to be the truest likeness of the general he ever saw; the brass chandeliers, made in Amsterdam in 1700 and installed here in 1724; and the clock, the oldest still running in an American public building. Try to visit when changes are rung on the bells, after the 11 am Sunday service; they bear the inscription, "We are the first ring of bells cast for the British Empire in North America." On the Sunday closest to April 18, descendants of the patriots reenact the raising of the lanterns in the church belfry during a special evening service. Visitors are welcome to drop in, but to see the bell-ringing chamber and the crypts, take the 30-minute behind-the-scenes tour ($6 ticket).

Behind the church is the **Washington Memorial Garden,** where volunteers cultivate a plot devoted to plants and flowers favored in the 18th century. ⊠ *193 Salem St., North End* ☎ *617/858-8231* ⊕ *www. oldnorth.com* Ⓜ *Haymarket, North Station.*

WORTH NOTING

FAMILY **Ebenezer Clough House.** Built in 1712, this house is now the only local survivor of its era aside from Old North Church, which stands nearby. Picture the streets lined with houses such as this, with an occasional grander Georgian mansion and some modest wooden-frame survivors of old Boston's many fires—this is what the North End looked like when Paul Revere was young. Today, the lower rooms serve as the Old North gift shop, with Captain Jackson's Colonial Chocolate Shop and the Printing Office of Edes & Gill, which offer an interactive look into the past. Watch a chocolate demonstration (and get a taste) and then learn how printers worked in the colonial era. ⊠ *21 Unity St., North End* ☎ *617/523–4848* ⊕ *oldnorth.com/printing-office-of-edes-gill* ⊙ *Closed Jan.*

FAMILY **Paul Revere House.** Originally on the site was the parsonage of the Second Church of Boston, home to the Rev. Increase Mather, the Second Church's minister. Mather's house burned in the great fire of 1676, and the house that Revere was to occupy was built on its location about four years later, nearly 100 years before Revere's 1775 midnight ride through Middlesex County. Revere owned it from 1770 until 1800, although he lived there for only 10 years and rented it out for the next two decades. Pre-1900 photographs show it as a shabby warren of storefronts and apartments. The clapboard sheathing is a replacement, but 90% of the framework is original; note the Elizabethan-style overhang and leaded windowpanes. A few Revere furnishings are on display here, and just gazing at his silverwork—much more of which is displayed at the Museum of Fine Arts—brings the man alive. Special events are scheduled throughout the year, many designed with children in mind.

The immediate neighborhood also has Revere associations. The little park in North Square is named after Rachel Revere, his second wife, and the adjacent brick **Pierce-Hichborn House** once belonged to relatives of Revere. The garden connecting the Revere house and the Pierce-Hichborn House is planted with flowers and medicinal herbs favored in Revere's day. ⊠ *19 North Sq., North End* ☎ *617/523–2338* ⊕ *www.paulreverehouse.org* ⊠ *$5 (cash only)* ⊙ *Jan.–Mar., closed Mon.* Ⓜ *Haymarket, Aquarium, Government Center.*

FAMILY **Paul Revere Mall** (*Prado*). This makes a perfect time-out spot from the Freedom Trail. Bookended by two landmark churches—Old North and St. Stephen's—the mall is flanked by brick walls lined with bronze plaques bearing the stories of famous North Enders. An appropriate centerpiece for this enchanting cityscape is Cyrus Dallin's equestrian **statue of Paul Revere.** Despite his depictions in such statues as this, the gentle Revere was stocky and of medium height—whatever manly dash he possessed must have been in his eyes rather than his physique. That physique served him well enough, however, for he lived to be 83 and saw nearly all of his Revolutionary comrades buried. ⊠ *Bordered by Tileston, Hanover, and Unity Sts., North End* Ⓜ *Haymarket, Aquarium, Government Center.*

CLOSE UP

Paul Revere's Ride

Test: Paul Revere was (1) a patriot whose midnight ride helped ignite the American Revolution; (2) a part-time dentist; (3) a silversmith who crafted tea services; (4) a printer who engraved the first Massachusetts state currency; (5) a talented metallurgist who cast cannons and bells; or (6) all of the above. The correct response is (6). But there's much more to this outsize Revolutionary hero—bell ringer for the Old North Church, founder of the copper mills that still bear his name, and father of 16 children.

Although his life spanned eight decades (1734–1818), Revere is most famous for that one night, April 18, 1775, when he became America's most celebrated Pony Express rider. *"Listen, my children, and you shall hear / Of the midnight ride of Paul Revere"* are the opening lines of Henry Wadsworth Longfellow's poem, which placed the event at the center of American folklore. Longfellow may have been an effective evangelist for Revere, but he was an indifferent historian.

Revere wasn't the only midnight rider. As part of the system set in motion by Revere and William Dawes Jr., also dispatched from Boston, there were at least several dozen riders, so that the capture of any one of them wouldn't keep the alarm from being sounded. It's also known that Revere never looked for the lantern signal from Charlestown. He told Robert Newman to hang two lanterns from Old North's belfry since the redcoats were on the move by water, but by that time Revere was already being rowed across the Charles River to begin his famous ride.

Revere and Dawes set out on separate routes, but had the same mission: to warn patriot leaders Samuel Adams and John Hancock that British regular troops were marching to arrest them, and alarm the countryside along the way. The riders didn't risk capture by shouting the news through the streets—and they never uttered the famous cry "The British are coming!," since Bostonians still considered themselves British. When Revere arrived in Lexington a few minutes past midnight and approached the house where Adams and Hancock were lodged, a sentry challenged him, requesting that he not make so much noise. "Noise!" Revere replied. "You'll have noise enough before long."

Despite Longfellow's assertion, Revere never raised the alarm in Concord, because he was captured en route. He was held and questioned by the British patrol, and eventually released, without his horse, to walk back to Lexington in time to witness part of the battle on Lexington Green.

Poetic license aside, this tale has become part of the collective American spirit. Americans dote on hearing that Revere forgot his spurs, only to retrieve them by tying a note to his dog's collar, then awaiting its return with the spurs attached. The resourcefulness he showed in using a lady's petticoat to muffle the sounds of his oars while crossing the Charles is greatly appreciated. Little wonder that these tales resonate in the hearts and imagination of America's citizenry, as well as in Boston's streets on the third Monday of every April, Patriots' Day, when Revere's ride is reenacted—in daylight—to the cheers of thousands of onlookers.

FAMILY **Rose Kennedy Greenway.** The Rose Kennedy Greenway, a winding series of parks marking the path the highway once took through the city, adds much-needed flora and fauna to the area and has turned into a delightful backyard playground for many residents. Lawn furniture, games, art installations, live performances, free Wi-Fi, and more make it a lively spot, especially in warmer months. The park's website has a map of its 15 acres; a pleasant stroll through all of them will take you from the North End to Chinatown. ⊠ *North End ✛ Between New Sudbury St. in North End and Beach St. in Chinatown ⊕ www.rosekennedygreenway. org* Ⓜ *State, Haymarket, Chinatown, Aquarium.*

St. Stephen's. Rose Kennedy, matriarch of the Kennedy clan, was christened here; 104 years later, St. Stephen's held mourners at her 1995 funeral. This is the only Charles Bulfinch church still standing in Boston, and a stunning example of the Federal style to boot. Built in 1804, it was first used as a Unitarian Church; since 1862 it has served a Roman Catholic parish. When the belfry was stripped during a major 1960s renovation, the original dome was found beneath a false cap; it was covered with sheet copper and held together with hand-wrought nails, and later authenticated as being the work of Paul Revere. ⊠ *401 Hanover St., North End* ☎ *617/523–1230* Ⓜ *Haymarket, Aquarium, Government Center.*

Salem Street. This ancient and constricted thoroughfare, one of the two main North End streets, cuts through the heart of the neighborhood and runs parallel to and one block west of Hanover. Between Cross and Prince streets, Salem Street contains numerous restaurants and shops. One of the best is Shake the Tree, one of the North End's trendiest boutiques, selling stylish clothing, gifts, and jewelry. The rest of Salem Street is mostly residential, but makes a nice walk to the Copp's Hill Burying Ground. ⊠ *Between Cross and Prince Sts., North End* Ⓜ *Haymarket.*

NEED A
BREAK

✕ **Bova's Bakery.** The allure of Bova's Bakery, a neighborhood institution, lies not only in its takeaway Italian breads, calzones, and pastries, but also in its hours: 24 a day (the deli closes at 1 am, however). ⊠ *134 Salem St., North End* ☎ *617/523–5601* ⊕ *bovabakeryboston.com* Ⓜ *Haymarket.*

CHARLESTOWN

Getting Oriented

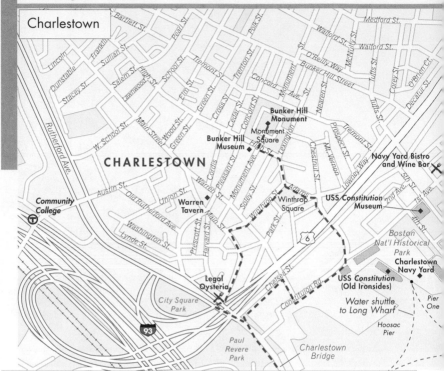

Charlestown

CHARLESTOWN

QUICK BITES

Legal Oysteria. This is a great place to down some freshly shucked oysters or enjoy a brick oven pizza. ✉ *10, City Square, Charlestown* ☎ *617/712–1988* ⊕ *www.legalseafoods.com/ restaurants/charlestown-legal-oysteria-104.*

Navy Yard Bistro and Wine Bar. Housed in a National Historic Site in the heart of the Charlestown Navy Yard, this restaurant offers French bistro fare at reasonable prices, with outdoor dining in summer. ✉ *6th St., on corner of 1st Ave., Charlestown* ⊕ *www.navyyard-bistro.com.*

TIMING AND SAFETY

Give yourself two to three hours for a Charlestown walk; the Charlestown Bridge calls for endurance in cold weather. You may want to save Charlestown's stretch of the Freedom Trail, which adds considerably to its length, for a second-day outing. You can always save time backtracking from the route by taking the MBTA water shuttle, which ferries back and forth between Charlestown's Navy Yard and Downtown Boston's Long Wharf and takes about 10 minutes, or call an Uber or Lyft ride.

The Charlestown Navy Yard is generally a safe area, but as always use common sense, as Boston is a big city. Stick to well-lighted streets at night and avoid walking alone.

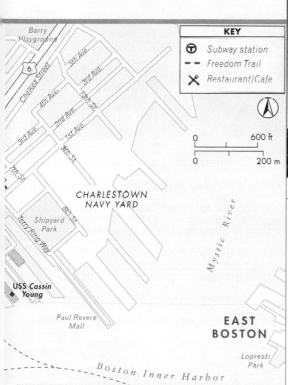

Barry Playground

CHARLESTOWN NAVY YARD

Mystic River

Shipyard Park

USS *Cassin Young*

Paul Revere Mall

EAST BOSTON

Lopresti Park

Boston Inner Harbor

TOP REASONS TO GO

■ Climb the 294 steps to the top of the Bunker Hill Monument, and enjoy the views of the city while reliving the battles of the past.

■ Tour the USS *Constitution*, and discover why the oldest commissioned warship still afloat in the world Is nicknamed "Old Ironsides."

■ Grab a pint at Warren Tavern, the same pub at which George Washington and Paul Revere once drank.

FREEDOM TRAIL SIGHTS

■ Bunker Hill Monument
■ USS *Constitution*

GETTING HERE AND AROUND

The closest subway stop to the Charlestown Navy Yard is North Station (accessible by the Green and Orange lines), about a 15-minute walk. Take Causeway Street northeast and make a left to walk over the Charlestown Bridge. Take a right on Chelsea Street and right again on Warren Street. Constitution Road will be your next left, and from here you can enter the Navy Yard. From Downtown Crossing, take the 93 Bus, which will drop you directly at the Navy Yard. If you are coming from Downtown, try the water shuttle from Long Wharf near the Aquarium. Boats run daily on the hour and half hour, and the ride is 10 minutes long.

Sightseeing
★★★
Dining
★★★
Lodging
★
Shopping
★
Nightlife
★★

Boston started here. Charlestown was a thriving settlement a year before colonials headed across the Charles River at William Blaxton's invitation to found the city proper. Today the district's attractions include two of the most visible—and vertical—monuments in Boston: the Bunker Hill Monument, which commemorates the grisly battle that became a symbol of patriotic resistance against the British, and the USS *Constitution*, whose masts continue to tower over the waterfront where it was built more than 200 years ago.

Updated by
Kim Foley
Mackinnon

The blocks around the Bunker Hill Monument are a good illustration of how gentrification has changed the neighborhoods. Along streets lined with gas lamps are impeccably restored Federal and mid-19th-century town houses; cheek by jowl are working-class quarters of similar vintage but more modest recent pasts. Near the Navy Yard along Main Street is City Square, the beginning of Charlestown's main commercial district, which includes City Square Park, with brick paths and bronze fish sculptures. On Phipps Street is the grave marker of John Harvard, a minister who in 1638 bequeathed his small library to the fledgling Cambridge College, thereafter renamed in his honor. The precise location of the grave is uncertain, but a monument from 1828 marks its approximate site.

TOP ATTRACTIONS

Fodor'sChoice
★

Bunker Hill Monument. Three misunderstandings surround this famous monument. First, the Battle of Bunker Hill was actually fought on Breed's Hill, which is where the monument sits today. (The real Bunker Hill is about ½ mile to the north of the monument; it's slightly taller than Breed's Hill.) Bunker was the originally planned locale for the battle, and for that reason its name stuck. Second, although the battle is generally considered a Colonial success, the Americans lost. It was a Pyrrhic victory for the British Redcoats, who sacrificed nearly half of their 2,200 men; American casualties numbered 400 to 600. And third: the famous war cry "Don't fire until you see the whites of their eyes" may never have been uttered by American Colonel William Prescott or General Israel Putnam, but if either one did shout it, he was quoting an old Prussian command made necessary by the notorious inaccuracy of the musket. No matter. The Americans did employ a deadly delayed-action strategy on June 17, 1775, and conclusively proved themselves worthy fighters, capable of defeating the forces of the British Empire.

Among the dead were the brilliant young American doctor and political activist Joseph Warren, recently commissioned as a major general but fighting as a private, and the British Major John Pitcairn, who two months before had led the Redcoats into Lexington. Pitcairn is believed to be buried in the crypt of Old North Church.

In 1823 the committee formed to construct a monument on the site of the battle chose the form of an Egyptian obelisk. Architect Solomon Willard designed a 221-foot-tall granite obelisk, a tremendous feat of engineering for its day. The Marquis de Lafayette laid the cornerstone of the monument in 1825, but because of a lack of funds, it wasn't dedicated until 1843. Daniel Webster's stirring words at the ceremony commemorating the laying of its cornerstone have gone down in history: "Let it rise! Let it rise, till it meets the sun in his coming. Let the earliest light of the morning gild it, and parting day linger and play upon its summit."

The monument's zenith is reached by a flight of 294 steps. There's no elevator, but the views from the observatory are worth the effort of the arduous climb. From April through June, due to high numbers, all visitors who wish to climb must first obtain a pass from the Bunker Hill Museum at 43 Monument Square. Climbing passes are free, but limited in number and offered on a first-come, first-served basis. The museum's artifacts and exhibits tell the story of the battle, while a detailed diorama shows the action in miniature. ⊠ *Monument Sq., Charlestown* ☎ *617/242–5641* ⊕ *www.nps.gov/bost/historyculture/ bhm.htm* 🎟 *Free* Ⓜ *Community College.*

NEED A BREAK

✕ **Pier 6.** For a meal on the waterfront, try Pier 6 in the Charlestown Navy Yard. It's got outstanding harbor views and the requisite New England seafood dishes. ⊠ *1 8th St., Pier 6, Charlestown* ☎ *617/337–0054* ⊕ *pier-6boston.com.*

FAMILY
Fodor'sChoice
★

USS *Constitution*. Better known as "Old Ironsides," the USS *Constitution* rides proudly at anchor in her berth at the Charlestown Navy Yard. The oldest commissioned ship in the U.S. fleet is a battlewagon of the old school, of the days of "wooden ships and iron men"—when she and her crew of 200 succeeded at the perilous task of asserting the sovereignty of an improbable new nation. Every July 4, she's towed out for a turnabout in Boston Harbor, the very place her keel was laid in 1797.

DID YOU KNOW?

The USS *Constitution* is a bit of an anachronism on the Freedom Trail. Though it is the oldest ship in the Navy, "Old Ironsides" wasn't launched until 1797—well after the American Revolution had been won.

The venerable craft has narrowly escaped the scrap heap several times in her long history. She was launched on October 21, 1797, as part of the nation's fledgling navy. Her hull was made of live oak, the toughest wood grown in North America; her bottom was sheathed in copper, provided by Paul Revere at a nominal cost. Her principal service was during Thomas Jefferson's campaign against the Barbary pirates, off the coast of North Africa, and in the War of 1812. In 42 engagements her record was 42–0.

The nickname "Old Ironsides" was acquired during the War of 1812, when shots from the British warship *Guerrière* appeared to bounce off her hull. Talk of scrapping the ship began as early as 1830, but she was saved by a public campaign sparked by Oliver Wendell Holmes's poem "Old Ironsides." She underwent a major restoration in the early 1990s. Today she continues, the oldest commissioned warship afloat in the world, to be a part of the U.S. Navy.

The navy personnel who look after the *Constitution* maintain a 24-hour watch. Instead of taking the T, you can get closer to the ship by taking MBTA Bus 93 to Chelsea Street from Haymarket. Or you can take the Boston Harbor Cruise water shuttle from Long Wharf to Pier 4. ✉ *Charlestown Navy Yard, 55 Constitution Rd., Charlestown* ☎ *617/242–7511* ⊕ *www.navy.mil/local/constitution* ✉ *Free* Ⓜ *North Station.*

> **A GOOD WALK**
>
> If you choose to hoof it to Charlestown, follow Hull Street from Copp's Hill Burying Ground to Commercial Street; turn left on Commercial and, two blocks later, right onto the bridge. The entrance to the **Charlestown Navy Yard** is on your right after crossing the bridge. Just ahead is the Charlestown Navy Yard Visitors Information Center; inside the park gate are the **USS Constitution** and the associated **USS Constitution Museum.** From here, the Red Line of the Freedom Trail takes you to the **Bunker Hill Monument.**

NEED A BREAK

✕ **Warren Tavern.** After a blustery walk at the Navy Yard, get a seat by the fireplace and warm yourself with a hearty chowder and Sam Adams draft at the Warren Tavern. Built in 1780, this restored colonial neighborhood pub was once frequented by George Washington and Paul Revere. It was one of the first buildings reconstructed after the Battle of Bunker Hill, which leveled Charlestown. ✉ *2 Pleasant St., Charlestown* ☎ *617/241–8142* ⊕ *www.warrentavern.com* Ⓜ *Community College.*

WORTH NOTING

FAMILY **Charlestown Navy Yard.** A National Park Service Historic Site since it was decommissioned in 1974, the Charlestown Navy Yard was one of six established to build warships. For 174 years, as wooden hulls and muzzle-loading cannons gave way to steel ships and sophisticated electronics, the yard evolved to meet the Navy's changing needs. Here are early-19th-century barracks, workshops, and officers' quarters; a ropewalk (an elongated building for making rope, not open to the public), designed in 1834 by the Greek Revival architect Alexander Parris and used by the Navy to turn out cordage for more than 125 years; and one of the oldest operational naval dry docks in the United States. The USS *Constitution* was the first to use this dry dock, in 1833. In addition to the ship itself, check out the *Constitution* Museum, the collections of the Boston Marine Society, and the USS *Cassin Young*, a World War II destroyer typical of the ships built here during that era. At the entrance of the Navy Yard is the **Charlestown Navy Yard Visitors Information Center,** with exhibits on ships and a fun little shop. A 10-minute movie about the Navy Yard runs every 15 minutes in a small theater. ⊠ *55 Constitution Rd., Charlestown* ☎ *617/242–5601* ⊕ *www.nps.gov/bost/historyculture/cny.htm* Ⓜ *North Station; MBTA Bus 92 to Charlestown City Sq. or Bus 93 to Chelsea St. from Haymarket; or Boston Harbor Cruise water shuttle from Long Wharf to Pier 4.*

USS Cassin Young. From a later date than the *Constitution*, this destroyer saw action in Asian waters during World War II. She served the Navy until 1960. Although not regularly open to the public, you can still walk beside her and take in her size. Check the website for special opening hours. ⊠ *Charlestown Navy Yard, 55 Constitution Rd., Charlestown* ☎ *617/242–5601* ⊕ *www.nps.gov/bost/historyculture/usscassinyoung.htm* 🎫 *Free* Ⓜ *North Station; MBTA Bus 92 to Charlestown City Sq. or Bus 93 to Chelsea St. from Haymarket; or Boston Harbor Cruise water shuttle from Long Wharf to Pier 4.*

FAMILY
Fodor's Choice
★

USS Constitution Museum. Artifacts pertaining to the USS *Constitution* are on display—firearms, logs, and instruments. One section takes you step by step through the ship's most important battles. Old meets new in a video-game battle "fought" at the helm of a ship. Kids will love to climb into hammocks and maybe even scrub the decks in interactive exhibits. ⊠ *Adjacent to USS Constitution, Charlestown Navy Yard, Charlestown* ☎ *617/426–1812* ⊕ *www.ussconstitutionmuseum.org* 🎫 *Suggested donation $5–$10* Ⓜ *North Station; MBTA Bus 92 to Charlestown City Sq. or Bus 93 to Chelsea St. from Haymarket; or Boston Harbor Cruise water shuttle from Long Wharf to Pier 4.*

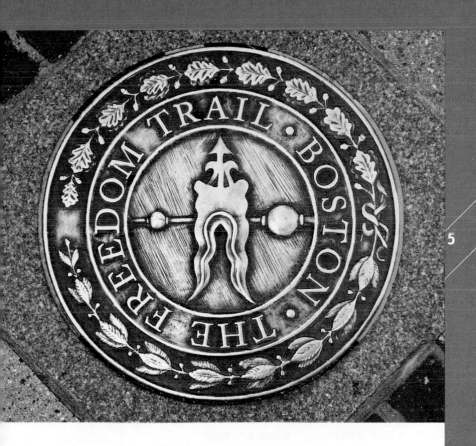

DOWNTOWN BOSTON

Getting Oriented

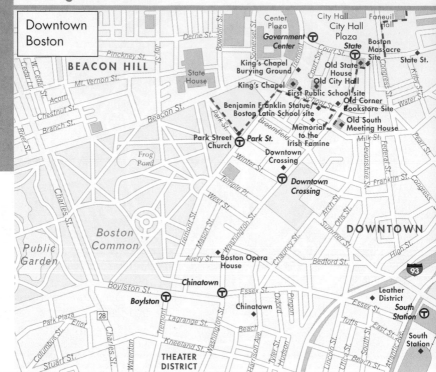

GETTING HERE AND AROUND	TIMING AND SAFETY

Downtown Boston is easily accessible by the T; take the Orange Line to Downtown Crossing, the Blue Line to Aquarium, or the Red Line to South Station or Downtown Crossing. If you are in a car, a garage is your best bet; the **Interpark Garage** (⌧ *270 Atlantic Ave.*) is near the New England Aquarium. The Children's Museum is a bit farther: either walk from South Station or park nearby at the **Atlantic Wharf Garage** (⌧ *280 Congress St.*).

This section of Boston has a generous share of attractions, so it's wise to save a full day for visiting Downtown, spending the bulk of it at the New England Aquarium or the Children's Museum. There are optimum times to catch some sights: dusk for a romantic stroll along the waterfront at Rowes Wharf, and at 2 pm on sunny days (except for Friday) at the observation deck at the top of the U.S. Custom House (now a Marriott) for a $4 fee. But there's no need to visit the aquarium at a special hour—feedings and trainings happen several times a day. Downtown is a safe area, but the Financial District empties out after 6 pm, so choose well-lighted streets when walking alone at night.

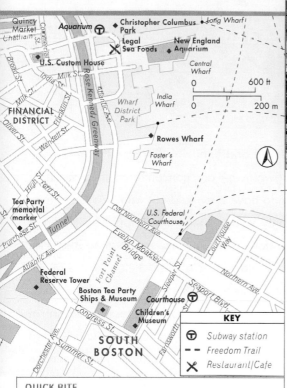

KEY

🚇 Subway station

-- Freedom Trail

✕ Restaurant/Cafe

TOP REASONS TO GO

■ Walk like a penguin and watch the seals play at the New England Aquarium.

■ Set the kids free in the two-story climbing maze at the Children's Museum.

■ Explore the stores of Downtown Crossing, an outdoor pedestrian mall.

■ Pretend to be a colonist and throw tea overboard at the Boston Tea Party Ships & Museum.

FREEDOM TRAIL SIGHTS

■ Benjamin Franklin Statue/ Boston Latin School

■ First Public School Site

■ King's Chapel and Burying Ground

■ Old Corner Bookstore Site

■ Old South Meeting House

■ Park Street Church

QUICK BITE

The quintessential Boston fish haunt, **Legal Sea Foods** (✉ 255 State St.) is at Long Wharf, steps from the New England Aquarium and other Downtown attractions. Stop in for a bowl of its famous clam chowder—just the thing to take the chill off a cool fall day. You can also pop into the Aquarium's food court for a variety of snacks and drinks.

DID YOU KNOW?

The Boston Tea Party occurred on Atlantic Avenue near Congress Street. The area was once a wharf—further evidence of Boston's relentless expansion into the harbor. There isn't much to see here now; look for the historical marker commemorating the event on the corner of Congress and Purchase streets. Head down Congress Street for the Boston Tea Party Ships & Museum to learn more.

Sightseeing
★★★★
Dining
★★★★
Lodging
★★★★
Shopping
★★★★★
Nightlife
★★★

Boston's commercial and financial districts—the area commonly called Downtown—are concentrated in a maze of streets that seem to have been laid out with little logic; they are, after all, only village lanes that happen to be lined with modern 40-story office towers. Just as the Great Fire of 1872 swept the old Financial District clear, more recent Downtown construction has obliterated many of the buildings in which 19th-century Boston businesspeople sat in front of rolltop desks. A number of the historic sites that remain tucked among the skyscrapers join together to make up a fascinating section of the Freedom Trail, and a lively theater scene keeps things hopping at night.

Updated by
Kim Foley
MacKinnon

The area is bordered by State Street to the north and by South Station and Chinatown to the south. Tremont Street and the Common form the west boundary, and the harbor wharves the eastern edge. Be prepared: the tangle of streets can be confusing.

Washington Street (aka Downtown Crossing) is Downtown's main commercial thoroughfare. It's a pedestrian street once marked by two venerable anchors of Boston's mercantile district, Filene's Basement (now closed), and Jordan Marsh (now Macy's). The block reeks of history—and sausage carts. Street vendors, flower sellers, and gaggles of teenagers, businesspeople, and shoppers throng the pedestrian mall. Shops like Primark and new eateries have been helping to revitalize the area after a dormant period.

Downtown is also the place for some of Boston's most idiosyncratic neighborhoods. The Leather District directly abuts Chinatown, which is also bordered by the Theater District (and the buildings of Tufts Medical Center) farther west. The Massachusetts Turnpike and its junction with the Southeast Expressway cut a wide swath through the area, isolating Chinatown from the South End.

Kids are entertained and educated at the Children's Museum.

TOP ATTRACTIONS

FAMILY
Fodor's Choice
★

Boston Tea Party Ships & Museum. This lively museum offers an interactive look at the past in a place as close as possible to the actual spot where the Boston Tea Party took place on December 16, 1773. Situated at the Congress Street Bridge where Griffin's Wharf once was, visitors can check out *The Beaver II,* a historic reproduction of one of the ships forcibly boarded and unloaded the night Boston Harbor became a teapot, along with a reproduction of the *Eleanor,* another of the ships (the third ship, the *Dartmouth,* is under construction with no firm date set for opening). The museum is big on visitor engagement. Actors in period costumes greet patrons, assign them a Colonial persona, and then ask a few people to heave boxes of tea into the water. Inside, there are 3-D holograms, talking portraits, and even the Robinson Half Tea Chest, one of two original tea chests known to exist. Outside, you can explore the replicas of the ships, meet reenactors, or drink a cup of tea in Abigail's Tea Room, which has one of the best views around. ⊠ *Fort Point Channel at Congress St. Bridge, Downtown* ⊕ *www.bostonteaparty-ship.com* ⌇ *$28 (check website for discounts)* Ⓜ *South Station.*

FAMILY
Fodor's Choice
★

Children's Museum. The country's second-oldest children's museum has always been ahead of the curve with creative hands-on exhibits, cultural diversity, and problem solving. Some of the most popular stops are also the simplest, like the bubble-making machinery and the two-story climbing maze. At the Japanese House you're invited to take off your shoes and step inside a two-story silk merchant's home from Kyoto. The "Boston Black" exhibit stimulates dialogue about ethnicity and community, and children can dig, climb, and build at the Construction Zone.

In the toddler PlaySpace, children under three can run free in a safe environment. There's also a full schedule of special exhibits, festivals, and performances. ⊠ *308 Congress St., Downtown* ☎ *617/426–6500* ⊕ *www.bostonkids.org* ✉ *$16, Fri. 5–9 $1* Ⓜ *South Station.*

FAMILY **New England Aquarium.** With one of the world's largest ocean-reef tanks
Fodor's Choice in the world and exhibits covering every sea creature imaginable, this
★ aquarium is a must for anyone curious about life under and around the sea. Its glass-and-steel exterior is constructed to mimic fish scales, and seals bark outside. Inside the main facility you'll see penguins, sea otters, sharks, and other exotic sea creatures—more than 30,000 animals, with 800 different species.

In the semi-enclosed outdoor space of the New Balance Foundation Marine Mammal Center, visitors can enjoy the antics of northern fur seals and sea lions while gazing out at Boston Harbor.

The real showstopper, though, is the four-story, 200,000-gallon ocean-reef tank. Ramps winding around the tank lead to the top level and allow you to view the inhabitants from many vantage points. Up top, the Yawkey Coral Reef Center features a seven-tank exhibit gallery that gives a close-up look at animals that might not be easily seen on the reef. Don't miss the five-times-a-day feedings; each lasts nearly an hour and takes divers 24 feet into the tank.

Another fascinating exhibit is Science of Sharks, which features sharks from around the world (did you know there are about 500 different species?) The aquarium also has one of the largest exhibits of jellies in the country, with thousands of jellyfish (some grown in the museum's labs). Get up close to sharks and rays at the Trust Family Foundation Shark and Ray Touch Tank, the largest of its kind on the East Coast. The Blue Planet Action Center is an interactive educational experience where visitors have the chance to see shark and lobster nurseries.

At the Edge of the Sea exhibit children can gingerly pick up starfish and other creatures. Whale-watch cruises leave from the aquarium's dock from April to October, and cost $53. The 6½-story-high IMAX theater takes you on virtual journeys from the bottom of the sea to the depths of outer space with its 3-D films. ■TIP→ If you are planning to see an IMAX show as well as check out the aquarium, buy a combo ticket; you'll save $5 for the adult ticket. Similarly, you'll save $7 with a combo ticket for the Aquarium and the whale-watch. ⊠ *1 Central Wharf, between Central and Milk Sts., Downtown* ☎ *617/973–5200* ⊕ *www.neaq.org* ✉ *$28, IMAX $10* Ⓜ *Aquarium, State.*

WORTH NOTING

Benjamin Franklin Statue/Boston Latin School. This stop on the Freedom Trail commemorates the famous revolutionary and inventor. His likeness also marks the original location of Boston Latin School, the country's oldest public school, which still molds young minds, albeit from the Fenway neighborhood today. Franklin attended Boston Latin with three other signers of the Declaration of Independence—Samuel Adams, John Hancock, and Robert Treat Paine—but he has the dubious distinction of being the only one of the four not to graduate. ✉ *School St. at City Hall Ave., Downtown* ☎ *617/357–8300* ⊕ *www. thefreedomtrail.org* Ⓜ *Park St.*

Boston Massacre Site. Directly in front of the Old State House a circle of cobblestones (on a traffic island) marks the site of the Boston Massacre. It was on the snowy evening of March 5, 1770, that nine British regular soldiers fired in panic upon a taunting mob of more than 75 Bostonians. Five townsmen died. In the legal action that followed, the defense of the accused soldiers was undertaken by John Adams and Josiah Quincy, both of whom vehemently opposed British oppression but were devoted to the principle of fair trial. All but two of the nine regulars charged were acquitted; the others were branded on the hand for the crime of manslaughter. Paul Revere lost little time in capturing the "massacre" in a dramatic engraving that soon became one of the Revolution's most potent images of propaganda. ✉ *Devonshire and Court Sts., Downtown* ⊕ *www.thefreedomtrail.org/freedom-trail/boston-massacre.shtml* Ⓜ *State.*

Boston Opera House. Originally the B. F. Keith Memorial Theatre in the days of vaudeville, this venue was designed in beaux arts style by Thomas Lamb and modeled after the Paris Opera House. The theater shut its doors in 1991, but a multimillion-dollar restoration completed in 2004 brought theater and dance performances, including touring Broadway shows and Boston Ballet performances, back to the Opera House. ✉ *539 Washington St., Downtown* ☎ *617/259–3400* ⊕ *bostonoperahouse.com* Ⓜ *Boylston.*

Chinatown. Boston's Chinatown may seem small, but it's said to be the third largest in the United States, after those in San Francisco and Manhattan. Beginning in the 1870s, Chinese immigrants started to trickle in, many setting up tents in a strip they called Ping On Alley. The trickle increased to a wave when immigration restrictions were lifted in 1968. As in most other American Chinatowns, the restaurants are a big draw; on Sunday many Bostonians head to Chinatown for dim sum. Today the many Chinese establishments—most found along Beach and Tyler streets and Harrison Avenue—are interspersed with Vietnamese, Korean, Japanese, Thai, and Malaysian eateries. A three-story pagoda-style arch at the end of Beach Street welcomes you to the district. ✉ *Bounded (roughly) by Essex, Washington, Marginal, and Hudson Sts., Chinatown* ⊕ *www.boston.gov/neighborhood/chinatown-leather-district* Ⓜ *Chinatown.*

NEED A BREAK

✕ **Eldo Cake House.** Never considered bean paste for dessert or eaten a Chinese-style pork bun? Expand your horizons at Eldo Cake House, which has both sweet and savory pastries. ✉ *36 Harrison Ave., Downtown* ☎ *617/350–7977* Ⓜ *Chinatown.*

Christopher Columbus Park (*Waterfront Park*). It's a short stroll from the Financial District to a view of Boston Harbor. This green space bordering the harbor and several of Boston's restored wharves is a pleasant oasis with benches and an arborlike shelter. Lewis Wharf and Commercial Wharf (north of the park), which long lay nearly derelict, had by the mid-1970s been transformed into condominiums, offices, restaurants, and upscale shops. Long Wharf's Marriott hotel was designed to blend in with the old seaside warehouses. There are sprinklers, a playground, and even free Wi-Fi. ✉ *Bordered by Atlantic Ave., Commercial Wharf, and Long Wharf, Downtown* ⊕ *www.foccp.org* Ⓜ *Aquarium.*

Federal Reserve Tower. On Atlantic Avenue, across from South Station, is this striking aluminum-clad building, designed in 1976 by Hugh Stubbins and Associates. The tower is mainly used for offices, and is not open to the public. ✉ *600 Atlantic Ave., Downtown* Ⓜ *South Station.*

King's Chapel. Both somber and dramatic, King's Chapel looms over the corner of Tremont and School streets. Its distinctive shape wasn't achieved entirely by design; for lack of funds, it was never topped with the steeple that architect Peter Harrison had planned. The first chapel on this site was erected in 1688, when Sir Edmund Andros, the royal governor whose authority temporarily replaced the original colonial charter, appropriated the land for the establishment of an Anglican place of worship. This rankled the Puritans, who had left England to escape Anglicanism and had until then succeeded in keeping it out of the colony.

It took five years to build the solid Quincy-granite structure. As construction proceeded, the old church continued to stand within the rising walls of the new, the plan being to remove and carry it away piece by piece when the outer stone chapel was completed. The builders then went to work on the interior, which remains essentially as they finished it in 1754; it's a masterpiece of proportion and Georgian calm (in fact, its acoustics make the use of a microphone unnecessary for Sunday sermons). The pulpit, built in 1717 by Peter Vintoneau, is the oldest pulpit in continuous use on the same site in the United States. To the right of the main entrance is a special pew once reserved for condemned prisoners, who were trotted in to hear a sermon before being hanged on the Common. The chapel's bell is Paul Revere's largest and, in his judgment, his sweetest sounding. For a behind-the-scenes look at the bell ("bell") or crypt ("bones"), buy a ticket at the chapel entrance (last tour at 4 pm). ✉ *58 Tremont St., at School St., Downtown* ☎ *617/523–1749* ⊕ *www.kings-chapel.org* ✎ *Self-guided tour of chapel, $2 suggested donation; Bells and Bones tour, $10 for both or $7 for one* Ⓜ *Park St., Government Center.*

King's Chapel Burying Ground. Legends linger in this oldest of the city's cemeteries. Glance at the handy map of famous grave sites (posted a short walk down the left path) and then take the path to the right from the entrance and then left by the chapel to the gravestone (1704) of Elizabeth Pain, the model for Hester Prynne in Nathaniel Hawthorne's *The Scarlet Letter.* Note the winged death's head on her stone. Also buried here is William Dawes Jr., who, with Dr. Samuel Prescott, rode out to warn of the British invasion the night of Paul Revere's famous ride. Other Boston worthies entombed here include the first Massachusetts governor, John Winthrop, and several generations of his descendants. The prominent slate monument between the cemetery and the chapel tells (in French) the story of the Chevalier de Saint-Sauveur, a young officer who was part of the first French contingent that arrived to help the rebel Americans in 1778. He was killed in a riot that began when hungry Bostonians were told they couldn't buy the bread the French were baking for their men, using the Bostonians' own wheat—a situation only aggravated by the language barrier. The chevalier's interment here was probably the occasion for the first Roman Catholic Mass in what has since become a city with a substantial Catholic population. ✉ *Tremont St. at School St., Downtown* ☎ *617/227 2155* ⊕ *www.thefreedom-trail.org/freedom-trail/kings-chapel-burying-ground.shtml* Ⓜ *Park St, Government Center.*

Leather District. Opposite South Station and inside the angle formed by Kneeland Street and Atlantic Avenue is a corner of Downtown that has been relatively untouched by high-rise development: the old Leather District. It's probably the best place in Downtown Boston to get an idea of what the city's business center looked like in the late 19th century. This was the wholesale supply area for raw materials in the days when the shoe industry was a regional economic mainstay; a few leather firms are still here, but most warehouses now contain expensive loft apartments. ✉ *Bordered by Kneeland St., Atlantic Ave., and Lincoln St., Downtown* Ⓜ *South Station.*

Memorial to the Irish Famine. A reminder of the rich immigrant past of this most Irish of American cities consists of two sculptures by artist Robert Shure, one depicting an anguished family on the shores of Ireland, the other a determined and hopeful Irish family stepping ashore in Boston. ✉ *Plaza outside Borders, Washington St. near School St., opposite Old South Meeting House, Downtown* Ⓜ *State, Downtown Crossing.*

Old City Hall. Just outside this site sits Richard S. Greenough's bronze statue (1855) of Benjamin Franklin, Boston's first portrait sculpture. Franklin was born in 1706 just a few blocks from here, on Milk Street, and attended the Boston Latin School, founded in 1635 near the City Hall site. (The school has long since moved to Louis Pasteur Avenue, near the Fenway.) As a young man, Franklin emigrated to Philadelphia, where he lived most of his long life. Boston's municipal government settled into the new City Hall in 1969, and the old Second Empire building now houses business offices and a restaurant. ✉ *41–15 School St., Downtown* ⊕ *www.oldcityhall.com* Ⓜ *State.*

Old Corner Bookstore Site. Through these doors, between 1845 and 1865, passed some of the century's literary lights: Henry David Thoreau, Ralph Waldo Emerson, and Henry Wadsworth Longfellow—even Charles Dickens paid a visit. Many of their works were published here by James T. "Jamie" Fields, who in 1830 had founded the influential firm Ticknor and Fields. In the 19th century the graceful, gambrel-roof early-Georgian structure—built in 1718 on land once owned by religious rebel Anne Hutchinson—also housed the city's leading bookstore. Today, somewhat sadly, the building is home to a fast-food joint. ✉ *1 School St., Downtown* ⊕ *www.thefreedomtrail.org/freedom-trail/old-corner-book-store.shtml* Ⓜ *State.*

Boston's Old City Hall is surrounded by modern buildings.

FAMILY **Old South Meeting House.** This is the second-oldest church building in Boston, and were it not for Longfellow's celebration of the Old North in "Paul Revere's Ride," it might well be the most famous. Today, visitors can learn about its history through exhibits and audio programs. Some of the fiercest of the town meetings that led to the Revolution were held here, culminating in the gathering of December 16, 1773, which was called by Samuel Adams to confront the crisis of three ships, laden with dutiable tea, anchored at Griffin's Wharf. The activists wanted the tea returned to England, but the governor would not permit it—and the rest is history. To cries of "Boston Harbor a teapot tonight!" and John Hancock's "Let every man do what is right in his own eyes," the protesters poured out of the Old South, headed to the wharf with their waiting comrades, and dumped 18,000 pounds' worth of tea into the water.

One of the earliest members of the congregation was an African slave named Phillis Wheatley, who had been educated by her owners. In 1773 a book of her poems was printed (by a London publisher), making her the first published African American poet. She later traveled to London, where she was received as a celebrity, but was again overtaken by poverty and died in obscurity at age 31.

The church suffered no small amount of indignity in the Revolution: its pews were ripped out by occupying British troops, and the interior was used for riding exercises by General John Burgoyne's light dragoons. A century later it escaped destruction in the Great Fire of 1872, only to be threatened with demolition by developers. Interestingly, it was the first successful preservation effort in New England. The building opened as an independent, nonprofit museum in 1877 and contains the last remaining example of a two-tiered gallery in a New England meetinghouse. The pulpit is a combination of two pulpits that were both original to the meetinghouse during points in the Victorian era. The white barrel portion of the pulpit dates from 1858 and the mahogany wine glass portion in the front dates from 1808.

The **Voices of Protest** exhibit celebrates Old South as a forum for free speech from Revolutionary days to the present. ⊠ *310 Washington St., Downtown* ☎ *617/482–6439* ⊕ *www.oldsouthmeetinghouse.org* ⌖ *$6* Ⓜ *State, Downtown Crossing.*

FAMILY

Fodor'sChoice

★

Old State House. This colonial-era landmark has one of the most recognizable facades in Boston, with its State Street gable adorned by a brightly gilded lion and unicorn, symbols of British imperial power. Today, it's an interactive museum with exhibits, artifacts, and 18th-century artwork, and tells the stories of Revolutionary Bostonians through costumed guides.

An interesting note is that the original figures were pulled down in 1776. For proof that bygones are bygones, consider not only the restoration of the sculptures in 1880 but also that Queen Elizabeth II was greeted by cheering crowds on July 4, 1976, when she stood on the Old State House balcony (from which the Declaration of Independence was first read in public in Boston and which overlooks the site of the Boston Massacre).

This was the seat of the colonial government from 1713 until the Revolution, and after the evacuation of the British from Boston in 1776 it served the independent Commonwealth until its replacement on Beacon Hill was completed in 1798. John Hancock was inaugurated here as the first governor under the new state constitution.

Like many other colonial-era landmarks, it fared poorly in the years that followed. Nineteenth-century photos show the old building with a mansard roof and signs in the windows advertising assorted businesses. In the 1830s the Old State House served as Boston's City Hall. When demolition was threatened in 1880 because the real estate was so valuable, the Bostonian Society organized a restoration, after which the Old State House reopened with a permanent collection that traces Boston's Revolutionary War history. Your ticket includes three different guided tours: the Boston Massacre Tour, the Old State House Tour, and the Revolutionary Boston Tour. ⊠ *206 Washington St., at State St., Downtown* ☎ *617/720–1713* ⊕ *www.bostonhistory. org* ⌖ *$10* Ⓜ *State.*

Rowes Wharf. Take a Beacon Hill redbrick town house, blow it up to the *n*th power, and you get this 15-story Skidmore, Owings & Merrill extravaganza from 1987, one of the more welcome additions to the Boston Harbor skyline. From under the complex's gateway six-story arch, you can get great views of Boston Harbor and the yachts docked at the marina. Water shuttles pull up here from Logan Airport—a gorgeous way to enter the city. A windswept stroll along the HarborWalk waterfront promenade at dusk makes for an unforgettable sunset on clear days. ⊠ *Atlantic Ave. south of India Wharf, Waterfront* Ⓜ *Aquarium.*

5

South Station. The colonnaded granite structure is the terminal for all Amtrak trains in and out of Boston as well as commuter trains originating from the west and south of the city. Next door on Atlantic Avenue is the terminal for Greyhound, Peter Pan, and other bus lines. Behind the station's grand 1900s facade, you'll find an airy, modern transit center. Thanks to its eateries, coffee bars, newsstand, flower stand, and other shops, waiting for a train here can actually be a pleasant experience. ✉ *Atlantic Ave. and Summer St., Downtown* ⊕ *www. south-station.net* Ⓜ *South Station.*

State Street. During the 19th century State Street was headquarters for banks, brokerages, and insurance firms; although these businesses have spread throughout the Downtown District, "State Street" still connotes much the same thing as "Wall Street" does in New York. The early commercial hegemony of State Street was symbolized by Long Wharf, built in 1710 and extending some 1,700 feet into the harbor. If today's Long Wharf doesn't appear to be that long, it's not because it has been shortened but because the land has crept out toward its end. State Street once met the water at the base of the Custom House; landfill operations were pursued relentlessly through the years, and the old coastline is now as much a memory as such colonial State Street landmarks as Governor Winthrop's 1630 house and the Revolutionary-era Bunch of Grapes Tavern, where Bostonians met to drink and wax indignant at their treatment by King George. ✉ *Between Cross and Congress Sts., Downtown* Ⓜ *State, Aquarium.*

U.S. Custom House. This 1847 structure resembles a Greek Revival temple that appears to have sprouted a tower. It's just that. This is the work of architects Ammi Young and Isaiah Rogers—at least, the bottom part is. The tower was added in 1915, at which time the Custom House became Boston's tallest building. It remains one of the most visible and best-loved structures in the city's skyline. To appreciate the grafting job, go inside and look at the domed rotunda. The outer surface of that dome was once the roof of the building, but now the dome is embedded in the base of the tower.

The federal government moved out of the Custom House in 1987 and sold it to the city of Boston, which, in turn, sold it to the Marriott Corporation, which has converted the building into hotel space and luxury time-share units, a move that disturbed some historical purists. You can now sip a cocktail in the hotel's bar after 6 pm, or visit the 26th-floor observation deck for a fee at 2 pm (except for Friday) and between 6 and 7 pm (with the purchase of a drink from the bar). The magnificent Rotunda Room sports maritime prints and antique artifacts, courtesy of the Peabody Essex Museum in Salem. ✉ *3 McKinley Sq., Downtown* ☎ *617/310–6300* 💲 *$4* Ⓜ *State, Aquarium.*

BACK BAY AND
THE SOUTH END

Getting Oriented

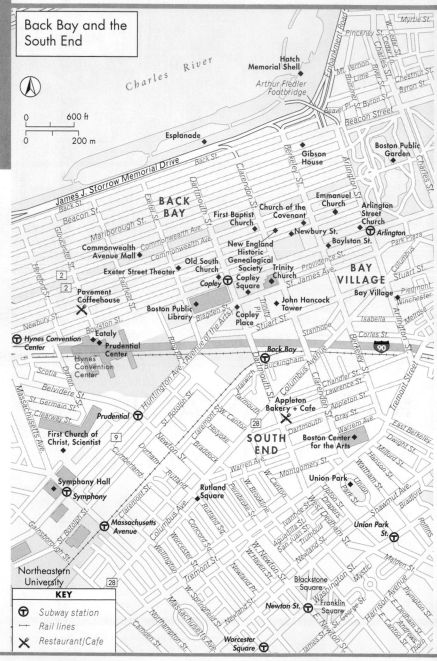

Back Bay and the
South End

0 ——— 600 ft
0 ——— 200 m

Charles River

Hatch
Memorial Shell

*Arthur Fiedler
Footbridge*

Boston Public
Garden

Esplanade

Gibson
House

Emmanuel
Church

Arlington
Street
Church

James J. Storrow Memorial Drive

**BACK
BAY**

First Baptist
Church

Church of the
Covenant

Newbury St.

Boylston St.

Arlington

Park Plaza

Commonwealth
Avenue Mall

Commonwealth Ave.

New England
Historic
Genealogical
Society

Columbus

Stuart St.

**BAY
VILLAGE**

Exeter Street Theater

Old South
Church

Copley

Copley
Square

Trinity
Church

St. James Ave.

Providence St.

Bay Village

Piedmont

Winchester

Pavement
Coffeehouse

Boston Public
Library

Blagden St.

Copley
Place

John Hancock
Tower

Isabella

Melrose

Hynes Convention
Center

Eataly

Prudential
Center

Boylston St.

Stuart St.

Stanhope

Corles St.

90

Hynes
Convention
Center

Avenue of the Arts

Back Bay

Buckingham

Columbus Avenue

Scotia

Belvidere St.

Huntington Ave.

Harwich

Yarmouth

Chandler St.

Lawrence St.

St. Germain St.

Clearway St.

Prudential

St. Botolph St.

Claremont

Holyoke

Canton

Appleton
Bakery + Cafe

Appleton St.

Gray St.

First Church of
Christ, Scientist

9

Cumberland

Durham

Newton St.

Braddock

28

**SOUTH
END**

Boston Center
for the Arts

Warren Ave.

Dwight St.

Milford St.

Symphony Hall

Symphony

Claremont St.

Rutland

Warren Ave.

W. Canton

Montgomery St.

Union Park

Waltham St.

Hanson St.

Rutland
Square

Pembroke St.

Ivanhoe St.

West Dedham St.

Union
Park St.

Drapers

Shawmut Ave.

Bradford

Massachusetts
Avenue

Columbus Avenue

Rutland Sq.

Concord Sq.

Aguadilla St.

San Juan St.

Trumbull St.

Union Park
St.

Northeastern
University

28

Worcester Sq.

Tremont St.

W. Newton St.

W. Haven St.

Newland Pl.

W. Brookline St.

Newland St.

W. Springfield St.

Blackstone
Square

Washington St.

Franklin
Square

Mystic

Malden St.

Plympton St.

Harrison Avenue

E. Dedham St.

KEY

- 🅣 Subway station
- ⊢ Rail lines
- ✕ Restaurant/Cafe

Newton St.

Camden St.

Northampton St.

Worcester
Square

GETTING HERE AND AROUND

There are myriad parking garages in Back Bay. Take the Orange Line to the Back Bay station or the Green Line to Copley for the heart of the shopping areas. The Arlington stop on the Green Line is the most convenient to the Public Garden.

The South End is easily accessible by the T; take the Orange Line to Back Bay and head south on Dartmouth Street to Columbus Avenue, or jump off the Silver Line at Union Park Street or East Berkeley Street to access the neighborhood.

TIMING

If you're not looking to max out your credit cards, then you can hurry past the boutiques and cover the Back Bay in about two hours. Allow at least half a day for a leisurely walk with frequent stops on Newbury Street and the shops at Copley Place and the Prudential Center. The reflecting pool at the Christian Science Church is a great time-out spot. Around the third week of April, magnolia time arrives, and nowhere do the flowers bloom more magnificently than along Commonwealth Avenue. In May the Public Garden bursts with color, thanks to its flowering dogwood trees and thousands of tulips. To stay oriented, remember that the north–south streets are arranged in alphabetical order, from Arlington to Hereford.

A few hours is perfect for exploring the South End; add a few more hours for a show at the Boston Center of the Arts or to dine at one of the many excellent restaurants in the area.

NEWBURY QUICK BITES

Pavement Coffeehouse. Enjoy coffee, snacks, and Wi-Fi access in this hip basement spot. ✉ *286 Newbury St., Back Bay* ☎ *617/859–9515* ⊕ *www.pavementcoffeehouse.com* Ⓜ *Hynes, Copley.*

TOP REASONS TO GO

■ Join the throngs of students, locals, and visitors window-shopping on Newbury Street.

■ Admire the architecture, revel in the artistry, and even enjoy an excellent lunch at the Boston Public Library—all without taking out a single book.

■ Visit the Public Garden on a sunny, late-spring day and take in the scenery from your seat on the Swan Boats. Don't forget to check out the bronze statues of the ducklings from Robert McCloskey's Boston classic *Make Way for Ducklings.*

■ Enjoy a play, concert, or art installation at the "people's" art-and-culture complex, the Boston Center for the Arts.

■ Shop Columbus Avenue and Tremont Street for the perfect additions to your home decor.

■ Walk the streets around Rutland Square, Union Park, and Bay Village. Architecture buffs will love the Victorian and Italianate row houses harking back to the neighborhood's 19th-century roots.

SOUTH END QUICK BITES

Appleton Bakery + Cafe. After a morning of gallery hopping in the South End, stop in for a bite at Appleton Bakery + Cafe. All the bakery goods are made fresh daily, and the breakfast burrito has many fans. ✉ *123 Appleton St., at Dartmouth St., Boston* ☎ *617/859–8222.*

6

Sightseeing
★★★★
Dining
★★★★
Lodging
★★★★
Shopping
★★★★★
Nightlife
★★★★★

In the roster of famous American neighborhoods, the Back Bay stands with New York's Park Avenue and San Francisco's Nob Hill as a symbol of propriety and high social standing. Before the 1850s it truly was a bay, a tidal flat that formed the south bank of a distended Charles River. The filling in of land along the isthmus that joined Boston to the mainland (the Neck) began in 1850, and resulted in the creation of the South End.

THE BACK BAY

Updated by
Kim Foley
MacKinnon

To the north a narrow causeway called the Mill Dam (later Beacon Street) was built in 1814 to separate the Back Bay from the Charles. By the late 1800s, Bostonians had filled in the shallows to as far as the marshland known as the Fenway, and the original 783-acre peninsula had been expanded by about 450 acres. Thus the waters of Back Bay became the neighborhood of Back Bay.

Heavily influenced by the then-recent rebuilding of Paris according to the plans of Baron Georges-Eugène Haussmann, the Back Bay planners created thoroughfares that resemble Parisian boulevards. The thorough planning included service alleys behind the main streets to allow provisioning wagons to drive up to basement kitchens. (Now they're used for waste pickup and parking.)

Today the area retains its posh spirit, but mansions are no longer the main draw. Locals and tourists alike flock to the commercial streets of Boylston and Newbury to shop at boutiques, galleries, and the usual mall stores. Many of the bars and restaurants have patio seating and bay windows, making the area the perfect spot to see and be seen while indulging in ethnic delicacies or an invigorating coffee. The Boston Public Library, Symphony Hall, and numerous churches ensure that high culture is not lost amid the frenzy of consumerism.

The Boston Public Library is a stunning cathedral of books.

TOP ATTRACTIONS

FAMILY
Fodor's Choice
★

Boston Public Garden. The Public Garden is America's oldest botanical garden, and is replete with gorgeous formal plantings. Keep in mind that the Boston Public Garden and Boston Common (not Commons!) are two separate entities with different histories and purposes and a distinct boundary between them at Charles Street. The Common has been public land since Boston was founded in 1630, whereas the Public Garden belongs to a newer Boston, occupying what had been salt marshes on the edge of the Common. By 1837 the tract was covered with an abundance of ornamental plantings donated by a group of private citizens. The area was defined in 1856 by the building of Arlington Street, and in 1860 the architect George Meacham was commissioned to plan the park.

The central feature of the Public Garden is its irregularly shaped pond, intended to appear, from any vantage point along its banks, much larger than its nearly 4 acres. The pond has been famous since 1877 for its foot-pedal-powered (by a captain) **Swan Boats** (⊕ *swanboats.com*), which make leisurely cruises during warm months. The pond is favored by ducks and swans, and for the modest price of a few boat rides you can amuse children here for an hour or more. Near the Swan Boat dock is what has been described as the world's smallest suspension bridge, designed in 1867 to cross the pond at its narrowest point.

The beds along the main walkways are replanted for spring and summer. The tulips during the first two weeks of May are especially colorful, and there's a sampling of native and European tree species.

The dominant work among the park's statuary is Thomas Ball's equestrian **George Washington** (1869), which faces the head of Commonwealth Avenue at the Arlington Street gate. This is Washington in a triumphant pose as liberator, surveying a scene that, from where he stood with his cannons at Dorchester Heights, would have included an immense stretch of blue water. Several dozen yards to the north of Washington (to the right if you're facing Commonwealth Avenue) is the granite-and-red-marble **Ether Monument**, donated in 1866 by Thomas Lee to commemorate the advent of anesthesia 20 years earlier at nearby Massachusetts General Hospital (you can visit the hospital to this day and see the famous Ether Dome). Other Public Garden monuments include statues of the Unitarian preacher and transcendentalist William Ellery Channing, at the corner opposite his Arlington Street Church; Edward Everett Hale, the author (*The Man Without a Country*) and philanthropist, at the Charles Street Gate; and the abolitionist senator Charles Sumner and the Civil War hero Colonel Thomas Cass, along Boylston Street.

The park contains a special delight for the young at heart; follow the children quack-quacking along the pathway between the pond and the park entrance at Charles and Beacon streets to the *Make Way for Ducklings* bronzes sculpted by Nancy Schön, a tribute to the 1941 classic children's story by Robert McCloskey. ⊠ *Bounded by Arlington, Boylston, Charles, and Beacon Sts., Back Bay* ☎ *617/522–1966 Swan Boats* ⊕ *friendsofthepublicgarden.org* ⌨ *Swan Boats $3.50* Ⓜ *Arlington.*

FAMILY
Fodor's Choice
★

Boston Public Library. This venerable institution is a handsome temple to literature and a valuable research library. The Renaissance Revival building was opened in 1895; a 1972 addition emulates the mass and proportion of the original, though not its extraordinary detail; this skylighted annex houses the library's circulating collections.

You don't need a library card to enjoy the magnificent art. The murals at the head of the staircase, depicting the nine muses, are the work of the French artist Puvis de Chavannes; those in the book-request processing room to the right are Edwin Abbey's interpretations of the Holy Grail legend. Upstairs, in the public areas leading to the fine-arts, music, and rare-books collections, is John Singer Sargent's mural series on the *Triumph of Religion*, shining with renewed color after its cleaning and restoration in 2003. The library offers free art and architecture tours daily. The corridor leading from the annex opens onto the Renaissance-style **courtyard**—an exact copy of the one in Rome's Palazzo della Cancelleria—around which the original library is built. A covered arcade furnished with chairs rings a fountain; you can bring books or lunch into the courtyard, which is open all the hours the library is open, and escape the bustle of the city. Beyond the courtyard is the main entrance hall of the 1895 building, with its immense stone lions by Louis St. Gaudens, vaulted ceiling, and marble staircase. The corridor at the top of the stairs leads to **Bates Hall,** one of Boston's most sumptuous interior spaces. This is the main reference reading room, 218 feet long with a barrel-arch ceiling 50 feet high. ⊠ *700 Boylston St., at Copley Sq., Back Bay* ☎ *617/536–5400* ⊕ *www.bpl.org* Ⓜ *Copley.*

The Houses of the Back Bay

The Back Bay remains a living museum of urban Victorian residential architecture. The earliest examples are nearest to the Public Garden (there are exceptions where showier turn-of-the-20th-century mansions replaced 1860s town houses), and the newer sites are out around the Massachusetts Avenue and Fenway extremes of the district. The height of Back Bay residences and their distance from the street are essentially uniform, as are the interior layouts, chosen to accord with lot width. Yet there's a distinct progression of facades, beginning with French academic and Italianate designs and moving through the various "revivals" of the 19th century. By the time of World War I, when development of the Back Bay was virtually complete, architects and their patrons had come full circle to a revival of the Federal period, which had been out of fashion for only 30 years when the building began. If the Back Bay architects had not run out of land, they might have gotten around to a Greek Revival revival.

The Great Depression brought an end to the Back Bay style of living, and today only a few of the houses are single-family residences. Most have been cut up into apartments, then expensive condominiums; during the boom years of the late 1990s some were returned to their original town-house status. Interior details have experienced a mixed fate: they suffered during the years when Victorian fashions were held in low regard and are undergoing careful restoration now that the aesthetic pendulum has reversed itself and moneyed condo buyers are demanding period authenticity. The original facades have survived on all but Newbury and Boylston streets, so the public face of the Back Bay retains much of the original charm and grandeur.

An outstanding guide to the architecture and history of the Back Bay is Bainbridge Bunting's *Houses of Boston's Back Bay* (Harvard, 1967). A few homes are open to the public.

✕ **Courtyard.** You can take a lunch break at the Courtyard or the MapRoom Café, adjoining restaurants in the Boston Public Library. Breakfast and lunch are served in the 1895 map room, and the main restaurant, which overlooks the courtyard, is open for lunch and afternoon tea. The library's newest venue, the Newsfeed Café, serves coffee, salads and pastries, and is also home to WGBH's satellite studio, where visitors might catch a taping of Boston Public Radio. ✉ *700 Boylston St., at Copley Sq., Back Bay* ☎ *617/859–2251* ⊕ *www.thecateredaffair.com/bpl/courtyard.*

Fodor's Choice ★ **Trinity Church.** In his 1877 masterpiece, architect Henry Hobson Richardson brought his Romanesque Revival style to maturity; all the aesthetic elements for which he was famous come together magnificently—bold polychromatic masonry, careful arrangement of masses, sumptuously carved interior woodwork—in this crowning centerpiece of Copley Square. A full appreciation of its architecture requires an understanding of the logistical problems of building it here. The Back Bay is a reclaimed wetland with a high water table. Bedrock, or at least stable glacial till, lies far beneath wet clay. Like all older Back Bay buildings, Trinity Church sits on submerged wooden pilings. But its central tower weighs 9,500 tons, and most of the 4,500 pilings beneath the building are under that tremendous central mass. The pilings are checked regularly for sinkage by means of a hatch in the basement.

Richardson engaged some of the best artists of his day—John LaFarge, William Morris, and Edward Burne-Jones among them—to execute the paintings and stained glass that make this a monument to everything that was right about the pre-Raphaelite spirit and the nascent aesthetic of Morris's Arts and Crafts movement. LaFarge's intricate paintings and ornamented ceilings received a much-needed overhaul during the extensive renovations completed in 2005. Along the north side of the church, note the Augustus Saint-Gaudens statue of Phillips Brooks—the most charismatic rector in New England, who almost single-handedly got Trinity built and furnished. Shining light of Harvard's religious community and lyricist of "O Little Town of Bethlehem," Brooks is shown here with Christ touching his shoulder in approval. For a nice respite, try to catch one of the Friday organ concerts beginning at 12:15. The 11:15 Sunday service is usually followed by a free guided tour. ⊠ *206 Clarendon St., Back Bay* ☎ *617/536–0944* ⊕ *trinitychurchboston.org* ✉ *Entrance free, guided and self-guided tours Tues.–Fri., $7* Ⓜ *Copley.*

6

WORTH NOTING

Arlington Street Church. Opposite the Park Square corner of the Public Garden, this church was erected in 1861—the first to be built in the Back Bay. Though a classical portico is a keynote and its model was London's St. Martin-in-the-Fields, Arlington Street Church is less picturesque and more Georgian in character. Note the Tiffany stained-glass windows. During the year preceding the Civil War the church was a hotbed of abolitionist fervor. Later, during the Vietnam War, this Unitarian-Universalist congregation became famous as a center of peace activism. ⊠ *351 Boylston St., Back Bay* ☎ *617/536–7050* ⊕ *www.ascboston.org* Ⓜ *Arlington.*

Boylston Street. Less posh than Newbury Street, this broad thoroughfare is the southern commercial spine of the Back Bay, lined with interesting restaurants and shops, and where you'll find the Boston Marathon Finish Line. ⊠ *Back Bay.*

Church of the Covenant. This 1867 Gothic Revival church, a National Historic Landmark at the corner of Newbury and Berkeley streets, has one of the largest collections of liturgical windows by Louis Comfort Tiffany in the country. It's crowned by a 236-foot-tall steeple—the tallest in Boston—that Oliver Wendell Holmes called "absolutely perfect." Inside, a 14-foot-high Tiffany lantern hangs from a breathtaking 100-foot ceiling. The church is now Presbyterian and United Church of Christ. ⊠ *67 Newbury St., enter at church office, Back Bay* ☎ *617/266–7480* ⊕ *www.cotcbos.org* Ⓜ *Arlington.*

Commonwealth Avenue Mall. The mall that extends down the middle of the Back Bay's Commonwealth Avenue, which serves as the green link between the Public Garden and the public parks system, is studded with statuary. One of the most interesting memorials, at the Exeter Street intersection, is a portrayal of naval historian and author Samuel Eliot Morison seated on a rock as if he were peering out to sea. The **Boston Women's Memorial,** installed in 2003, sculpted by Meredith Bergmann, is between Fairfield and Gloucester streets. Statues of Abigail Adams, Lucy Stone, and Phillis Wheatley celebrate the progressive ideas of these three women and their contributions to Boston's history.

A dramatic and personal memorial near Dartmouth Street is the **Vendome Monument,** dedicated to the nine firemen who died in a 1972 blaze at the Back Bay's Vendome Hotel, which, now office space, is across the street. The curved black-granite block, 29 feet long and waist high, is etched with the names of the dead. A bronze cast of a fireman's coat and hat is draped over the granite. ⊠ *Commonwealth Ave. between Arlington St. and Massachusetts Ave., Back Bay* Ⓜ *Arlington, Copley.*

Copley Place. Two modern structures dominate Copley Square—the **John Hancock Tower** off the southeast corner and the even more assertive Copley Place skyscraper on the southwest. An upscale, glass-and-brass urban mall built between 1980 and 1984, Copley Place includes two major hotels: the high-rise Westin and the Marriott Copley Place. Dozens of shops, restaurants, and offices are attractively grouped on several levels, surrounding bright, open indoor spaces. ⊠ *100 Huntington Ave., Back Bay* ⊕ *www.simon.com/mall/copley-place* Ⓜ *Copley.*

FAMILY **Copley Square.** Every April thousands find a glimpse of Copley Square the most wonderful sight in the world: this is where the runners of the Boston Marathon end their 26.2-mile race. The civic space is defined by three monumental older buildings. One is the stately, bowfront 1912 **Fairmont Copley Plaza Hotel,** which faces the square on St. James Avenue and serves as a dignified foil to its companions, two of the most important works of architecture in the United States: Trinity Church—Henry Hobson Richardson's masterwork of 1877—and the Boston Public Library, by McKim, Mead & White. The John Hancock Tower looms in the background. To honor the runners who stagger over the marathon's finish line, bronze statues of the Tortoise and the Hare engaged in their mythical race were cast by Nancy Schön, who also did the much-loved *Make Way for Ducklings* group in the Boston Public Garden. From May through October, a popular farmers' market draws crowds. ⊠ *Bounded by Dartmouth, Boylston, and Clarendon Sts. and St. James Ave., Back Bay* Ⓜ *Copley.*

Emmanuel Church. Built in 1860, this Back Bay Gothic Episcopal church is popular among classical music lovers—every Sunday morning at 10, from September to May, as part of the liturgy, a Bach cantata is performed; guest conductors have included Christopher Hogwood and Seiji Ozawa. ⊠ *15 Newbury St., Back Bay* ☎ *617/536–3355* ⊕ *www. emmanuelboston.org* Ⓜ *Arlington.*

FAMILY **Esplanade.** Near the corner of Beacon and Arlington streets, the Arthur Fiedler Footbridge crosses Storrow Drive to the 3-mile-long Esplanade and the **Hatch Memorial Shell.** The free concerts here in summer include the Boston Pops' immensely popular televised July 4 performance. For shows like this, Bostonians haul lawn chairs and blankets to the lawn in front of the shell; so bring a takeout lunch from a nearby restaurant, find an empty spot—no mean feat, so come early—and you'll feel right at home. An impressive stone bust of the late maestro Arthur Fiedler watches over the walkers, joggers, picnickers, and sunbathers who fill the Esplanade's paths on pleasant days. Here, too, is the turn-of-the-20th-century **Union Boat Club Boathouse,** headquarters for the country's oldest private rowing club. ⊠ *Back Bay* ⊕ *www.esplanadeassociation.org.*

Exeter Street Theater. This massive Romanesque structure was built in 1884 as a temple for the Working Union of Progressive Spiritualists. Beginning in 1911, it enjoyed a long run as a movie theater, then served a turn as a bookstore. Today, it's home to a private school. ⊠ *26 Exeter St., at Newbury St., Back Bay* ⊕ *www.fst.org/exeter.htm* Ⓜ *Copley.*

First Baptist Church. This 1872 structure, at the corner of Clarendon Street and Commonwealth Avenue, was architect Henry Hobson Richardson's first foray into Romanesque Revival. It was originally erected for the Brattle Square Unitarian Society, but Richardson ran over budget and the church went bankrupt and dissolved. In 1882, the building was bought by the Baptists. The figures on each side of its soaring tower were sculpted by Frédéric Auguste Bartholdi, the sculptor who designed the Statue of Liberty. The friezes represent four points at which God enters an individual's life: baptism, communion, marriage, and death. If you phone ahead for an appointment on a weekday, you may be given an informal tour. ⊠ *110 Commonwealth Ave., Back Bay* ☎ *617/267-3148* 🖙 *Free* Ⓜ *Copley.*

First Church of Christ, Scientist. The world headquarters of the Christian Science faith mixes the traditional with the modern—marrying Bernini to Le Corbusier by combining an old-world basilica with a sleek office complex designed by I. M. Pei & Partners and Araldo Cossutta, Associated Architects. Mary Baker Eddy's original granite First Church of Christ, Scientist (1894) has since been enveloped by a domed Renaissance Revival basilica, added to the site in 1906, and both church buildings are now surrounded by the offices of the Christian Science Publishing Society, where the *Christian Science Monitor* is produced, and by Cossutta's complex of church-administration structures completed in 1973. You can hear all 13,000-plus pipes of the church's famed Aeolian-Skinner organ during services. Free tours are offered Tuesday through Sunday on the hour and half-hour and last about 20 minutes. ⊠ *275 Massachusetts Ave., Back Bay* ☎ *617/450-2000* ⊕ *www. christianscience.com/church-of-christ-scientist/the-mother-church-in-boston-ma-usa* 🖙 *Free* Ⓜ *Hynes, Symphony.*

Gibson House. Through the foresight of an eccentric bon vivant, this house provides an authentic glimpse into daily life in Boston's Victorian era. One of the first Back Bay residences (1859), the Gibson House is relatively modest in comparison with some of the grand mansions built during the decades that followed; yet its furnishings, from its 1795 Willard clock to the raised and gilded wallpaper to the multipiece faux-bamboo bedroom set, seem sumptuous to modern eyes. Unlike other

Back Bay houses, the Gibson family home has been preserved with all its Victorian fixtures and furniture intact. The house serves as the meeting place for the New England chapter of the Victorian Society in America; it was also used as an interior for the 1984 Merchant-Ivory film *The Bostonians.* ⊠ *137 Beacon St., Back Bay* ☎ *617/267–6338* ⊕ *www. thegibsonhouse.org* ⊠ *$9* ⊙ *Closed Mon. and Tues.* Ⓜ *Arlington.*

John Hancock Tower. In the early 1970s, the tallest building in New England became notorious as the monolith that rained glass from time to time. Windows were improperly seated in the sills of the blue rhomboid tower, designed by I. M. Pei. Once the building's 13 acres of glass were replaced and the central core stiffened, the problem was corrected. Bostonians originally feared the Hancock's stark modernism would overwhelm nearby Trinity Church, but its shimmering sides reflect the older structure's image, actually enlarging its presence. The tower is closed to the public. ⊠ *200 Clarendon St., Back Bay* ⊕ *www.200clarendon.com* Ⓜ *Copley.*

Newbury Street. Eight-block-long Newbury Street has been compared to New York's 5th Avenue, and certainly this is the city's poshest shopping area, with branches of Chanel, Diane von Furstenberg, Burberry, Kate Spade, Marc Jacobs, and other top names in fashion. But here the pricey boutiques are more intimate than grand, and people live above the trendy restaurants and ubiquitous hair salons, giving the place a neighborhood feel. Toward the Massachusetts Avenue end, cafés proliferate and the stores get funkier, ending with Newbury Comics and Urban Outfitters. ⊠ *From Arlington St. to Massachusetts Ave., Back Bay* ⊕ *www.newbury-st.com* Ⓜ *Hynes, Copley.*

New England Historic Genealogical Society. Are you related to Miles Standish or Priscilla Alden? The answer may lie here. If your ancestors were pedigreed New Englanders—or if you're just interested in genealogical research of any kind—you can trace your family tree with the help of the society's collections. The society dates from 1845, and is the oldest genealogical organization in the country. ⊠ *101 Newbury St., Back Bay* ☎ *888/296–3447* ⊕ *www.americanancestors.org* ⊠ *$20 for nonmembers to use facility* ⊙ *Closed Sun.* Ⓜ *Copley.*

NEED A BREAK

Trident Booksellers & Café. Folks gather at the two-story Trident Booksellers & Café to review literary best sellers, thumb through the superb magazine selection, and chow down on items from the perpetual breakfast menu. The restaurant also serves lunch and dinner and has an excellent beer selection, as well as wine. Readings and other events are held at the bookstore. It's open from 8 am until midnight daily. ⊠ *338 Newbury St., Back Bay* ☎ *617/267–8688* ⊕ *www.tridentbookscafe.com* Ⓜ *Hynes.*

Old South Church. Members of the Old South Meeting House, of Tea Party fame, decamped to this new site in 1873, a move not without controversy. In an Italian Gothic style inspired by the art critic John Ruskin and an interior decorated with Venetian mosaics and stained-glass windows, the "new" structure could hardly be more different from the plain meetinghouse they vacated. The sanctuary is free and open to the public seven days a week. ⊠ *645 Boylston St., Back Bay* ☎ *617/536–1970* ⊕ *www.oldsouth.org* Ⓜ *Copley.*

FAMILY **Prudential Center.** The 52-story Prudential Tower, or the "Pru," dominates the acreage between Boylston Street and Huntington Avenue. Its enclosed shopping mall is connected by a glass bridge to the more upscale Copley Place. The popular food emporium, Eataly, located in the Pru, offers a great spot for a quick bite. As for the Prudential Tower itself, the architectural historian Bainbridge Bunting made an acute observation when he called it "an apparition so vast in size that it appears to float above the surrounding district without being related to it." Later modifications to the Boylston Street frontage of the Prudential Center effected a better union of the complex with the urban space around it, but the tower itself floats on, vast as ever. **Prudential Center Skywalk Observatory,** a 50th-floor observatory atop the Prudential Tower, offers panoramic vistas of Boston, Cambridge, and the suburbs to the west and south—on clear days, you can even see Cape Cod. Your ticket includes an audio tour, admission to the Dreams of Freedom Museum, and the multimedia theater. You can go two floors up to the Top of the Hub for drinks or dinner. ⊠ *800 Boylston St., Back Bay* ☏ *800/746-7778, 617/859-0648 for Skywalk* ⊕ *www.prudentialcenter.com* ☏ *Skywalk $19* Ⓜ *Prudential Center, Copley Station.*

Hynes Convention Center. The Hynes Convention Center hosts conferences, trade shows, and conventions. It's connected to the Prudential Center, where visitors can find a branch of the Greater Boston Visitors Bureau in the center court of the mall. ⊠ *900 Boylston St., Back Bay* ☏ *617/954-2000* ⊕ *www.massconvention.com* Ⓜ *Hynes Convention Center Station.*

Symphony Hall. While Boston's Symphony Hall—the home of the Boston Symphony Orchestra and the Boston Pops—is considered among the best in the world for its sublime acoustics, it's also worth visiting to enjoy its other merits. The stage is framed by an enormous organ facade and an intricate golden proscenium. Above the second balcony are 16 replicas of Greek and Roman statues, which, like the rest of the Hall, marry the acoustic and aesthetic by creating niches and uneven surfaces to enhance the acoustics of the space. Although acoustical science was a brand-new field of research when Professor Wallace Sabine planned the interior, not one of the 2,500 seats is a bad one—the secret is the box-within-a-box design. ⊠ *301 Massachusetts Ave., Back Bay* ☏ *888/266-1200 box office, 617/638-9390 tours* ⊕ *www. bso.org* Ⓜ *Symphony.*

THE SOUTH END

The South End lost many residents to the Back Bay in the late 19th century, but in the late 1970s, middle-class professionals began snapping up town houses at bargain prices and restoring them. Solidly back in fashion now, the South End's redbrick row houses in various states of refurbished splendor now house a mix of ethnic groups, the city's largest gay community, and some excellent shops and restaurants.

Today a large African American community resides along Columbus Avenue and Mass Ave. (short for Massachusetts Avenue), which marks the beginning of the predominantly black neighborhood of Roxbury. Boston's gay community also has a strong presence in the South End. If you like to shop, you'll have a blast in this area, which focuses on home furnishings and accessories, with a heavy accent on the unique and handmade. At the northern tip of the South End, where Harrison Avenue and Washington Street lead to Chinatown, are several Chinese supermarkets. South of Washington Street is the "SoWa" District, home to a large number of art galleries, many of which have relocated here from pricey Newbury Street. From May through October, the excellent SoWa Open Market on Sunday is a great excursion, packed with artists, food trucks, and a farmers' market.

TOP ATTRACTIONS

Rutland Square. Reflecting a time when the South End was the most prestigious Boston address, this slice of a park is framed by lovely Italianate bowfront houses. ⊠ *Rutland Sq. between Columbus Ave. and Tremont St., South End.*

Union Park. Cast-iron fences, Victorian-era town houses, and a grassy area all add up to one of Boston's most charming mini-escapes. ⊠ *Union Park St. between Shawmut Ave. and Tremont St., South End.*

NEED A BREAK

✕ **Flour Bakery + Café.** A good spot to refuel on a budget is Flour Bakery + Café, a perennial candidate for Boston's best sandwiches and stuffed bread. Also superb are the fresh pizzas, dinner specials, and delicious pastries. You may end up taking home one of their cookbooks as a sweet keepsake. ⊠ *1595 Washington St., South End* ☎ *617/267–4300* ⊕ *www.flourbakery. com* Ⓜ *Back Bay/South End.*

WORTH NOTING

Bay Village. This pocket of early-19th-century brick row houses, near Arlington and Piedmont streets, is a fine, mellow neighborhood (Edgar Allan Poe was born here). Its window boxes and short, narrow streets make the area seem a toylike reproduction of Beacon Hill. Note that, owing to the street pattern, it's nearly impossible to drive to Bay Village, and it's easy to miss on foot. ⊠ *Bounded (roughly) by Arlington, Stuart, Charles, and Marginal Sts., South End* ⊕ *www.bayvillage.net.*

Boston Center for the Arts. Of Boston's multiple arts organizations, this nonprofit arts-and-culture complex is one of the most lively and diverse. Here you can see the work of budding playwrights, check out rotating exhibits from contemporary artists, or stop in for a curator's talk and other special events. The BCA houses six performance spaces, a community music center, the Mills Art Gallery, and studio space for some 40 Boston-based contemporary artists. ⊠ *539 Tremont St., South End* ☎ *617/426–5000* ⊕ *www.bcaonline.org* ⊠ *Free* Ⓜ *Back Bay/South End.*

7

THE FENWAY

Getting Oriented

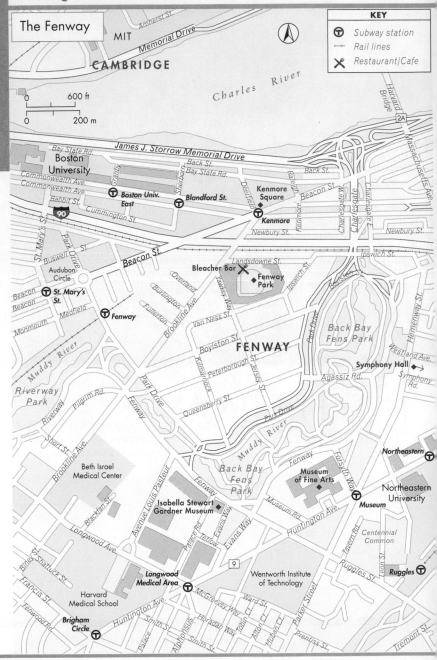

The Fenway

MIT

CAMBRIDGE

Charles River

KEY
🚇 Subway station
— Rail lines
✕ Restaurant/Cafe

Amherst St.

Memorial Drive

Harvard Bridge

0 ——— 600 ft
0 ——— 200 m

2A

James J. Storrow Memorial Drive

Bay State Rd.

Boston University

Back St.

Bay State Rd.

Back St.

Commonwealth Ave.
Commonwealth Ave.

Granby St.

Sherborn St.

Deerfield St.

Kenmore Square

Raleigh St.

Beacon St.

Charlesgate W.

Charlesgate E.

Massachusetts Ave.

Newbury St.

🚇 Boston Univ. East

Babbit St.

90

Cummington St.

Blandford St. 🚇

🚇 Kenmore

Newbury St.

Kenmore St.

St. Mary's St.

Buswell St.

Park Drive

Beacon St.

Landsdowne St.

Bleacher Bar ✕

Fenway Park

Ipswich St.

Ipswich St.

Lansdowne St.

Audubon Circle

🚇 St. Mary's St.

Beacon St.

Beacon

Medfield St.

🚇 Fenway

Burlington Ave.

Fullerton St.

Brookline Ave.

Overland St.

Yawkey Way

Van Ness St.

Brookline St.

Park Drive

Back Bay Fens Park

Boylston St.

Hemenway St.

Monmouth St.

FENWAY

Westland Ave.

Muddy River

Kilmarnock St.

Peterborough St.

Jersey St.

Agassiz Rd.

Symphony Hall

Symphony Rd.

Riverway Park

Park Drive

Queensberry St.

Park Drive

Riverway

Pilgrim Rd.

Fenway

Muddy River

Short St.

Brookline Ave.

Back Bay Fens Park

Fenway

Forsyth Way

Northeastern 🚇

Beth Israel Medical Center

Avenue Louis Pasteur

Museum of Fine Arts

Museum Rd.

Northeastern University

Blackfan St.

Isabella Stewart Gardner Museum

Palace Rd.

Evans Way

Huntington Ave.

🚇 Museum

Centennial Common

Longwood Ave.

Tetlow St.

Evans Way

Leon St.

Binney St.

Shattuck St.

Harvard Medical School

Longwood Medical Area 🚇

9

Wentworth Institute of Technology

Ruggles St.

Parker Street

Ruggles 🚇

Francis St.

Brigham Circle 🚇

Palace St.

Huntington Ave.

McGreevey Way

Smith St.

Horadan Way

Ward St.

Tavern Rd.

Tremont St.

Fenwood Rd.

Alphonsus St.

Robin Ct.

Afton Ct.

Huban Ct.

Prentiss St.

GETTING HERE AND AROUND

The Green Line is the way to go when it comes to getting to the Fenway; get off at the Kenmore or Fenway stop for a short walk to the ballpark. Also know that it *is* possible to drive around this part of town. With a little hunting, on-street parking can usually be found on nongame days; if not, many lots and garages are within reasonable walking distance of Fenway Park.

TIMING AND SAFETY

Although this area can be walked through in a couple of hours, art lovers could spend a week here, thanks to the glories of the MFA and the Isabella Stewart Gardner Museum. (If you want to do a museum blowout, avoid Tuesday, when the Gardner is closed.) To cap off a day of culture, plan for dinner in the area and then a concert at nearby Symphony Hall. Another option, if you're visiting between spring and early fall, is to take a tour of Fenway Park — or better yet, catch a game.

The Fenway and Kenmore Square area is generally safe, and is home to thousands of college students attending Boston University, Wheelock, Simmons, and Emmanuel, to name only a few of the nearby institutions. While the main strips—Beacon Street, Commonwealth Avenue, and Brookline Avenue—can be choked with pedestrians during game day, the marshy area of the Fens is quiet and poorly lighted: avoid walking there alone at night.

QUICK BITES

Nothing beats a dog and a beer at Fenway when you're enjoying the game on a warm summer's night. But even if you don't have a ticket, you can enjoy the same vibe at **Bleacher Bar** (⊠ *82A Landsdowne St.*), a hidden-away bar in Fenway Park with a view into center field, and enough historical Red Sox memorabilia to open its own museum.

TOP REASONS TO GO

■ Root for the home team (the *only* team in the eyes of Red Sox Nation) at Fenway Park.

■ Immerse yourself in masterpieces at the MFA and the Isabella Stewart Gardner Museum.

■ Relish the perfect acoustics of a concert at Symphony Hall.

BALLPARK TIP

If you plan on catching a game at Fenway in the spring, bring warm clothes or a blanket. It can get chilly in Boston, especially if you're sitting up in the stands. April lows are in the 40s and in May it can still get down to 50.

FENWAY PARK TOURS

If you can't see the Sox, you can still see the Green Monster up close by going on a tour of the park. The one-hour Fenway walking tours run year-round, and if you go on the day's last tour on a home-game day, you can watch batting practice. Tours run hourly from 9 am to 5 pm (or four hours before game time) and cost $20. Check the site for info on premium tours. ☎ *617/226–6666* ⊕ *boston. redsox.mlb.com/bos/ballpark/ tour.jsp.*

7

Sightseeing
★★★★
Dining
★★★
Lodging
★★★
Shopping
★★
Nightlife
★★★★

The Back Bay Fens marshland gave this neighborhood its name, but two iconic institutions give it its character: Fenway Park, which in 2004 saw the triumphant reversal of an 86-year drought for Boston's beloved Red Sox, and the Isabella Stewart Gardner Museum, the legacy of a high-living Brahmin who attended a concert at Symphony Hall in 1912 wearing a headband that read "Oh, You Red Sox." Not far from the Gardner is another major cultural magnet: the Museum of Fine Arts. Kenmore Square, a favorite haunt for Boston University students, adds a bit of youthful flavor to the mix.

Updated by
Kim Foley
MacKinnon

After the outsize job of filling in the bay had been completed, it would have been small trouble to obliterate the Fens with gravel and march row houses straight through to Brookline. But the planners, deciding that enough pavement had been laid between here and the Public Garden, hired vaunted landscape architect Frederick Law Olmsted to turn the Fens into a park. Olmsted applied his genius for heightening natural effects while subtly manicuring their surroundings; today the Fens park consists of irregularly shaped reed-bound pools surrounded by broad meadows, trees, and flower gardens.

The Fens marks the beginning of Boston's Emerald Necklace, a loosely connected chain of parks designed by Olmsted that extends along the Fenway, Riverway, and Jamaicaway to Jamaica Pond, the Arnold Arboretum, and Franklin Park.

A GOOD WALK

With Boston's two major art museums on this itinerary, a case of museum fatigue could set in. However, both the Museum of Fine Arts and the Isabella Stewart Gardner Museum are surrounded by the sylvan glades of the Fenway—a perfect oasis and time-out location when you're suffering from gallery overload. From the intersection of Massachusetts and Huntington avenues, with the front entrance of Symphony Hall on your right, walk down Huntington Avenue. On your left is the New England Conservatory of Music and, on Gainsborough Street, its recital center, Jordan Hall. Between Huntington Avenue and the Fenway is the **Museum of Fine Arts (MFA)** and, just around the corner, the **Isabella Stewart Gardner Museum.** If you prefer to pay homage to the Red Sox: from Symphony Hall, go north on Mass Ave., turn left on Commonwealth Avenue, and continue until you reach **Kenmore Square**; from here it's a 10-minute walk down Brookline Avenue to Yawkey Way and **Fenway Park.**

TOP ATTRACTIONS

Fodor's Choice ★ **Fenway Park.** For 86 years, the Boston Red Sox suffered a World Series dry spell, a streak of bad luck that fans attributed to the "Curse of the Bambino," which, stories have it, struck the team in 1920 when they sold Babe Ruth (the "Bambino") to the New York Yankees. All that changed in 2004, when a maverick squad broke the curse in a thrilling seven-game series against the team's nemesis in the series semifinals. This win against the Yankees was followed by a four-game sweep of St. Louis in the finals. Boston, and its citizens' ingrained sense of pessimism, hasn't been the same since. The repeat World Series win in 2007, and again in 2013, cemented Bostonians' sense that the universe had finally begun working correctly and made Red Sox caps the residents' semiofficial uniform. ⊠ *4 Yawkey Way, between Van Ness and Lansdowne Sts., The Fenway* ☎ *877/733–7699 box office, 617/226–6666 tours* ⊕ *www.redsox.com* ⊟ *Tours $20* Ⓜ *Kenmore.*

Fodor's Choice ★ **Isabella Stewart Gardner Museum.** A spirited society woman, Isabella Stewart came in 1860 from New York to marry John Lowell Gardner, one of Boston's leading citizens. "Mrs. Jack" promptly set about becoming the most un-Bostonian of the Proper Bostonians. She built a Venetian palazzo to hold her collected arts in one of Boston's newest neighborhoods. Her will stipulated that the building remain exactly as she left it—paintings, furniture, and the smallest object in a hall cabinet—and that is as it has remained.

Gardner's palazzo includes such masterpieces as Titian's *Europa,* Giotto's *Presentation of Christ in the Temple,* Piero della Francesca's *Hercules,* and John Singer Sargent's *El Jaleo.* Spanish leather panels, Renaissance hooded fireplaces, and Gothic tapestries accent salons; eight balconies adorn the majestic Venetian courtyard. There's a Raphael Room, Spanish Cloister, Gothic Room, Chinese Loggia, and a magnificent Tapestry Room for concerts, where Gardner entertained Henry James and Edith Wharton.

On March 18, 1990, the Gardner was the target of a sensational art heist. Thieves disguised as police officers stole 12 works, including Vermeer's *The Concert*. None of the art has been recovered, despite a $5 million reward. Because Mrs. Gardner's will prohibited substituting other works for any stolen art, empty expanses of wall identify spots where the paintings once hung.

The modern addition to the museum opened in 2012. The Renzo Piano–designed building houses a music hall, exhibit space, and conservation labs, where Gardner's works can be repaired and preserved. ■ TIP→ A quirk of the museum's admission policy waives entrance fees to anyone named Isabella and on your birthday. ✉ *25 Evans Way, The Fenway* ☏ *617/566–1401, 617/566–1088 café* ⊕ *www.gardnermuseum.org* ⧉ *$15* ⊙ *Closed Tues.* Ⓜ *Museum.*

FAMILY
Fodor'sChoice
★

Museum of Fine Arts. The MFA's collection of approximately 450,000 objects was built from a core of paintings and sculpture from the Boston Athenæum, historical portraits from the city of Boston, and donations by area universities. The MFA has more than 70 works by John Singleton Copley; major paintings by Winslow Homer, John Singer Sargent, Fitz Henry Lane, and Edward Hopper; and a wealth of American works ranging from native New England folk art and Colonial portraiture to New York abstract expressionism of the 1950s and 1960s.

More than 30 galleries contain the MFA's European painting and sculpture collection, dating from the 11th century to the 20th. Contemporary art has a dynamic home in the MFA's dramatic I. M. Pei–designed building. ✉ *465 Huntington Ave., The Fenway* ☏ *617/267–9300* ⊕ *www.mfa.org* ⧉ *$25 (good for 2 days in a 10-day period)* Ⓜ *Museum.*

WORTH NOTING

Kenmore Square. Two blocks north of Fenway Park is Kenmore Square, where you'll find shops, restaurants, and the city's iconic sign advertising Citgo gasoline. The red, white, and blue neon sign from 1965 is so thoroughly identified with the area that historic preservationists fought, successfully, to save it. The old Kenmore Square punk clubs have given way to a block-long development of pricey stores and restaurants, as well as brick sidewalks, gaslight-style street lamps, and tree plantings. In the shadow of Fenway Park between Brookline and Ipswich is **Lansdowne Street,** a nightlife magnet for the trendy who have their pick of dance clubs and pregame bars. The urban campus of Boston University begins farther west on Commonwealth Avenue, in blocks thick with dorms, shops, and restaurants. ✉ *Convergence of Beacon St., Commonwealth Ave., and Brookline Ave., The Fenway* Ⓜ *Kenmore.*

BOSTON
OUTSKIRTS

Getting Oriented

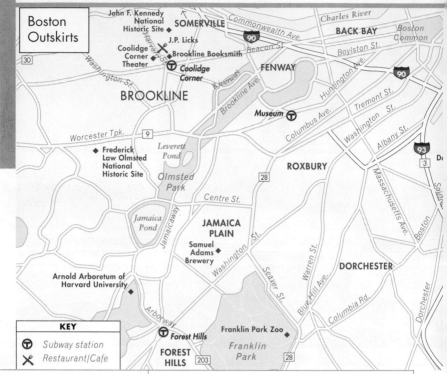

Boston Outskirts

GETTING HERE AND AROUND	TOP REASONS TO GO
Although driving to these suburbs is relatively painless, they're not called the "streetcar suburbs" for nothing. To get to South Boston, hop off the Red Line at Broadway. To reach the Arnold Arboretum in Jamaica Plain, take the Orange Line to the end at Forest Hills. Brookline is accessible via the C and D lines of the Green Line.	■ Marvel at the architectural wonder cantilevered over Boston Harbor that houses the Institute of Contemporary Art.
	■ Relive the history of Camelot with a visit to the John F. Kennedy Library and Museum.
	■ Tour the Samuel Adams Brewery, home to Boston's own award-winning beers. Free samples at the end are the highlight of the tour.

TIMING AND SAFETY

Timing all depends on which areas you decide to explore. Each neighborhood merits a half day, especially factoring in travel time from Boston proper and a leisurely lunch or dinner.

Generally, most of these neighborhoods are safe, particularly in the areas where these attractions reside. But use common sense: stick to well-lighted areas and avoid walking alone late at night.

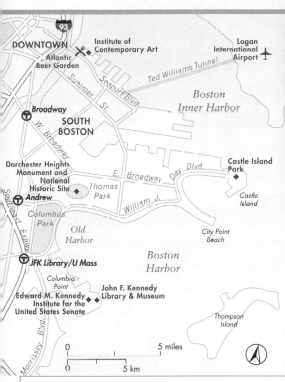

BOSTON'S ICONIC BEER

Before Prohibition, Jamaica Plain was home to a thriving beer industry, the remnants of which can be seen in the neighborhood's 19th-century brick breweries, long since converted to offices and lofts.

Samuel Adams Brewery. Free tastings at the Samuel Adams Brewery are the highlight of the first-come, first-served tours. ✉ *30 Germania St., Jamaica Plain* ☎ *617/368–5080* ⊕ *www.samueladams. com* ☞ *$2 suggested donation* ⊙ *Closed Sun.* Ⓜ *Green.*

8

QUICK BITES

Atlantic Beer Garden. If you happen to be visiting the ICA, take a break at the Atlantic Beer Garden. Just steps from the art museum, the bar and restaurant has dozens of flat screens to catch every game, and gorgeous views of the harbor and the ICA from the deck, where you can dine alfresco in summer. ✉ *146 Seaport Blvd., Waterfront* ☎ *617/357–8000* ⊕ *www.atlanticbeergarden.com.*

A GOOD WALK

A stroll down Brookline's Harvard Street is a great way to spend a few hours if you're in the neighborhood. Browse the bookshelves at **Brookline Booksmith** (✉ *279 Harvard St.*), an excellent local bookstore; or take in an independent film at the **Coolidge Corner Theater** (✉ *290 Harvard St.*). After window-shopping, treat yourself to a few scoops at **J. P. Licks** (✉ *311 Harvard St.*), arguably some of the Boston area's best ice cream.

Sightseeing
★★★
Dining
★★
Lodging
★★
Shopping
★★★
Nightlife
★★

The expansion of Boston in the 1800s was not confined to the Back Bay and the South End. Toward the close of the century, as the working population of the Downtown district swelled and public transportation (first horsecars, then electric trolleys) linked outlying suburbs with the city, development of the "streetcar suburbs" began. These areas answered the housing needs of the rising native-born middle class as well as the growing second-generation immigrant families. Today, most of these neighborhoods are technically in the city of Boston, yet have retained their own distinct personalities and charms.

Updated by
Kim Foley
MacKinnon

The landfill project that became South Boston—known as "Southie" and not to be confused with the South End—isn't a true streetcar suburb; its expansion predates the era of commuting. Some of the brick bowfront residences along East Broadway in City Point date from the 1840s and 1850s, but the neighborhood really came into its own with the influx of Irish around 1900, and Irish Americans still hold sway here. Southie is a Celtic enclave, as the raucous annual St. Patrick's Day parade attests.

Among the streetcar suburbs are Dorchester and Jamaica Plain (now part of Boston proper)—rural retreats barely more than a century ago that are now thick with tenements and Boston's distinctive three- and six-family triple-decker apartment houses. Dorchester is almost exclusively residential, tricky to navigate by car, and accessible by the T only if you know exactly where you're going. Jamaica Plain is a hip, young neighborhood with a strong lesbian and ecofriendly population; brunch and a wander through the neighborhood's quirky stores or through the Arnold Arboretum make for a relaxing weekend excursion. Both towns border Franklin Park, an Olmsted creation of more than 500 acres, noted for its zoo. Farther west, Brookline is composed of a mixture of the affluent and students.

SOUTH BOSTON

TOP ATTRACTION

Fodor's Choice ★ **Institute of Contemporary Art.** Housed in a breathtaking cantilevered edifice that juts out over the Boston waterfront, the ICA moved to this site in 2006 as part of a massive reinvention that has made the museum one of Boston's most exciting attractions. Since its founding in 1936, the institute has cultivated its cutting-edge status: it's played host to works by Edvard Munch, Egon Schiele, and Oskar Kokoschka. Early in their careers, Andy Warhol, Robert Rauschenberg, and Roy Lichtenstein each mounted pivotal exhibitions here. The ICA's permanent collection showcases work by contemporary artists featured in ICA exhibitions, many at seminal moments in their careers. ⊠ *100 Northern Ave., South Boston* ☎ *617/478–3100* ⊕ *www.icaboston.org* ☞ *$15, free Thurs. 5–9, free for families last Sat. of month (except Dec.)* ☉ *Closed Mon.* Ⓜ *Courthouse.*

WORTH NOTING

FAMILY **Castle Island Park.** South Boston projects farther into the harbor than any other part of Boston except Logan Airport, and the views of the Harbor Islands from along Day Boulevard or Castle Island are expansive. At L Street and Day Boulevard is the L Street Beach, where an intrepid group called the L Street Brownies swims year-round, including a celebratory dip in the icy Atlantic every New Year's Day. Castle Island Park is no longer on an island, but **Fort Independence,** when it was built here in 1801, was separated from the mainland by water. The circular walk from the fort around Pleasure Bay, delightful on a warm summer day, has a stunning view of the city's skyline late at night. If you get peckish, stop by Sullivan's (open February through November), a Castle Island institution for more than 60 years, for a hot dog and fries. To get here by the T, take the Red Line to Broadway Station. Just outside the station, catch Bus 9 or 11 going east on Broadway, which takes you to within a block of the waterfront. From the waterfront park you can walk the loop, via piers, around the island. ⊠ *Off William J. Day Blvd., South Boston* ☎ *617/727–5290* ⊕ *www.mass.gov/eea/agencies/dcr/massparks/region-boston/castle-island-pleasure-bay-m-street-and-carson-beach.html* ☞ *Tours Memorial Day–Labor Day, call for specific tour times* Ⓜ *Broadway Station.*

8

DORCHESTER

TOP ATTRACTIONS

FAMILY **Edward M. Kennedy Institute for the United States Senate.** Located adjacent to the JFK Library and Museum, the Edward M. Kennedy Institute for the United States Senate offers another view of the workings of the U.S. government, this one through the lens of the Senate and one of its most influential members. Interactive exhibits take visitors through a day in the life of a senator and the highlight is the stunning full-scale representation of the Senate Chamber. In addition, there's an exact reproduction of Senator Kennedy's office, complete with photos of his family, model ships, and letters from his mother. It's definitely worth planning to visit both Kennedy attractions. ⊠ *Colombia Point, Dorchester* 🕾 *617/740–7000* ⊕ *www.emkinstitute.org* 💷 *$14* ◐ *Closed Mon.* Ⓜ *JFK/UMass, then free shuttle bus every 20 min.*

FAMILY   **Franklin Park Zoo.** Lion and tiger habitats, the Giraffe Savannah, and a 4-acre mixed-species area called the Serengeti Crossing that showcases zebras, ostriches, warthogs, and wildebeests keep this zoo roaring. The Tropical Forest, with its Western Lowland Gorilla environment, is a big draw, and kookaburras, emus, and kangaroos populate the Outback Trail. From May to September butterflies flit and flutter at Butterfly Landing, where docents are on hand to answer questions and give advice on attracting the colorful insects to your own garden. Franklin Farm entices children with sheep, goats, and other farm animals. In winter, call in advance to find out which animals are braving the cold. The park, 4 miles from downtown, is reached by Bus 16 from the Forest Hills (Orange Line) or Andrew (Red Line) T stops; there's plenty of parking. ⊠ *1 Franklin Park Rd., Dorchester* 🕾 *617/541–5466* ⊕ *www. zoonewengland.com* 💷 *$20* Ⓜ *Forest Hills.*

Fodor's Choice   **John F. Kennedy Library & Museum.** The library-museum is both a center
★   for serious scholarship and a focus for Boston's nostalgia for her native son. The stark, white, prowlike building (another modernist monument designed by I. M. Pei) at this harbor-enclosed site pays homage to the life and presidency of John F. Kennedy and to members of his family, including his wife, Jacqueline, and brother Robert.

The Kennedy Library is the official repository of his presidential papers; the museum displays a trove of Kennedy memorabilia, including re-creations of his desk in the Oval Office and of the television studio in which he debated Richard M. Nixon in the 1960 election. At the entrance, high and dry during the summer months, is the president's 26-foot sailboat; inside, two theaters show a film about his life. The museum exhibits, ranging from the Cuban missile crisis to his assassination, include 20 video presentations. There's also a permanent display on the late Jacqueline Kennedy Onassis, including such personal mementos as a first edition of *One Special Summer,* the book she and her sister wrote and illustrated shortly after a 1951 trip to Paris. A re-creation of the office Robert Kennedy occupied as attorney general from 1961 to 1964 complements "legacy" videos of John's idealistic younger brother. The facility also includes a store and a small café. ⊠ *Columbia Point, Dorchester* 🕾 *617/514–1600* ⊕ *www.jfklibrary.org* 💷 *$14* Ⓜ *JFK/UMass, then free shuttle bus every 20 min.*

WORTH NOTING

Dorchester Heights Monument and National Historic Site. In 1776 Dorchester Heights hill commanded a clear view of central Boston, where the British had been under siege since the preceding year. Here George Washington set up the cannons that Henry Knox, a Boston bookseller turned soldier, and later secretary of war, had hauled through the wilderness after their capture at Fort Ticonderoga. The artillery did its job of intimidation, and the British troops left Boston, never to return. The view of Boston from the site is magnificent. Sadly, the tower is not open to the public, but the lovely park grounds are a destination on their own on a warm day. ⌧ *Thomas Park off Telegraph St., near G St., Dorchester* ☎ 617/242–5642 ⊕ *www.nps.gov/bost/historyculture/ dohe.htm* ⍾ *Free* |M| *Broadway, then City Point Bus (9 or 11) to G St.*

JAMAICA PLAIN

TOP ATTRACTIONS

FAMILY

Fodor'sChoice
★

Arnold Arboretum of Harvard University. This 281-acre living laboratory established in 1872 in accordance with the terms of a bequest from New Bedford merchant James Arnold contains more than 4,000 kinds of woody plants, most from the hardy north temperate zone. The rhododendrons, azaleas, lilacs, magnolias, and fruit trees are eye-popping when in bloom, and something is always in season from early April through September. The Larz Anderson bonsai collection contains individual specimens imported from Japan. In the visitor center there is a 40-to-1 scale model of the arboretum (with 4,000 tiny trees). If you visit during May, Lilac Sunday on Mother's Day is a celebration of blooming trees and picnicking (the only day it's allowed). The arboretum, 6 miles from downtown Boston, is accessible by the MBTA Orange Line or Bus 39 from Copley Square to the Custer Street stop in Jamaica Plain (three blocks away). ⌧ *125 Arborway, at Centre St., Jamaica Plain* ☎ 617/524–1718 ⊕ *www.arboretum.harvard.edu* ⍾ *Donations accepted* |M| *Forest Hills.*

8

BROOKLINE

TOP ATTRACTION

Frederick Law Olmsted National Historic Site. Frederick Law Olmsted (1822–1903) is considered the nation's preeminent creator of parks. In 1883, at age 61, while immersed in planning Boston's Emerald Necklace of parks, Olmsted set up his first permanent office at Fairsted, an 18-room farmhouse dating from 1810, to which he added another 18 rooms for his design offices. Plans and drawings on display include such projects as the U.S. Capitol grounds, Stanford University, and Mount Royal Park in Montréal. You can also tour the design rooms (some now in use as an archive library) where Olmsted and staff drew up their plans; highlights include a 1904 "electric blueprint machine," a kind of primitive photocopier. The 1¾-acre site incorporates many trademark Olmstedian designs, including areas of meadow, wild garden, and woodland; Olmsted believed body and spirit could be healed through close association with nature. The site became part of the National Park Service in 1980; Olmsted's office played an influential role in the creation of this federal agency. Call ahead to inquire about house tour hours, which change with the seasons. ⊠ *99 Warren St., Brookline* ☎ *617/566–1689* ⊕ *www.nps.gov/frla/index.htm* ✉ *Free* Ⓜ *Brookline Hills.*

WORTH NOTING

John F. Kennedy National Historic Site. This was the home of the 35th president from his birth on May 29, 1917, until 1921, when the family moved to nearby Naples and Abbottsford streets. Rose Kennedy provided the furnishings for the restored 2½-story, wood-frame structure. You can pick up a brochure for a walking tour of young Kennedy's school, church, and neighborhood. To get here, take the MBTA Green Line to Coolidge Corner and walk north on Harvard Street four blocks. The house is open by appointment only November through May. ⊠ *83 Beals St., Brookline* ☎ *617/566–7937* ⊕ *www.nps.gov/jofi* ✉ *Free* Ⓜ *Coolidge Corner.*

CAMBRIDGE

Getting Oriented

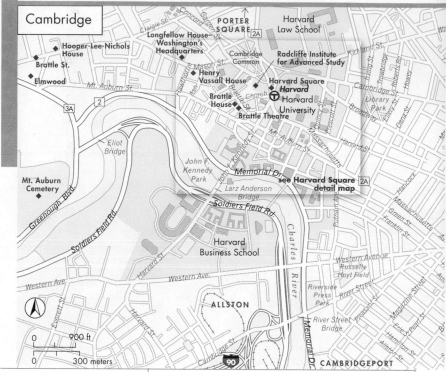

Cambridge

TIMING	GETTING HERE AND AROUND
Harvard Square is worth an afternoon; be sure to take a tour. Most visitors don't go beyond Harvard Square and Harvard Yard, but this is a one-of-a-kind town filled with funky restaurants, independent shops, unique art installations, important historic sites, and a large concentration of independent bookstores. If you plan to visit Harvard's natural history or art museums or explore other Cambridge neighborhoods, give yourself a day or two here. *See "It's Hip to Be Square," below, for ideas on where to go.*	Just minutes from Boston, Cambridge is easily reached by taking the Red Line train (otherwise known as the T) outbound to any stop past Charles/MGH station. There are stops at MIT (Kendall Square), Central Square, Harvard Square, Porter Square, Davis Square (actually in Somerville), and Alewife. Harvard Square is the best place to begin any visit to Cambridge, but driving (and parking) here is a small nightmare. Do yourself a favor and take the T. If you insist on driving, suck it up and park in a garage. (Street parking is usually limited to two hours, and most spots are reserved for Cambridge residents.) Driving is less of a pain in other parts of Cambridge, but you're still better off getting around via the T. Try to spend as much time as possible exploring on foot. This is a walking town, and you'll miss a lot of Cambridge's quirkiness if you're moving too fast.

KEY

🚇 Subway station

— Rail lines

✕ Restaurant/Cafe

TOP REASONS TO GO

■ Browse the new and used-book stores, trawl the artsy boutiques, and people-watch in Harvard Square. Take a break at one of the local coffee shops.

■ Do the museum circuit: The Harvard Art Museums; the Semitic Museum for ancient Near Eastern collections; the Peabody and the Natural History Museum for artifacts and culture.

■ Visit MIT to wander the halls, visit its museum, and see Frank Gehry's Seuss-like Stata Center.

■ Breathe the rarefied air of Harvard on an official tour (or an irreverent unofficial one), then return to real life with a burger from Mr. Bartley's.

■ Amble down Brattle Street, visiting the 1700s-era homes of Tory Row (Washington really did sleep here).

VISITOR INFORMATION

Cambridge Visitor Information Booth. A good place to start is the Cambridge Visitor Information Booth, outside the T station in Harvard Square. Free maps, brochures, historical walking tours, an excellent list of bookstores in the area, and a guide to seasonal events are available. ✉ *Harvard Sq., near MBTA station entrance, Harvard Square* ☎ *617/441–2884* 🌐 *www.cambridgeusa.org* Ⓜ *Harvard.*

QUICK BITES

All the squares in Cambridge are surrounded by great restaurants. Near Harvard Square try **Mr. Bartley's Burger Cottage** (✉ *1246 Massachusetts Ave.*), a Harvard institution with a menu that includes dozens of riffs on the humble burger. Cafés abound on Brattle Street; good bets include **Felipe's Taqueria** (✉ *21 Brattle St.*) and **Cardullo's Gourmet Shop** (✉ *6 Brattle St.*), both of which make great sandwiches.

MOBILE TOUR

The Cambridge Office for Tourism offers a walking tour for your mobile device on its website 🌐 *www.cambridge-usa.org.*

9

Sightseeing
★★★★
Dining
★★★★★
Lodging
★★
Shopping
★★★★
Nightlife
★★★★★

Updated by
Kim Foley
MacKinnon

Boston's Left Bank—an uberliberal academic enclave—is a must-visit if you're spending more than a day or two in the Boston area. It's packed with world-class cultural institutions, quirky shops, and restaurants galore.

The city is punctuated at one end by the funky architecture of MIT and at the other by the grand academic fortress that is Harvard University. Civic life connects the two camps into an urban stew of 100,000 residents who represent nearly every nationality in the world, work at every kind of job from tenured professor to taxi driver, and are passionate about living on this side of the river.

The Charles River is the Cantabrigians' backyard, and there's virtually no place in Cambridge more than a 10-minute walk from its banks. Strolling, running, or biking is one of the great pleasures of Cambridge, and your views will include graceful bridges, the distant Boston skyline, crew teams rowing through the calm water, and the elegant spires of Harvard soaring into the sky.

No visit to Cambridge is complete without an afternoon (at least) in Harvard Square. It's a hub, a hot spot, and home to every variation of the human condition: Nobel laureates, homeless buskers, trust-fund babies, and working-class Joes. Farther along Massachusetts Avenue is Central Square, an ethnic melting pot of people and restaurants. Ten minutes more bring you to MIT, with its eclectic architecture from postwar pedestrian to Frank Gehry's futuristic fantasyland. In addition to providing a stellar view, the Massachusetts Avenue Bridge, spanning the Charles from Cambridge to Boston, is also notorious in MIT lore for its Smoot measurements.

HARVARD SQUARE

In Cambridge all streets point toward Harvard Square. In addition to being the gateway to Harvard University and its various attractions, Harvard Square is home to the tiny yet venerable folk-music venue Club Passim (Bob Dylan played here, and Bonnie Raitt was a regular during her time at Harvard), first-run and vintage movie theaters, concert and

lecture venues, and a tempting collection of eclectic, independent shops. Harvard Square is a multicultural microcosm. On a warm day street musicians coax exotic tones from their Andean pan flutes and *erhus,* Chinese stringed instruments, while cranks and local pessimists pass out pamphlets warning against all sorts of end-of-the-world scenarios. You will hear people speaking dozens of languages. In the small plaza atop the main entrance to the Harvard T station known as "the Pit," students like to hang out at all hours and quiet clusters study the moves and strategy of the chess players seated outside Au Bon Pain. It's a wonderful circus of humanity.

TOP ATTRACTIONS

Fodor'sChoice   **Harvard Art Museums.** In late 2014, the combined collections of the
★   Busch-Reisinger, Fogg, and Arthur M. Sackler museums were united under one glorious, mostly glass roof, under the umbrella name Harvard Art Museums. Housed in a facility designed by award-winning architect Renzo Piano, the 204,000-square-foot museum is spread over seven levels, allowing more of Harvard's 250,000-piece art collection to be seen in one place. Highlights include American and European paintings, sculptures, and decorative arts from the Fogg Museum; and works by German expressionists, materials related to the Bauhaus, and postwar contemporary art from German-speaking Europe from the Busch-Reisinger Museum. In addition to the gallery spaces, there's a 300-seat theater, a café, plus conservation and research labs. ⊠ *32 Quincy St., Harvard Square* ☎ *617/495–9400* ⊕ *www.harvardartmuseums.org* 🖼 *$15* Ⓜ *Harvard.*

FAMILY   **Harvard Museum of Natural History.** The Harvard Museum of Natural
Fodor'sChoice   History (which exhibits specimens from the Museum of Compara-
★   tive Zoology, Harvard University Herbaria, and the Mineralogical and Geological Museum) displays some 12,000 specimens, including dinosaurs, rare minerals, hundreds of mammals and birds, and Harvard's world-famous Blaschka Glass Flowers. The museum combines historic exhibits drawn from the university's vast collections with new and changing multimedia exhibitions such as *New England Forests and Mollusks: Shelled Masters of the Marine Realm,* and the renovated Earth & Planetary Sciences gallery. ⊠ *26 Oxford St., Harvard Square* ☎ *617/495–3045* ⊕ *www.hmnh.harvard.edu* 🖼 *$12; ticket includes admission to adjacent Peabody Museum* Ⓜ *Harvard.*

FAMILY   **Harvard Square.** Tides of students, tourists, political-cause proponents,
Fodor'sChoice   and bizarre street creatures are all part of the nonstop pedestrian flow
★   at this most celebrated of Cambridge crossroads.

Harvard Square is where Massachusetts Avenue, coming from Boston, turns and widens into a triangle broad enough to accommodate a brick peninsula (above the T station). The restored 1928 kiosk in the center of the square once served as the entrance to the MBTA station. Harvard Yard, with its lecture halls, residential houses, libraries, and museums, is one long border of the square; the other three are composed of clusters of banks and a wide variety of restaurants and shops.

On an average afternoon you'll hear earnest conversations in dozens of foreign languages; see every kind of youthful uniform from Goth to impeccable prep; wander by street musicians playing Andean flutes, and doing excellent Stevie Wonder or Edith Piaf imitations; and watch an outdoor game of pickup chess between a street-tough kid and an older gent wearing a beret. An afternoon in the square is people-watching raised to high art.

The historic buildings are worth noting. It's a thrill to walk though the big brick-and-wrought-iron gates to Harvard Yard on up to Widener Library, the University's flagship library. More than 50 miles of bookshelves snake around six stories above and four stories below ground, holding more than 3 million volumes. The imposing neoclassical structure was designed by one of the nation's first major African American architects, Julian Abele.

Across Garden Street, through an ornamental arch, is **Cambridge Common,** decreed a public pasture in 1631. It's said that under a large tree that once stood in this meadow George Washington took command of the Continental Army on July 3, 1775. A stone memorial now marks the site of the "Washington Elm." Also on the Common is the Irish Famine Memorial by Derry artist Maurice Herron, unveiled in 1997 to coincide with the 150th anniversary of "Black '47," the deadliest year of the potato famine. At the center of the Common a large memorial commemorates the Union soldiers who lost their lives in the Civil War. On the far side of the Common is a fantastic park. ⊠ *Harvard Square* ⊕ *www.harvardsquare.com* Ⓜ *Harvard.*

Harvard University. The tree-studded, shady, and redbrick expanse of Harvard Yard—the very center of Harvard University—has weathered the footsteps of Harvard students for hundreds of years. In 1636 the Great and General Court of the Massachusetts Bay Colony voted funds to establish the colony's first college, and a year later chose Cambridge as the site. Named in 1639 for John Harvard, a young Charlestown clergyman who died in 1638 and left the college his entire library and half his estate, Harvard remained the only college in the New World until 1693, by which time it was firmly established as a respected center of learning. Local wags refer to Harvard as WGU—World's Greatest University—and it's certainly the oldest and most famous American university.

Although the college dates from the 17th century, the oldest buildings in Harvard Yard are from the 18th century (though you'll sometimes see archaeologists digging here for evidence of older structures). Together the buildings chronicle American architecture from the Colonial era to the present. **Holden Chapel,** completed in 1744, is a Georgian gem. The graceful **University Hall** was designed in 1815 by Charles Bulfinch. An 1884 statue of John Harvard by Daniel Chester French stands outside; ironically for a school with the motto of "Veritas" ("Truth"), the model for the statue was a member of the class of 1882 and not Harvard himself. **Sever Hall,** completed in 1880 and designed by Henry Hobson Richardson, represents the Romanesque revival that was followed by the neoclassical (note the pillared

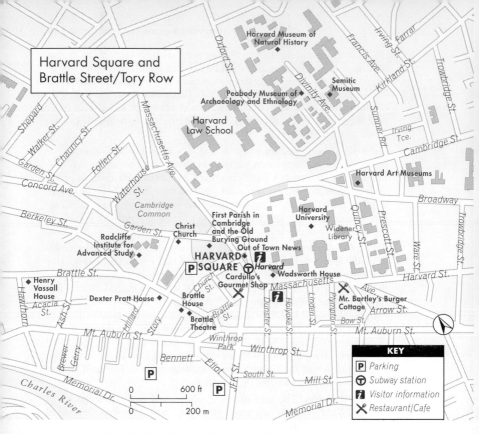

Harvard Square and Brattle Street/Tory Row

Harvard Museum of Natural History

Semitic Museum

Peabody Museum of Archaeology and Ethnology

Harvard Law School

Harvard Art Museums

Cambridge Common

First Parish in Cambridge and the Old Burying Ground

Harvard University

Christ Church

Radcliffe Institute for Advanced Study

Widener Library

Out of Town News

HARVARD SQUARE

Harvard

Cardullo's Gourmet Shop

Wadsworth House

Henry Vassall House

Dexter Pratt House

Brattle House

Mr. Bartley's Burger Cottage

Brattle Theatre

Winthrop Park

Winthrop St.

KEY

P Parking
T Subway station
i Visitor information
✕ Restaurant/Cafe

0   600 ft
0   200 m

facade of Widener Library) and the neo-Georgian, represented by the sumptuous brick houses along the Charles River, many of which are now undergraduate residences. **Memorial Church,** a graceful steepled edifice of modified Colonial Revival design, was dedicated in 1932. Just north of the Yard is **Memorial Hall,** completed in 1878 as a memorial to Harvard men who died in the Union cause; it's High Victorian both inside and out. It also contains the 1,166-seat Sanders Theatre, which serves as the university's largest lecture hall, site of year-round concerts by students and professionals, and the venue for the festive Christmas Revels.

Many of Harvard's cultural and scholarly facilities are important sights in themselves, but most campus buildings, other than museums and concert halls, are off-limits to the general public.

The **Harvard Information Center,** in the Smith Campus Centre, has a small exhibit space, distributes maps of the university area, and offers free student-led tours of Harvard Yard. The tour doesn't include visits to museums, and it doesn't take you into campus buildings, but it provides a fine orientation. The information center is open year-round (except during spring recess and other semester breaks). From the end of June through August, guides offer tours every half hour; however, it's best to call ahead to confirm times.

✉ *Bounded by Massachusetts Ave. and Mt. Auburn, Holyoke, and Dunster Sts., 1350 Massachusetts Ave., Harvard Square* ☎ *617/495–1573 Information Center* ⊕ *www.harvard.edu* Ⓜ *Harvard.*

Peabody Museum of Archaeology & Ethnology. With one of the world's outstanding anthropological collections, the Peabody focuses on Native American and Central and South American cultures. The Hall of the North American Indian is particularly outstanding, with art, textiles, and models of traditional dwellings from across the continent. The Mesoamerican room juxtaposes ancient relief carvings and weavings with contemporary works from the Maya and other peoples. ✉ *11 Divinity Ave., Harvard Square* ☎ *617/496–1027* ⊕ *www.peabody.harvard.edu* Ⓜ *Harvard.*

WORTH NOTING

Christ Church. This modest yet beautiful gray clapboard structure was designed in 1761 by Peter Harrison, the first architect of note in the colonies (he designed King's Chapel). During the Revolution, members of its mostly Tory congregation fled for their lives. The organ was melted down for bullets and the building was used as a barracks during the Siege of Boston. (Step into the vestibule to look for the bullet hole left during the skirmish.) Martha Washington requested that the church reopen for services on New Year's Eve in 1775. The church's historical significance extends to the 20th century: Teddy Roosevelt was a Sunday-school teacher here (and famously fired because he remained Dutch Reformed rather than becoming an Episcopalian), and Martin Luther King Jr. spoke from the pulpit to announce his opposition to the Vietnam War. ✉ *0 Garden St., Harvard Square* ☎ *617/876–0200* ⊕ *www.cccambridge.org* Ⓜ *Harvard.*

NEED A BREAK

Out of Town News. Need a news fix? Out of Town News has got you covered. Browse the world at this fascinating international news seller. Peruse the racks at this fabled landmark for international publications in languages from around the world. It's definitely worth a browse. ✉ *0 Harvard Square, Harvard Square* ☎ *617/354–1441* Ⓜ *Harvard.*

First Parish in Cambridge and the Old Burying Ground. Next to the imposing church on the corner of Church Street and Mass Ave., a spooky-looking colonial graveyard houses 17th- and 18th-century tombstones of ministers, early Harvard presidents, and Revolutionary War soldiers. The wooden Gothic Revival church, known locally as "First Church" or "First Parish," was built in 1833 by Isaiah Rogers. The congregation dates to two centuries earlier, and has been linked to Harvard since the founding of the college. ✉ *3 Church St., Harvard Square* ☎ *617/876–7772* ⊕ *www.firstparishcambridge.org* Ⓜ *Harvard.*

Forum. The church sponsors the popular lecture series Forum on Wednesday at 7 pm September through May, featuring well-known authors and academics. It's one of public radio's longest-running public affairs programs. ✉ *3 Church St., Harvard Square* ☎ *617/495–2727* ⊕ *www.cambridgeforum.org* Ⓜ *Harvard.*

9

Semitic Museum. An almost unknown gem, this Harvard institution serves as an exhibit space for Egyptian, Mesopotamian, and ancient Near East artifacts and as a center for archaeological exploration. Who knew that the Sphinx may have had curls? The museum's extensive collection rotates and there are temporary exhibits, so you never know what you might see here. The building also houses the Department of Near Eastern Languages and Civilization, with offices tucked among the artifacts. ⊠ 6 *Divinity Ave., Harvard Square* ☎ *617/495–4631* ⊕ *www.fas.harvard. edu/~semitic* 🖼 *Free; donations appreciated* ⊙ *Closed Sat.* Ⓜ *Harvard.*

Wadsworth House. On the Harvard University side of Harvard Square stands the Wadsworth House, a yellow clapboard structure built in 1726 as a home for Harvard presidents. It served as the first headquarters for George Washington, who arrived on July 2, 1775, to take command of the Continental Army, which he did the following day. The building, closed to the public, now houses general Harvard offices. ⊠ *1341 Massachusetts Ave., Harvard Square* ⊕ *www.harvard. edu* Ⓜ *Harvard.*

BRATTLE STREET/TORY ROW

Brattle Street remains one of New England's most elegant thoroughfares. Elaborate mansions line both sides from where it meets JFK Street to Fresh Pond Parkway. Brattle Street was once dubbed Tory Row, because during the 1770s its seven mansions, on land that stretched to the river, were owned by staunch supporters of King George. These properties were appropriated by the patriots when they took over Cambridge in the summer of 1775. Many of the historic houses are marked with blue signs, and although only two (the Hooper-Lee-Nichols House and the Longfellow National Historic Site) are fully open to the public, it's easy to imagine yourself back in the days of Ralph Waldo Emerson and Henry David Thoreau as you stroll the brick sidewalks. Mt. Auburn Cemetery, an exquisitely landscaped garden cemetery, is less than 2 miles down Brattle Street from Harvard Square.

TOP ATTRACTIONS

Brattle House. This 18th-century, gambrel-roof Colonial once belonged to the Loyalist William Brattle. He moved to Boston in 1774 to escape the patriots' anger, then left in 1776 with the British troops. From 1831 to 1833 the house was the residence of Margaret Fuller, feminist author and editor of *The Dial*. Today it's the office of the Cambridge Center for Adult Education, and is listed on the National Register of Historic Places. ⊠ *42 Brattle St., Harvard Square* ☎ *617/547–6789* ⊕ *www.ccae. org* Ⓜ *Harvard.*

NEED A BREAK

✕ **Algiers Coffee House.** Algiers Coffee House, upstairs from the Brattle Theatre, is a favorite evening hangout for young actors and artists. Linger over mint tea or a plate of hummus, or enjoy a glass of wine on the second-floor terrace and watch the world go by. ⊠ *40 Brattle St., Harvard Square* ☎ *617/492–1557* Ⓜ *Harvard.*

Brattle Theatre. For the last half century, the Brattle Theatre has served as the square's independent movie house, screening indie, foreign, obscure, and classic films, from nouveau to noir. Occupying a squat, barnlike building from 1890, it is set improbably between a modern shopping center and a colonial mansion. The resident repertory company gained notoriety in the 1950s when it made a practice of hiring actors blacklisted as Communists by the U.S. government. Check the website for current offerings and events. ⊠ *40 Brattle St., Harvard Square* ☎ *617/876–6837* ⊕ *www.brattlefilm.org* Ⓜ *Harvard.*

Longfellow House-Washington's Headquarters. Henry Wadsworth Longfellow, the poet whose stirring tales of the Village Blacksmith, Evangeline, Hiawatha, and Paul Revere's midnight ride thrilled 19th-century America, once lived in this elegant mansion. One of several original Tory Row homes on Brattle Street, the house was built in 1759 by John Vassall Jr., and George Washington lived (and slept!) here during the Siege of Boston from July 1775 to April 1776. Longfellow first boarded here in 1837 and later received the house as a gift from his father-in-law on his marriage to Frances Appleton, who burned to death here in an accident in 1861. For 45 years Longfellow wrote his famous verses here and filled the house with the exuberant spirit of his own work and that of his literary circle, which included Ralph Waldo Emerson, Nathaniel Hawthorne, and Charles Sumner, an abolitionist senator. Longfellow died in 1882, but his presence in the house lives on—from the Longfellow family furniture to the wallpaper to the books on the shelves (many the poet's own). The home is preserved and run by the National Park Service; guided tours of the house are offered May through October. The formal garden is the perfect place to relax; the grounds are open year-round. Longfellow Park, across the street, is the place to stand to take photos of the house. The park was created to preserve the view immortalized in the poet's "To the River Charles." ⊠ *105 Brattle St., Harvard Square* ☎ *617/876–4491* ⊕ *www. nps.gov/long* 🎫 *Free* Ⓜ *Harvard.*

Mt. Auburn Cemetery. A cemetery might not strike you as a first choice for a visit, but this one is an absolute pleasure, filled with artwork and gorgeous landscaping. Opened in 1831, it was the country's first garden cemetery, and more than 90,000 people have been buried here—among them Henry Wadsworth Longfellow, Mary Baker Eddy, Winslow Homer, Amy Lowell, Isabella Stewart Gardner, and architect Charles Bulfinch. The grave of engineer Buckminster Fuller bears an engraved geodesic dome. In spring local nature lovers and bird-watchers come out of the woodwork to see the warbler migrations and the glorious blossoms. Brochures, maps, and audio tours are at the entrance. ⊠ *580 Mt. Auburn St., Harvard Square* ☎ *617/547–7105* ⊕ *www.mountauburn. org* Ⓜ *Harvard; then Watertown (71) or Waverly (73) bus to cemetery.*

Radcliffe Institute for Advanced Study. The famed women's college, situated around a serene yard, was founded in 1879 and partnered with Harvard University in 1977. It officially merged with Harvard in 1999, and its name changed to the Radcliffe Institute for Advanced Study at Harvard. ⊠ *10 Garden St., Harvard Square* ⊕ *www.radcliffe.edu* Ⓜ *Harvard.*

9

MIT's Stata Center was designed by Frank Gehry.

WORTH NOTING

Dexter Pratt House. Also known as the "Blacksmith House," this yellow Colonial is now owned by the Cambridge Center for Adult Education. The tree itself is long gone, but this spot inspired Longfellow's lines: "Under a spreading chestnut tree, the village smithy stands." The blacksmith's shop, today commemorated by a granite marker, was next door, at the corner of Story Street. From October to December, the celebrated Blacksmith House Poetry Series runs most Monday nights. Tickets are $3. ⊠ *56 Brattle St., Harvard Square* ⊕ *ccae.org/blacksmithpoetry* Ⓜ *Harvard.*

NEED A BREAK

✕ **L.A. Burdick Chocolates.** Chocolate lovers may be seduced by the aromas emanating from L.A. Burdick Chocolates; rich confections or elegant, life-changing hot cocoa may be just the things to restore flagging spirits or weary feet. ⊠ *52 Brattle St., Harvard Square* ☎ *617/491–4340* ⊕ *www.burdickchocolate.com* Ⓜ *Harvard.*

Elmwood. Shortly after its construction in 1767, this three-story Georgian house was abandoned by its owner, colonial governor Thomas Oliver. Elmwood House was home to the accomplished Lowell family for two centuries. Elmwood is now the Harvard University president's residence, ever since student riots in 1969 drove President Nathan Pusey from his house in Harvard Yard. ⊠ *33 Elmwood Ave., Harvard Square* Ⓜ *Harvard.*

Henry Vassall House. Brattle Street's seven houses known as "Tory Row" were once occupied by wealthy families linked by friendship, if not blood. This one may have been built as early as 1636. In 1737 it was purchased by John Vassall Sr.; four years later he sold it to his younger brother Henry. It was used as a hospital during the Revolution, and the traitor Dr. Benjamin Church was held here as a prisoner. The house was remodeled during the 19th century. It's now a private residence, but from the street you can view the Colonial home with its black-shuttered windows and multiple dormers. ☒ *91 Brattle St., Harvard Square* Ⓜ *Harvard.*

Hooper-Lee-Nichols House. Now headquarters of the Cambridge Historical Society, this is one of two Tory-era homes on Brattle Street fully open to the public. The Emerson family gave it to the society in 1957. Built between 1685 and 1690, the house has been remodeled at least six times, but has maintained much of the original structure. The downstairs is elegantly, although sparsely, appointed with period books, portraits, and wallpaper. An upstairs bedroom has been furnished with period antiques, some belonging to the original residents. Tours are offered on the last Sunday of the month April through September for $10. Visits are also available by appointment. Check the website for special events and to see a virtual tour of the house. ☒ *159 Brattle St., Harvard Square* 🕾 *617/547–4252* ⊕ *www.cambridgehistory.org* Ⓜ *Harvard.*

KENDALL SQUARE/MIT

Harvard Square may be the center of the "People's Republic of Cambridge," but the Kendall Square neighborhood is the city's hard-driving capitalist core. Gritty industrial buildings share space with sleek office blocks and the sprawling Massachusetts Institute of Technology. Although the MIT campus may lack the ivied elegance of Harvard Yard, major modern architects, including Alvar Aalto, Frank Gehry, I. M. Pei, and Eero Saarinen, created signature buildings here. To reach MIT, take the Red Line T to Kendall station; if you're headed for the MIT Museum on the western edge of the campus, the Central Square station is more convenient.

TOP ATTRACTIONS

List Visual Arts Center. Founded by Albert and Vera List, pioneer collectors of modern art, this MIT center has three galleries showcasing exhibitions of cutting-edge art and mixed media. Works from the center's collection of contemporary art, such as Thomas Hart Benton's painting *Fluid Catalytic Crackers* and Harry Bertoia's altarpiece for the MIT Chapel, are on view here and around campus. The center's website includes a map indicating the locations of more than 25 of these works. ☒ *20 Ames St., Bldg. E 15, Kendall Square* 🕾 *617/253–4680* ⊕ *listart. mit.edu* ☒ *Free* ☉ *Closed Mon.* Ⓜ *Kendall/MIT.*

Massachusetts Institute of Technology. Founded in 1861, MIT moved to Cambridge from Copley Square in the Back Bay in 1916. Once dissed as "the factory," particularly by its Ivy League neighbor, Harvard University, MIT mints graduates that are the sharp blades on the edge of the information revolution. It's perennially in the top five of *U.S. News and World Report*'s college rankings. It has long since fulfilled the predictions of its founder, the geologist William Barton Rogers, that it would surpass "the universities of the land in the accuracy and the extent of its teachings in all branches of positive science." Its emphasis shifted in the 1930s from practical engineering and mechanics to the outer limits of scientific fields.

Architecture is important at MIT. Although the original buildings were obviously designed by and for scientists, many represent pioneering designs of their times. The **Kresge Auditorium,** designed by Eero Saarinen, with a curving roof and unusual thrust, rests on three, instead of four, points. The nondenominational **MIT Chapel,** a circular Saarinen design, is lighted primarily by a roof oculus that focuses natural light on the altar and by reflections from the water in a small surrounding moat; it's topped by an aluminum sculpture by Theodore Roszak. The serpentine **Baker House,** now a dormitory, was designed in 1947 by the Finnish architect Alvar Aalto in such a way as to provide every room with a view of the Charles River. Sculptures by Henry Moore and other notable artists dot the campus. The latest addition is the newly minted Green Center, punctuated by the splash of color that is Sol LeWitt's 5,500-square-foot mosaic floor.

The East Campus, which has grown around the university's original neoclassical buildings of 1916, also has outstanding modern architecture and sculpture, including the stark high-rise **Green Building** by I. M. Pei, housing the Earth Science Center. Just outside is Alexander Calder's giant stabile (a stationary mobile) *The Big Sail.* Another Pei work on the East Campus is the **Wiesner Building,** designed in 1985, which houses the **List Visual Arts Center.** Architect Frank Gehry made his mark on the campus with the cockeyed, improbable **Ray & Maria Stata Center,** a complex of buildings on Vassar Street. The center houses computer, artificial intelligence, and information systems laboratories, and is reputedly as confusing to navigate on the inside as it is to follow on the outside. East Campus's **Great Dome,** which looms over neoclassical Killian Court, has often been the target of student "hacks" and has at various times supported a telephone booth with a ringing phone, a life-size statue of a cow, and a campus police cruiser. Nearby, the domed **Rogers Building** has earned unusual notoriety as the center of a series of hallways and tunnels dubbed "the infinite corridor." Twice each winter the sun's path lines up perfectly with the corridor's axis, and at dusk students line the third-floor hallway to watch the sun set through the westernmost window. The phenomenon is known as "MIT-henge."

MIT maintains an information center in the Rogers Building, and offers free tours of the campus weekdays at 11 and 3. Check the schedule, as the tours are often suspended during school holidays. General hours for the information center are weekdays 9 to 5. ⊠ *77 Massachusetts Ave., Kendall Square* ☎ *617/253–4795* ⊕ *www.mit.edu* Ⓜ *Kendall/MIT.*

WHERE TO EAT

Updated by
Victoria Abbott
Riccardi

In a city synonymous with tradition, Boston chefs have spent recent years rewriting culinary history. The stuffy, wood-paneled formality is gone; the endless renditions of *chow-dah*, lobster, and cod have retired; and the assumption that true foodies better hop the next Amtrak to New York is also—thankfully—a thing of the past.

In their place, a crop of young chefs has ascended, opening small, upscale neighborhood spots that use local New England ingredients to delicious effect. Traditional eats can still be found (Durgin-Park remains the best place to get baked beans), but many diners now gravitate toward innovative food in understated environs. Whether you're looking for casual French, down-home Southern cooking, some of the best sushi in the country, or Vietnamese banh mi sandwiches, Boston restaurants are ready to deliver. Eclectic Japanese spot o ya and iconic French restaurant L'Espalier have garnered widespread attention, while a coterie of star chefs like Barbara Lynch, Lydia Shire, and Ken Oringer have built mini-empires and thrust the city to the forefront of the national dining scene.

The fish and shellfish brought in from nearby shores continue to inform the regional cuisine, along with locally grown fruits and vegetables, handmade cheeses, and humanely raised heritage game and meats. But don't expect boiled lobsters and baked apple pie. Today's chefs, while showcasing New England's bounty, might offer you lobster cassoulet with black truffles, bacon-clam pizza from a wood-burning oven, and a tomato herb salad harvested from the restaurant's rooftop garden. In many ways, though, Boston remains solidly skeptical of trends. To wit: the cupcake craze and food truck trend hit here later than other cities; the Hawaii-inspired poke movement has only recently arrived. And over in the university culture of Cambridge, places like the Harvest and Oleana espoused the locavore and slow-food movements before they became buzzwords.

BOSTON DINING PLANNER

EATING OUT STRATEGY

Where should we eat? With hundreds of eateries competing for your attention, it may seem like a daunting question. But fret not—our expert writers and editors have done most of the legwork. The 100-plus selections here represent the best the city has to offer. Search Best Bets for top recommendations by price, cuisine, and experience, and sample local flavor in the neighborhood features. Or find a review quickly in the listings, organized alphabetically within neighborhoods. Delve in and enjoy!

RESERVATIONS

Reservations generally need to be made at least a few nights in advance, but this is easily done by your concierge, online at *www.opentable.com*, or by calling the restaurant directly. Tables can be hard to come by if you want to dine between 7 and 9, or on Friday or Saturday night. But most restaurants will get you in if you show up and are willing to wait.

HOURS

Boston's restaurants close relatively early; most shut their doors by 10 or 11 pm, and a few have bars that stay open until 1 am. Restaurants that serve breakfast often do so until 11 am or noon, at which point they start serving lunch. Unless otherwise noted, the restaurants listed in this guide are open daily for lunch and dinner.

WHAT TO WEAR

Boston is a notch or two more reserved in its fashion than New York or Los Angeles. Its dining dress code normally hovers at the level of casual chic. Few of the city's most formal restaurants require jackets, and even at some of the most expensive places jeans are acceptable as long as they're paired with a dressy top and posh shoes. Shorts are appropriate only in the most casual spots. When in doubt, call and ask.

PRICES

Entrée prices fluctuate with the state of the economy. Top-tier restaurants remain impervious to market changes, but more restaurants are accommodating every price range with small or half portions at a lower price.

Credit cards are widely accepted, but some restaurants accept only cash. If you plan to use a credit card, it's a good idea to double-check when making reservations or before sitting down to eat.

10

WHAT IT COSTS			
$	$$	$$$	$$$$
Restaurant	under $18	$18–$24	$25–$35	over $35

Price per person for a median main course or equivalent combination of smaller dishes.

TIPPING AND TAXES

Never tip the maître d'. In most restaurants, tip the waiter at least 15% to 20% (to figure the amount quickly, double the 7% tax on the bill and add a little more). Bills for parties of six or more sometimes include service. Tip at least $1 per drink at the bar and $1 for each coat checked.

TOURS

To eat like an Italian, you've got to know your sfogliatelle from your amaretti. Local foodie Michele Topor schools visitors on the "right" kind of olive oil and the primo places to buy Italian pastries during three-hour tours with her Boston Food Tours **North End Market Tour** (✉ *6 Charter St.* ☎ *617/523–6032*), which get off the beaten Hanover Street path. The $54 tour includes a few sample noshes. Due to high demand, Topor also offers a Gluten-free North End Market Tour with cookie samples included, $57.

CHILDREN

Though it's unusual to see children in the dining rooms of Boston's most elite restaurants, dining with youngsters does not have to mean culinary exile. Many of the restaurants reviewed in this chapter are excellent choices for families and are accordingly marked.

SMOKING

In both Boston and Cambridge, smoking is prohibited in all enclosed public spaces, including restaurants and bars.

USING THE MAPS

Throughout the chapter, you'll see mapping symbols and coordinates (such as 3:F2) after property names or reviews. To locate the property on a map, turn to the Boston Dining and Lodging Atlas at the end of this chapter. The first number after the symbol indicates the map number. Following that are the property's coordinates on the map grid.

RESTAURANT REVIEWS

Listed alphabetically within neighborhoods.

BOSTON

BEACON HILL AND BOSTON COMMON

Eminently walkable, this is one of Boston's smallest and most historic neighborhoods filled with brick sidewalks, shimmering gas lamps, and 19th-century row houses with brass knockers and flower boxes. On the food front you'll find an appealing blend of fancy and casual restaurants, as well as cafés, along the main pedestrian path of Charles Street, where you'll see mothers with strollers, young professionals, and patrician elderly couples, who live right around the corner, all going about their day.

$$$

MIDDLE EASTERN

✗ **Lala Rokh.** A rotating gallery of Persian art adorns the walls of this pearl-gray eatery specializing in home-style Iranian dishes. Along with classics such as *fesejan*, duck leg in a satiny pomegranate-walnut sauce, you'll find brain fritters, smoky eggplant puree, *pollo* (rice dishes), kebabs, and richly spiced lamb stews, including one seasoned with dried lime. **Known for:** authenic Persian cuisine; home-style dishes; exotic, yet approachable, seasonings;. ⑤ *Average main: $26* ✉ *97 Mt. Vernon St., Beacon Hill* ☎ *617/720–5511* ⊕ *www.lalarokh.com* ☺ *No lunch* Ⓜ *Charles/MGH* ✛ *1:D6.*

$$$$
STEAKHOUSE

✗ **Mooo....** Inside the swanky XV Beacon hotel lies Mooo..., a luxurious, refined steak house that remains civilized despite the restaurant's somewhat goofy name. Look for the succulent (and very popular) Wagyu beef dumpling appetizer, along with dry-aged steaks with your choice of sauces, such as Bearnaise, and classic sides (creamed spinach, whipped potatoes, sautéed mushrooms). **Known for:** top-grade steaks; attentive service; impressive wine list. ⑤ *Average main: $59* ⊠ *XV Beacon Hotel, 15 Beacon St., Beacon Hill* ☎ *617/670–2515* ⊕ *mooorestaurant.com* Ⓜ *Park St.* ✛ *1:E6.*

$$$$
EUROPEAN
Fodor's Choice
★

✗ **No. 9 Park.** The stellar cuisine at chef Barbara Lynch's first restaurant continues to draw plenty of well-deserved attention from its place in the shadow of the State House's golden dome. Settle into the plush but unpretentious dining room and indulge in pumpkin risotto with rare lamb or the memorably rich prune-stuffed gnocchi drizzled with bits of foie gras, the latter of which is always offered even if you don't see it on the menu. **Known for:** upscale French-Italian dishes; polished service; prune-stuffed gnocchi with foie gras. ⑤ *Average main: $46* ⊠ *9 Park St., Beacon Hill* ☎ *617/742–9991* ⊕ *www.no9park.com* Ⓜ *Park St.* ✛ *1:E6.*

$$$
ITALIAN

✗ **Scampo.** In the Liberty Hotel—the former site of the infamous Charles Street Jail—this Beacon Hill hot spot has a prison-chic vibe, complete with barred windows and a sign on the wall reminding patrons that "crime doesn't pay." The restaurant's Italian fare, however, is anything but institutional: the house-made mozzarella bar, crusty pizzas, and handmade pastas (several gluten-free) are all exceptional. Take note of the King Crab Cocktail: thick slices of buffalo mozzarella cheese and slices of avocado mixed with warm buttery Alaskan King Crab and drizzled with green mustard oil. **Known for:** bold Italian fare; tandoori-oven cooked breads, pizzas, and skewers; happening atmosphere. ⑤ *Average main: $36* ⊠ *215 Charles St., Beacon Hill* ☎ *617/536–2100* ⊕ *www.scampoboston.com* Ⓜ *Charles/MGH* ✛ *1:D5.*

GOVERNMENT CENTER AND THE NORTH END
GOVERNMENT CENTER

Government Center is home to Faneuil Hall, a tourist magnet, packed with fast-food concessions as well as some more serious alternatives. If you're not on a schedule, and if you've seen enough of Faneuil Hall and want a change of scene, you shouldn't rule out a walk to the North End.

$$
AMERICAN

✗ **Durgin-Park Market Dining Room.** You should be hungry enough to cope with enormous portions, yet not so hungry you can't tolerate a long wait (or sharing a table with others). Durgin-Park was serving its same hearty New England fare (Indian pudding, baked beans, corned beef and cabbage, and a prime rib that hangs over the edge of the plate) back when Faneuil Hall was a working market instead of a tourist attraction. **Known for:** solid, Yankee classics; purposely brusk waitstaff; huge portions. ⑤ *Average main: $20* ⊠ *340 Faneuil Hall Market Pl., North Market Bldg.* ☎ *617/227–2038* ⊕ *www.arkrestaurants.com/durgin_park.html* Ⓜ *Government Center* ✛ *1:G5.*

10

$$$
SEAFOOD
✕ **Union Oyster House.** Established in 1826, this is Boston's oldest continuing restaurant, and a must-see destination. Eat what Daniel Webster had—oysters on the half shell at the ground-floor raw bar, which is the oldest part of the restaurant and still the best. **Known for:** oldest Boston restaurant; long waits on weekends; oysters. ⑤ *Average main: $28* ✉ *41 Union St., Government Center* ☎ *617/227–2750* ⊕ *www. unionoysterhouse.com* Ⓜ *Haymarket* ✛ *1:F5.*

THE NORTH END

As the city's oldest residential area, the North End contains some remarkable Revolutionary War history, including Paul Revere's home, and some really remarkable Italian food. The narrow side streets can be eerily quiet during the day, save for a gathering of grandmothers sitting on lawn chairs outside an apartment building, but then transform into vibrant meeting places come evening, as twentysomething hipsters return home from work and couples of all ages take advantage of the romantic opportunities afforded by the neighborhood's small, rustic restaurants and cannoli-filled cafés.

$$
ITALIAN
Fodor'sChoice
★
✕ **Antico Forno.** Many of the menu choices here come from the eponymous wood-burning brick oven, which turns out surprisingly delicate pizzas simply topped with tomato and fresh buffalo mozzarella. Though its pizzas receive top billing, Antico excels at a variety of Italian country dishes, like veal parmigiana, osso buco with pork shanks, chicken saltimbocca, and handmade pastas; the specialty, gnocchi, is rich and creamy but light. **Known for:** wood-fired, brick-oven pizza; Italian country classics; casual, jovial atmosphere. ⑤ *Average main: $18* ✉ *93 Salem St., North End* ☎ *617/723–6733* ⊕ *www.anticofornoboston.com* Ⓜ *Haymarket* ✛ *1:G4.*

$$$$
ITALIAN
✕ **Bricco.** A sophisticated but unpretentious enclave of nouveau Italian, Bricco has carved out quite a following. And no wonder: the handmade pastas alone are argument for a reservation. **Known for:** sophisticated Italian classics; dark, elegant atmosphere; pillowy homemade pastas. ⑤ *Average main: $38* ✉ *241 Hanover St., North End* ☎ *617/248–6800* ☽ *No lunch* Ⓜ *Haymarket* ✛ *1:G5.*

$$
SEAFOOD
Fodor'sChoice
★
✕ **Daily Catch.** You've just got to love this shoebox-size place—for the noise, the intimacy, the complete absence of pretense, and, above all, the food, which proved so popular, it spawned two other locations (one in Brookline and another in Boston's Seaport area). With garlic and olive oil forming the foundation for almost every dish, this cheerful, bustling spot specializes in calamari, black squid-ink pastas, and linguine with clam sauce, all served in the skillets in which they were cooked, hot from the stove. **Known for:** garlic-rich preparations; luscious seafood skillet pastas; intimate, elbow-to-elbow dining. ⑤ *Average main: $21* ✉ *323 Hanover St., North End* ☎ *617/523–8567* ⊕ *thedailycatch.com* ▭ *No credit cards* Ⓜ *Haymarket* ✛ *1:G4.*

$$$
ITALIAN
✕ **Mamma Maria.** Don't let the clichéd name fool you: Mamma Maria is far from a typical red-sauce joint. From the handmade pappardelle layered with braised rabbit to the authentic sauces and entrées to some of the best desserts in the North End, you can't go wrong here. **Known for:** white-cloth Italian cuisine; charming setting; good service. ⑤ *Average main: $30* ✉ *3 North Sq., North End* ☎ *617/523–0077* ⊕ *www. mammamaria.com* ☽ *No lunch* Ⓜ *Haymarket* ✛ *1:G4.*

COFFEE TALK

Café culture is alive and well in the North End. **Caffe Vittoria** (✉ *290–296 Hanover St.* ☎ *617/227–7606* 1:G4), established in 1929, is Boston's oldest Italian café. With four levels of seating, three bars that serve aperitifs, and one massive, ancient espresso maker, this old-fashioned café will make you want to lose yourself in these surroundings. At **Caffé Paradiso** (✉ *255 Hanover St.* ☎ *617/742–1768* 1:G5) spectacular coffee drinks await, along with the richest gelato in the neighborhood, weighing in at a decadent 14% milk fat (versus the 8% used in traditional versions). **Caffe dello Sport** (✉ *308 Hanover St.* ☎ *617/523–5063* 1:G4) is an Italianate version of a sports bar, with two wide screens transmitting live soccer; order espressos, cordials, and gelato. If you're not able to kill a whole afternoon sipping cappuccino, stop by **Polcari's Coffee** (✉ *105 Salem St.* ☎ *617/227–0786* 1:G4), selling dried goods by the pound—coffees, teas, herbs, and spices displayed in antique brass bins.

$$$
SEAFOOD
Fodor's Choice
★

✕ **Neptune Oyster.** This *piccolo* oyster bar, the first of its kind in the neighborhood, has only 22 chairs, but the long marble bar adorned with mirrors has extra seating for 15 more patrons, who can watch the oyster shuckers deftly undo handfuls of more than a dozen different kinds of bivalves to savor as an appetizer or on a *plateau di frutti di mare*, a gleaming tower of oysters and other raw-bar items piled over ice that you can order from the slip of paper they pass out listing each day's crustacean options. Dishes change seasonally, but a couple of year-round favorites include the North End Cioppino (fish stew) and the signature lobster roll that, hot or cold, overflows with meat. **Known for:** casual setting; Italian-style seafood; generously packed lobster roll. ⑤ *Average main: $30* ✉ *63 Salem St., North End* ☎ *617/742–3474* ⊕ *www.neptuneoyster.com* Ⓜ *Haymarket* ✛ 1:G5.

$$$$
MODERN ITALIAN

✕ **Prezza.** Chef Anthony Caturano pays homage to his Italian grandmother at this warm, convivial eatery by naming it after the tiny Abruzzese village where she was born and then putting a modern twist on the rustic dishes she would have cooked. Favorites include polenta smothered with sausage-meatball-rib sauce; wood-grilled veal porterhouse; and buttery ricotta-stuffed ravioli. **Known for:** scrumptious country-style Italian; generous portions; impressive Italian wine list. ⑤ *Average main: $37* ✉ *24 Fleet St., North End* ☎ *617/227–1577* ⊕ *www.prezza.com* ▭ *No credit cards* ✛ 1:G4.

$$
ITALIAN

✕ **Regina Pizzeria.** This North End institution owned by the Polcari family has been doing what it does best since 1926—creating thin-crusted, brick-oven-charred pizzas with fresh toppings, excellent sauce, and just the right amount of cheese. With 17 locations, they only offer what they excel in: incredibly well-made pies, like the Margherita, which contains fresh basil leaves baked into the cheese so they don't burn. **Known for:** excellent thin-crust pizzas; good prices; no-frills atmosphere. ⑤ *Average main: $20* ✉ *11½ Thatcher St., North End* ☎ *617/227–0765* ⊕ *www.pizzeriaregina.com* ✛ 1:F4.

10

$$$
ITALIAN

✕**Ristorante Euno.** Unassuming and friendly, Euno is the North End's culinary mouse that roars, hitting just the right notes from the starter bowls of buttery olives to handmade pastas and risottos to the chef's catch of the day. The rustic, two-story space, which used to be a butcher shop (the meat hooks still stud the wall, doubling as coat hangers), often fills on weekends, but those wise enough to make reservations might snag a table in the romantic downstairs dining room. **Known for:** traditional Italian favorites; reasonable prices; rustic interior. ⑤ *Average main: $28* ✉ *119 Salem St., North End* ☎ *617/573–9406* ⊕ *www. eunoboston.com* ⊙ *No lunch* Ⓜ *Haymarket* ✛ *1:G4.*

$$$
ITALIAN

✕**Terramia Ristorante.** Nearly everything on the menu at this cozy restaurant with a honeyed glow and exposed wooden beams tastes home-cooked and authentic, from the fresh homemade pastas tossed with equally fresh ingredients to the perfectly cooked, powerfully flavored risottos and the succulent, 16-ounce grilled veal chop with veal porcini reduction. The dessert list stops after tiramisu, bread pudding, and a flourless chocolate cake, but who needs more choices than those? **Known for:** simple Italian classics; cozy, rustic setting; family-friendly atmosphere. ⑤ *Average main: $30* ✉ *98 Salem St., North End* ☎ *617/523–3112* ⊕ *www.terramiaristorante.com* ⊙ *No lunch* Ⓜ *Haymarket* ✛ *1:G4.*

CHARLESTOWN

English colonists founded this little neighborhood across Boston Harbor before they established Boston. Notable for its historic houses and buildings, including the Bunker Hill Monument and the USS *Constitution*, it also contains a vibrant mix of affordable eateries, mainly along Main Street and in City Square, that cater to the artists, working families, and young couples who live in the area.

$$$
MOROCCAN

✕**Tangierino.** Chef-owner Samad Naamad draws visitors into his enchanting Moroccan fantasy with hearty, spice-driven food, fragrant cocktails, and binightly belly-dancing shows. Indulge in small plates like calamari rubbed with *harissa* aioli; then enjoy a drawn-out meal of entrées cooked in a tagine (a clay pot used for slow cooking). **Known for:** Moroccan tagines and couscous; sultry atmosphere; hookah bar. ⑤ *Average main: $28* ✉ *83 Main St., Charlestown* ☎ *617/242–6009* ⊕ *www.tangierino.com* Ⓜ *Community College* ✛ *1:E2.*

DOWNTOWN BOSTON

Boston's Downtown scene revs up at lunchtime, but the streets get quiet after 5 pm, when everyone goes back to the suburbs. The city center is great for after-hours dining, though, especially in the hideaway restaurants around the former Leather District.

$
ITALIAN
FAMILY

✕**Babbo Pizzeria.** With his signature ponytail and orange clogs, celebrity chef Mario Batali is the name behind this bountiful pizzeria with three bars and a 1,000-degree wood-burning oven churning out blistered, chewy crusted rounds topped with everything from kid-friendly tomato, basil, and mozzarella to more esoteric combos like goat cheese, pistachios, red onion, and truffle honey. The generous menu also features flavor-rich antipasti, vegetable dishes, cured meats, cheese, seafood, pastas, and grilled and fried goodies. **Known**

for: golden-crusted pizzas; umami-rich menu; lively, spacious setting. $ *Average main: $16* ⊠ *11 Fan Pier Blvd., Downtown* ☎ *617/421–4466* ⊕ *babbopizzeria.com* ✛ *1:H6.*

$$
ASIAN FUSION
✕ **Blue Dragon.** Old Shanghai meets stylish South Boston at TV-star chef Ming Tsai's uber-popular Asian gastropub, set in an abandoned triangular diner in the Fort Point neighborhood. Folks regularly stop in to slurp up Tsai's East-meets-West cocktails and share succulent braised short-rib pot stickers, spicy Dan Dan noodles, tiny teriyaki bison cheese burgers, and salt and pepper shrimp. **Known for:** funky Asian mash-ups; chocolate chip cookie, ice cream, soy caramel dessert. $ *Average main: $19* ⊠ *324 A St., Downtown* ☎ *617/338–8585* ⊕ *www.ming.com/blue-dragon.htm* ✛ *2:H2.*

$$$
SEAFOOD
FAMILY
✕ **Legal Sea Foods.** What began as a tiny restaurant adjacent to a Cambridge fish market has grown to important regional status, with more than 30 East Coast locations, including almost a dozen in Boston. The hallmark is the freshest possible seafood, whether you have it wood-grilled, in New England chowder, or doused in an Asia-inspired sauce. **Known for:** classic, superfresh New England seafood; family-friendly setting. $ *Average main: $30* ⊠ *26 Park Sq., Downtown* ☎ *617/426–4444* ⊕ *www.legalseafoods.com* Ⓜ *Arlington* ✛ *2:D2.*

$$$
FRENCH
✕ **Les Zygomates.** The French expression for the facial muscles that make you smile is *les zygomates* and this combination wine bar–bistro inarguably lives up to its name, making diners happy with quintessential French bistro fare like the tiered, ice-packed house platter (*plateau maison*) filled with oysters, clams, shrimp, and snow crab claws, and the unctuous beef short-rib bourguignonne, simply made (with many local ingredients) and simply delicious. The dinner menu beautifully matches the ever-changing wine list, with 20 reds and 20 whites by the glass and hundreds of bottles, including some dating back to 1970, like Château Margaux. **Known for:** French bistro offerings; tiered seafood platter; extensive wine-by-the-glass offerings. $ *Average main: $32* ⊠ *129 South St., Downtown* ☎ *617/542–5108* ⊕ *www.winebar129.com* ☾ *Closed Sun. No lunch Sat.* Ⓜ *South Station* ✛ *2:F2.*

$$$$
FRENCH
✕ **Menton.** If price is no object, head over to the Fort Point neighborhood to experience Barbara Lynch's Italian-meets-French Relais & Chateaux eatery, named for a French town near Italy's border. In addition to several luxurious lunch and dinner tasting menus, the restaurant offers seasonal à la carte options, including signature favorites, like the seafood-enriched butter soup and foie gras tart, along with a more casual (and affordable) Gold Bar menu (only available at the bar) featuring crostini, a Wagyu burger, and foie gras frankfurter. **Known for:** opulent tasting menus; extravagant prices; hushed atmosphere. $ *Average main: $150* ⊠ *354 Congress St., Fort Point Channel, Downtown* ☎ *617/737–0099* ⊕ *www.mentonboston.com* ☾ *No lunch weekends* Ⓜ *South Station* ✛ *2:H2.*

$$$$
JAPANESE
Fodor's Choice
★
✕ **o ya.** Despite its side-street location and hidden door, o ya isn't exactly a secret: dining critics from the *New York Times*, *Bon Appetit*, and *Food & Wine* have all named this tiny, improvisational sushi spot among the best in the country, so much so, it now has a branch in Manhattan.

10

Chef Tim Cushman's small plate menu features squid-ink bubbles, homemade potato chips, and foie gras, along with dozens of other dishes, some paying homage to New England, like the wild Maine uni toast with truffled honey and local smoked bluefish with wasabi vinaigrette. **Known for:** creative small-plate Japanese; mind-blowing Omakase. $ *Average main: $60* ⊠ *9 East St., Downtown* ☎ *617/654–9900* ⊕ *www.oyarestaurantboston.com* ☾ *Closed Sun. and Mon. No lunch* Ⓜ *South Station* ⊹ *2:G2.*

$$$ ✕ **Row 34.** This boisterous, self-proclaimed "workingman's oyster bar"
SEAFOOD   with soaring ceilings and a warehouse chic decor, reels customers in with its menu devoted to raw, cured, smoked, pickled, and cooked seafood. Whatever marine delicacy sails into Boston that morning will appear on the restaurant's menu that night, whether it's roasted bluefish with sweet potatoes, onions, and bacon or Dijon-crusted cod. **Known for:** local oysters from restaurant's oyster farm; superfresh seafood; bustling vibe. $ *Average main: $26* ⊠ *383 Congress St., Downtown* ☎ *617/553–5900* ⊕ *www.row34.com* ☾ *No lunch Sun.* ⊹ *1:H6.*

$ ✕ **Silvertone.** Devotees of this retro-cool basement restaurant with strong
AMERICAN   cocktails and reasonable prices swear by the no-fuss menu options, such as a truly addictive macaroni and cheese topped with crispy bacon, meat loaf with mashed potatoes, and steak tips. The wine list is compact but varied and has one of the lowest markups in the city. **Known for:** strong cocktails; comfort food; laid-back feel. $ *Average main: $16* ⊠ *69 Bromfield St., Downtown* ☎ *617/338–7887* ⊕ *www.silvertone-downtown.com* ☾ *Closed Sun.* Ⓜ *Park St.* ⊹ *1:F6.*

$$ ✕ **Sportello.** Barbara Lynch, the queen of Boston's dining scene (see also
ITALIAN   No. 9 Park, B&G Oysters, and The Butcher Shop), had the foresight to create a culinary triad in the city's burgeoning Fort Point Channel neighborhood: the posh restaurant Menton, the adjacent below-street-level bar, DRINK, and the upstairs Italian trattoria Sportello, modeled after a diner and serving rustic, market-fresh fare like deep bowls of truffled gnocchi with peas and plates of spicy smoked pork with roasted onions and farro to enjoy with a tantalizing selection of artisanal wines. **Known for:** homey Italian dishes; lunch-counter layout; quality ingredients. $ *Average main: $22* ⊠ *348 Congress St., Fort Point Channel, Downtown* ☎ *617/737–1234* ⊕ *www.sportelloboston.com* Ⓜ *South Station* ⊹ *2:H2.*

$$$ ✕ **Yvonne's.** For a big, brassy, bountiful night out in an iconic Boston
CONTEMPORARY building, head to this glamorous reimagined supper club inside the former 1862 Locke-Ober restaurant, now a wildly ornate setting where the buffed and beautiful sink into plush chairs in the book-packed library or at the original mahogany mirrored bar to swill down ice-cold martinis and large format whiskey drinks. Should cocktails morph into dinner, white-clothed tables glowing with votives behind the boisterous bar provide a cushy place to share plates of globally inspired comfort food, like grilled octopus with charred romesco salad, steak tartare, and any one of the feasts for two, such as the garlicky 2-pound rib eye with golden fries. **Known for:** glamorous supper club concept; historic setting; large-format cocktails and shared feasts. $ *Average main: $30* ⊠ *2 Winter Pl., Downtown* ☎ *617/267–0047* ⊕ *yvonnesboston.com* ⊹ *1:E6.*

CHINATOWN

Boston's Chinatown is the focal point of Asian cuisines of all types, from authentic Cantonese and Vietnamese to Malaysian, Japanese, and Mandarin. Many places are open after midnight, while the rest of the city sleeps or lurks. It's definitely worth the trek, especially if you're trying to track down live-tank seafood prepared Hong Kong or Chiu Chow style.

$ **✕ Dumpling Cafe.** Discerning diners stream into this no-frills Taiwan-
TAIWANESE ese and Szechuan eatery to slurp down the house specialty—wobbly,
FAMILY Mini Juicy Buns (soup dumplings) crafted from thin noodle wrappers plumped up with pork or pork and crab meat and a rich, flavorful broth that's—be careful—hot enough to scald your chin. In addition to authentic dishes featuring stinky tofu, pork intestine, and duck tongue, the menu has plenty of crowd-pleasing options, like fluffy braised chicken meatballs with crisp bok choy, spicy beef with long horn peppers, and Szechuan-style flounder, swimming in fiery broth with sweet cabbage. **Known for:** Taiwanese/Szechuan dishes; soup dumplings; unusual ingredients, like intestines. $ *Average main: $16* ✉ *695 Washington St., Chinatown* ☎ *617/338–8858* ⊕ *www.dumplingcafe. com* Ⓜ *Chinatown* ✛ *2:E2.*

$ **✕ Q Restaurant.** For a more upscale Chinatown experience, look no far-
ASIAN ther than this sleek Asian outpost with a full cocktail menu, extensive
FAMILY sushi bar, and addictive hot pot menu featuring rich, robust broths, ranging from the meaty *mala*, fired up with spices and herbs, to vegetarian, all served with a fleet of herbs, chilis, and ginger should you wish to season the broth further. Ask for the divided hot pot, which accommodates two broths, and then order whatever vegetables, seafood, meats, and noodles you want to cook at the table, from paper-thin slices of Wagyu rib eye and honeycomb beef tripe to fish balls and shelled shrimp to pea sprouts and exotic mushrooms. **Known for:** Asian hot pots; good cocktails; sleek setting. $ *Average main: $15* ✉ *660 Washington St., Chinatown* ☎ *857/350–3968* ⊕ *www.thequsa.com* Ⓜ *Chinatown* ✛ *2:E2.*

WATERFRONT

Tourists flock to Faneuil Hall and the Marketplace almost year-round, so tried-and-true cuisine tends to dominate there. However, some of Boston's most famous seafood restaurants are, naturally, on the waterfront.

$$$ **✕ Barking Crab Restaurant.** Decked out in cheery colors of yellow, red,
SEAFOOD and green, this is, believe it or not, a real seaside clam shack located
FAMILY smack dab in the middle of Boston with stunning views of the financial district (and prices to match). An outdoor patio and lobster tent in summer, in winter it retreats indoors to a warmhearted version of a waterfront dive, where you'll encounter a classic New England clambake—chowder, Maine lobster, steamed Cape Cod clams, corn on the cob—or oysters and littlenecks from the raw bar, followed by meaty, golden crab cakes. **Known for:** traditional New England clambake; beachy feeling; kitchy confines. $ *Average main: $35* ✉ *88 Sleeper St., Northern Ave. Bridge, Waterfront* ☎ *617/426–2722* ⊕ *www.bark-ingcrab.com* Ⓜ *South Station* ✛ *2:H1.*

10

$$$$
EUROPEAN

✕ **Meritage Restaurant + Wine Bar.** Inside the stately Boston Harbor Hotel with one of the city's finest waterfront views, you'll find this elegant restaurant reflecting Chef Daniel Bruce's passion for pairing wine and New England's bounty. Via separate white wine and red wine menus, you'll find seasonal appetizers and entrées, such as foie gras with pine nuts and plum and pan-roasted local halibut, each paired with the perfect white wine suggestion; juicy duck breast with cranberry and short ribs with shallots are both offered with just the right reds. **Known for:** vineyard-to-table fare; wine selection; harbor views. ⑤ *Average main: $49* ⊠ *Boston Harbor Hotel at Rowes Wharf, 70 Rowes Wharf, Waterfront* 🕾 *617/439–3995* ⊕ *www.meritagetherestaurant.com* ☉ *Closed Sun. and Mon. No lunch* Ⓜ *Aquarium* ✛ *1:H6.*

$$$
MEDITERRANEAN

✕ **Trade.** Crowds slip into this Waterfront District eatery for quiet lunches of globally inspired fare, like salmon crudo with chickpea crackers and plates of soul-warming rigatoni with lamb ragu. Come evening, the boisterous buzz begins and the lofty, white windowed space fills with the city's professionals, eager to unwind over cocktails and plates of roasted chicken with fried potatoes and lemon aioli, seared salmon, and blistered flatbreads (try the tomato four-cheese with arugula) that fly out of the open-hearth pizza oven—perfect for sharing and perfectly delicious. **Known for:** Mediterranean small plates; Downtown convenience; after-work crowds. ⑤ *Average main: $27* ⊠ *540 Atlantic Ave., Waterfront* 🕾 *617/451–1234* ⊕ *trade-boston.com* ▭ *No credit cards* ☉ *No lunch Sun.* Ⓜ *South Station* ✛ *2:G1.*

BACK BAY AND THE SOUTH END
BACK BAY

Easily the ritziest section of Boston, Back Bay is where you'll find historic landmarks such as Copley Square and the Boston Public Library rubbing shoulders with stylish boutiques like Valentino and Max Mara. The restaurant scene follows suit with landmark steak houses and seafood spots sharing sidewalk space with more chic, more global options. But don't feel like you have to win the lottery to eat in this area. While lots of fine-dining establishments dot the neighborhood, you'll also find plenty of affordable spots including Irish taverns, burrito and burger joints, and Eataly, star-chef Mario Batali's massive Italian food emporium in the Prudential Center with groceries, bakeries, seafood, cheese, and meat markets, a dozen eateries, and public café tables to sit at and enjoy takeout.

$$$$
STEAKHOUSE

✕ **Abe & Louie's.** Go ahead: live the fantasy of the robber baron feasting in a setting of cavernous fireplaces and deep-textured, plush mahogany booths. Abe & Louie's may be a tad Disney-esque in its decor, but its menu lives up to the promise with gorgeous, two-tiered raw seafood platters and juicy rib-eye steaks under velvety hollandaise. **Known for:** excellent meats; top-brass service; business-style setting. ⑤ *Average main: $49* ⊠ *793 Boylston St., Back Bay* 🕾 *617/536–6300* ⊕ *www. abeandlouies.com* Ⓜ *Copley* ✛ *2:A2.*

$$$
SEAFOOD
Fodor's Choice
★

✕ **Atlantic Fish Co.** Designed to look like an ocean vessel with gorgeous wood finishes and nautical artwork, this local seafood restaurant delivers first-class fish, so fresh that the extensive menus are printed daily to reflect the day's catch served broiled, baked, blackened, fried, grilled, or pan-seared. Unsnap your starched napkin and begin with a platter of chilled seafood (lobster, little necks, oysters, crab, and shrimp), followed by any one of the specialties ranging from whole-bellied fried Ipswich clams to pan-seared bass with lobster ravioli in an unctuous lobster cream sauce. **Known for:** elegant seafood; solicitous service in a lux atmosphere. $ *Average main: $31* ✉ *761 Boylston St., Back Bay* ☎ *617/267–4000* ⊕ *www.atlanticfishco.com* ▭ *No credit cards* Ⓜ *Copley* ✢ *2:A2.*

$$$$
STEAKHOUSE

✕ **The Capital Grille.** A carnivore's utopia awaits within the clubby, dark-wood walls of this beloved steak house favored by those on expense accounts. Adjust your starched napkin and tuck into such staples as lobster and crab cakes, a massive shellfish platter, and succulent meats such as the 24-ounce dry-aged porterhouse. **Known for:** clubby feel; great steaks; swell crowd. $ *Average main: $40* ✉ *900 Boylston St., Back Bay* ☎ *617/262–8900* ⊕ *www.thecapitalgrille.com* ☽ *No lunch weekends* Ⓜ *Hynes* ✢ *2:A3.*

$$$$
ITALIAN
Fodor's Choice
★

✕ **Davio's.** Comfy armchairs and a grand, high-ceilinged dining room give diners a heightened sense of self-importance, beginning with lunch when the city's power elite stop in for great pastas (half portions are available) and oversize salads. For dinner, some patrons snag quick, pretheater bites at the bar while others opt for a more leisurely experience, lingering over sophisticated Italian dishes like grilled swordfish with tomatoes, olives, and capers and succulent grilled veal chops with creamy potatoes and Port wine sauce. **Known for:** delectable Italian classics; generous portions; elegant setting and service. $ *Average main: $39* ✉ *75 Arlington St., Back Bay* ☎ *617/357–4810* ⊕ *www.davios.com* ☽ *No lunch weekends* Ⓜ *Arlington* ✢ *2:D2.*

$$$
MODERN
AMERICAN

✕ **Deuxave.** At the corner of two avenues (Commonwealth and Massachusetts), which is how this restaurant got its name (deux is French for "two"), you'll find this snazzy, dark-wood enclave serving sophisticated combos of local ingredients, like lobster gnocchi with grapes and walnuts, which sounds odd but works beautifully, tender duck with ginger jus, and richly spiced lamb, all available with a bottle from the thoughtfully crafted and surprisingly affordable wine list. **Known for:** modern French food; warm gnocchi with lobster; reasonably priced wine list. $ *Average main: $35* ✉ *375 Commonwealth Ave., Back Bay* ☎ *617/517–5915* ⊕ *www.deuxave.com* ▭ *No credit cards* Ⓜ *Hynes* ✢ *3:H2.*

10

$$$$
STEAKHOUSE
Fodor's Choice
★

✕ **Grill 23 & Bar.** Pinstripe suits, dark paneling, Persian rugs, and waiters in white jackets give this single-location steak house a posh tone, and the kitchen places a premium on seasonal, organic ingredients and sustainable and humanely raised meats. Choose from seasonally dressed tartares (steak and tuna), cuts of all-natural beef like the 14-ounce dry-aged New York sirloin, and seafood specialties such as grilled branzino with a velvety lemon butter sauce that give steak sales a run for their money. **Known for:** nonchain steak house status; excellent meats; party dress vibe. $ *Average main: $40* ✉ *161 Berkeley St., Back Bay* ☎ *617/542–2255* ⊕ *grill23.com* ☽ *No lunch* Ⓜ *Back Bay/South End* ✢ *2:C2.*

$$
AMERICAN

✕ **Joe's American Bar & Grill.** Despite its classy Newbury Street address, Joe's (with another location on the waterfront) dishes up kitschy July 4 decor, along with myriad burgers, hearty salads, clam chowder, and affordable kid-friendly options like pasta with butter and grilled cheese sandwiches served with a complimentary hot fudge sundae (or a fruit cup for those health-conscious parents). The warm oversize chocolate chip cookie brought to the table in a small black skillet crowned with vanilla ice cream, chocolate sauce, and candied pecans, however, is reason enough to stop by. **Known for:** kid-friendly offerings; affordable prices; unfussy American classics. $ *Average main: $21* ⊠ *181 Newbury St., Back Bay* ☎ *617/536–4200* ⊕ *www.joesamerican.com* ▬ *No credit cards* Ⓜ *Copley* ✛ *2:B2.*

$$$$ ✕ **L'Espalier.** Located next door to the Mandarin Oriental Hotel, this

FRENCH elegant French restaurant, with floor-to-ceiling windows and modern

Fodor's Choice decor, is the sort of place where locals come to splurge with either a

★ five- or eight-course tasting menu, including a vegetarian one. Chefowner Frank McClelland's dishes—from caviar and roasted foie gras to beef sirloin and smoked Maine lobster—are as delicious as they are artful and often include ingredients harvested that morning from McClelland's own farm. **Known for:** masterful French cuisine; sumptuous cheese trolley; special occasion atmosphere. $ *Average main: $98* ⊠ *774 Boylston St., Back Bay* ☎ *617/262–3023* ⊕ *www.lespalier. com* Ⓜ *Copley* ✛ *2:A2.*

$$$$ ✕ **Ostra.** Boston has plenty of great seafood restaurants, but this

SEAFOOD sophisticated option near the Theater District turns out delicate and exquisitely prepared catches of the day fit for a king (and some say costing a king's ransom). Settle in with a seasonal cocktail in the sleek, pearl-white dining room before tucking into any one of the glistening raw fish tartares followed by a simply prepared entrée, whether it's a salt-crusted branzino for two or local halibut with mushrooms and black truffle. **Known for:** exquisite seafood dishes; lustrous setting; fancy atmosphere. $ *Average main: $42* ⊠ *1 Charles St., Back Bay* ☎ *617/421–1200* ⊕ *ostraboston.com* ☾ *No lunch* ✛ *2:D2.*

$$$$ ✕ **Porto.** In a spanking white space next to the Prudential Center, chef/

SEAFOOD co-owner Jody Adams, former owner of the shuttered Rialto restaurant, takes seafood up a notch, both in terms of presentation and pricing. In addition to plenty of raw options—oysters, crudo, and caviar—you'll find starters like steamed clams with guanciale, and mains such as whole roasted lobster with lemon and feta cheese. **Known for:** artful seafood preparations; bountiful raw bar; elegant Back Bay setting. $ *Average main: $35* ⊠ *Next door to Saks 5th Ave., Ring Rd., Back Bay* ☎ *617/536–1234* ⊕ *www.porto-boston.com* ✛ *2:B2.*

$$$ ✕ **Post 390.** This hopping "urban tavern" tantalizes diners with cre-

AMERICAN ative gastropub fare like sizzled crab cakes with champagne-pickled shallots, herb-marinated swordfish, lemon-pepper roast chicken, and a swoon-worthy Valrhona hot fudge sundae with salty cashews. Every week the restaurant serves a Farm-to-Post three-course menu based on ingredients from a featured American farm or fishery and prepared in the cooking style of where that farm or fishery resides, whether it's New Orleans or New Hampshire. **Known for:** creative gastropub cuisine; cozy multilevel space; weekly Farm-to-Post three-course meal. $ *Average main: $34* ⊠ *406 Stuart St., Back Bay* ☎ *617/399–0015* ⊕ *www. post390restaurant.com* ☾ *No lunch Sat.* Ⓜ *Back Bay* ✛ *2:C2.*

$$$
SEAFOOD
Fodor'sChoice
★

✕ **Saltie Girl.** Step into this snug Back Bay raw bar specializing in snappy cocktails and luscious preparations of all things seafood and you'll fall hook, line, and sinker for everything on the menu, including platters of fresh-shucked oysters on crushed ice, torched salmon belly with charred avocado, smoked fish that would make a New York deli owner proud, seafood-topped toasts, and easily the best warm lobster roll in the city, a butter-drenched affair overflowing with fresh lobster meat. Rounding out the menu and decorating the restaurant's walls are 80-plus tins of domestic and imported gourmet fish and shellfish (including caviar!) served in all their oily goodness with bread, butter, smoked salt, lemon, and sweet pepper jam. **Known for:** yummy seafood tapas; huge tinned seafood selection; big, buttery, warm lobster roll. ⑤ *Average main: $25* ✉ *281 Dartmouth St., Back Bay* ☎ *617/267–0691* ⊕ *saltiegirl.com* ⊗ *Closed Mon.* ✛ *2:B2.*

$$$$
SEAFOOD
Fodor'sChoice
★

✕ **Select Oyster Bar.** Snug quarters and no desserts can't quell the stream of diners pouring into this uptown enclave eager to savor oysters and such seductive seafood combinations as salmon crudo with pistachio oil, Maine lobster cabbage-kale Thai salad, and tomato bouillabaisse with saffron aioli. With 70% of the restaurant's catch coming from New England, plus a thoughtful libations list and polished service, you have all the ingredients for a good time, whether you're sitting at the bar, the front communal table, or in the three-season alfresco area out back. **Known for:** lip-smacking seafood dishes; 20% pretax service charge automatically added to each bill; cozy, relaxed atmosphere. ⑤ *Average main: $36* ✉ *50 Gloucester St., Back Bay* ☎ *857/293–8064* ⊕ *www.selectboston.com* ✛ *2:A2.*

$$$
AMERICAN

✕ **Sonsie.** Café society blossoms along Newbury Street, particularly at Sonsie (a favorite haunt of the Patriot's Tom Brady), where a well-heeled crowd sips coffee up front or angles for places at the bar. Lunch and dinner dishes veer toward basic bistro fare with an American twist such as kale Caesar salad with grilled chicken and pan-roasted salmon with potatoes, chard, and beet "ketchup." The restaurant is a terrific place for weekend brunch, when the light pours through the long windows, and is at its most vibrant in warm weather, when the open doors make for colorful people-watching. **Known for:** American bistro favorites; sceney vibe; Sunday brunch. ⑤ *Average main: $25* ✉ *327 Newbury St., Back Bay* ☎ *617/351–2500* ⊕ *sonsieboston.com* Ⓜ *Hynes* ✛ *3:H2.*

$$$$
ITALIAN

✕ **Sorellina.** Set in an all-white dining room, everything about this upscale Italian spot is oversized, from its space near Copley Square to its flavor-packed portions of grilled octopus with squid-ink couscous, homemade pasta with Wagyu meatballs, and bone-in veal chops over soft polenta. Just save room for dessert: it's always a highlight here. **Known for:** modern Italian cooking; bountiful portions; edgy decor. ⑤ *Average main: $42* ✉ *1 Huntington Ave., Back Bay* ☎ *617/412–4600* ⊕ *www.sorellinaboston.com* ⊗ *No lunch* Ⓜ *Copley, Back Bay* ✛ *2:B2.*

$$
AMERICAN
FAMILY

✕ **Summer Shack.** Boston uberchef Jasper White has given New England seafood an urban tweak in his boisterous, bright, fun eatery next to the Prudential Center (he also has one in Cambridge), where creamy clam chowder and fried Ipswich clams share menu space with golden crab cakes and cedar-planked, maple-lemon glazed salmon. In addition to a handful of chicken and meat dishes for those not into seafood, White features the most succulent lobsters in the city (he has a patented process

10

for cooking them), all brought to you by an eager-to-please staff. **Known for:** fresh seafood; succulent lobster; fun, casual atmosphere. $ *Average main: $24 ⊠ 50 Dalton St., Back Bay ☎ 617/867–9955 ⊕ www. summershackrestaurant.com ▭ No credit cards ☞ Lunch menu is only offered weekdays. Weekend visitors, even at 11:30 am, receive dinner menu* Ⓜ *Hynes* ✛ *3:H3.*

$$$$
FRENCH FUSION
Fodor's Choice
★

✕ **Troquet on South.** Despite having what might well be Boston's longest wine list, with nearly 500 vintages (more than 50 of which are available by the glass), plus an interactive Champagne cart, this French fusion spot flies somewhat under the radar. Still, locals know that Troquet offers all the ingredients for a lovely and delectable evening: a generous space for drinking and dining, a knowledgeable yet unpretentious staff, and decadent fare, beginning with chewy rolls and farm-churned butter scooped from a bucket, and entrées like roasted suckling pig and rosy duck with lentils and mandarin. **Known for:** exceptional wine selection; mouthwatering bistro fare; excellent cheese cart. $ *Average main: $42 ⊠ 107 South St., Theater District ☎ 617/695–9463 ⊕ troquetboston.com ☉ No lunch ☞ Valet parking available Tues.–Sat.* Ⓜ *Boylston* ✛ *2:F2.*

$$$$
ASIAN FUSION

✕ **Uni.** Inside the tasteful boutique Eliot Hotel lies an innovative *izakaya* (informal Japanese gastropub) offering boldly flavored renditions of Asian street food—steamed buns stuffed with pickled vegetables and pork belly; green curry crab fried rice; chicken waffles with kimchee; and dozens of raw fish bites like tuna poke with sweet onion and seaweed and hamachi with ponzu powder and pickled chili. Although the bites can add up price-wise, the menu has a sprinkling of inexpensive dishes, like Indian spiced carrots, crispy potatoes with herbed mayonnaise, and bone marrow rice balls. **Known for:** creative raw fish options; trendy feel; small plate format. $ *Average main: $45 ⊠ Eliot Hotel, 370 Commonwealth Ave., Back Bay ☎ 617/536–7200 ⊕ www.uni-boston. com ☉ No lunch* Ⓜ *Hynes* ✛ *3:H2.*

THE SOUTH END

Home to lovely Victorian brownstones, art galleries, and the city's most diverse crowd, the South End is Boston's cultural engine. It's also ground zero for local foodies, who flood the scores of ethnic resto-bars that morph from neighborhood bistros into packed hot spots as the evening progresses. Some of the city's most popular restaurants inhabit the small square between Berkeley Street and Massachusetts Avenue to the west, and Harrison Avenue and Columbus Avenue to the north.

$$$
SEAFOOD

✕ **B&G Oysters.** B&G Oysters' Chef Barbara Lynch (of No. 9 Park, the Butcher Shop, Sportello, DRINK, and Menton fame) has made yet another fabulous mark on Boston with a style-conscious seafood restaurant that updates New England's traditional bounty with such offerings as smoked mussels with mustard mayonnaise, shrimp ceviche with tomatillo and avocado, potato gnocchi with seared calamari and a BLT with lobster. Designed to imitate the inside of an oyster shell, the iridescent bar glows with silvery, candlelighted tiles and a sophisticated crowd that in warm weather fills the hidden outdoor patio strung with tiny white lights. **Known for:** creative seafood preparations; delicate portions; stylish setting. $ *Average main: $30 ⊠ 550 Tremont St., South End ☎ 617/423–0550 ⊕ www.bandgoysters.com* Ⓜ *Back Bay* ✛ *2:D4.*

$$$ ✕**The Butcher Shop.** Chef Barbara Lynch has remade the classic meat
AMERICAN market as a polished wine bar–cum–hangout, serving those who either
want to stop in for a glass of wine and a casual, quick snack of home-
made prosciutto and a plate of artisanal cheeses or relax longer over
dinner specials like tagliatelle Bolognese, roasted bone marrow with
grilled bread, and beef tenderloin with crispy potatoes. **Known for:**
excellent cooked and cure meats; rustic atmosphere; friendly service.
⑤ *Average main: $30* ⊠ *552 Tremont St., South End* ☎ *617/423–4800*
⊕ *www.thebutchershopboston.com* Ⓜ *Back Bay* ✛ *2:D4.*

$$$ ✕**Estragon Tapas.** The urbane 1930s decor makes this South End Spanish
SPANISH restaurant feel high-class, but the tapas plates and easy-to-share fish and
meat dishes make dining here an entirely casual experience. A selection
of traditional tapas, such as grilled Spanish sausage on toast and grilled
leeks *romesco* (spicy red pepper–almond sauce) can easily fill up two
people when coupled with entrées like paella (vegetarian or nonvegetar-
ian) or the grilled lamb skewers. **Known for:** tapas/rice dishes; authentic
flavors; comfortable setting. ⑤ *Average main: $30* ⊠ *700 Harrison Ave.,
South End* ☎ *617/266–0443* ⊕ *www.estragontapas.com* ☾ *Closed Sun.
No lunch* Ⓜ *Newton* ✛ *2:D5.*

$ ✕**Flour Bakery + Café.** When folks need coffee, a great sandwich, or
AMERICAN an irresistible sweet, like a pecan sticky bun, lemon tart, or double
FAMILY chocolate cookie—or just a place to sit and chat—they come to one
Fodor's Choice of owner Joanne Chang's six Flour bakeries, including this one in the
★ South End. A communal table in the middle acts as a gathering spot,
around which diners enjoy morning pastries, homemade soups, hearty
bean and grain salads, and specialty sandwiches like grilled chicken with
Brie, roasted peppers, caramelized onions, and arugula, or a BLT with
applewood-smoked bacon. **Known for:** scrumptious sweets; delicious
salads and sandwiches; laid-back setting. ⑤ *Average main: $9* ⊠ *1595
Washington St., South End* ☎ *617/267–4300* ⊕ *www.flourbakery.com*
Ⓜ *Massachusetts Ave.* ✛ *2:C5.*

$$ ✕**The Franklin Café.** With a full menu served until 1:30 pm, this place has
AMERICAN jumped to the head of the class by keeping things simple yet effective,
from the well-crafted cocktails to the homey cuisine: think skillet-smoked
mussels, succulent turkey meat loaf, and braised beef brisket with roasted
vegetables. The vibe tends to feel more like a bar than a restaurant (hence
the many bartender awards), so be forewarned that it can get loud and the
wait for a table (there are only seven booths and two tables) can be long.
Known for: gastropub fare; neighborhood feel; open late. ⑤ *Average
main: $20* ⊠ *278 Shawmut Ave., South End* ☎ *617/350–0010* ⊕ *www.
franklincafe.com* ☾ *No lunch* Ⓜ *Union Park* ✛ *2:D4.*

$$$ ✕**Kava.** Despite Boston's many ethnic restaurants, good Greek food
GREEK served in an inviting atmosphere has been missing, until the opening of
Fodor's Choice this sweet little white-washed taverna serving authentic Greek cuisine
★ with many ingredients imported from the Mediterranean, such as the
feta, fish, and octopus. Order some crisp white wine off the mainly Greek
wine list to sip with a parade of home-style entrées, including jumbo
white beans in tomato sauce, chunky Greek salad, grilled loukaniko
sausage spritzed with lemon, and charred sea bass served with a side of
scordalia (garlic whipped potatoes) and *horta* (cooked greens with olive

10

oil). **Known for:** authentic Greek favorites; taverna feel; high-quality ingredients. $ *Average main: $27* ✉ *315 Shawmut Ave., South End* ☎ *617/356–1100* ⊕ *www.kavaneotaverna.com* ☉ *Lunch on weekends only* ✛ *2:D4.*

$$$$ FRENCH **Fodor's**Choice ★ ✗**Mistral.** Boston's fashionable set flocks to this long-popular South End restaurant with polished service and upscale yet unpretentious French-Mediterranean cuisine with fail-safe favorites like tuna tartare, duck with cherries, and French Dover sole. The seasonally tweaked menu rarely changes—but no one's complaining. **Known for:** sophisticated Mediterranean cuisine; superb service; white-cloth, country French decor. $ *Average main: $36* ✉ *223 Columbus Ave., South End* ☎ *617/867–9300* ⊕ *mistralbistro.com* ☉ *No lunch* Ⓜ *Back Bay* ✛ *2:C3.*

$$ CHINESE **Fodor's**Choice ★ ✗**Myers + Chang.** Pink and orange dragon decals cover the windows of this all-day Chinese café, where Joanne Chang (of Flour bakery fame) taps her familial cooking roots to create shareable platters of creative dumplings, wok-charred udon noodles, and stir-fries brimming with fresh ingredients and plenty of hot chili peppers, garlic, fresh herbs, crushed peanuts, and lime. The staff is young and fun, and the crowd generally follows suit. **Known for:** Asian soul food; fabulous cocktails; punchy decor. $ *Average main: $18* ✉ *1145 Washington St., South End* ☎ *617/542–5200* ⊕ *www.myersandchang.com* Ⓜ *Back Bay* ✛ *2:E4.*

$$$ JAPANESE ✗**Oishii Boston.** Although the entrance to this superb sushi restaurant may elude you, simply follow the crowds of raw fish fans streaming into the sleek, gray industrial space, to find edible aquatic enchantment in the form of tuna tartare with caviar and crispy shallots tempura, lobster maki in a daikon radish wrapper, and seafood risotto in a sizzling hot pot. The vibe is stylish and so are the diners. **Known for:** high-end Japanese sushi; quiet atmosphere; minimalist decor. $ *Average main: $35* ✉ *1166 Washington St., South End* ☎ *617/482–8868* ⊕ *www.oishiiboston.com* ⊟ *No credit cards* ☉ *Closed Mon.* Ⓜ *East Berkeley* ✛ *2:E4.*

$$$ ITALIAN ✗**SRV.** SRV, short for Serene Republic of Venice, bills itself as a bacaro, or Italian wine bar, which here in the South End translates into a happening cocktail scene, where the chic set gathers to sip on Aperol Spritz and negroni *bianco* before tucking into tantalizing small plates and hand-crafted pastas made from flour the chefs mill themevles from durham wheat berries. Sharing is the way to go and once you've forked up some two-bite pork-beef meatballs, marinated artichoke hearts, baby clams with guanciale—ask for extra bread to sop up the spicy briney juices—it's time for pastas and risottos, like the richly sauced lumache with seafood and green garlic risotto perked up with Pecorino Romano.

Known for: Venetian bar bites; cocktail party buzz; casual, fun feel. ⑤ *Average main: $35* ✉ *569 Columbus St., South End* ☎ *617/536–9500* ⊕ *www.srvboston.com* ◷ *No lunch* ✛ *2:A5.*

$$$

SPANISH

Fodor'sChoice

★

✕ **Toro.** The opening buzz from chefs Ken Oringer and Jamie Bissonnette's tapas joint, which now has an outpost in Manhattan, still remains loud—for good reason. Small plates such as grilled corn with aioli and cotija cheese are hefty enough to make a meal out of a few, or you can share the regular or vegetarian paella with a group. **Known for:** excellent traditional tapas; cozy, small dining room; cult following. ⑤ *Average main: $35* ✉ *1704 Washington St., South End* ☎ *617/536–4300* ⊕ *www.toro-restaurant.com* Ⓜ *Massachusetts Ave.* ✛ *2:B6.*

THE FENWAY AND KENMORE SQUARE

No longer just a place to grab a slice of pizza before a Red Sox game, this area adjacent to Fenway Park and Boston University blooms with restaurants along tree-lined streets that specialize in BBQ, oysters, tacos, and faculty-friendly bistro fare.

$$$

AMERICAN

Fodor'sChoice

★

✕ **Eastern Standard Kitchen and Drinks.** A vivid red awning beckons patrons of this spacious brasserie-style restaurant with menus for breakfast, lunch, midday, dinner, and late-night (until 1:30 am). The bar area and red banquettes fill most nights with Boston's power players (members of the Red Sox management are known to stop in), thirtysomethings, and students from the nearby universities all noshing on raw-bar specialties and comfort dishes such as lamb-sausage rigatoni, steak frites, and burgers. **Known for:** brasserie fare; terrific craft cocktails; Parisian-style decor. ⑤ *Average main: $25* ✉ *528 Commonwealth Ave., Kenmore Square* ☎ *617/532–9100* ⊕ *www.eastern-standardboston.com* Ⓜ *Kenmore* ✛ *3:F2.*

$$$

SEAFOOD

Fodor'sChoice

★

✕ **Island Creek Oyster Bar.** As the name indicates, this Hotel Commonwealth restaurant specializes in seafood, beginning with oysters that come fresh from the restaurant's own oyster farm in nearby Duxbury Bay, as well as Maine, Prince Edward Island, and Puget Sound (Washington). Beyond raw options, look for pan-fried crab cakes, steamed little neck clams, chowders, bisques, and daily fish selections ranging from cornmeal-crusted skate wing and herb-crusted cod to grilled Maine salmon and New Bedford monkfish with Maine yellow eye beans and chorizo. **Known for:** superb oysters; delish seafood dishes; loud, fun feel. ⑤ *Average main: $34* ✉ *500 Commonwealth Ave., Kenmore Square* ☎ *617/532–5300* ⊕ *www.islandcreekoysterbar.com* ▬ *No credit cards* Ⓜ *Kenmore* ✛ *3:F2.*

$$

SOUTHERN

Fodor'sChoice

★

✕ **Sweet Cheeks.** Red Sox fans, foodies, and Fenway residents flock to this meat-lover's mecca, where Texas-style BBQ is the name of the game. Hefty slabs of dry-rubbed heritage pork, great northern beef brisket, and plump chickens cook low and slow in a jumbo black smoker then come to the table heaped on a tray lined with butcher paper, along with homemade sweet pickles, shaved onion, and your choice of "hot scoops" (collard greens, mac 'n' cheese) or "cold scoops" (coleslaw, potato salad). **Known for:** finger-licking barbecue; scrumptious sides; jeans and T-shirt atmosphere. ⑤ *Average main: $22* ✉ *1381 Boylston St., The Fenway* ☎ *617/266–1300* ⊕ *www.sweetcheeksq.com* ▬ *No credit cards* Ⓜ *Fenway* ✛ *3:E4.*

10

$$ ✕ **Tiger Mama.** Chef-owner Tiffany Faison of the beloved barbecue spot,
ASIAN FUSION   Sweet Cheeks, has hit another home run in Fenway with this spacious,
FAMILY   brightly colored Asian eatery. Tiki cocktails and a bevy of umami-rich
plates, like ginger-chili ribs with peanut crumble, coconut marinated
chicken with tamarind sauce, and curried Singapore street noodles tan-
gled with greens, pay homage to South East Asia. **Known for:** sassy Asian
fare; tiki drinks; casual setting. $ *Average main: $18* ✉ *1363 Boylston St.,
The Fenway* ☎ *617/425–6262* ⊕ *www.tigermamaboston.com* ✛ *3:E3.*

BOSTON OUTSKIRTS

JAMAICA PLAIN

This neighborhood is a kind of mini-Cambridge: multiethnic and
filled with cutting-edge artists, graduate students, political idealists,
and yuppie families. Recently the area, known for its affordable and
unusual ethnic spots, has seen a swell of a more gentrified—but no less
creative—sort.

$$ ✕ **Bella Luna & The Milky Way.** Tucked away in The Brewery Complex,
ITALIAN   home to myriad small businesses, including Samuel Adams beer, this res-
FAMILY   taurant-cum-nightclub offers sci-fi jokes written throughout a spaced-
out menu of eccentric pizzas, calzones, and Italian standards. Menu
favorites include "The Gypsy King" topped with red sauce, caramelized
onion, spinach, and ricotta; and "The Brewery Burger," a tender bun
cradling a gut-busting heap of grilled ground beef, sautéed mushrooms,
cheese, aioli, arugula, and truffle fries (yes, the fries are inside the bun).
Known for: pizzas and hot sandwiches; playful vibe; local feeling. $ *Av-
erage main: $20* ✉ *Samuel Adams Brewery complex, 284 Amory St.,
Jamaica Plain* ☎ *617/524–3740* ⊕ *www.milkywayjp.com* ☾ *No lunch*
Ⓜ *Stony Brook* ✛ *3:C6.*

$$ ✕ **Centre Street Café.** Nearby farms provide the bulk of the ingredients for
ITALIAN   simple yet sublime appetizers, homemade pastas, and main dishes at this
laid-back, 34-seat Italian eatery. Expect menu items like red bean hummus,
grilled octopus, rigatoni with pork Bolognese, and chicken Parmesan with
creamy polenta. **Known for:** farm-fresh comfort food; intimate setting;
friendly service. $ *Average main: $24* ✉ *669A Centre St., Jamaica Plain*
☎ *617/524–9217* ⊕ *www.centrestreetcafejp.com* Ⓜ *Green St.* ✛ *3:C6.*

$ ✕ **El Oriental de Cuba.** This light, airy haven with wooden tables and walls
CUBAN   full of artwork—featuring tropical fruit, Cuban street life, and magazine
covers—serves a large variety of excellent Cuban food, including a restor-
ative chicken soup, a classic Cuban sub, superb rice and beans (opt for
the red beans over the black), and sweet "tropical shakes." The menu,
written in both English and Spanish, begins with breakfast, mainly vari-
ous preparations of eggs with added ham, chorizo, or cheese, and Cuban
espresso or Cuban iced coffee with milk. *Tostones* (twice-fried plantains)
are beloved during cold New England winters by the city's many Cuban
transplants, who will also find such dishes as oxtail, braised beef tongue,
and *monfongo* (fried mashed green plantains with pork rinds and garlic
oil). **Known for:** simple, quality Cuban cuisine; generous menu selection;
homey setting. $ *Average main: $15* ✉ *416 Centre St., Jamaica Plain*
☎ *617/524–6464* ⊕ *www.elorientaldecuba.net* Ⓜ *Stony Brook* ✛ *3:C6.*

$$$ ✗ **Ten Tables.** Jamaica Plain's postage stamp–size, candlelit space is an
FRENCH enchanting mix of Gallic elegance and chummy neighborhood rev-
elry—both in the atmosphere and the food. Simple but high-quality
dishes such as lamb meatballs with tomato jam, duck-fat dumplings
with Cognac cream, and house-made pasta with garden vegetables
seamlessly seal the deal. **Known for:** New England bistro fare; locally
sourced ingredients; snug feel. ⑤ *Average main: $27* ✉ *597 Centre St.,
Jamaica Plain* ☎ *617/524–8810* ⊕ *tentables.net* ⊙ *No lunch* Ⓜ *Stony
Brook* ✛ *3:C6.*

BROOKLINE

Going to Brookline is a nice way to get out of the city without really
leaving town. Although it's surrounded by Boston on three sides,
Brookline has its own suburban flavor, seasoned with a multitude of
historic—and expensive—houses and garnished with a diverse ethnic
population that supports a string of sushi bars and a small list of kosher
restaurants. Most Brookline eateries are clustered in the town's com-
mercial centers: Brookline Village, Washington Square, Longwood, and
bustling Coolidge Corner.

$ ✗ **Cutty's.** Don't be fooled by this self-named "sandwich shop," which
AMERICAN belies the care, creativity, and culinary quality of the luscious offerings
Fodor'sChoice found in this diminutive establishment featured on the Food Network's
★ Diners, Drive-Ins, and Dives. The owners' cooking school experience
and recipe development work in a magazine test kitchen helps explain
why their offerings will blow your socks off—whether it's a brioche
breakfast sandwich stuffed with egg, homemade chorizo, mozzarella,
and cilantro or the succulent roast beef and roasted shallot sandwich
with cheddar and Thousand Island dressing. **Known for:** superb sand-
wiches; locally sourced ingredients; no-frills setting. ⑤ *Average main:
$10* ✉ *284 Washington St., Coolidge Corner* ☎ *617/505–1844* ⊕ *www.
cuttyfoods.com* ⊙ *Closed Sun. No dinner* ⊟ *No credit cards* Ⓜ *Brook-
line Village* ✛ *3:A6.*

$$ ✗ **FuGaKyu.** The name in Japanese means "house of elegance" and the
JAPANESE gracious and efficient service hits the mark at this flagship location,
along with the interior's tatami mats, rice-paper partitions, and wooden
ships circling a moat around the sushi bar. The extensive menu is both
elegant and novel, with thick slabs of superfresh sashimi, inventive maki
rolls, and plenty of cooked items, like panko-crusted pork cutlet and
chicken teriyaki for those not into seafood or raw fish. **Known for:** excellent sushi and sashimi; attentive service; private, screened-in booths.
⑤ *Average main: $22* ✉ *1280 Beacon St., Brookline* ☎ *617/734–1268*
⊕ *www.fugakyu.net* Ⓜ *Coolidge Corner* ✛ *3:A4.*

$ ✗ **Mei Mei Restaurant.** After hitting the culinary jackpot with their wildly
ASIAN FUSION successful Chinese-American comfort-food truck several years ago, sib-
lings Andrew, Margaret, and Irene Li brought the same concept to this
casual exposed-brick and hardwood eatery, which, like their food truck
(and kiosk in The Innovation and Design Building in the Seaport District), uses as many local, sustainable, and humanely raised ingredients
as possible to create a lusty menu featuring The Double Awesome scal-
lion pancake sandwich packed with pesto, local greens, gooey cheddar,
and two wobbly eggs; golden, sweet corn fritter balls with dipping

10

sriracha aioli; and creamy mac and cheese cradling tender nuggets of soft pulled pork. Curries, noodle dishes, dumplings, and salads round out the restaurant's offerings, along with a carefully chosen selection of Asian cocktails, beer, and wine. **Known for:** Asian comfort food; The Double Awesome sandwich; cheerful service. $ *Average main: $11* ✉ *506 Park Dr., Brookline* ☎ *857/250–4959* ⊕ *www.meimeiboston. com* ◷ *Closed Mon.* ✛ *3:D2.*

$$
AMERICAN

✕ **The Publick House.** What started as a simple neighborhood beer bar has reached cultlike status for Brookline-ites and beyond. Serving more than 175 out-of-the-ordinary and artisanal beers, the bar also offers tasty sandwiches, smaller entrées, and main dishes (try the lobster mac and cheese), many of which have beer incorporated into them, such as the steamed mussels (served with golden frites). **Known for:** standout beer selection; great pub fare; chummy feel. $ *Average main: $20* ✉ *1648 Beacon St., Brookline* ☎ *617/277–2880* ⊕ *www.thepublickhousebeer-bar.com* ☞ *No reservations accepted* Ⓜ *Washington Sq.* ✛ *3:A4.*

$$
INDIAN

✕ **Rani Bistro.** This Indian bistro serves complex, richly spiced cuisine in the Hyderabadi style, which incorporates sweet and salty northern and southern flavors to create an impressive variety of specialty breads, along with mains like the tender and juicy *Murg musalam,* roast chicken in a fragrant brown sauce, and fork-tender tandoori dishes designed for beginners. The sleek interior fills up nightly with locals looking for a change of pace from downtown's more casual Indian spreads. **Known for:** Hyderabadi-style Indian cuisine; polite service; excellent lunch buffet. $ *Average main: $20* ✉ *1353 Beacon St., Brookline* ☎ *617/734–0400* ⊕ *www.ranibistro.com* Ⓜ *Coolidge Corner* ✛ *3:A4.*

$$
SPANISH

✕ **Taberna de Haro.** With a cozy, saffron yellow interior, Boston's first tapas bar has a nearly all-Spanish wine list (more than 320 bottles, 60 of which are Sherry and Manzanilla). The menu includes hot and cold tapas and *raciones* (medium-size plates) including such classics as a tortilla Española, shrimp in garlic oil, braised eggplant, and jamón Serrano. **Known for:** authentic Spanish tapas; warm atmosphere; bountiful Sherry and Manzanilla selection. $ *Average main: $20* ✉ *999 and 1001 Beacon St., Brookline* ☎ *617/277–8272* ⊕ *www.tabernaboston. com* ◷ *No lunch* Ⓜ *Coolidge Corner* ✛ *3:D3.*

$
AMERICAN
FAMILY

✕ **Zaftigs.** How refreshing to have a contemporary version of a Jewish delicatessen offering genuinely lean corned beef, a modest slice of cheesecake, low-sugar homemade borscht, and a lovely whitefish-salad sandwich. If you believe breakfast is the most important meal, know it's served all day, meaning you can skip the hour-long weekend brunch waits and enjoy a plate of the area's best pancakes and stuffed French toast any weekday. Just try to leave room for one of the goodies (cupcakes, conga bars) in the bakery case. **Known for:** contemporary Jewish food; great breakfasts; friendly service. $ *Average main: $17* ✉ *335 Harvard St., Brookline* ☎ *617/975–0075* ⊕ *www.zaftigs.com* Ⓜ *Coolidge Corner* ✛ *3:A4.*

CAMBRIDGE

Among other collegiate enthusiasms, Cambridge has a long-standing fascination with ethnic eateries. Another kind of great restaurant has also evolved here, mixing world class cooking with a studied informality, particularly around the red-hot Technology Square area near MIT where chefs cook with wood fires and borrow flavors from every continent. For more posh tastes and the annual celebrations that come with college life (or the end of it), Cambridge also has its share of linen-cloth tables.

$$$
MODERN
AMERICAN

✗ **Alden & Harlow.** This boisterous subterranean restaurant with a 30-seat bar and industrial-chic design specializes in rustic, seasonal snacks and small plates layered with flavor. Start with an expertly made cocktail and perhaps some chips and three-onion dip before sharing little dishes like clams with smoked pig's tail; smoked carrots with feta cream; crisp pork belly hunks over warm grits; and the Ubiquitous Kale Salad, which rivals all others with its creamy pistachio dressing. **Known for:** flavor-packed sharing plates; terrific cocktails; boisterous feel. ⑤ *Average main: $28* ✉ *40 Brattle St., Harvard Square* ☎ *617/864–2100* ⊕ *www.aldenharlow.com* ☺ *No lunch* ═ *No credit cards* Ⓜ *Harvard* ✛ *4:A2.*

$
AMERICAN

✗ **All Star Sandwich Bar.** This brightly colored place with about a dozen tables turns out fresh, high-quality sandwiches all served with coleslaw, dill pickle, and a smile. Beyond multiple beef burgers, you'll find classics like crispy, overstuffed Reubens and the famous Atomic Meatloaf Meltdown, which has been highlighted on a number of foodie networks. **Known for:** chef-quality sandwiches; creative combinations; simple setting. ⑤ *Average main: $12* ✉ *1245 Cambridge St., Cambridge* ☎ *617/868–3065* ⊕ *www. allstarsandwichbar.com* Ⓜ *Central/Inman* ✛ *4:F2.*

$$
MODERN
AMERICAN
Fodor's Choice
★

✗ **Area Four.** A bona fide hit from day one, everything at this glass-enclosed eatery in the avant-garde Technology Square area is scrumptious—from the morning sticky buns and excellent dark coffee at the café to the wood-fire-oven-cooked food in the dining room; blistered pizzas (try the clam-bacon one) mac and cheese served in your own skillet, and crackly skinned chicken best enjoyed with a side of market veggies, like charred greens with miso and candied peanuts. You will find only local, seasonal, and sustainable cooking here. **Known for:** crisp, blistered pizzas; market-fresh salads and mains; relaxed feel. ⑤ *Average main: $18* ✉ *500 Technology Sq., Cambridge* ☎ *617/758–4444* ⊕ *www. areafour.com* ═ *No credit cards* ✛ *4:G5.*

$$$
ITALIAN
Fodor's Choice
★

✗ **Benedetto.** Chef Michael Pagliarini, whose devoted fan base will wait hours for his mouthwatering pastas and Italian food at Giulia up the street, is turning out an even more ambitious menu of seasonal Italian small bites, silky pastas, and mains. Start with a cocktail and some ricotta and smoked trout crostini and spicy grilled octopus while you figure out whether to get the linguine with clams or the spelt pasta *cacio e pepe* before your entrée of grilled beef with charred leeks, veal sausages over lentils, or roasted catch-of-the day. **Known for:** masterful Italian cooking; elegant airy setting; incredible pastas. ⑤ *Average main: $33* ✉ *1 Bennett St., Harvard Square* ☎ *617/661–5050* ⊕ *www. benedettocambridge.com* ☺ *No lunch* ✛ *4:A3.*

10

$$$ ✕ **Café ArtScience.** Harvard professor and innovator David Edwards,
MEDITERRANEAN an inventor of edible food packaging, creates mad scientist-like
cocktails infused with ingredients that have been smoked, turned
into essences, and vaporized, as well as gorgeously plated food that
offers a lesson in physics. Menu items might include light and fresh
tartares and salads and more hefty courses, like hanger steak with a
nutty brown butter bernaise. **Known for:** inventive cocktails; creative
food; funky setting. ⑤ *Average main: $30* ⊠ *650 Kendall St., Kendall
Square* ☎ *857/999–2193* ⊕ *www.cafeartscience.com* ⊘ *Closed Sun.
No lunch Sat.* ✢ *1:A4.*

$$$$ ✕ **Craigie on Main.** This soulful, white-cloth restaurant is the project
FRENCH of chef-owner Tony Maws, one of Boston's landmark chefs. With a
passion for all things fresh, local, and organic, he changes the menu
daily, so options can range from a Spanish-style octopus to black
bass to pork done three ways. **Known for:** nose-to-tail fare; locally
sourced ingredients; white-cloth service. ⑤ *Average main: $38* ⊠ *853
Main St., Cambridge* ☎ *617/497–5511* ⊕ *www.craigieonmain.com*
Ⓜ *Central* ✢ *4:F5.*

$$$ ✕ **Dante.** With one of the best patio views of the Charles River, Dante
MEDITERRANEAN almost resembles a seaside café on the Amalfi coast. Kick off dinner
with some Prosecco and a handful of *sfizi* (small bites), followed by a
silky pasta (several are gluten-free) with richly flavored sauce, a perfectly charred steak with crushed potatoes, or an Aqua Pazza of cod,
shrimp, and clams in a rich tomato broth. **Known for:** coastal Italian
cuisine; carefully prepared selections; Charles River views. ⑤ *Average
main: $27* ⊠ *Royal Sonesta Hotel, 40 Edwin H. Land Blvd., Cambridge*
☎ *617/497–4200* ⊕ *www.restaurantdante.com* ⊘ *No lunch* Ⓜ *Lechmere* ✢ *1:B4.*

$$ ✕ **Full Moon.** Here's a happy reminder that dinner with children doesn't
AMERICAN have to mean hamburgers and juice for everyone. While the youngsters
FAMILY race around the designated play space with sippy cups before noshing
on hot dogs and homemade mac and cheese, parents can sip sangria,
beer, or any one of the carefully chosen wines before tucking into more
sophisticated fare, such as grilled salmon or sirloin with blue-cheese but-
ter, arugula, and fries. **Known for:** simple family-friendly menu; spirits
for adults; designated place space for kids. ⑤ *Average main: $20* ⊠ *344
Huron Ave., Cambridge* ☎ *617/354–6699* ⊕ *www.fullmoonrestaurant.
com* ⊘ *No lunch* Ⓜ *Harvard* ✢ *4:A1.*

$$$ ✕ **Giulia.** With exposed brick walls and soft lighting, this welcom-
ITALIAN ing Italian restaurant has a back communal pasta table that doubles
Fodor's Choice as a counter that the kitchen uses for rolling out superlative pastas.
★ Just as delicious are the various antipasti, as well as mains like the
house-made sausage with fennel risotto. If you don't (or can't get) a
reservation on a preferred night, give your name to the hostess and
grab a drink (or two) at the bar or up the street; chances are you'll get
seated sooner or later. **Known for:** excellent Italian food; silky pastas;
warm, softly-lit space. ⑤ *Average main: $28* ⊠ *1682 Massachusetts
Ave., Harvard Square* ☎ *617/441–2800* ⊕ *www.giuliarestaurant.com*
⊘ *Closed Sun.* ✢ *4:B1.*

$$ ✗ **Green Street.** The tables may be small and the service casual, but the
AMERICAN relatively inexpensive New England menu speaks to the young, artistic
community that now claims the neighborhood. Lobster fettuccine with
Wellfleet clams and chorizo is a highlight from the menu, which mostly
features modern comfort fare. **Known for:** great cocktails; upscale com-
fort food; artsy atmosphere. $ *Average main: $22* ✉ *280 Green St.,
Cambridge* ☎ *617/876–1655* ⊕ *www.greenstreetgrill.com* ⊘ *No lunch*
Ⓜ *Central* ✛ *4:E5.*

$$$ ✗ **Harvest.** Once a favorite of former Cambridge resident Julia Child, this
AMERICAN sophisticated shrine to New England cuisine remains a perennial go-to
Fodor'sChoice spot for Harvard students when their parents are in town. The seasonal
★ menu could feature Cape scallop crudo, fresh pasta with braised veal
and pesto, or fresh Cape lobster with lemon hollandaise. **Known for:**
elegant New England cuisine; expansive wine list; pretty patio dining
area. $ *Average main: $34* ✉ *44 Brattle St., on walkway, Cambridge*
☎ *617/868–2255* ⊕ *harvestcambridge.com* Ⓜ *Harvard* ✛ *4:A2.*

$$ ✗ **The Helmand.** The area's first Afghan restaurant, named after the coun-
AFGHAN try's most important river, welcomes you into its cozy Kendall Square con-
Fodor'sChoice fines with Afghan rugs, a wood-burning oven, and exotic, yet extremely
★ approachable food. Standouts, beyond the chewy warm bread, include
terrific *aushak* (leek stuffed ravioli over yogurt with beef ragu and mint),
chapendaz (marinated grilled beef tenderloin served with cumin-spiced
hot pepper–tomato puree), and a vegetarian baked pumpkin platter.
Known for: excellent Afghan fare; enveloping atmosphere; incredible
breads. $ *Average main: $21* ✉ *143 1st St., Cambridge* ☎ *617/492–4646*
⊕ *helmandrestaurant.com* ⊘ *No lunch* Ⓜ *Lechmere* ✛ *1:B4.*

$$ ✗ **Henrietta's Table.** This cheerful, country-style restaurant in The Charles
AMERICAN Hotel was named after the owner's pet pig, Henrietta, whose picture
(including one with President and Secretary Clinton) hangs by the
entrance area, where a U-shape bar offers a relaxing spot to enjoy a
preprandial coffee or cocktail. Chef-owner Peter Davis's passion for
working with small area farms, as well as harvesting veggies and honey
from the restaurant's rooftop garden and hives, is evident in his fresh,
honest, wholesome, New England–style dishes, like red flannel breakfast hash, creamy Maine crab-corn chowder, and juicy pot roast with
mashed potatoes. **Known for:** farm-fresh comfort food; inviting, sunny
setting; New England farm-sourced ingredients. $ *Average main: $24*
✉ *1 Bennett St., Harvard Square* ☎ *617/661–5005* ⊕ *www.henrietta-
stable.com* ▭ *No credit cards* Ⓜ *Harvard* ✛ *4:A3.*

$ ✗ **Le's.** Vietnamese noodle soup called *pho* is the name of the game in
VIETNAMESE this quick and casual eatery (it's set inside the Garage, a small mall in
FAMILY Harvard Square). At less than $10, it's a meal unto itself. **Known for:**
terrific Vietnamese; low prices; fast service. $ *Average main: $9* ✉ *35
Dunster St., Cambridge* ☎ *617/864–4100* ⊕ *www.lescambridge.com*
Ⓜ *Harvard* ✛ *4:B2.*

$$$ ✗ **Les Sablons.** The talented team behind the Island Creek Oyster empire
EUROPEAN opened this elegant French brasserie cum London gastropub in the
Fodor'sChoice historic Conductor's building. Chefs Jeremy Sewall and Brian Rae's
★ deftly prepared cuisine, like fresh oysters and salmon crudo in cucumber
water, rye spaghetti with pesto and mushrooms, and perfectly cooked

10

salmon over sorrel cream—plus a thoughtful wine list, attentive service, and welcoming ambience—explain why diners depart with such satisfied smiles. **Known for:** elegant bistro fare; terrific wine list; historic setting. $ *Average main: $34* ⊠ *2 Bennett St., Harvard Square* ☎ *617/268–6800* ⊕ *www.lscambridge.com* ✛ *4:A2.*

$$
FUSION

✕ **Little Donkey.** Dream team chef-owners, Jamie Bissonnnette and Ken Oringer (of Coppa, Toro) serve crazy-good small plates made from big, bold, unexpected combos: think Vietnamese-accented cabbage with bologna and fried squid, matzo ball ramen, and farro kimchi fried rice. Brunch menu standouts include the miso-banana bread Toad-in-a-Hole served with creamed spinach and habanero sausage. **Known for:** bold-flavored small plates. $ *Average main: $24* ⊠ *505 Massachusetts Ave., Central Square* ☎ *617/945–1008* ⊕ *www.littledonkeybos.com* ✛ *4:E5.*

$$$
MEDITERRANEAN
Fodor's Choice
★

✕ **Oleana.** With three restaurants (Sofra in Cambridge and Sarma in Somerville) and a cookbook to her name, chef-owner Ana Sortun continues to bewitch area diners with her intricately spiced Eastern Mediterranean *meze* (small plates) made with fresh-picked produce from her husband's nearby Siena Farms. Oleana's menu changes often but look for the hot, crispy-fried mussels starter and Sultan's Delight (tamarind-glazed beef with smoky eggplant puree) along with Turkish-spiced lamb and lemon chicken. **Known for:** eastern Mediterranean menu; mouthwatering small plates; deft use of spices. $ *Average main: $27* ⊠ *134 Hampshire St., Cambridge* ☎ *617/661–0505* ⊕ *www.oleanarestaurant. com* ◐ *No lunch* Ⓜ *Central* ✛ *4:F3.*

$
LATIN AMERICAN
Fodor's Choice
★

✕ **Orinoco.** Don't miss this red clapboard, Latin American restaurant located down an alleyway in Harvard Square. Owner Andres Banger's dream to bring bountiful plates of superfresh family fare from his home country of Venezuela to Cambridge (as well as Brookline and the South End) rewards diners with delectable, palm-sized *arepas*, or crispy, hot, corn-flour pockets stuffed with beans, cheese, chicken, or pork; *pabellon criollo*, moist shredded beef with stewed beans, rice, and plantains; and red chili adobo–marinated, charred *pollo* (chicken). **Known for:** Venezuelan specialties; generous portions; great value. $ *Average main: $17* ⊠ *56 JFK St., Harvard Square* ☎ *617/354–6900* ⊕ *www.orinocokitchen.com* ⊟ *No credit cards* ◐ *Closed Mon.* ✛ *4:A3.*

BOSTON DINING AND LODGING ATLAS

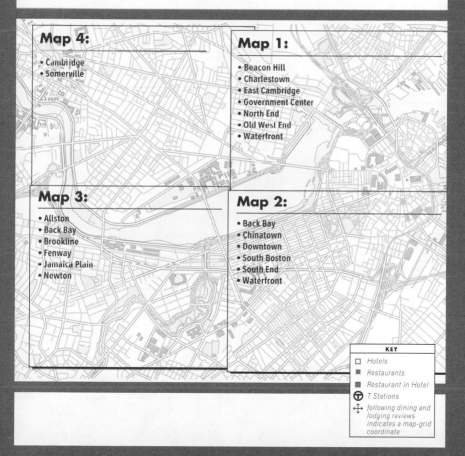

Map 4:
- Cambridge
- Somerville

Map 1:
- Beacon Hill
- Charlestown
- East Cambridge
- Government Center
- North End
- Old West End
- Waterfront

Map 3:
- Allston
- Back Bay
- Brookline
- Fenway
- Jamaica Plain
- Newton

Map 2:
- Back Bay
- Chinatown
- Downtown
- South Boston
- South End
- Waterfront

KEY
- ☐ Hotels
- ■ Restaurants
- ■ Restaurant in Hotel
- 🅣 T Stations
- ⬌ following dining and lodging reviews indicates a map-grid coordinate

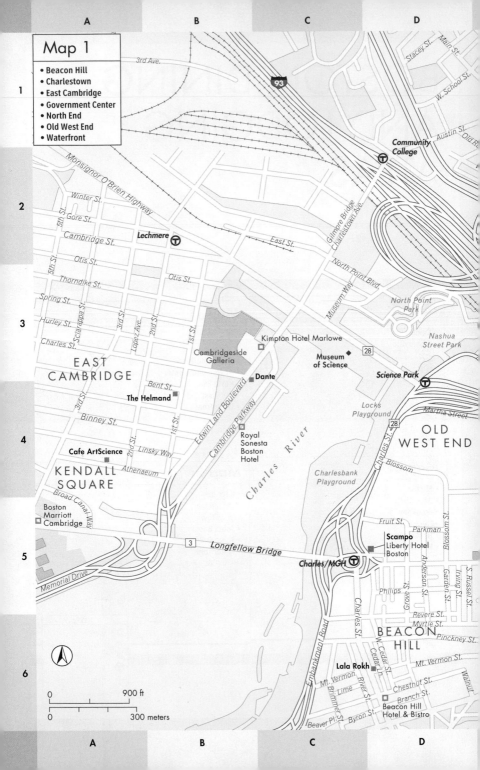

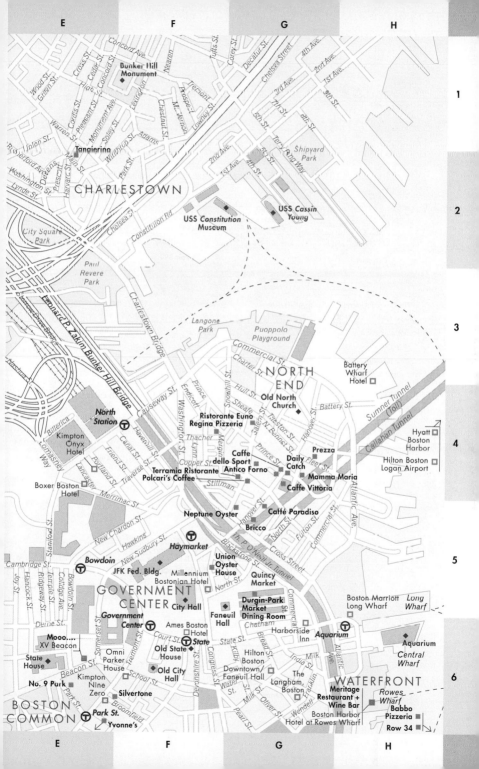

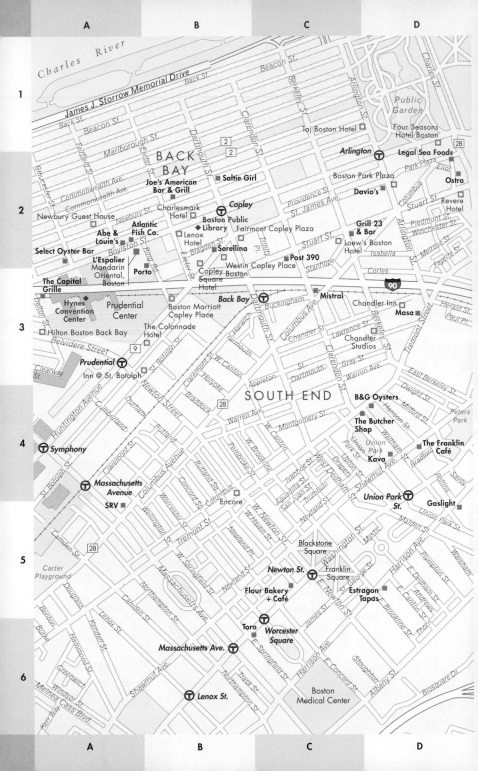

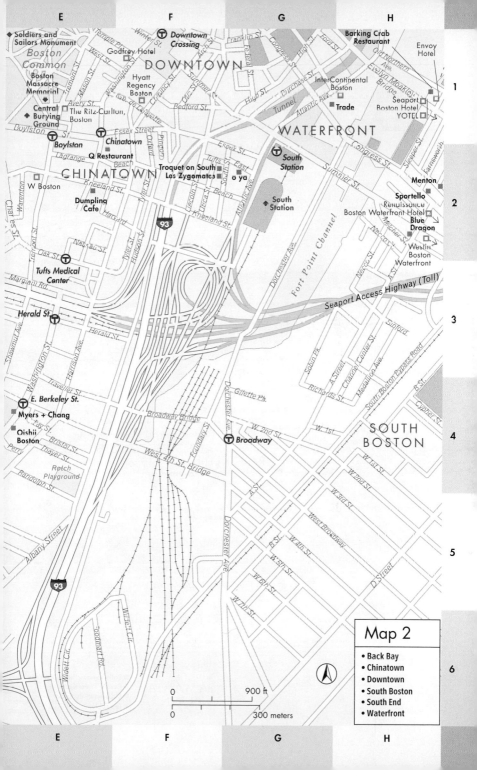

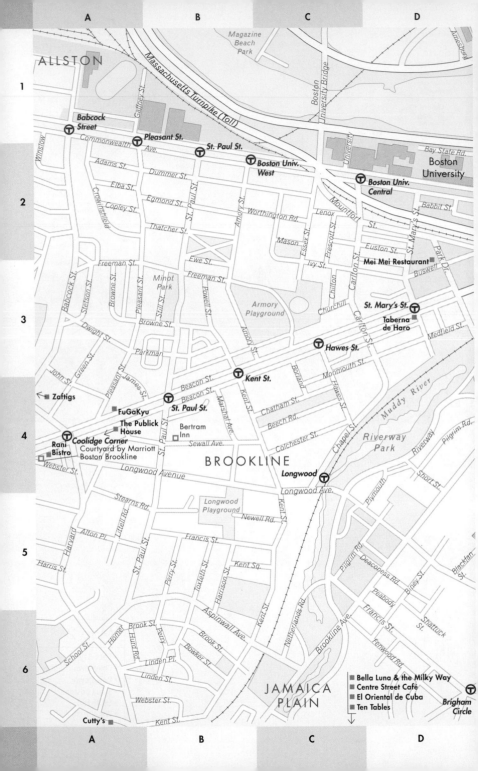

ALLSTON

Magazine Beach Park

Massachusetts Turnpike (Toll)

Boston University Bridge

Bay State Rd.

Boston University

Babcock Street

Commonwealth Ave.

Pleasant St.

St. Paul St.

Boston Univ. West

Boston Univ. Central

Winslow

Gaffney St.

Adams St.

Elba St.

Copley St.

Crowninshield

Dummer St.

Egmond St.

Thatcher St.

St. Paul St.

Amory St.

Worthington Rd.

Lenox

Mason

Essex St.

Prescott St.

Mountfort St.

Babbit St.

Euston St.

Park Dr.

Mei Mei Restaurant

Buswell

Babcock St.

Stetson St.

Browne St.

Pleasant St.

Minot Park

Freeman St.

Ewe St.

Powell St.

Freeman St.

Armory Playground

Amory St.

Ivy St.

Chilton

Churchill

Carlton St.

St. Mary's St.

Medfield St.

Taberna de Haro

Dwight St.

Browne St.

Parkman

Hawes St.

Borland

Monmouth St.

Hawes St.

Muddy River

John St.

Green St.

James St.

Pleasant St.

Beacon St.

Beacon St.

Kent St.

Kent St.

Marshal Ave.

Chatham St.

Beech Rd.

Colchester St.

Chapel St.

Riverway Park

Riverway

Pilgrim St.

Zaftigs

FuGaKyu

The Publick House

St. Paul St.

Bertram Inn

Sewall Ave.

Coolidge Corner

Courtyard by Marriott Boston Brookline

Rani Bistro

Webster St.

Longwood Avenue

BROOKLINE

Longwood

Longwood Ave.

Short St.

Stearns Rd.

Littell Rd.

Longwood Playground

Newell Rd.

Kent St.

Plymouth

Pilgrim Rd.

Deaconess Rd.

Briney St.

Blackfan St.

Harvard

Alton Pl.

St. Paul St.

Perry St.

Francis St.

Harris St.

Toxteth St.

Harrison St.

Kent Sq.

Kent St.

Netherlands Rd.

Brookline Ave.

Francis St.

Peabody

Shattuck St.

Fenwood Rd.

School St.

Harriet

Hurd Rd.

Brook St.

Perry

Linden Pl.

Linden St.

Bowker St.

Brook St.

Aspinwall Ave.

JAMAICA PLAIN

Bella Luna & the Milky Way
Centre Street Café
El Oriental de Cuba
Ten Tables

Brigham Circle

Webster St.

Cutty's

Kent St.

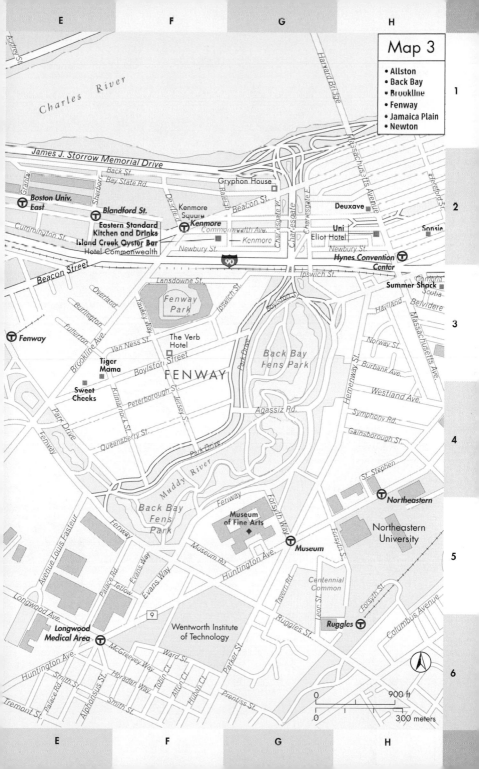

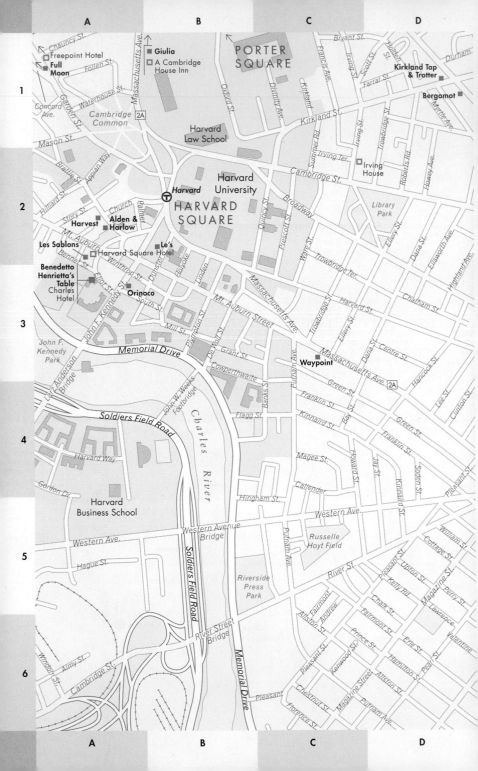

Dining

Abe & Louie's, 2:A2
Alden & Harlow, 4:A2
All Star Sandwich Bar, 4:F2
Antico Forno, 1:G5
Area Four, 4:G5
Atlantic Fish Co., 2:A2
B&G Oysters, 2:D4
Babbo Pizzeria, 1:H6
Barking Crab Restaurant, 2:H1
Bella Luna & the Milky Way, 3:C6
Benedetto, 4:A3
Blue Dragon, 2:H2
Bricco, 1:G5
The Butcher Shop, 2:D4
Café ArtScience, 1:A4
The Capital Grille, 2:A3
Centre Street Café, 3:C6
Craigie on Main, 4:F5
Cutty's, 3:A6
Daily Catch, 1:G4
Dante, 1:B4
Davio's, 2:D2
Deuxave, 3:H2
Dumpling Cafe, 2:F2
Durgin-Park Market Dining Room, 1:G5
Eastern Standard Kitchen and Drinks, 3:F2
El Oriental de Cuba, 3:C6
Estragon Tapas, 2:D5
Flour Bakery + Cafe, 2:C5
The Franklin Cafe, 2:D4
Full Moon, 4:A1
FuGaKyu, 3:A4
Giulia, 4:B1
Green Street, 4:E5
Grill 23 & Bar, 2:C2

Harvest, 4:A2
The Helmand, 1:B4
Henrietta's Table 4:A3
Island Creek Oyster Bar 3:F2
Kava, 2:D4
Joe's American Bar & Grill, 2:B2
Lala Rokh, 1:D6
Legal Seal Foods, 2:D2
Le's, 4:B2
Les Sablons, 4:A2
Les Zygomates, 2:F2
L'Espalier, 2:A2
Little Donkey, 4:E5
Mamma Maria, 1:G4
Mei Mei Restaurant, 3:D2
Menton, 2:H2
Meritage Restaurant + Wine Bar, 1:H6
Mike's Pastry, 1:G4
Mistral, 2:C3
Mooo...., 1:E6
Myers + Chang, 2:E4
Neptune Oyster, 1:G5
No. 9 Park, 1:E6
o ya, 2:G2
Oishii Boston, 2:E4
Oleana, 4:F3
Orinoco, 4:A3
Ostra, 2:D2
Porto, 2:B2
Post 390, 2:C2
Prezza, 1:G4
The Publick House, 3:A4
Q Restaurant, 2:F2
Rani Bistro, 3:A4
Regina Pizzeria, 1:F4
Ristorante Euno, 1:G4
Row 34, 1:H6

Saltie Girl, 2:B2
Select Oyster Bar, 2:A2
Scampo, 1:D5
Silvertone, 1:F6
Sonsie, 3:H2
Sorellina, 2:B2
Sportello, 2:H2
SRV, 2:A3
Summer Shack, 3:H3
Sweet Cheeks, 3:E4
Taberna de Haro, 3:D3
Tangierino, 1:E2
Ten Tables, 3:C6
Terramia Ristorante, 1:G4
Tiger Mama, 3:E3
Toro, 2:B6
Trade, 2:G1
Troquet on the South, 2:F2
Uni, 3:H2
Union Oyster House, 1:F5
Yvonne's, 1:E6
Zaftigs, 3:A4

Lodging

A Cambridge House Inn, 4:B1
Ames Boston Hotel, 1:F6
Battery Wharf Hotel, 1:H3
Beacon Hill Hotel & Bistro, 1:D6
Bertram Inn, 3:B4
Boston Harbor Hotel at Rowes Wharf, 1:H6
Boston Marriott Cambridge, 1:A5
Boston Marriott Long Wharf, 1:H5

Boston Park Plaza Hotel & Towers, 2:D2
Boxer Boston Hotel, 1:E3
Chandler Inn, 2:D3
Chandler Studios, 2:D3
Charles Hotel, 4:A3
Charlesmark Hotel, 2:B2
Colonnade Hotel, 2:B3
Copley Square Hotel, 2:B2
Courtyard by Marriott Boston Brookline, 3:A4
Eliot Hotel, 3:H2
Encore, 2:B4
Envoy Hotel, 2:H1
Fairmont Copley Plaza, 2:B2
Four Seasons, 2:D1
Freepoint Hotel, 4:A1
Godfrey Hotel, 2:F1
Gryphon House, 3:G2
Harborside Inn, 1:G6
Harvard Square Hotel, 4:A2
Hilton Boston Back Bay, 2:A3
Hilton Boston Downtown Faneuil Hall, 1:G6
Hilton Boston Logan Airport, 1:H4
Hotel Commonwealth, 3:F2
Hotel Marlowe, 1:C3
Hyatt Boston Harbor, 1:H4
Hyatt Regency Boston, 2:F1
The Inn at Longwood Medical, 3:D5
Inn@St. Botolph, 2:B3
InterContinental Boston, 2:H1

Irving House, 4:C2
John Jeffries House, 1:C5
Kendall Hotel, 4:H5
Langham Hotel, 1:G6
Le Meridien Cambridge, 4:F5
Lenox Hotel, 2:B2
Liberty Hotel Boston, 1:D5
Loew's Boston Hotel, 2:C2
Mandarin Oriental Boston, 2:A2
Marriott Hotel at Copley Place, 2:B3
Millennium Bostonian Hotel, 1:F5
Newbury Guest House, 2:A2
Nine Zero, 1:E6
Omni Parker House, 1:F6
Onyx Hotel, 1:E4
Renaissance Boston Waterfront Hotel, 2:H2
Revere Hotel, 2:D2
Ritz-Carlton Boston Common, 2:E1
Royal Sonesta Hotel, 1:B4
Seaport Boston Hotel, 2:H1
Sheraton Commander, 4:A1
Taj Boston Hotel, 2:C1
The Verb Hotel, 3:F3
Westin Boston Waterfront, 2:H2
Westin Copley Place Boston, 2:B2
W Boston, 2:E2
XV Beacon, 1:E6
Yotel, 2:H1

WHERE TO STAY

Updated
by Megan
Johnson

At one time, great lodging was scarce in Boston. If you were a persnickety blue blood in town to visit relatives, you checked into the Charles or the old Ritz on Newbury. If you were a parent in town to see your kid graduate from one of the city's many universities, you suffered through a stay at a run-down chain. And if you were a young couple in town for a little romance, well, you could just forget it. A dearth of suitable rooms practically defined Boston. Oh, how things have changed.

In the early 2000s, Boston finally got wise to modernization, and a rush of new construction took the local hotel scene by storm. Sleek, boutique accommodations began inviting guests to Cambridge and Downtown, areas once relegated to the alumni and business traveler sets. New, megaluxury lodgings like the Mandarin Oriental and the Taj (the latter in that old Ritz spot) infiltrated posh Back Bay, while high-end, hipster-friendly spots like the W Boston and Ames are drawing visitors to up-and-coming areas in Downtown. Even mostly residential areas like the South End now draw discerning boarders, thanks to the revamped Chandler and the nearby Inn@St. Botolph.

Speaking of revamped, it seems that nearly every hotel in town just got a face-lift. From spruced-up decor (good-bye, grandma's bedspread; hello, puffy white duvets) to hopping restaurant-bars to new spas and fitness centers, Boston's lodgings are feeling the competitive heat and acting accordingly. You don't just get a room anymore—you get an experience.

Many properties have stellar weekend deals, so you may be able to try an upscale Fodor's Choice even if you thought it was out of your budget.

BOSTON LODGING PLANNER

LODGING STRATEGY

Where should we stay? With so many new and improved Boston hotels, it may seem like a daunting question. But fret not—our expert writers and editors have done most of the legwork. The selections here represent the best this city has to offer—from the best affordable picks to the sleekest designer hotels. Or find a review quickly in the listings—search by neighborhood, then alphabetically. Happy hunting!

RESERVATIONS

Commencement weekends in May and June book months in advance; prices can be triple the off-season rate, with minimum stays of two to four nights. Leaf-peepers arrive in early October, and fall conventions bring waves of business travelers, especially in the Seaport District. Events such as the Boston Marathon in April and the Head of the Charles in October are busy times for large hotels and small inns alike.

PRICES

The hotel tax in Boston adds 14.95% to your bill; some hotels also tack on energy, service, or occupancy surcharges. Though it's not an absolute necessity, many visitors prefer to bring a car, but then parking is another expense to consider. Almost all lodgings have parking, and most charge for the privilege—anywhere from $15 per day for self-garaging to $35 for valet. When looking for a hotel, don't write off the pricier establishments immediately. Price categories are determined by "rack rates"—the list price of a hotel room, which is usually discounted. Specials abound, particularly in Downtown on weekends. With so many new rooms in Boston, pricing is very competitive, so always check out the hotel website in advance for current special offers.

WHAT IT COSTS FOR HOTELS			
$	$$	$$$	$$$$
Hotel	under $200	$200–$299	$300–$399	over $399

Prices are for two people in a standard double room in high season, excluding 14.95% tax and service charges.

USING THE MAPS

Throughout the chapter, you'll see mapping symbols and coordinates (such as 3:F2) after property names or reviews. To locate the property on a map, turn to the Boston Dining and Lodging Atlas at the end of the Where to Eat chapter. The first number after the symbol indicates the map number. Following that are the property's coordinates on the map grid.

WHERE SHOULD I STAY?

Neighborhood	Vibe	Pros	Cons
Beacon Hill and Boston Common	Old brick and stone buildings host luxe boutique hotels and B&Bs on the hill or along busy, preppy Charles Street; some skyscraper lodging right on Boston Common.	Safe, quaint area with lamp-lighted streets; chain-free upscale shopping and dining; outdoor fun abounds in the park; good T access.	Street parking is extremely hard to come by; not budget-friendly; close to noisy hospital; hills can be steep.
Downtown Boston	The city's Financial District hums with activity and busy hotels during the week; new boutique lodging is moving in to compete with the big-box chains.	Excellent area for business travelers; frequent low weekend rates; good T and bus access; walking distance to Theater District and some museums.	All but dead at night; expensive garage parking during the day; Downtown Crossing is mobbed at lunchtime and on weekends; poorly marked streets.
The Back Bay	High-priced hotels in the city's poshest neighborhood, home to shops, restaurants, bars, spas, and salons. Commonwealth Avenue is lined with historic mansions.	Easy, central location; safe, beautiful area to walk around at night; ample T access; excellent people-watching.	Rooms, shopping, and eating can be ridiculously expensive; Newbury Street is overcrowded with tourists on weekends.
The South End	Small, funky lodgings in a hip and happening (and gay-friendly) area packed with awesome independent restaurants and shops.	The city's best dining scene; easy T and bus access; myriad parks; walking distance from the Back Bay and Downtown; safe along the main avenues at night.	Some bordering blocks turn seedy after dusk; difficult street parking (and few garages); only a handful of hotel options.
The Fenway and Kenmore Square	A sampling of large and small hotels and inns, plus two hostels; the area is a mix of students, young professionals, and diehard Sox fans.	Close to Fenway Park (home of the Red Sox); up-and-coming dining scene; less expensive than most 'hoods; accessible by the T.	Impossible street parking on game days (and pricey garages); expect big crowds for concerts and sporting events; some bars are loud and tacky.
Boston Outskirts	Mostly mid-size chain hotels in student neighborhoods full of coffee shops, convenience stores, and rowdy college bars, except for sweet inns in lovely Brookline.	Serviceable airport lodging near Logan; cheap rates on rooms in Brighton and parts of Brookline; easier driving than in Downtown.	No overnight street parking in Brookline; far from Boston center, museums, shopping, and the river; some areas get dicey at night; T rides into the city proper can take an hour.
Cambridge	A mix of grand and small hotels peppers the hip, multiuniversity neighborhood; expect loads of young freethinkers and efficient (if laid-back) service.	Hallowed academia; verdant squares; good low- and high-cost eating and lodging; excellent neighborhood restaurants; few chain anythings.	Spotty T access; less of a city feel; a few areas can be quiet and slightly dodgy at night; lots of one-way streets make driving difficult.

HOTEL REVIEWS

Listed alphabetically within neighborhoods. For expanded hotel reviews, visit Fodors.com.

BOSTON

BEACON HILL AND BOSTON COMMON

If you want calm, serenity, and class, then stay on Beacon Hill. This is one of the poshest neighborhoods in Boston. Its streets are lined with elegant brick buildings holding unique shops and boutique hotels. Meanwhile, the hip Boston Common shares a vibe of busyness with Boylston and Newbury streets.

$
HOTEL

Beacon Hill Hotel & Bistro. This home away from home—or, rather, full-service version of home where you hardly have to lift a finger—is within walking distance of the Public Garden, Back Bay, Government Center, and the river Esplanade. **Pros:** free Wi-Fi; many nearby shops and restaurants; executive chef Lucas Sousa's decadent Sunday brunch at the ground-floor bistro. **Cons:** neighborhood parking is nonexistent; the rooms are somewhat small; no room service. $ *Rooms from: $199* ⊠ *25 Charles St., Beacon Hill* ☎ *617/723-7575* ⊕ *www.beaconhillhotel.com* ⇆ *13 rooms* ⎮Ol *No meals* Ⓜ *Arlington, Charles/MGH* ✛ *1:D6.*

$$$
HOTEL
Fodor'sChoice
★

Liberty Hotel Boston. Since it opened in late 2007, the buzz surrounding the chic Liberty—formerly Boston's Charles Street Jail—was at first deafening, with bankers, tech geeks, foreign playboys, and fashionistas all scrambling to call it their own; a few years later, the Liberty has evolved into what is part retreat, part nightclub. **Pros:** Lydia Shire's popular restaurant Scampo is on the first floor; bustling nightlife; proximity to the Esplanade and Beacon Hill. **Cons:** loud in-house nightlife; long waits at bars and restaurants; parking is expensive. $ *Rooms from: $369* ⊠ *215 Charles St., Beacon Hill* ☎ *617/224-4000* ⊕ *www.libertyhotel.com* ⇆ *298 rooms* ⎮Ol *No meals* Ⓜ *Charles/MGH* ✛ *1:D5.*

$$$$
HOTEL

XV Beacon. The 1903 beaux arts exterior of the city's first small luxury boutique hotel is a study in sophistication and elegance. **Pros:** hotel's modern steak house Mooo…. provides 24-hour room service; courtesy Lexus car service; dogs of any size welcome for no fee; complimentary Wi-Fi. **Cons:** some rooms are small; can be expensive on weekends during peak months (May, June, September, October); no view from classic rooms. $ *Rooms from: $575* ⊠ *15 Beacon St., Beacon Hill* ☎ *617/670-1500, 877/982-3226* ⊕ *www.xvbeacon.com* ⇆ *63 rooms* ⎮Ol *No meals* Ⓜ *Government Center, Park St.* ✛ *1:E6.*

DOWNTOWN BOSTON

This is the place to be whether you're here on business (the closer you are to the Financial District the more business-oriented the hotels become) or pleasure; think High Tea at the Langham Hotel or a stroll through its adjacent park, Post Office Square.

$$$ **Ames Boston Hotel.** Located in the iconic Ames Building, this 15-story
HOTEL   hotel is now part of the Curio Collection by Hilton. **Pros:** Molton Brown
bath products; complimentary bicycles; great proximity to the Freedom
Trail and Beacon Hill. **Cons:** far from South End and Back Bay shopping;
no swimming pool or spa; parking is expensive. ⑤ *Rooms from: $375* ✉ *1
Court St., Downtown* ☎ *617/979–8100, 888/697–1791* ⊕ *www.ameshotel.com* ⬦ *114 rooms* ⦿| *No meals* Ⓜ *State, Government Center* ✛ *1:F6.*

$$$$ **Battery Wharf Hotel.** One of the growing number of lodgings clustered
HOTEL   along Boston's ever-expanding Harborwalk—a pretty pedestrian path
FAMILY   that runs from Charlestown to Dorchester—the Battery Wharf Hotel
looks more like a gated community than a chain hotel. **Pros:** walking
distance to more than 80 world-class restaurants; on-site Exhale Spa has
discounted spa services and fitness classes for hotel guests; great North
End location; water taxi stand on-site. **Cons:** far from Newbury Street
and South End shopping; 15- to 20-minute walk to nearest T stations;
hotel is in two separate buildings. ⑤ *Rooms from: $499* ✉ *3 Battery
Wharf, North End* ☎ *877/794–6218* ⊕ *www.batterywharfhotelboston.
com* ⬦ *150 rooms* ⦿| *No meals* Ⓜ *Haymarket, North Station* ✛ *1:H4.*

$$$$ **Boston Harbor Hotel at Rowes Wharf.** Boston has plenty of iconic land-
HOTEL   marks, but none are as synonymous with uber-hospitality as the Boston
Fodor's Choice   Harbor Hotel, with its 80-foot-tall outdoor archway and rotunda and
★   classic city and harbor views. **Pros:** high-quality Meritage Restaurant +
Wine Bar and Rowes Wharf Sea Grille restaurants; easy walk to Faneuil
Hall, financial district, and the Greenway; water shuttle to Logan Air-
port. **Cons:** pricey; the spa gets booked up early; less convenient to the
Back Bay and South End. ⑤ *Rooms from: $495* ✉ *70 Rowes Wharf,
Downtown* ☎ *617/439–7000, 800/752–7077* ⊕ *www.bhh.com* ⬦ *230
rooms* ⦿| *No meals* Ⓜ *Aquarium, South Station* ✛ *1:H6.*

$$ **Boston Marriott Long Wharf.** Families favor this spot that looks like a big
HOTEL   brick ship docked in Boston Harbor. **Pros:** next door Tia's bar is a must
FAMILY   for outdoor happy hour; good weekend rates (check the Web for deals);
great location for first-time visitors. **Cons:** area is packed with tourists;
traffic in the area can be horrible; parking is difficult to find. ⑤ *Rooms
from: $229* ✉ *296 State St., Downtown* ☎ *617/227–0800* ⊕ *www.mar-
riott.com/boston* ⬦ *412 rooms* ⦿| *No meals* Ⓜ *Aquarium* ✛ *1:H5.*

$$ **Boxer Boston Hotel.** Steps from the TD Garden and an easy walk from
HOTEL   Government Center, Faneuil Hall, and the North End, the nine-floor,
80-room boutique hotel with a crisp, contemporary look is a great
value—if you don't mind tiny accommodations. **Pros:** great group rates;
free Internet; close to North Station and the T. **Cons:** small rooms
and lobby; staff can be indifferent; area can be rowdy at night by the
TD Garden. ⑤ *Rooms from: $220* ✉ *107 Merrimac St., Downtown*
☎ *617/624–0202, 877/267–1776* ⊕ *www.theboxerboston.com* ⬦ *80
rooms* ⦿| *No meals* Ⓜ *North Station* ✛ *1:E4.*

$$$$ **Envoy Hotel.** Visitors and locals like to hang out at the Envoy, whose
HOTEL   design-forward aesthetic provides a comfortable yet stylish vibe. **Pros:** fit-
ness center includes Peloton bikes; full restaurant menu is available for in-
room dining; beautiful views overlooking the Fort Point Channel. **Cons:**
bar crowds can be loud and rowdy; not within walking distance to Back
Bay shopping and sights; alarm clocks only available by request; Wi-Fi

isn't free. ⑤ *Rooms from: $499* ✉ *70 Sleeper St., Downtown* ☎ *617/338–3030* ⊕ *www.theenvoyhotel.com* ⇨ *136 rooms* ❌ *No meals* ✛ *2:H1.*

$$ 🏨 **Godfrey Hotel.** A welcome addition to downtown Boston's hotel scene, the bustling boutique hotel is popular with business folk, who like the ease of walking to the nearby Financial District. **Pros:** Frette linens; short walking distance from Boston Common and Beacon Hill; ideal for business travelers. **Cons:** Downtown Crossing can get a little sketchy at night; expensive valet parking; no airport shuttle. ⑤ *Rooms from: $200* ✉ *505 Washington St., Downtown* ☎ *617/804–2000, 855/649–4500* ⊕ *www.godfreyhotelboston.com* ⇨ *242 rooms* ❌ *No meals* Ⓜ *Downtown Crossing* ✛ *2:F1.*

HOTEL

$$ 🏨 **Harborside Inn.** With rates that are considerably lower than most Waterfront hotels—as low as $119 in the off season—this hotel with an understated charm is an exceptional value. **Pros:** free Wi-Fi; close to Quincy Market and the New England Aquarium; nearby water taxi. **Cons:** the area might be too touristy for some leisure travelers; no turndown service; no valet. ⑤ *Rooms from: $250* ✉ *185 State St., Downtown* ☎ *617/723–7500, 888/723–7565* ⊕ *harborsideinnboston.com* ⇨ *116 rooms* ❌ *No meals* Ⓜ *Aquarium* ✛ *1:G6.*

HOTEL
Fodor's Choice
★

$$ 🏨 **Hilton Boston Downtown/Faneuil Hall.** If you're looking for comfortable downtown lodging, you'll find it at this classic business hotel with 24-hour fitness and business centers. **Pros:** well maintained; clean and quiet; ideal for business travelers and those with pets. **Cons:** $15 daily Wi-Fi fee, or free on first floor; corporate vibe; doesn't have a Hilton Honors lounge. ⑤ *Rooms from: $259* ✉ *89 Broad St., Downtown* ☎ *617/556–0006* ⊕ *www.hilton.com* ⇨ *428 rooms* ❌ *No meals* Ⓜ *State* ✛ *1:G6.*

HOTEL

$$$ 🏨 **Hyatt Regency Boston.** The Hyatt Regency Boston sits amid the colorful Downtown Crossing neighborhood, a convergence of discount stores and crowds of 9-to-5 office dwellers that work in the area. **Pros:** steps from Boston Common and Faneuil Hall; indoor, saline swimming pool; good for business travelers. **Cons:** views of office buildings from guest rooms; thin walls; noise of neighborhood's construction may bug some guests. ⑤ *Rooms from: $379* ✉ *1 Ave. de Lafayette, Downtown* ☎ *617/912–1234, 800/233–1234* ⊕ *www.regencyboston.hyatt.com* ⇨ *502 rooms* ❌ *No meals* Ⓜ *Chinatown, Downtown Crossing* ✛ *2:F1.*

HOTEL
FAMILY

$$$$ 🏨 **InterContinental Boston.** The 424-room InterContinental, facing both the waterfront and the Rose Kennedy Greenway, consists of two opulent, 22-story towers wrapped in blue glass. **Pros:** upper-floor rooms have great views; cool bathrooms; close to Financial District and South Station. **Cons:** limited breakout rooms for large conventions; far from Newbury Street and Copley Square shopping; guests say the soundproofing could be better. ⑤ *Rooms from: $429* ✉ *510 Atlantic Ave., Downtown* ☎ *617/747–1000, 866/493–6495* ⊕ *www.intercontinental-boston.com* ⇨ *424 rooms* ❌ *No meals* Ⓜ *South Station* ✛ *2:H1.*

HOTEL

$$ 🏨 **Kimpton Nine Zero.** If it's all about location, the Kimpton Nine Zero can't be beat. **Pros:** pet- and kid-friendly; lobby wine tasting every evening (from 5 to 6); Atelier Bloem bath products. **Cons:** smallish rooms; high parking fees; small gyms. ⑤ *Rooms from: $249* ✉ *90 Tremont St., Downtown* ☎ *617/772–5800, 866/906–9090* ⊕ *www.ninezero.com* ⇨ *190 rooms* ❌ *No meals* Ⓜ *Park St., Government Center* ✛ *1:E6.*

HOTEL
FAMILY
Fodor's Choice
★

$$ **☷ Kimpton Onyx Hotel.** A sexy, supper-club atmosphere oozes from this
HOTEL recently renovated, contemporary Kimpton Group hotel, located a
block from North Station. **Pros:** good location for catching a sport-
ing event or concert at the Garden; near North Station commuter
rail and T stop; near several inexpensive restaurants and bars. **Cons:**
smallish rooms and bathrooms; small gym; neighborhood can get
noisy at night. ⑤ *Rooms from: $229 ⊠ 155 Portland St., Downtown*
☎ *617/557–9955, 866/660–6699 ⊕ www.onyxhotel.com ↩ 112 rooms*
☷○☷ *No meals* Ⓜ *North Station ✛ 1:E4.*

$$$ **☷ The Langham, Boston.** This 1922 Renaissance Revival landmark
HOTEL (the former Federal Reserve Building) strikes an admirable balance
between historic, old-world charm and sleek, modern appointments.
Pros: ideal Downtown location for business travelers; fabulous Sunday brunch and Saturday Chocolate Bar at Café Fleuri; guests enjoy
special deals at the Chuan Body + Soul spa. **Cons:** Downtown location feels remote on weekends; pricey during the week; expensive
valet parking. ⑤ *Rooms from: $395 ⊠ 250 Franklin St., Downtown*
☎ *617/451–1900, 800/543–4300 ⊕ www.boston.langhamhotels.com*
↩ *335 rooms* ☷○☷ *No meals* Ⓜ *South Station ✛ 1:G6.*

$$$ **☷ Millennium Bostonian Hotel.** Near historic Faneuil Hall, the Bostonian
HOTEL has guest rooms featuring Frette linens, pillowtop mattresses, and
FAMILY 40-inch TVs—many also have French doors with step-out balconies
showcasing city views and the popular North End. Warmed up with
red wall coverings, the lobby provides sofas and arm chairs, perfect
for relaxing with a book chosen from one of the floor-to-ceiling book-
shelves. **Pros:** updated fitness center; great location for sightseeing; free
Wi-Fi. **Cons:** some rooms still get street noise; Faneuil Hall can get
clogged with tourists; parking is expensive. ⑤ *Rooms from: $309 ⊠ Fa-
neuil Hall Marketplace, 26 North St., Downtown* ☎ *617/523–3600,*
866/866–8086 ⊕ www.millenniumhotels.com ↩ 201 rooms ☷○☷ *No*
meals Ⓜ *Haymarket, Aquarium ✛ 1:F5.*

$$$ **☷ Omni Parker House.** If any hotel says "Boston," it's this one, where
HOTEL JFK proposed to Jackie, and Charles Dickens gave his first reading
FAMILY of "A Christmas Carol"; there's more than a century and a half of
rich and varied history within these walls. **Pros:** overflowing with
history; great location on the Freedom Trail; newly renovated public
areas. **Cons:** small rooms, some of which are a bit dark; thin-walled
rooms can be noisy; area parking is very expensive. ⑤ *Rooms from:*
$339 ⊠ 60 School St., Downtown ☎ *617/227–8600, 800/843–6664*
⊕ *www.omniparkerhouse.com ↩ 572 rooms* ☷○☷ *No meals* Ⓜ *Govern-*
ment Center, Park St. ✛ 1:F6.

$ **☷ Renaissance Boston Waterfront Hotel.** Set along the working wharves of
HOTEL Boston Harbor, near the must-visit Institute of Contemporary Art, the
Renaissance plays to a watery theme. **Pros:** sleek new lobby Capiz Bar
and Lounge; close to the Silver Line (airport transportation) and convention center; Sapore Ristorante + Bar fuses Italian cuisine with seasonal New England ingredients. **Cons:** some guest-room harbor views
are more industrial than scenic; hordes of conventioneers; far from
Back Bay and Boston Common. ⑤ *Rooms from: $159 ⊠ 606 Congress*
St., Downtown ☎ *617/338–4111, 888/796–4664 ⊕ renaissance-hotels.*

marriott.com/renaissance-boston-waterfront-hotel ⟿ *471 rooms* ❍*No meals* Ⓜ *World Trade Center* ✛ *2:H2.*

$$
HOTEL
Fodor's Choice
★

🏨 **Revere Hotel.** The Revere Hotel experienced a $28 million renovation in 2017, and the stylish spot now embraces New England history, but with a twist. **Pros:** rooftop pool and bar has amazing city views; balconies in every room; ideal location where Back Bay meets Downtown Boston. **Cons:** expensive parking; elevators can get congested; no three-meal restaurant on-site. Ⓢ *Rooms from: $249* ✉ *200 Stuart St., Downtown* ☎ *617/482–1800* ⊕ *www.reverehotel.com* ⟿ *356 rooms* ❍*No meals* Ⓜ *Arlington* ✛ *2:D2.*

$$$$
HOTEL
FAMILY

🏨 **The Ritz-Carlton, Boston.** With a great downtown location and a multimillion-dollar redesign for all guest rooms and suites, the Ritz is looking great. **Pros:** excellent service; central location just off Boston Common; spacious rooms and suites. **Cons:** fee to access Equinox Sports Club, unless you're staying on Club Level; food service is brutally expensive; valet parking costs a pretty penny. Ⓢ *Rooms from: $550* ✉ *10 Avery St., Downtown* ☎ *617/574–7100, 800/542–8680* ⊕ *www.ritzcarlton.com* ⟿ *193 rooms* ❍*No meals* ☞ *Pets are welcome for $125 deep-cleaning fee* Ⓜ *Boylston* ✛ *2:E1.*

$$
HOTEL

🏨 **Seaport Boston Hotel.** Chances are, if you've ever been to Boston on business, you've already stayed at the Seaport, where guest rooms are among the biggest in the city. **Pros:** beautiful on-site Wave Health & Fitness Club; close to a newly developed restaurant scene offering 20 dining options; free Wi-Fi. **Cons:** far from city center; hotel elevators can be swamped during conventions. Ⓢ *Rooms from: $209* ✉ *World Trade Center, 1 Seaport La., Waterfront* ☎ *617/385–4000, 800/440–3318* ⊕ *www.seaportboston.com* ⟿ *428 rooms* ❍*No meals* Ⓜ *World Trade Center* ✛ *2:H1.*

$$$
HOTEL

🏨 **W Boston.** This 238-room tower is fronted by a metal-and-glass "awning" that is outfitted with soft, color-changing neon lights that cast a cheeky glow on passersby, but inside, the nature-inspired decor is modern through and through, with typical W brand touches like a sleek, scene-y lobby lounge (complete with falling water display and open fireplace) and a host of room categories such as the standard Wonderful and expanded WOW lodgings. **Pros:** on-site Bliss spa; signature W feather-top beds; fashion scene; dogs have their own room service menu. **Cons:** Wi-Fi isn't free in every room type; area theater and bar crowds can be loud; expensive parking. Ⓢ *Rooms from: $350* ✉ *100 Stuart St., Downtown* ☎ *617/261–8700* ⊕ *www.whotels.com/boston* ⟿ *238 rooms* ❍*No meals* Ⓜ *Boylston, Tufts Medical Center* ✛ *2:E2.*

$$$
HOTEL

🏨 **Westin Boston Waterfront.** Located in Boston's Seaport district, the Westin is connected to the Boston Convention & Exhibition Center and provides comfortable accomodations and exceptional service. **Pros:** close to the stellar Institute of Contemporary Art; pet-friendly for animals up to 40 lbs. (pet beds and bowls provided); Westin's signature "heavenly" beds. **Cons:** clusters of meeting-goers; lobby can get hectic; not within walking distance of Back Bay and South End. Ⓢ *Rooms from: $305* ✉ *425 Summer St., Downtown* ☎ *617/532–4600* ⊕ *www.westinbostonwaterfront.com* ⟿ *814 rooms* ❍*No meals* Ⓜ *World Trade Center* ✛ *2:H2.*

$$ 📺 **Yotel.** The second YOTEL to open in the United States, YOTEL Boston
HOTEL fits perfectly in the city's rapidly developing "Innovation District" with
tech-forward innovations like airline-style self-service check-in, and Tech-
nowalls in the rooms that allow guests to stream movies and music from
their own devices. **Pros:** free Wi-Fi; allergen-free cabins; digital check-in.
Cons: not within walking distance to Back Bay and Newbury Street;
those who aren't fans of technology won't appreciate the high-tech style;
rooms are smallish; valet parking is expensive. ⑤ *Rooms from: $259*
✉ *65 Seaport Blvd., Waterfront* ☎ *617/377–4747* ⊕ *www.yotel.com/en/
hotels/yotel-boston* ⤳ *326 rooms* ⦿ *No meals* Ⓜ *Courthouse* ⊕ *2:H1.*

THE BACK BAY AND THE SOUTH END

The Back Bay and the South End are what locals call the "well-heeled"
sections of Boston, meaning money talks here—think the likes of Man-
darin Oriental or Fairmont Copley Plaza. The streets are lined with
upscale, stylish hotels (old and new), boutique hotels, and inns.

THE BACK BAY

$ 📺 **Boston Marriott Copley Place.** It's busy-busy, with throngs of tourists
HOTEL and business travelers, but you can't beat the location of this 38-story
FAMILY megahotel. **Pros:** good service; comfortable beds; prime Copley Square
location; on-site Starbucks. **Cons:** chaotic lobby; not for those who
want an intimate, boutique experience; massive in size. ⑤ *Rooms from:
$159* ✉ *110 Huntington Ave., Back Bay* ☎ *617/236–5800, 800/228–
9290* ⊕ *www.marriott.com* ⤳ *1,147 rooms* ⦿ *No meals* Ⓜ *Copley,
Back Bay* ⊕ *2:B3.*

$ 📺 **Boston Park Plaza.** Step into a true piece of Boston history at the
HOTEL 2016-renovated Park Plaza, one of the city's most identifiable land-
FAMILY marks. **Pros:** 20,000-square-foot health club; helpful concierge; tons
of historic value; on-site Starbucks. **Cons:** bathrooms are small; guest
rooms vary in size and can be small; guests expecting the old decor may
be surprised by renovation. ⑤ *Rooms from: $199* ✉ *50 Park Plaza,
at Arlington St., Back Bay* ☎ *617/426–2000, 800/225–2008* ⊕ *www.
bostonparkplaza.com* ⤳ *1,054 rooms* ⦿ *No meals* ⌇ *Pets allowed for
$50 cleaning fee, weight limit may apply* Ⓜ *Arlington* ⊕ *2:D2.*

$$ 📺 **Charlesmark Hotel.** Hipsters and romantics who'd rather spend their
HOTEL cash on a great meal than a hotel bill have put this late-19th-century
former residential row house on the map. **Pros:** fantastic price for the
location; free Wi-Fi; all rooms have safes and refrigerators. **Cons:**
some might feel crowded by compact rooms and hallways; no valet;
no turndown service. ⑤ *Rooms from: $239* ✉ *655 Boylston St., Back
Bay* ☎ *617/247–1212* ⊕ *www.thecharlesmarkhotel.com* ⤳ *40 rooms*
⦿ *Breakfast* Ⓜ *Copley* ⊕ *2:B2.*

$ 📺 **The Colonnade Hotel.** The Colonnade showcases clean, modern envi-
HOTEL rons injected with hues of khaki, chocolate, and chrome. **Pros:** roof-
FAMILY deck pool; across from Prudential Center shopping; close to Hynes
Convention Center. **Cons:** Huntington Avenue can get clogged with
rush-hour traffic; on summer days the pool is packed by 11 am; parking
is expensive. ⑤ *Rooms from: $199* ✉ *120 Huntington Ave., Back Bay*
☎ *617/424–7000, 800/962–3030* ⊕ *www.colonnadehotel.com* ⤳ *385
rooms* ⦿ *No meals* Ⓜ *Back Bay, Prudential Center* ⊕ *2:B3.*

11

$$$ ⛺ **Copley Square Hotel.** Thanks to an $18 million renovation, the
HOTEL Copley Square Hotel has hurtled into the present with high-tech
registration pods, cushy mattresses, and in-room iPod docks—not
too shabby for a place that opened in 1891 and has provided respite
to a century of celebrities like Babe Ruth, Ella Fitzgerald, and Billie
Holiday. **Pros:** free Wi-Fi; free nightly wine tastings; cool bar and
club scene. **Cons:** small rooms; rooms facing Huntington Avenue
can be noisy; not ideal for older couples seeking peace and quiet.
⑤ *Rooms from: $350* ✉ *47 Huntington Ave., Back Bay* ☎ *617/536–
9000* ⊕ *www.copleysquarehotel.com* ⤳ *143 rooms* ⦿ *No meals*
Ⓜ *Copley, Back Bay* ✛ *2:B2.*

$$$$ ⛺ **Eliot Hotel.** One of the city's best small hotels is on posh Common-
HOTEL wealth Avenue, modeled after Paris's epic Champs-Élysées, and it
Fodor's Choice expertly merges the old blue-blood Boston aesthetic with modern flair
★ (like contemporary rugs mingling with crystal chandeliers); everyone
from well-heeled Sox fans to traveling CEOs to tony college parents
have noticed. **Pros:** great location near Fenway and Newbury Street;
top-notch restaurant; pet-friendly; beautiful rooms. **Cons:** very expen-
sive; some complain of elevator noise; parking is expensive. ⑤ *Rooms
from: $485* ✉ *370 Commonwealth Ave., Back Bay* ☎ *617/267–1607,
800/443–5468* ⊕ *www.eliothotel.com* ⤳ *96 rooms* ⦿ *No meals*
Ⓜ *Hynes* ✛ *3:H2.*

$$$ ⛺ **Fairmont Copley Plaza.** Past guests, including one Judy Garland, felt
HOTEL at home in this decadent, unabashedly romantic hotel that underwent
FAMILY a $20 million renovation in early 2012. **Pros:** prime Back Bay loca-
Fodor's Choice tion, centrally located in Copley Square; luxurious gym; 24-hour daily
★ in-room dining. **Cons:** small bathrooms; charge for Internet access
(no charge on Fairmont President's Club level); due to the historical
nature, room sizes vary greatly. ⑤ *Rooms from: $369* ✉ *138 St. James
Ave., Back Bay* ☎ *617/267–5300, 866/540–4417* ⊕ *www.fairmont.
com/copley-plaza-boston* ⤳ *383 rooms* ⦿ *No meals* Ⓜ *Copley, Back
Bay* ✛ *2:B2.*

$$$$ ⛺ **Four Seasons Hotel Boston.** This Public Garden–facing spot keeps a
HOTEL surprisingly low profile in Boston—and that's OK by the jeans-clad
FAMILY millionaires and assorted business types who cluster in the glossy lobby
or use the Mercedes courtesy car. **Pros:** close to Newbury Street and
the Public Garden; signature Four Seasons service; pet-friendly. **Cons:**
pricey during peak times; valet service can be slow; can be hard to get
a table at The Bristol. ⑤ *Rooms from: $675* ✉ *200 Boylston St., Back
Bay* ☎ *617/338–4400, 800/819–5053* ⊕ *www.fourseasons.com/boston*
⤳ *273 rooms* ⦿ *No meals* Ⓜ *Arlington* ✛ *2:D1.*

$$ ⛺ **Hilton Boston Back Bay.** Rooms at the Back Bay Hilton are relatively
HOTEL spacious, with plush "Serenity" bedding, Suite Dreams mattresses, and
cozy, down-filled comforters. **Pros:** oversize showers; good 7th-floor
fitness center; free Wi-Fi in the lobby. **Cons:** fee for Internet in guest
rooms unless you are a Hilton honors member; expensive breakfast;
parking is expensive. ⑤ *Rooms from: $249* ✉ *40 Dalton St., Back Bay*
☎ *617/236–1100, 888/874–0663* ⊕ *www.bostonbackbay.hilton.com*
⤳ *395 rooms* ⦿ *No meals* Ⓜ *Prudential, Hynes* ✛ *2:A3.*

$$
B&B/INN
FAMILY
Fodor's Choice
★

⬚ **Inn@St. Botolph.** The posh yet homey 16-room Inn@St. Botolph follows a groundbreaking new hotel model—no front desk, no restaurant, no keys, and no valet (there is, however, an office on-site that is staffed 24/7). **Pros:** guests get 25% off meals at Columbus Hospital Group restaurants; free Wi-Fi; free transit to select restaurants. **Cons:** DIY parking; no traditional front desk check-in services; may be too "off the beaten path" for some. ⑤ *Rooms from: $299* ✉ *99 St. Botolph St., Back Bay* ☎ *617/236–8099* ⊕ *www.innatstbotolph.com* ⇗ *16 rooms* ⦿ *Breakfast* Ⓜ *Prudential* ✚ *2:B3.*

$$
HOTEL
FAMILY

⬚ **Lenox Hotel.** A good alternative to chain-owned, big-box Back Bay hotels, the family-owned Lenox with top-notch service continues to please a well-groomed clientele. **Pros:** mini-refrigerator in every room; fantastic Copley Square location; historic/architectural charm; free Wi-Fi. **Cons:** some bathrooms are small; no minibar; costly parking. ⑤ *Rooms from: $215* ✉ *61 Exeter St., Back Bay* ☎ *617/536–5300, 800/225–7676* ⊕ *www.lenoxhotel.com* ⇗ *214 rooms* ⦿ *No meals* Ⓜ *Back Bay, Copley* ✚ *2:B2.*

$$$$
HOTEL
FAMILY

⬚ **Loews Boston Hotel.** The former headquarters of the Boston Police Department now houses the sleek Loews Boston Hotel. **Pros:** delicious restaurant with a great patio; welcoming staff; pet-friendly. **Cons:** bar side can be loud; parking is expensive; restaurant is pricey. ⑤ *Rooms from: $459* ✉ *154 Berkeley St., Back Bay* ☎ *617/266–7200, 855/495–6397* ⊕ *www.loewshotels.com/boston-hotel* ⇗ *225 rooms* ⦿ *No meals* Ⓜ *Back Bay* ✚ *2:C2.*

$$$$
HOTEL

⬚ **Mandarin Oriental, Boston.** With too many amenities to list, the 148-room hotel has helped redefine luxury in town (pay attention, Ritz and Four Seasons) since opening in 2008. **Pros:** amazing service; very quiet; good-size rooms. **Cons:** small fitness center; rates are exorbitant; valet parking is expensive. ⑤ *Rooms from: $545* ✉ *776 Boylston St., Back Bay* ☎ *617/535–8888* ⊕ *www.mandarinoriental.com/boston* ⇗ *148 rooms* ⦿ *No meals* Ⓜ *Prudential, Copley, Back Bay* ✚ *2:A2.*

$$
B&B/INN

⬚ **Newbury Guest House.** A homey feel and personalized service are at the soul of this elegant brownstone at the heart of Boston's most fashionable shopping street. **Pros:** cozy and homey; great location on Newbury Street; perfect base for shopping. **Cons:** rooms go quickly year-round; small bathrooms; limited parking. ⑤ *Rooms from: $259* ✉ *261 Newbury St., Back Bay* ☎ *617/670–6000, 800/437–7668* ⊕ *www.newburyguesthouse. com* ⇗ *32 rooms* ⦿ *Breakfast* Ⓜ *Back Bay, Hynes, Copley* ✚ *2:A2.*

$$
HOTEL
FAMILY

⬚ **Taj Boston Hotel.** Standing guard at the corner of fashionable Newbury Street and the Public Garden, the old-school elegant Taj features plush new robes and towels in guest rooms, new carpets, Molton Brown bath amenities, and vibrant floral displays in the lobby. **Pros:** white-glove service; amazing views; proximity to shopping, dining, and the park. **Cons:** all this luxury will cost you; rooms on the 16th floor are under the roof-deck party space; guest rooms need an update. ⑤ *Rooms from: $299* ✉ *15 Arlington St., Back Bay* ☎ *617/536–5700* ⊕ *www.thetajboston.com* ⇗ *273 rooms* ⦿ *No meals* Ⓜ *Arlington* ✚ *2:C1.*

$$$
HOTEL

⬚ **Westin Copley Place Boston.** If the idea of sleeping in an upscale mall appeals to you, meet your new favorite hotel. **Pros:** great location close to shopping and tourist spots; guided running tours in the summer and fall; clean, spacious rooms. **Cons:** big and busy feeling; pool area is nothing special; some say it's overpriced. $ *Rooms from: $349* ✉ *10 Huntington Ave., Back Bay* ☎ *617/262–9600, 888/937–8461* ⊕ *www. westincopleyplaceboston.com* 📞 *945 rooms* ⦿ *No meals* Ⓜ *Copley, Back Bay* ✛ *2:B2.*

THE SOUTH END

$

B&B/INN

🎫 **Chandler Inn.** In 2012, the Chandler received a major update by big-shot local designers Dennis Duffy and Eric Roseff. **Pros:** can't beat the price; friendly staff; the South End is a prime location for foodies. **Cons:** area parking is brutally hard or expensive; rooms can be noisy. $ *Rooms from: $175* ✉ *26 Chandler St., South End* ☎ *617/482–3450, 800/842–3450* ⊕ *www.chandlerinn.com* 📞 *56 rooms* ⦿ *No meals* 🐾 *Pets only up to 25 pounds allowed, and can never be left alone in room* Ⓜ *Back Bay* ✛ *2:D3.*

$

B&B/INN

🎫 **Chandler Studios.** For folks who prefer a home away from home, the Chandler Studios are like your very own luxury apartment in Boston's uberhip South End neighborhood. **Pros:** prime South End location; huge bathrooms; DirectTV in all studios. **Cons:** check-in is around the corner at Chandler Inn; not for those who want hotel staff at their disposal; area parking is very expensive. $ *Rooms from: $169* ✉ *54 Berkeley St., South End* ☎ *617/482–3450* ⊕ *www.chandlerstudiosboston.com* 📞 *12 studios* ⦿ *No meals* Ⓜ *Back Bay* ✛ *2:D3.*

$

B&B/INN

🎫 **Encore.** Innkeepers Reinhold Mahler and David Miller, who are a retired architect and creative set designer, respectively, have pooled their creative energies into this South End lodging gem, proving that they know a thing or two about ambience. **Pros:** trendy South End location; free Wi-Fi; Bang & Olufsen sound systems; breakfast pastries from Flour; Aveda amenities in bathrooms. **Cons:** small breakfast nook; two-night minimum on weekends in July and August, three-night minimum in September and October; no elevator. $ *Rooms from: $155* ✉ *116 W. Newton St., South End* ☎ *617/247–3425* ⊕ *www.encorebandb.com* 📞 *4 rooms* ⦿ *Breakfast* Ⓜ *Back Bay, Massachusetts Ave.* ✛ *2:B4.*

THE FENWAY AND KENMORE SQUARE

If you have tickets for a Red Sox baseball game at Fenway Park, this is the area you want to stay in. If you're a museum hound, you'll also be able to walk to the Museum of Fine Arts and Isabella Stewart Gardner Museum as well as to Downtown. Boston University is a stone's throw from here and lots of students means lots of visiting parents. Book early.

$$$

B&B/INN

Fodor's Choice

★

🎫 **Gryphon House.** The staff in this value-packed, four-story 19th-century brownstone is helpful and friendly, and the suites are thematically decorated: one evokes rustic Italy; another is inspired by neo-Gothic art. **Pros:** elegant suites are lush and spacious; gas fireplaces in all rooms; free Wi-Fi. **Cons:** may be too fussy for some; no elevator; no wheelchair access. $ *Rooms from: $300* ✉ *9 Bay State Rd., Kenmore Square* ☎ *617/375–9003, 877/375–9003* ⊕ *www.innboston.com* 📞 *8 suites* ⦿ *Breakfast* Ⓜ *Kenmore* ✛ *3:G2.*

$$$

HOTEL

Fodor's Choice

★

🎫 **Hotel Commonwealth.** Luxury and service without pretense make this hip spot a solid choice. **Pros:** down bedding; perfect locale for Red Sox fans; happening bar scene at Eastern Standard; free Wi-Fi. **Cons:** area is absolutely mobbed during Sox games; small gym; pricey rates.

$ *Rooms from: $399* ⊠ *500 Commonwealth Ave., Kenmore Square* ☎ *617/933–5000, 866/784–4000* ⊕ *www.hotelcommonwealth.com* ⟿ *245 rooms* ❣◎❣ *No meals* Ⓜ *Kenmore* ✢ *3:F2.*

$ ⊡ **The Verb Hotel.** A rock 'n' roll reimagining of a classic midcentury
HOTEL hotel, the stylish Verb is filled to the brim with carefully curated historic music memorabilia. **Pros:** stylish pool scene; Bigelow bath products in the showers; free Wi-Fi. **Cons:** may be too unique for some people; one-way cooling/heating system; valet only parking option. $ *Rooms from: $139* ⊠ *1271 Boylston St., The Fenway* ☎ *855/695–6678* ⊕ *www.theverbhotel.com* ⟿ *94 rooms* ❣◎❣ *No meals* Ⓜ *Fenway* ✢ *3:F3.*

BOSTON OUTSKIRTS

BROOKLINE

If you don't want to pay Boston or Cambridge prices, then staying in Brookline is your best bet. Located four miles from Boston, Brookline is an easy T ride into the city.

$$ ⊡ **Courtyard by Marriott Boston Brookline.** If you don't mind the anonymity
HOTEL and predictability of a chain hotel—and don't mind staying outside of
FAMILY Boston proper—this is a decent choice. **Pros:** kid-friendly with adjoining rooms; 1 mile from Fenway Park and Longwood Medical Center; roomy bathrooms; free Wi-Fi. **Cons:** staff can be indifferent; dull decor; might be too far of a walk to downtown Boston for some people. $ *Rooms from: $209* ⊠ *40 Webster St., Brookline* ☎ *617/734–1393, 866/296–2296* ⊕ *www.marriott.com/bosbl* ⟿ *188 rooms* ❣◎❣ *No meals* Ⓜ *Beacon St.* ✢ *3:A4.*

EAST BOSTON (LOGAN AIRPORT)

This waterfront neighborhood is undergoing a renaissance, making it one of the most highly coveted areas in the city thanks to its proximity to Logan International Airport, easy commute downtown, and of course, amazing harbor views. Eastie, as it's locally known, attracts tourists and locals alike for its plethora of Italian and Latin American restaurants.

$ ⊡ **Hilton Boston Logan Airport.** Quiet rooms, competitive prices, and the
HOTEL only on-airport location make this modern Hilton a good choice for in-and-out visitors to Boston. **Pros:** easy access to Logan Airport; short drive from Downtown Boston; day-use rooms available. **Cons:** Internet and parking fees can add up; not walking distance to attractions, restaurants, or shopping; not directly connected to Terminals B & C. $ *Rooms from: $199* ⊠ *1 Hotel Dr.* ☎ *617/568–6700, 800/445–8667* ⊕ *www.bostonlogan.hilton.com* ⟿ *599 rooms* ❣◎❣ *No meals* Ⓜ *Airport* ✢ *1:H4.*

$$ ⊡ **Hyatt Boston Harbor.** Half the rooms at the Hyatt Boston Harbor
HOTEL have sweeping views of either the city skyline or the ocean; the others overlook planes taking off and landing. **Pros:** close to airport; pool area has skyline views; competent, can-do staff. **Cons:** close to airport; overpriced restaurant; airport shuttle is frustratingly slow. $ *Rooms from: $265* ⊠ *101 Harborside Dr.* ☎ *617/568–1234, 800/233–1234* ⊕ *www.bostonharbor.hyatt.com* ⟿ *270 rooms* ❣◎❣ *No meals* Ⓜ *Airport* ✢ *1:H4.*

CAMBRIDGE

Cambridge is much more provincial than Boston, giving the hotels in Cambridge a more intimate feel. Several are on tree-lined streets surrounded by college "yards" or campuses.

$
B&B/INN
A Cambridge House Inn. This sweet Cambridge spot, a restored 1892 National Register of Historic Places house, has richly carved cherry paneling, a grand fireplace, elegant antiques, and polished wood floors overlaid with Oriental rugs. **Pros:** most rooms have fireplaces; free parking (first come, first serve) and Wi-Fi; complimentary coffee, tea, and hot chocolate; old school B&B charm with modern hospitality. **Cons:** very quiet area; no elevator; a little farther north of Harvard Square than most people would like; doesn't serve a full hot breakfast. *$ Rooms from: $149 ⊠ 2218 Massachusetts Ave., Cambridge ☎ 617/491–6300, 800/232–9989 ⊕ www.acambridgehouse.com ⇆ 33 rooms ⊚ Breakfast Ⓜ Davis ✛ 4:B1.*

$$$
HOTEL
Boston Marriott Cambridge. Traveling businesspeople and families like the modern look and efficiency of this 26-story high-rise hotel in Kendall Square, steps from the subway and MIT. **Pros:** top-floor rooms have stunning views; comfy bed linens; decent cost-saving packages on weekends. **Cons:** has the "chain hotel" feel; smallish pool; lots of business travelers and people with children. *$ Rooms from: $339 ⊠ 2 Cambridge Center, 50 Broadway, Cambridge ☎ 617/494–6600, 888/228–9290 ⊕ www.marriotthotels.com/boscb ⇆ 444 rooms ⊚ No meals Ⓜ Kendall/MIT ✛ 1:A5.*

$$$
HOTEL
FAMILY
Fodor's Choice
★
Charles Hotel. It used to be that the Charles was *the* place to stay in Cambridge, and while other luxury hotels have since arrived to give it a little healthy competition, this Harvard Square staple is standing strong. **Pros:** two blocks from the T Red Line to Boston; on-site jazz club and hip Noir bar; on-site 4,000-square-foot Corbu Spa & Salon. **Cons:** luxury comes at a price; restricted pool hours for children; coffee pots and tea kettles are available by request only. *$ Rooms from: $399 ⊠ 1 Bennett St., Cambridge ☎ 617/864–1200, 800/882–1818 ⊕ www.charleshotel.com ⇆ 294 rooms ⊚ No meals Ⓜ Harvard ✛ 4:A3.*

$
HOTEL
Freepoint Hotel. The modern and eclectic style of the Freepoint Hotel, which burst onto the scene in early 2017, fits into tech-forward Cambridge perfectly. **Pros:** free Wi-Fi; complimentary shuttle to Alewife T station and Harvard Square; on-site Starbucks; Living Proof hair products. **Cons:** not close to major attractions; not within walking distance to the T; no suites. *$ Rooms from: $199 ⊠ 220 Alewife Brook Pkwy., Cambridge ☎ 617/491–8000 ⊕ www.freepointhotel.com ⇆ 121 rooms ⊚ No meals Ⓜ Alewife ✛ 4:A1.*

$
HOTEL
Harvard Square Hotel. Don't feel like shelling out a week's salary to stay at the venerable Charles? Check in to the next-door Harvard Square Hotel, where you'll get the location and convenience for half the cost. **Pros:** awesome location; all guest room windows open; Wi-Fi, tea, and coffee in the lobby café are all complimentary. **Cons:** parking costs extra; no gym; no restaurant. *$ Rooms from: $189 ⊠ 110 Mt. Auburn St., Cambridge ☎ 617/864–5200, 800/458–5886 ⊕ www.harvardsquarehotel.com ⇆ 73 rooms ⊚ No meals Ⓜ Harvard ✛ 4:A2.*

$ ⬚ **Irving House.** On a residential street three blocks from Harvard Square,
B&B/INN this four-story gray clapboard guest house is a bargain. **Pros:** free Wi-Fi;
         good location and price; coffee, tea, and pastries are available until 10
         pm. **Cons:** small parking lot is first come, first served; some rooms with
         shared baths; four floors are not served by elevator; dining room is in the
         basement. ⑤ *Rooms from: $85* ⊠ *24 Irving St., Cambridge* ☎ *617/547–
         4600, 877/547–4600* ⊕ *www.irvinghouse.com* ↵ *44 rooms* ¶⊙¶ *Breakfast*
         Ⓜ *Harvard* ✛ *4:C2.*

$$$ ⬚ **Kendall Hotel.** You might think a place in such a high-tech neighbor-
HOTEL   hood would be all stainless steel and chrome; think again: the Kend-
         all Hotel is homey and ultrafriendly, bright-hued and lively—and it's
         convenient, with a T stop just one block away. **Pros:** quiet rooms; hot
         buffet breakfast included; free Wi-Fi and passes to local gym. **Cons:** too
         many tchotchkes; no swimming pool; not for those who dislike kitsch.
         ⑤ *Rooms from: $390* ⊠ *350 Main St., Cambridge* ☎ *617/577–1300,
         866/566–1300* ⊕ *www.kendallhotel.com* ↵ *77 rooms* ¶⊙¶ *Breakfast*
         Ⓜ *Kendall/MIT* ✛ *4:H5.*

$ ⬚ **Kimpton Hotel Marlowe.** If Alice in Wonderland dreamed up a hotel, it
HOTEL   might look a bit like the Kimpton Marlowe—vivid stripes, swirls, and
         other geometric patterns lend the decor a wild, lively aesthetic. **Pros:**
         family and pet-friendly; fun, eclectic atmosphere; free wine tastings.
         Cons: a cab or T ride or walk from central Boston; not for formal
         decor purists; short walk required to get to nearby nonchain restau-
         rants. ⑤ *Rooms from: $199* ⊠ *25 Edwin H. Land Blvd., Cambridge*
         ☎ *617/868–8000, 800/825–7140* ⊕ *www.hotelmarlowe.com* ↵ *236
         rooms* ¶⊙¶ *No meals* Ⓜ *Lechmere* ✛ *1:C3.*

$$ ⬚ **Le Meridien Cambridge.** When the Meridien chain took over the cult
HOTEL   favorite geek-chic Hotel at MIT, with its tech-savvy rooms and sur-
         roundings, some fans worried the Cambridge spot would lose its charm;
         but the new owners only amped up the offerings—and added some
         luxe touches—by displaying cool interactive lobby art from MIT and
         refurbishing the guest rooms with platform beds, puffy white duvets,
         flat-screen TVs, and ergonomically designed furniture. **Pros:** walk
         to many excellent restaurants in Central Square; close to the T (Red
         Line Central); 24-hour fitness center; free Wi-Fi. **Cons:** pricey high-
         season rates; tons of tech people; not really walkable to Boston sights.
         ⑤ *Rooms from: $219* ⊠ *20 Sidney St., Cambridge* ☎ *617/577–0200,
         800/543–4300* ⊕ *www.lemeridien.com/cambridge* ↵ *210 rooms* ¶⊙¶ *No
         meals* Ⓜ *Central, Kendall/MIT* ✛ *4:F5.*

$$$ ⬚ **Royal Sonesta Boston.** Right next to the Charles River, the certified-
HOTEL   green Sonesta has one of the best city skylines and sunset views in
FAMILY   Boston. **Pros:** walk to Museum of Science and T to Downtown Bos-
Fodor's Choice ton; complimentary shuttle to Cambridge-area attractions; nice pool.
★   **Cons:** parking is not free; river view guest rooms have much better
         view than Cambridge view rooms; ArtBar's fire pits are first come first
         serve. ⑤ *Rooms from: $379* ⊠ *40 Edwin Land Blvd., off Memorial
         Dr., Cambridge* ☎ *617/806–4200, 800/766–3782* ⊕ *www.sonesta.com/
         boston* ↵ *400 rooms* ¶⊙¶ *No meals* Ⓜ *Lechmere* ✛ *1:B4.*

NIGHTLIFE AND PERFORMING ARTS

Updated
by Megan
Johnson

Boston's cultural attractions are a bracing mix of old-world aesthetics and new-world experimentation. At the classical end of the spectrum, revered institutions like the Museum of Fine Arts, the Boston Symphony Orchestra and Boston Pops, and the Isabella Stewart Gardner Museum offer refined experiences. For less reverential attitudes toward the arts, the Institute of Contemporary Art (ICA) features edgy electronic concerts, and graffiti and multimedia exhibitions. Museums like the MFA, the Gardner, and the ICA also host special shows and festivals in strikingly handsome performance spaces.

For live shows, head to the compact Theater District to see traveling Broadway revues, national comedy, opera companies, rock bands, and premiere previews headed to New York. Perennial favorites Blue Man Group and Shear Madness offer fun experiences. Enjoy cocktails at Bina Osteria or the Ritz's Avery Bar, where performers at the nearby Paramount Theater often unwind after shows. Or share a quiet chat about the play at Troquet's cozy wine bar.

For casual, less costly alternatives, indie rock and music clubs abound, dance clubs and lounges cater to party types and night owls, and bars in every neighborhood blare plasma-screen games—good luck, though, during high season trying to catch games not involving the Red Sox, Celtics, Bruins, or Patriots. Scan the crowd over a late-night bite at Miel in the waterfront InterContinental Hotel or at House of Blues on Lansdowne Street for both local and visiting celebrities. Whether it's cheering on the Bruins, Revolution (soccer), Sox, Celtics, or Pats at a watering hole, rocking out at an underground club, applauding a symphonic or ballet performance, or just chillin' in an elegant lounge, Boston has cultural amusements to suit all types and moods.

NIGHTLIFE PLANNER

COVERS

Cover charges for local acts and club bands generally run $8 to $20; big-name acts can be double that. Dance clubs usually charge a cover of $8 to $20. Nearly all nightlife spots accept major credit cards; cash-only places are noted.

LAST CALL

Because Boston retains vestiges of its puritanical blue laws, last call for alcoholic beverages in bars and restaurants remains at 1 am, and doors close at 2 am. Mayor Marty Walsh recently stumped for an extension to 3:30 am, but Beacon Hill legislators rebuffed the move. The only places "serving" after the official 2 am closing time for bars and clubs are a few restaurants in Chinatown (ask for "cold tea" and you might get a beer) and all-night diners, which won't serve alcohol. Bars may also close up shop early if business is slow or the weather is bad. Blue laws also prohibit bars from offering happy-hour drink specials, although happy-hour food specials abound. That said, the MBTA (lovingly, the "T") keeps the subway and major bus routes running weekends until 2:30 am.

GETTING INFORMED

The best source of arts and nightlife information is the *Boston Globe*'s "Arts & Entertainment" section (⊕ *www.boston.com/thingstodo*). Also worth checking out are the Thursday "Calendar" section of the *Boston Globe*; the Friday "Scene" section of the *Boston Herald*; and the calendar listings in free magazines in drop boxes around town, like *DigBoston* (⊕ *www.digboston.com*) and the *Improper Bostonian*. The *Globe, Dig,* and specialized sites as diverse as the thoroughly classical *Boston Musical Intelligencer* (⊕ *www.classicalscene.org*) and the scruffy indie-rock broadside *Boston Hassle* (⊕ *www.bostonhassle.com*), provide up-to-the-minute information online. Other reliable websites include the comprehensive ⊕ *artsfuse.org* and The ARTery at ⊕ *wbur. org*, the radio station of Boston University.

GETTING TICKETS

Boston's supporters of the arts are an avid group; tickets often sell out well in advance. Buy tickets when you make your hotel reservations.

BosTix. This Ticketmaster outlet has two locations that sell half-price tickets for same-day performances and for select advance shows online. Full-price tickets for local attractions like Boston Duck Tours, Freedom Trail Walking Tours, and New England Aquarium are available. On Friday, Saturday, or Sunday, show up a half hour before the booth opens. Booths are in Faneuil Hall and Copley Square. ⊕ *www.bostix.org*.

Broadway Across America—Boston. This organization brings Broadway shows to Boston in pre- and post-Broadway runs. Call between 10 am and 5 pm on weekdays. ☎ 866/523–7469 ⊕ *www.boston.broadway.com*.

Live Nation. This huge ticket outlet handles top and trending tours of country, rock, and arena shows at major Boston venues such as TD Garden, Xfinity Center, Gillette Stadium, House of Blues, Blue Hills Bank Pavilion, and Paradise Rock Club. Transactions are conducted online. ⊕ *www.livenation.com*.

12

Ticketmaster. The ticket juggernaut has outlets in local stores (check online for locations), or you can order by phone, but note that Ticketmaster phone charges allow neither refunds nor exchanges. ☎ *800/653–8000 existing orders, 800/745–3000 new orders, 866/448–7849 Ticketmaster Express* ⊕ *www.ticketmaster.com.*

NIGHTLIFE

Boston is a Cinderella city, aglow with delights that for some end all too soon. With the T (subway and bus) making its final runs between midnight and 1 am and taxis sometimes scarce, most nightspots follow accordingly, with "last call" typically by 2 am. Though night owls may be disappointed by the meager late-night options, except in Chinatown, visitors find plenty of possibilities for stepping out on the early side. The martini set may stroll Newbury and Boylston streets in the Back Bay or Downtown, selecting from swank restaurants, lounges, and clubs. Coffee- and tea drinkers can find numerous cafés in Cambridge and Somerville, particularly Harvard and Davis squares. Microbrew enthusiasts find viable options at sports bars and brewpubs, especially near campuses and sports arenas. For dancing, Lansdowne and Boylston streets near Fenway Park have a stretch of student-friendly hangs, DJ rooms, and techno clubs. The thriving "lounge" scene in Downtown's cooler hybrid bar-restaurant-clubs provides a mellower, more mature alternative to the collegiate indie clubs. Tourists crowd Faneuil Hall for its pubs, comedy spots, and dance scenes. The South and North ends, as well as Cambridge and Somerville, cater to the "dinner-and-drinks" set, while those seeking rock clubs should explore Allston and Cambridge, especially Central Square. College-owned concert halls regularly host homegrown and visiting ensembles. Prominent among these are Harvard University's Sanders Theatre, New England Conservatory's Jordan Hall, Berklee College of Music's Performance Center, MIT's Kresge Auditorium, and Agganis Arena at Boston University.

BOSTON

BEACON HILL AND THE OLD WEST END

Charles and Cambridge streets mark the livelier borders of the majestic State House and leafy, patrician enclave of Beacon Hill. You'll find art galleries, cozy pubs, and small restaurants along Charles, and Old West Church, Harrison Otis House, and major hospitals Mass General and Mass Eye and Ear on Cambridge. Opposite the stunning glass-and-steel Charles Street T station looms the old jailhouse, now housing the swank Liberty Hotel. Towards the harbor, the TD Garden, playground of the Celtics and Bruins, dominates North Station and its satellite brewpubs, sports bars, and restaurants.

BARS

Boston Beer Works. Located near the TD Garden, this BBW branch serves up the same array of well-crafted draft beers and ales to Celtics and Bruins fans as its brother spot outside Fenway Park does to thirsty Red

12

Sox fans. It sports six pool tables and prodigious copper brewing vessels that spew clean drafts like Hub Light and Boston Red Ale. ■TIP→ Expect packed crowds on game nights. ✉ *112 Canal St., Old West End* ☎ *617/896-2337* ⊕ *www.beerworks.net* Ⓜ *North Station.*

Cheers. The upstairs pub—dismantled in England, shipped to Boston, and reassembled—later became the inspiration for the now-classic TV series *Cheers*. Enjoy a quality burger at the model bar of the Hollywood set and imagine Sam and Diane walking in the door and calling your name. ■TIP→ You'll find many a tourist in Cheers, but locals tend to stay away to avoid the crowds. ✉ *Hampshire House, 84 Beacon St., Beacon Hill* ☎ *617/227-9605* ⊕ *www.cheersboston.com* Ⓜ *Arlington, Park St., Charles/MGH.*

The Fours. Just outside the TD Garden, all-for-sports Fours has two floors packed with fans on game and concert nights, but you can enjoy good fish, chowder, and wings every day. ✉ *166 Canal St., Old West End* ☎ *617/720-4455* ⊕ *www.thefours.com* Ⓜ *North Station.*

Harp. Find a crowded, rollicking atmosphere at this watering hole by North Station and TD Garden. A sort-of Irish pub, the Harp's two floors of bars serve postgame and concert crowds, sports addicts, and ticketless fans wanting in on the action. ■TIP→ Expect lines on weekend nights, when this area can get a little rowdy. ✉ *85 Causeway St., Old West End* ☎ *617/742-1010* ⊕ *www.harpboston.com* Ⓜ *North Station.*

Fodor'sChoice
★
The Sevens Ale House. Serving beer and wine, this classic dive bar is an easygoing alternative to Beacon Hill's tony stuffiness, with its dark tones, simple bar setup, well-peppered dartboard, perfectly poured pints, and decent wines. It's pleasantly untrendy. ✉ *77 Charles St., Beacon Hill* ☎ *617/523-9074* Ⓜ *Charles/MGH.*

21st Amendment. Named for the amendment that ended Prohibition, this convivial pub across from the State House draws legislators, lobbyists, and neighborhood regulars who trade gossip and insider info on notched wooden tables over beers, burgers, and BBQ chicken salad—the food is surprisingly good. ✉ *150 Bowdoin St., Beacon Hill* ☎ *617/227-7100* ⊕ *www.21stboston.com* Ⓜ *Park St.*

GOVERNMENT CENTER

The seat of Boston's city hall and financial center, the Center hosts concerts and circuses on its plaza, shelters popular food trucks serving up sidewalk gourmet grub, and overlooks those historic brick beehives of activity, Old State House and Faneuil Hall, and the haunting, transparent New England Holocaust Memorial. The Rose F. Kennedy Greenway, a mile-long parkland built over the depressed central artery, links the North End to Chinatown with gardens and trees, and parallels the hotel-rich stretch of the Harborwalk.

BARS

Bell in Hand Tavern. America's oldest continuously operating pub (founded 1795) is named after its original owner, town crier Jimmy Wilson, whose bell-ringing wooden sign still hangs on the wall. On the edge of the Freedom Trail, this glassed-in flatiron pub hosts live bands nightly downstairs, and DJs spin Top 40 for dancers Thursday through

Saturday upstairs. ■**TIP**➔ Expect long lines of twentysomethings on the weekends. ✉ *45–55 Union St., Government Center* ☎ *617/227–2098* ⊕ *www.bellinhand.com* Ⓜ *Haymarket.*

Black Rose. Hung with 20 bright county banners, decorated with pictures of Ireland and portraits of Samuel Beckett, Lady Gregory, and James Joyce, the Rose draws as many tourists as locals. Friendly Irish bartenders serve up pints, blarney, and far more Irish whiskeys (42) than Scotches (14). Nightly shows by traditional Irish and contemporary musicians confirm its abiding Gaelic good cheer, or *craic.* ✉ *160 State St., Government Center* ☎ *617/742–2286* ⊕ *www.blackroseboston.com* Ⓜ *Aquarium, State.*

Cheers. The owners of the former Bull & Finch in Beacon Hill established this Faneuil Hall outpost in 2001 by popular demand, re-creating a replica of the studio set, complete with Sam's Red Sox jacket. Despite overpriced burgers and seafood, tourists pour in, but don't expect to find locals hanging out here; they tend to avoid the massive crowds of the area. ✉ *Faneuil Hall Marketplace, Government Center* ☎ *617/227–0150* ⊕ *www.cheersboston.com* Ⓜ *Government Center, Haymarket.*

Durgin-Park. Steeped in history and serving Yankee classics like roast beef rib and Indian pudding since 1828, Durgin-Park is mostly visited by tourists looking to see some old-time Boston character. Happy hour brings in Faneuil Hall 9-to-5ers looking for cheap beer and snacks, like the $3 hot dog and fries. ✉ *340 N. Market St.* ☎ *617/227–2038* ⊕ *www.arkrestaurants.com/durgin_park.html* Ⓜ *Haymarket.*

Green Dragon Tavern. Less rowdy than its Faneuil Hall neighbors, this now-Irish bar claims to have housed the "Headquarters of the Revolution" and was the inn where silversmith Paul Revere overheard plans for a British assault on Lexington and Concord, prompting his famous ride. Today it's known more for Irish music—soloists play in the evenings from 5 to 9 Wednesday through Friday, and bands bring it on nightly beginning at 9. Regular lunch and seafood specials are served by a friendly waitstaff. ■**TIP**➔ College kids and young professionals tend to crowd the bar in the evenings. ✉ *11 Marshall St., Government Center* ☎ *617/367–0055* ⊕ *www.somerspubs.com* Ⓜ *Haymarket, Government Center.*

Hennessy's. Grab a seat by the windows overlooking Faneuil Hall on hot summer days, or cozy up to a coal fireplace in winter, and enjoy your pint. There's lots of live music in Hennessy's, as well as plenty of rowdy crowds that overrun the yellow-and-black confines for Top 40 cover bands on weekends from 9 pm to 1 am. ✉ *25 Union St., Government Center* ☎ *617/742–2121* ⊕ *www.somerspubs.com* Ⓜ *Haymarket, Government Center.*

MUSIC CLUBS

Hard Rock Cafe. This famed chain draws rock music and memorabilia fans to its large space with a double bar—decorated with hundreds of Zildjian cymbals—dance floor, bandstand, restaurant (wall art of signed photos, LPs, guitars, and gear), and private party room. When Cavern Club welcomes name or tribute bands (Rubix Cube, Doors, Aerosmith, and Pixies) occasionally on weekends, cover may range

$10–$20. ✉ 22–24 Clinton St., Government Center ☎ 617/424–7625
⊕ www.hardrock.com/boston ☞ No cover for drinks/dinner; shows will
vary Ⓜ Haymarket, Government Center.

THE NORTH END

Third generation Italians may have decamped to the suburbs, yet today's
North End still echoes with brass parades in summer street fairs honoring
saints. The friendly neighborhood attracts resident young professionals
with convenient and safe housing, and entices all by wafting aromas of
bitter espresso, pastries, fish specialties, red-sauce pasta, and pizza.

CAFÉS AND COFFEEHOUSES

Fodor'sChoice **Caffe Vittoria.** The glorious matriarch of North End cafés, glistening with
★ marble-topped tables, mirrors, and shiny machines, lets you glimpse
la dolce vita on Hanover Street as baristas pump steaming espresso
machines from 7 am until midnight. Skip the frenzy at tourist trap
Mike's Pastry next door; relax as you sip caffe latte or grappa and nib-
ble authentic gelati and pastries—tiramisu, sfogliatelle, cannoli. Cash
only, per favore. ✉ 290–296 Hanover St., North End ☎ 617/227–7606
⊕ www.caffevittoria.com Ⓜ Haymarket.

CHARLESTOWN

The historic waterfront along the harbor and Mystic River affords
Charlestown sweeping views of the USS *Constitution,* the Navy Yard
and Admiralty, and Boston itself, to which Charlestown is linked by
bike paths and Prison Point and Zakim bridges. Bunker Hill's needle
monument presides over a quiet, elegant neighborhood, while Main
Street and City Square attract visitors to restaurants and taverns.

BARS

Fodor'sChoice **Warren Tavern.** This venerable Colonial-era watering hole, rebuilt in
★ 1780, was frequented by Paul Revere; even George Washington had
a few drinks here. Today tourists and locals stop by for a glass and
passable grub en route to the historic Navy Yard. Try the house made
potato chips with your ale of choice. ✉ 2 Pleasant St., Charlestown
☎ 617/241–8142 ⊕ www.warrentavern.com Ⓜ Community College.

DOWNTOWN AND SOUTH BOSTON

Boston's historic heart beats at the conjunction of Boston Common and
the Public Garden: here shoppers and strollers cross paths with students
and workers along Tremont and Boylston streets, with Chinatown and
the Theater District tucked in between. The Greenway opens up the city
center and the burgeoning Seaport beyond the Fort Point Channel to
great benefit and beauty, with gateway boulevards connecting to North
Station, South Bay, Long Wharf, and South Station.

BARS

Fodor'sChoice **Beantown Pub.** Right on the Freedom Trail, this is the only pub in Bos-
★ ton where you can enjoy a Sam Adams lager while pondering the grave
of that Founding Father himself. It's a fine place to watch multiple
sports events, shoot pool, or people-watch. The standard pub menu,
available until 2 am, includes great burgers, soups, salads, mains, and
sandwiches, many named after local heroes and patriots buried in the
Granary Burying Ground (founded 1660) across the street—Mother
Goose, Paul Revere, John Hancock, Robert Treat Paine, and yes, Mr.

Adams (Cajun chicken with Vermont cheddar). ⊠ *100 Tremont St., Downtown* ☎ *617/426–0111* ⊕ *www.beantownpub.com* Ⓜ *Park St., Downtown Crossing.*

Bond Restaurant and Lounge. The stylish Bond belies its location in the somewhat conservative yet tony Langham Boston Hotel with its glittery lounge scene of sophisticates sipping house mixologists' seasonal cocktails and nibbling on modern American fare. ■**TIP→ A dinner menu is served until 10 pm, while a bar menu is served until 11 pm.** ⊠ *250 Franklin St., Downtown* ☎ *617/956–8765* ⊕ *www.bondboston. com* Ⓜ *State.*

Fodor's Choice
★

Drink. This area favorite lounge in a brick Fort Point Channel warehouse offers a short beer, wine, and food list, but no cocktail menu. Patrons rely on the highly knowledgeable bartenders to concoct libations on the spot according to drinkers' preferences. The space has an underground, modern speakeasy feel. Chat with the bartender to create your perfect drink; hint: if you like creative Manhattans, ask for a "Fort Point." ⊠ *348 Congress St., Fort Point, South Boston* ☎ *617/695–1806* ⊕ *drinkfortpoint.com* Ⓜ *South Station.*

Good Life. This funky bar in a heritage flatiron building mixes exotic martinis and fresh-juice cocktails, and boasts a whopping selection of international vodkas. The menu is broad, reasonable, and healthy. Subterranean Afterlife Lounge draws eclectic crowds for hip-hop, House, and party jams. Occasional live bands play and it's open until 2 am weekends, but closed Sunday. ⊠ *28 Kingston St., Downtown* ☎ *617/451–2622* ⊕ *www.goodlifebar.com* Ⓜ *Downtown Crossing.*

Howl at the Moon. Dueling pianos and hammy singers lure in bachelorettes, tourists, and friends to this party spot that's open nightly 'til 2 am. The performers fill requests on the spot for Lady Gaga, '80s and '90s Top 40, Elvis, Katy Perry, Taylor Swift—you get it. ⊠ *184 High St., Downtown* ☎ *617/292–4695* ⊕ *www.howlatthemoon.com* ⊗ *Closed Sun.* Ⓜ *Government Center, South Station.*

Kinsale. Deconstructed in Ireland piece by piece, the Kinsale was reassembled here to give it an air of Celtic authenticity. By day, businesspeople come in for lunch and a pint to admire the woodwork; by night, revelers pour in from nearby Faneuil Hall. Come Wednesday for trivia, and Thursday for karaoke. On Saturday, live bands play with no cover. ■**TIP→ The Kinsale also serves up a delicious brunch on weekends, including a full Irish breakfast.** ⊠ *2 Center Plaza, Downtown* ☎ *617/742–5577* ⊕ *www.classicirish.com* Ⓜ *Government Center.*

Last Hurrah. The mahogany club chairs and silver-tray service might make you feel like a Boston Brahmin, even if only for a martini or two. The historic setting and location inside the Omni Parker House right on the Freedom Trail make it an easy stop en route to King's Chapel or Ben Franklin's statue. ⊠ *60 School St., Downtown* ☎ *617/227–8600 hotel* Ⓜ *Downtown Crossing, Park St.*

Limelight Stage + Studios. Sing privately or go big time: bold karaoke patrons belt out their favorite tunes to the audience, while shy types can rent a "studio" room and croon with friends at this dedicated singers' bar. Expect theatrics, hamming, and a lively crowd with plenty of students from neighboring Emerson College. ■ **TIP→ Patrons must be 21-plus, except in private rooms before 10 pm.** ⊠ *204 Tremont St., Downtown* ☎ *617/423–0785, 877/557–8271* ⊕ *www.limelightboston. com* Ⓜ *Boylston, Park St.*

Lucky's Lounge. This is a subterranean dive with gritty charisma. Live bands hit the stage Thursday to Sunday, including one of the hotspot's most popular events: Sinatra Sundays, where a live Sinatra Band takes the stage at 8 pm. The story goes: when its signboard wasn't ready for the 2001 opening, the owners shrugged, "Ah, so what?" and let the joint go incognito. ⊠ *355 Congress St., Fort Point, South Boston* ☎ *617/357–5825* ⊕ *luckyslounge.com* Ⓜ *South Station.*

RumBa. In the InterContinental hotel, RumBa highlights two disparate spirits: rum (more than 70 varieties) and champagne (more than two dozen types). Slip into the hidden champagne lounge area behind sliding mahogany doors for quieter, secluded celebrations—you must book in advance. ■ **TIP→ Summertime is the perfect time to visit as the patio overlooks the glittering Fort Point Channel.** ⊠ *510 Atlantic Ave., Downtown* ☎ *617/747–1000* ⊕ *www.intercontinentalboston.com/dining/rumba.aspx* Ⓜ *South Station, Aquarium.*

COMEDY CLUBS

Comedy Connection [Wilbur Theatre]. This pretty white-and-gold bandbox, now 103 years old, is the happy home of Comedy Connection, presenting comedians like Amy Schumer, Michael Che, Jim Gaffigan, T.J. Miller, and Kevin James. Musical legends also take the stage—Chris Botti, Gordon Lightfoot, and Graham Nash are just a few. ⊠ *246 Tremont St., in Wilbur Theatre, Theater District* ☎ *617/248–9700* ⊕ *thewilbur.com* Ⓜ *Boylston.*

Nick's Comedy Stop. Boston's oldest comedy club, yukking it up since 1977, presents mainly local comics Friday and Saturday at 8 pm. Well-known comedians occasionally pop in. Jay Leno reportedly got his start here. Reservations are advised, tickets are $20. Bar available. ⊠ *100 Warrenton St., Theater District* ☎ *617/963–6261* ⊕ *www.nickscomedystop.com* Ⓜ *Boylston.*

DANCE CLUBS

Icon. This is the place to dance, dance, dance. International students and college kids looking to get down flock here to listen to DJs spin all types of music: especially hip-hop, Latin, and Europop. It's open 10 pm–2 am nightly. Make sure you dress to impress; if you're wearing sneakers, you may be denied entry. ⊠ *100 Warrenton St., Theater District* ☎ *617/422–0045* ⊕ *www.iconnightclub.com* ⊠ *Varies; $10 minimum* Ⓜ *NE Medical Center.*

Venu. International jet-setters, weekend warriors, and clubby wannabes converge on this 6,500-square-foot glittery dungeon evoking Miami's South Beach. It may not be 80 degrees, yet a warm energy sets Venu apart from the pack of techno industrial clubs. The diverse clientele mixes stylish students with downtown suits cutting loose. International Fridays bring DJs that play house and Latin, while Saturdays are Top 40 hits and hip-hop. ■ **TIP→ Sign up online for the guest list to snag the reduced entry price.** ⊠ *100 Warrenton St., Theater District* ☎ *617/338–8061* ⊕ *venuboston.com* Ⓜ *Boylston, Arlington.*

Whiskey Saigon. With its rich red velvet and crystal chandeliers, the former Gypsy Bar calls to mind the decadence of a dark European castle. You'll find a multitude of international students bopping their heads at the bar, dressed to the nines. Be ready to stand in line if you're planning on heading in late on the weekends. ✉ *116 Boylston St., Theater District* ☎ *617/482–7799* ⊕ *www.whiskysaigon.com* Ⓜ *Boylston.*

GAY AND LESBIAN

Alley Bar. Tucked away in an alley, this long-standing gay bar has recently been revamped with multiple TVs and large booth seating in the downstairs area. Although it was once largely known to attract the Bear subset, the crowd is diversifying thanks to monthly theme nights like Sunday Karaoke. ■TIP➔ It's cash only. ✉ *14 Pi Alley (Washington St.), Theater District* ⊕ *thealleybar.com* Ⓜ *Boylston.*

Fodor's Choice
★

Jacque's Cabaret. There's nothing traditional about Jacque's Cabaret, an institution for more than 60 years. Nightly drag-queen shows draw bachelorette parties and locals looking to swill cocktails from plastic cups. Be sure to make reservations if you're going in a group, and don't show up late; they may give your table away if you aren't seated before showtime. Because of a long-running licensing dispute with sleepy Bay Villagers, the whole carnival shuts down nightly at midnight. ✉ *79 Broadway, Theater District* ☎ *617/426–8902* ⊕ *www.jacques-cabaret.com* Ⓜ *Arlington.*

Royale. Largely a concert venue and nightclub, the Royale's spacious interior resembles a 20th-century ballroom. but this club is hardly sedate. It throws theme nights such as "Full on Fridays" and "WCKD Saturdays." Watch for concerts with bands like Clean Bandit, Dillinger Escape Plan, and Above And Beyond. Sunday evening hosts the gay/lesbian scene, with additional gay nights thrown in on three-day weekends. ✉ *279 Tremont St., Theater District* ☎ *617/338–7699* ⊕ *www.royaleboston.com* Ⓜ *Boylston.*

BACK BAY

Though the name says it, it's hard to believe that this broad street grid running from Boston Public Garden up elegant Beacon Street and Commonwealth Avenue, divided by a center strip of statues and magnolia trees, was, until the 1830s, landfilled dockland. Dominated by the John Hancock Tower and the Prudential, Back Bay is studded with beautiful churches around Copley Square and lively Newbury Street.

BARS

Bristol Bar. This restaurant and bar boasts floor-to-ceiling views of the Public Garden and a relaxed luxury setting that's enjoyable at nearly any time of day. On weekdays, power breakfasts and lunches are followed by a vibrant dinner scene, and weekends offer three meals a day plus a lively bar scene with signature cocktails. Don't hesitate to take a stroll around the room; quite often, you'll find a famous face or two enjoying a drink. ✉ *200 Boylston St., Back Bay* ☎ *617/338–4400* ⊕ *www.fourseasons.com/boston/dining/the_bristol_lounge.html* Ⓜ *Arlington, Boylston.*

Bukowski Tavern. This narrow barroom has a literary flair and more than 100 brews for your sipping pleasure. You'll see many a beer nerd hanging out at the bar, but hungry folks also come to the funky joint for the high-quality cuisine. Food is served until 1 am Sunday through

Wednesday (1:30 am Thursday through Sunday). ■TIP➔ All regular menu items drop to $6.99 after midnight. ✉ *50 Dalton St., Back Bay* ☎ *617/437-9999* ⊕ *www.bukowskitavern.net* Ⓜ *Hynes.*

Champions Sports Bar. Located inside Copley Place, this bar calls all sports fans (rabid, yet civilized) with 40 TV screens—including a 12' x 24' whopper where you surely won't miss a play. Visiting-team fans are welcome but may expect to be drowned out by cheers for home teams. Champions is not just about sports and beer (36 taps and scores of bottles); there's smooth waitstaff, a wine and cocktail list, and lengthy menu from Connections restaurant next door. ✉ *Boston Marriott Copley Pl., Copley Pl. Mall, 2nd level, 110 Huntington Ave., Back Bay* ☎ *617/927-5304* ⊕ *www.championsboston.com* Ⓜ *Prudential Center.*

Oak Long Bar + Kitchen. This flagship bar in the 1912 Fairmont Copley Plaza Hotel underwent a centennial stem-to-stern makeover that added new oak paneling and a flashy pizza oven. Now a "see and be seen" hotspot, restoration of the original sky-high coffered ceilings also opened up catbird views over Copley Square. Seated at outdoor tables perusing a menu of signature martinis, single malts, shareable platters, and desserts, you can people-watch and enjoy a panorama that encompasses the Boston Public Library and Trinity Church. ✉ *Fairmont Copley Plaza, 138 St. James Ave., Back Bay* ☎ *617/267-5300* ⊕ *www. fairmont.com/copleyplaza* Ⓜ *Copley.*

Fodor's Choice ★ **Sonsie.** The crowd spilling through French doors onto the sidewalk café in warm weather consists of trendy cosmopolitans, fun-loving professionals, local sports celebs, and scenesters. Founding owner-chef Bill Poirier's offerings of contemporary Americana have been a Back Bay standout for 20 years. The sophisticated jazz-rock soundtrack remains at a civilized volume as you dine, sip, and people-watch. Hungry? There's breakfast after 9, with specialty coffees from a Presse espresso coffee-bar, a weekday lunch, weekend brunches from 11 to 3:30 pm, and daily dinner and late-night menus until 12:30 am. ✉ *327 Newbury St., Back Bay* ☎ *617/351-2500* ⊕ *sonsieboston.com* Ⓜ *Hynes.*

Top of the Hub. At 52 floors up, this in-the-clouds lounge has incomparable views of Boston Harbor, Back Bay, Logan Airport, and the far suburbs. Hip jazz combos swing for starry-eyed dancers, and cheerful servers pour from an extensive drinks and fine wine list. Live jazz bands play nightly after 7:30 pm, and during Sunday brunch. There's no cover at the bar, but there's a $24 per person minimum at lounge tables after 8 pm. ✉ *Prudential Tower, 800 Boylston St., 52nd fl., Back Bay* ☎ *617/536-1775* ⊕ *topofthehub.net* Ⓜ *Prudential, Hynes, Copley.*

CAFÉS AND COFFEEHOUSES

Trident Booksellers & Café. Browse an eccentric collection of books and magazines at this crowded, pleasant café, then have coffee or tea while you read. This is a nice spot for a meal with a date, solo journal writing or reading at the bar, or surfing the net with free Wi-Fi. The windows facing Newbury Street (not to mention the patio) are great for people-watching. Open daily from 8 am until midnight. ✉ *338 Newbury St., Back Bay* ☎ *617/267-8688* ⊕ *www.tridentbookscafe.com* Ⓜ *Hynes.*

MUSIC CLUBS

Red Room @ Cafe 939. By day a Berklee College coffee and snack bar, the Cafe by night opens its tidy, scarlet, 200-capacity concert space. Run, booked, and played by students, it's an ideal all-ages venue for aspiring student bands and indies on the rise; everyone from Hozier to Karmin has played here. Refreshments are light (soft drinks, noodles), and so is the cover charge, which varies based on the event. There are a dozen eateries within 200 yards. ✉ *939 Boylston St., Back Bay* ☎ *617/747–2261* ⊕ *www.cafe939.com* Ⓜ *Hynes.*

THE SOUTH END

Sedate tree-lined streets of newly repointed brick town houses cast demure impressions, but the South End is a truly "hoppin' hood" with cafés, restaurants, theaters, parks, and recreational enclaves. A stroll along long, narrow Southwest Corridor Park (reclaimed as the Orange Line was built) links walkers from Copley Square (Back Bay Station) to Forest Hills Station, 5 miles away. Along winding lanes of flowering crab trees and community and butterfly gardens, an array of moms with strollers, bikers, dogwalkers, and skateboarders pass tennis courts, summer lawn concerts at Titus Sparrow Park, and kids playing basketball.

BARS

Clerys. Open-windowed, multiroomed Clerys can be your neighborhood bar, Irish pub, dance hall, sports hub, painting studio (Tuesday) or trivia source (Wednesday). Expect long lines on weekend nights in this high-traffic club near Copley Square; its several rooms bustle with young professionals local 9-to-5ers. ✉ *113 Dartmouth St., South End* ☎ *617/262–9874* ⊕ *www.clerysboston.com* Ⓜ *Copley.*

Fodor's Choice
★ **Darryl's Corner Bar & Kitchen.** This longtime neighborhood soul-food and jazz hangout still looks spiffy, and features real southern cooking and live bands nearly nightly at light cover charges. Come for glorified chicken and waffles on Wednesday and on Sunday there is a blues brunch starting at 10:30 am. Theatergoers receive dining discounts. ✉ *604 Columbus Ave., South End* ☎ *617/536–1100* ⊕ *www.dcbkboston.com* ☞ *Closed Mon.* Ⓜ *Massachusetts Ave.*

Delux Café. This unpretentious, cozy bar on a quiet corner attracts old-timers and young professionals with modest drinks and affordable comfort food. The quesadillas are worth the wait for a table. Yellowing posters, dim lights, and a '60s soundtrack add to the quirky, retro vibe. Wine list? Couple of reds, whites, sparklers. Entertainment? Talk to the bartender or your friends. Cash only. ✉ *100 Chandler St., South End* ☎ *617/338–5258* Ⓜ *Back Bay/South End.*

Franklin Café. A neighborhood institution for 20 years, The Franklin's renowned for creative cocktails, local microbrews, fine wines, and modern American food. There's no sign: just look for the white martini logo (or folks waiting for a dinner table) to know you're there. A full menu is served until 1:30 am every single night of the week, but sweet tooths beware: there's no dessert. ✉ *278 Shawmut Ave., South End* ☎ *617/350–0010* ⊕ *www.franklincafe.com* Ⓜ *Back Bay.*

12

Fodor's Choice ★ **JJ Foley's Cafe.** Family-owned and operated since 1909, JJ Foley's Cafe (or "Foley's," as regulars call it) is one of the most authentic Irish bars in Boston. There's an intimate dining room, as well as a more casual bar area where everyone from former Boston mayors to Justin Timberlake have enjoyed a pint. The pub food is great; order a sky-high plate of nachos if you dare. ■ TIP➜ Don't mistake this Foley's with the JJ Foley's Bar & Grill in Downtown Boston; despite similar names, the South End Foley's is the real thing. ⊠ *117 E. Berkeley St., South End* 🕾 *617/728–9101* ⊕ *www.jjfoleyscafe.com* Ⓜ *Tufts Medical Center.*

Lion's Tail. A sleek, high-energy cocktail bar in the massive Ink Block complex, Lion's Tail is a new urban-chic enclave where cocktails take center stage like the New York Streets Swizzle made with caramelized pineapple-infused Plymouth gin, or our favorite, the "Good Luck Finding a DJ Who Can Move & Shake Like Thisssss," a Wedding Singer–inspired fusion of Clyde May's bourbon, Hurricane rum, and a few other things. Co-owned by industry veteran Jarek Mountain and Dropkick Murphy's front-man Ken Casey, the hot spot has a creative and contemporary menu that features elevated bar bites, shared plates, hearty entrées, and a few sweet treats. ⊠ *300 Harrison Ave., South End* 🕾 *857/239–9276* ⊕ *www.lionstailboston.com* Ⓜ *Tufts Medical Center.*

GAY AND LESBIAN

Club Café. This smart multiroom club and restaurant for Boston gays, lesbians, and their straight friends is livelier than ever going into its fourth decade. Behind a stylish restaurant, patrons dance in the "video lounge" or watch classic music videos, cult flicks, and TV shows. There are trivia, karaoke, and Edge Boston events weekly; Napoleon Cabaret hosts singers nightly. A $10 cover charge on Friday and Saturday does not deter long lines. ⊠ *209 Columbus Ave., South End* 🕾 *617/536–0966* ⊕ *www.clubcafe.com* Ⓜ *Back Bay/South End.*

The Trophy Room. Tucked under the Chandler Inn, this gay sports bar is popular with the local after-work crowd and the sports teams that it sponsors. Casually dressed locals drop by for the large beer list and steak and eggs during the hopping weekend brunches (10 am–3 pm), which feature long, tall mimosas. ⊠ *26 Chandler St., South End* 🕾 *617/482–4428* ⊕ *www.trophyroomboston.com* Ⓜ *Back Bay/South End.*

MUSIC CLUBS

Fodor's Choice ★ **Beehive.** An underground bohemian bistro featuring delicious food, libations, and live music nightly, the Beehive is nestled under the historic Cyclorama building. The performers are a mix of jazz, blues, R&B, reggae, and Latin music artists, while patrons enjoy sipping craft cocktails and wines. Dine on Mediterranean mezze platters, daily special pastas, and comfort entrées. If jazz is your jam, don't miss the weekend jazz brunch from 10 am to 3 pm, and Sunday nights feature blues. ⊠ *541 Tremont St., South End* 🕾 *617/423–0069* ⊕ *www.beehiveboston.com* ☾ *Closed Mon.* Ⓜ *Back Bay.*

Fodor's Choice ★ **Wally's Café.** A rare gem for jazz and blues fans, Wally's Café, founded in 1947, is the oldest continuously operating family-owned jazz club in America. Patrons may see nostalgic stars like Branford Marsalis or Esperanza Spalding drop by, because the place is internationally renowned for its steady stream of heated performances by local bands and guests. Wally's diverse crowd attracts regulars from the South End and Roxbury, and music-hungry students, especially from Berklee College of Music. It's jammed every night of the year and there's never a cover. Monday it's blues and Thursday it's Latin jazz. Daily jam sessions run from 6 to 9 pm; bring your horn! Arrive early if you want a seat, because the line can be brutal. ✉ *427 Massachusetts Ave., South End* ☎ *617/424–1408* ⊕ *www.wallyscafe.com* ✉ *Free* Ⓜ *Massachusetts Ave., Symphony.*

THE FENWAY

Along the fens unclaimed by Back Bay, where Olmstead's Emerald Necklace winds along museum row, you'll find ball fields, the Kelleher Rose Garden, and extensive, lovingly maintained victory gardens in the shadow of Fenway Park and lively upper Boylston Street. Along "Avenue of the Arts" (aka Huntington Avenue) are Symphony Hall, New England Conservatory, Northeastern University, the Museum of Fine Arts, the Isabella Stewart Gardner Museum, and Museum College of Art. In the middle are Berklee College of Music, Boston Conservatory, and the Massachusetts Historical Society.

BARS

Boston Beer Works. Standing opposite Fenway Park since 1992, this brewery has all its works exposed—the tanks, pipes, and gleaming stainless-steel and copper kettles. Seasonal brews, in addition to 20 microbrews on tap, draw students, young adults, and tourists alike to the original location (its sibling by the TD Garden is popular, too). The atmosphere is too electric and noisy for quiet chats, and good luck trying to get in on a Sox game day. There are 20 small screens to view sports events, but the real action here is the busy brewers. Full bar service features West Coast wines. ✉ *61 Brookline Ave., The Fenway* ☎ *617/536–2337* ⊕ *www.beerworks.net* Ⓜ *Kenmore.*

House of Blues. Around the corner from Fenway Park and girded with bars and restaurants, the city's juggernaut among nightclubs books a wide array of bands into its barnlike music hall nightly. Tickets are $20–$40, with VIP box seats usually $10–$15 more. The Foundation Room (upscale VIP lounge) opens to the public for an additional $20, and promises "high-class debauchery." ✉ *15 Lansdowne St., Kenmore Square* ☎ *888/693–2583* ⊕ *www.houseofblues.com* Ⓜ *Kenmore.*

BOWLING ALLEYS AND POOL HALLS

Jillian's Boston. Often called the city's best (and certainly biggest) playground for grown-ups, this multistory complex has something for (almost) everyone. Home to Jillian's, an upscale pool hall, and Lucky Strike Lanes, there are 25 pool tables, 12 plasma screens, 16 bowling lanes, and an 80-foot video wall blasting sports and music videos. ✉ *145 Ipswich St., The Fenway* ☎ *617/437–0300* ⊕ *www.jilliansboston.com* Ⓜ *Kenmore.*

GAY AND LESBIAN

Machine. The granddaddy of Boston gay bars, Machine, is still cranking, and you can chalk your cue at the downstairs Pool Room. They host various theme nights like All-Star Mondays, a raucous weekly drag show. On Friday and Saturday, the crowd is age 18-plus. ✉ *1254 Boylston St., The Fenway* ☎ *617/536–1950* ⊕ *www.machineboston. club* Ⓜ *Fenway*.

12

BOSTON OUTSKIRTS

ALLSTON

A haven for students and international culture, this area bristles with music clubs, beer saloons, and ethnic eateries. Union Square, a prime locale, has cheerful, informal restaurants serving foods from Brazil, Colombia, El Salvador, Thailand, Vietnam, and Russia, as well as superbar Deep Ellum crafting superior Tex-Mex and La Befana serving up knockout wood-fired pizzas.

BARS

Fodor'sChoice
★

Sunset Grill & Tap. In the heart of student heaven, the Sunset looks, at first glance, like any neighborhood hangout. But venture inside and you'll be bowled over by its good promise to host the "365-days-a-year beer festival" with a staggering 500 choices of beer, 112 of them on tap. Forget pallid domestics: try an unpronounceable but appetizing brew from faraway places—seasonals, cask-conditioned, Belgians, wheats, stouts. If you're really thirsty, order a "half-yard"; if curious, order a flight sampler. There are ciders and meads, too. Brewing excellence is matched by fine eats like steam burgers and mile-high nachos served until 1 am. ✉ *130 Brighton Ave., Allston* ☎ *617/254–1331* ⊕ *www. allstonsfinest.com* Ⓜ *Harvard*.

MUSIC CLUBS

Brighton Music Hall. This spacious, popular venue connected with Paradise offers bands nightly, some open to all ages, often double bills. ✉ *158 Brighton Ave., Allston* ☎ *617/779–0140* ⊕ *crossroadspresents. com/brighton-music-hall* Ⓜ *Harvard Ave*.

Great Scott. Crowds of cool Allston students and greater Boston music fans rock hard until closing at Great Scott, which books an impressive lineup of local and visiting indie rock bands (from 9 pm) in live double and triple bills on a varying rotation nearly every night. ✉ *1222 Commonwealth Ave., Allston* ☎ *617/566–9014* ⊕ *www.greatscottboston. com* Ⓜ *Harvard Ave*.

Paradise Rock Club. This iconic bandbox near Boston University is famed for bringing up big-name talent (think U2), hosting Coldplay, and nurturing local rock and hip-hop acts. Two tiers of booths provide good sight lines from all angles, even some intimate, out-of-the-way corners. Four bars quench the crowd's thirst, and food is available. Some shows are for 18-plus only; many sell out. The newer Paradise Lounge next door is a more intimate space to catch local (often acoustic) songsters, literary readings, poetry slams, and other artsy events. ✉ *967–969 Commonwealth Ave., Allston* ☎ *617/562–8800* ⊕ *crossroadspresents.com/ paradise-rock-club* Ⓜ *Pleasant St*.

Scullers Jazz Club. Since 1989, this intimate and amiable venue overlooking the Charles River has presented top names—Harry Connick Jr., Chris Botti, Michael Bublé, and Wynton Marsalis, to name a few—in jazz, Latin, and contemporary, but also blues, soul, R&B, cabaret, and world music. There are full bar and cocktail menus, as well as food and dessert selections. Performances are Thursday through Saturday 8 and 10 pm; tickets range from $25 to $50 and are discounted if you come for dinner. Advance purchase is recommended. ⊠ *Doubletree Suites by Hilton Hotel, 400 Soldiers Field Rd., Allston* 🕾 *617/562–4111* ⊕ *www.scullersjazz.com* Ⓜ *BU West, Bus 47, or CT2.*

JAMAICA PLAIN

Great swaths of green—the Arboretum, Jamaica Pond, and Emerald Necklace stretching miles to the Fenway—set "J.P." apart from other streetcar suburbs. Centre Street runs the cultural gamut with Cuban, Mexican, Indian, Irish, and Dominican restaurants. Cafés and bars are wide open to gays and lesbians and everyone else.

BARS

Fodor's Choice
★
Doyle's Cafe. Truly an institution since 1892—and the first pub to put Sam Adams on tap—this friendly, crowded neighborhood Irish pub is a political as well as cultural landmark. Candidates for office from Boston City Council to U.S. Senate drop by to eat corned beef and cabbage, sample from 30 tap brews or 60 single-malt scotches, speechify, and "press the flesh." Non-Irish noshes include trout burgers, award-winning clam "chowdah," and kale-linguica soup. ⊠ *3484 Washington St., Jamaica Plain* 🕾 *617/524–2345* ⊕ *www.doylescafeboston.com* Ⓜ *Green St., Forest Hills.*

BREWPUBS AND BEER GARDENS

Boston Beer Company. Tour the Boston Beer Company's Jamaica Plain facility, where it conducts research and develops new products (the bulk of Samuel Adams production is done elsewhere). The entertaining hour-long tour is free to all, and includes a tasting for those over 21. Smell and taste the components of brewing: hops, malt, and barley; look at the flavoring process and hear about—perhaps even see—new beers in development. On fair-weather weekends, arrive early to avoid long waits. Tours run continuously 10 am–3 pm weekdays and Saturday, until 5:30 on Friday, closed Sunday and holidays. ■TIP→ Parking is limited, so consider taking the T to Stony Brook. ⊠ *30 Germania St., Jamaica Plain* 🕾 *617/368–5080* ⊕ *www.samueladams.com* Ⓜ *Stony Brook.*

GAY AND LESBIAN

Midway Café. This very popular Jamaica Plain café books a lively mix of nightly rock bands, DJs, and noise artists. There's punk, soul, R&B, and Thursday a raucous lesbian (straights, too) dance party and "queeraoke." Cover varies nightly. ⊠ *3496 Washington St., Jamaica Plain* 🕾 *617/524–9038* ⊕ *www.midwaycafe.com* Ⓜ *Green St., Forest Hills.*

CAMBRIDGE

Town meets gown at Harvard Square, and glitz meets not-so-nerdy MIT at biotech-booming Kendall Square. As "Mass Ave." (Massachusetts Avenue) bends beyond the Charles, it connects both campuses and Porter Square's ethnic restaurants and jolly scenesters. Inman Square's music spots, Brattle Street's patrician serenity, and the bustle of Cambridgeside's mall and hotel pubs and dining rooms enrich the fabric.

12

BARS

Alden & Harlow. This subterranean haunt adjacent to Brattle Theater provides fascinating pre- or postmovie dining with provocative locally sourced, rustic American fare like cheesy smoked grits, charred broccoli, or a burger that you once needed a secret code to order. Bartenders pour creative cocktails, local craft brews, and a fluid list of 50 edgy boutique wines. The late-night menu (to 1 am weeknights, 2 am weekends) offers favored fried smelts, broiled oysters with bacon, and crispy rabbit. ⊠ *40 Brattle St., Cambridge* ☎ *617/864–2100* ⊕ *www.aldenharlow. com* Ⓜ *Harvard Sq.*

Cambridge Brewing Company. This collegial, cavernous microbrewery has been the happy haunt for MIT techies and craft-brew geeks since its 1989 founding. Order CBC's Cambridge Amber, Charles River Porter, and Tall Tale Pale Ale fresh in pints, or go for a "tower" (an 83-ounce glass "yard"). In warm weather, try to nab a coveted patio table, a catbird seat for people-watching across bricky Kendall Square. Cheerful staff serve above-average pub grub, even at weekend "beerunches." ⊠ *1 Kendall Sq., Bldg. 100, at Hampshire St. and Broadway, Cambridge* ☎ *617/494–1994* ⊕ *www.cambridgebrewingcompany.com* Ⓜ *Kendall/MIT.*

Druid. You can feel like you're in Dublin here, sipping well-poured pints, eyeing the dusky atmosphere, eating black-and-white pudding or rib eye in Guinness. Located in vibrant Inman Square, Druid welcomes tourists and locals, a mix of Portuguese- and Italian-Americans, Harvard and MIT students, and young families. Irish musicians jam Tuesday evening and Saturday afternoon; there's trivia Wednesday at 8 pm and a DJ Thursday at 10 pm. ⊠ *1357 Cambridge St., Cambridge* ☎ *617/497–0965* ⊕ *www.druidpub.com* Ⓜ *Central, Harvard.*

Grendel's Den. This quintessential grad-student hangout is low lit and brick-walled. During happy hour, tasty entrées like crab dip, burritos, nachos, and burgers are half-priced with a $3-per-person drink (inside only; not on outdoor patio). ⊠ *89 Winthrop St., Cambridge* ☎ *617/491–1160* ⊕ *www.grendelsden.com* Ⓜ *Harvard.*

John Harvard's Brewery & Ale House. A convivial gathering place for the Crimsonites from the nearby Yard, John Harvard's Brew House dispenses ales, lagers, pilsners, wheats, and stouts brewed on the premises, just like an English pub. The food is no-frills and hearty. Pizza dough is made with spent-grains from the brewing process. Trivia is on Monday. ⊠ *33 Dunster St., Cambridge* ☎ *617/868–3585* ⊕ *www.johnharvards. com* Ⓜ *Harvard.*

Fodor's Choice
★   **Middlesex Lounge.** For those looking to avoid the uber-sceney clubs of Boston's Theater District, the Middlesex is a welcoming, laid-back club for all sorts of people looking to dance the night away. Rolling settees, movable in varied seating configurations for trivia, games, and nerd nights, are usually cleared by 9 pm, when a $10 cover kicks in for DJs spinning crowd-pleasing EDM and hip-hop. Feed on small plates and pressed sandwiches. The lounge is only Thursday through Saturday, 7 pm–2 am. ✉ *315 Massachusetts Ave., Cambridge* ☎ *617/868–6739* ⊕ *www.middlesexlounge.us* Ⓜ *Central.*

Noir. Cary Grant and Katharine Hepburn would feel at their ease in this nightspot in the Charles Hotel, with its after-hours feel and rotating menu of classic and signature cocktails. Sink back into a voluptuous black-leather couch, sip a sultry Black Dahlia, and cloak yourself in an air of mystery. Wear evening or casual attire. There's a small bites and snack menu. ✉ *Charles Hotel, 1 Bennett St., Cambridge* ☎ *617/661–8010* ⊕ *www.noir-bar.com* Ⓜ *Harvard.*

The Plough & Stars. This genuine Irish pub has doubled as a bohemian oasis for 40 steady years. Drink Guinness and Bass on tap and many Irish whiskeys; hear light rock, Irish, or country music nightly, usually by 10:30. Narrow and cozy, the Plough is a comfy, noisy den for locals and students, yet a fine place to have lunch alone. The cover charge varies. Fun fact: literary magazine *Ploughshares* was founded here. ✉ *912 Massachusetts Ave., Cambridge* ☎ *617/576–0032* ⊕ *www. ploughandstars.com* Ⓜ *Central, Harvard.*

Temple Bar. The chef here emphasizes house-made everything—entreés to condiments. After exploring Cambridge, kick back with a signature barrel-aged cocktail and savory gin or rum concoctions at the copper bar. Be prepared to be impressed by lamb sliders and garganelli Bolognese. There is no live entertainment; events are taste-oriented, like Negroni Week. ■TIP➔ There's free parking in the rear after 6 pm. ✉ *1688 Massachusetts Ave., Cambridge* ☎ *617/547–5055* ⊕ *templebar-cambridge.com* Ⓜ *Porter, Harvard.*

Fodor's Choice
★   **Toad.** Bands, beers, and burgers sum up this amiable little Porter Square club attached to Christopher's. The bar is maple, the toads ceramic. Nightly music comes in many a stripe, and usually in double bills at 7 and 10 pm. Check out Sunday spins after 5 pm: bring your own vinyl. Twelve taps, Toad T-shirts, and never a cover charge: What's not to like? ✉ *1912 Massachusetts Ave., Cambridge* ☎ *617/497–4950 recording* ⊕ *www.toadcambridge.com* Ⓜ *Porter.*

BOWLING ALLEYS AND POOL HALLS

Flat Top Johnny's. In a mixed commercial and high-tech business park in Kendall Square, Flat Top Johnny's wears its hipster cred on its sleeve. This genuine pool hall (12 tournament-size, red-felt tables, $6/hour 11–6 pm, $12/hour 6 pm–1 am) also offers darts and pinball. Artwork by local painters hangs on exposed-brick walls; the sonic landscape veers between alternative rock and metal, chosen by the tattooed and pierced staff. Bartenders tap from Cambridge's finest craft brews, and that's saying something. Local musicians hang out here when not gigging and rehearsing. ⊠ *1 Kendall Sq., Bldg. 200, Cambridge* ☎ *617/494–9565* ⊕ *www.flattopjohnnys.com* Ⓜ *Kendall/MIT.*

CAFÉS AND COFFEEHOUSES

Café Algiers. Cozy, clustered tables fill both floors at this genuine Middle Eastern café, where you can peer at soaring, wood-paneled cathedral ceilings as you listen to classical music. The updated menu at this beloved Harvard Square landmark includes beer and wine, as well as pita bread, hummus, tabbouleh, varied salads, exotic teas, and strong coffee—Arabic or Turkish, brewed in a brass *briki* (brass or copper pot). Service tends toward low key; visit when you're in the mood to linger over conversation or a novel. ⊠ *40 Brattle St., Cambridge* ☎ *617/492–1557* Ⓜ *Harvard.*

Club Passim. Joan Baez, Bob Dylan, Josh Ritter, Lake Street Dive—thousands of folkies have strummed and warbled their way through Club Passim, one of America's oldest (1958) and most renowned clubs for Americana and roots music. The cozy brick basement has a new kitchen that's open for weekday lunch to all, but dinner is only available to ticket holders. If you travel with your guitar, call about open-mike nights. Classes and workshops at their school around the corner carry on folk traditions. Acoustic bands perform here nightly; expect to pay a $10–$20 cover. ⊠ *47 Palmer St., Cambridge* ☎ *617/492–7679 box office* ⊕ *www.passim.org* Ⓜ *Harvard.*

1369 Coffeehouse. Quirky characters rub elbows with book-writing professors and tweeting students at this Cambridge institution devoted to espresso and cold-brewed iced coffee (also delivered in growlers). Staffers pride themselves on intensive "barista jedi" training, though locally sourced spiced apple cider is favored in the cool months. Serving pastries galore, daily quiches, cookies, sandwiches, and salads, this café and its Central Square location (757 Massachusetts Avenue) are packed until 10 pm. ⊠ *1369 Cambridge St., Cambridge* ☎ *617/576–1369* ⊕ *www.1369coffeehouse.com* Ⓜ *Bus 69, 83, or 91.*

COMEDY CLUBS

Comedy Studio. Located on the third floor at the Hong Kong in Harvard Square, this comedy club serves up platters of silly offerings, including a host of local and touring comedians. Feast on reasonably priced Chinese dishes (and a Scorpion Bowl or two) between smiles. ∎TIP➔ **All shows begin at 8 pm.** ⊠ *1238 Massachusetts Ave., Cambridge* ☎ *617/661–6507* ⊕ *www.thecomedystudio.com* 🎫 *$10–$15* Ⓜ *Harvard.*

Fodor's Choice ★ **Improv Asylum.** Comedians weave audience suggestions into shows (seven nights a week, and Saturday matinees) that blend comic improv and topical sketches. Shows are never the same; midnight performances on Friday and Saturday have raucous, R-rated comedy. Most shows (ranging from $15 to $28) tend to sell out, so get there early or call ahead. ⊠ *216 Hanover St., North End* ☎ *617/263–6887* ⊕ *www.improvasylum.com* 🎫 *$15–$28* Ⓜ *Haymarket, North Station.*

ImprovBoston. This Central Square venue flips audience cues into situation comedy, complete with theme songs and commercials. Be careful when you go to the restroom—you might be pulled onstage. Performers may face off in improv competitions judged by audiences. Shows

Candlepin Bowling

Pool halls in Boston make a popular winter refuge for teens and collegiates (though some ban under-18s). Forget Paul Newman and smoky interiors: Boston likes its billiards halls swanky and well-lit, with polished brass and dark wood. Many do double duty as bowling alleys. Be forewarned, however, that in New England bowling is often "candlepin," with smaller balls and different rules.

It was back in 1880 that Justin White trimmed the size of his pins at his Worcester, Massachusetts, bowling hall, giving birth to candlepin bowling, a locally popular pint-size version of tenpin bowling. Now played almost exclusively in northern New England and in the Canadian Maritime Provinces, candlepin bowling is a game of power and accuracy.

Paradoxically, candlepin bowling is both easier and far more difficult than regular bowling. The balls are significantly smaller, like boccie balls, weigh less than 3 pounds, and have no finger holes. Thus, players of all ages and abilities can whip the ball down the alley. But because both the ball and the pins are lighter, it is more difficult to bowl strikes and spares. Players are allowed three throws per frame, and bowlers may hit fallen pins ("wood" or "deadwood") to knock down other pins. There has never been a perfect "300" score: the world record is 245. Good players will score around 100 to 110, and novice players should be proud of a score of 90.

Among the handful of alleys in and around Boston, many maintain and celebrate their own quirky charm and history.

Boston Bowl. This Dorchester mainstay is open 24 hours a day, and attracts a more adult crowd. It has pool tables, a game room, both tenpin and candlepin bowling, and a restaurant and bar. ■TIP➜ Call ahead to reserve a lane as bowling leagues snap them up pretty quickly. ⊠ *820 Morrissey Blvd., Dorchester* ☎ *617/825–3800* ⊕ *www.bostonbowl.com* Ⓜ *JFK/UMass.*

Needham Bowlaway. Founded in 1917, this tiny alley's eight cramped lanes are tucked away down a flight of stairs. Fans say Bowlaway is like bowling in your own basement. The charge is $25 per lane per hour. Note that this is a drive-to destination, though it's a short walk from Needham Center train station. ⊠ *16 Chestnut St., Needham* ☎ *781/449–4060* ⊕ *www.needhambowl.com.*

Sacco's Bowl Haven. The '50s decor here "makes bowling the way it was, the way it is." Run by the Sacco family until 2010, the building and alleys in the heart of Davis Square were bought and are maintained by Flatbread Company pizzeria. Its 10 lanes are open daily until midnight (11 pm Sunday), and cost $30 per hour; there's a $3 fee to rent shoes. You can bowl away and enjoy organic pizza. ⊠ *45 Day St., Somerville* ☎ *617/776–0552* ⊕ *www.flatbread-company.com/sacco.*

run Wednesday through Sunday, $10 to $18. You may need that beer and wine bar. ⊠ *40 Prospect St., Cambridge* ☏ *617/576–1253* ⊕ *www. improvboston.com* Ⓜ *Central.*

Laugh Boston. Located in the Westin Waterfront Hotel in the rapidly developing Waterfront neighborhood, Laugh Boston is the stand-up sibling to the North End's Improv Asylum. Known for bringing in local and national acts like Michael Ian Black and Jamie Lee, shows are at 8 pm on Wednesday and Thursday and at 8 and 10:15 pm on Friday and Saturday. A light fare menu of appetizers, panini, and desserts is available. ■TIP➔ **Laugh is 18plus, unless accompanied by an adult.** ⊠ *Westin Waterfront Hotel, 425 Summer St., Waterfront* ☏ *617/725–2844* ⊕ *www.laughboston.com* Ⓜ *South Station.*

MUSIC CLUBS

Beat Brasserie. An American brasserie and bar located in the heart of Harvard Square, Beat is inspired by the hippie and beat movements of the mid-twentieth century. There's daily live music by cutting-edge musicians in jazz, blues, and world music, and the bar celebrates American spirits and American artisanal wines crafted by small-batch winemakers with heart and soul. A fresh, seasonal, and wholesome menu includes dishes that draw influence and flavors from around the world. ⊠ *13 Brattle St., Harvard Square* ☏ *617/499–0001* ⊕ *www.beatbrasserie. com* Ⓜ *Harvard.*

Fodor's Choice ★ **Cantab Lounge.** This place hums every night with live bands cranking out rhythm and blues, soul, funk, rock, or bluegrass. The theme-driven bar hosts open-mike performers (Monday) bluegrass (Tuesday), poetry slams (Wednesday), and soul and funk (Thursday). Its diverse twenties-to-forties crowd is friendly and informal, and loves to get up and dance. ⊠ *738 Massachusetts Ave., Cambridge* ☏ *617/354–2685* ⊕ *www.cantab-lounge.com* Ⓜ *Central.*

Lizard Lounge. Low-key Lizard Lounge is a subterranean nightspot that features experimental and cult bands. Seven nights a week hear folk, pop, rock, acid jazz, reggae, and neo-funk band Club d'Elf, and cabaret. Poetry is featured Sunday and open-mike night is Monday. There's a full bar, cocktail list, and 30 brews on tap, and the dinner menu is available every night until midnight. ⊠ *1667 Massachusetts Ave., between Harvard and Porter Sqs., Cambridge* ☏ *617/547–0759* ⊕ *www.lizard-loungeclub.com* Ⓜ *Harvard, Porter.*

Fodor's Choice ★ **Middle East & ZuZu Restaurant & Nightclub.** This nightclub has balanced its kebab-and-falafel menu with three ever-active performance spaces to carve its niche as one of New England's most eclectic alternative-rock venues. National and local acts vie for the large upstairs and cavernous downstairs rooms, while intimate combos play ZuZu's and the tiny Corner. Phenoms like the Mighty Mighty Bosstones got their start here. Music-world celebs drop by when playing in town. There's also belly dancing, folk, jazz, country-rock, and dancing at ZuZu. Nightly shows at 8 pm usually run $10 to $20. ⊠ *472–480 Massachusetts Ave., Cambridge* ☏ *617/497–0576, 617/864–3278 recorded line* ⊕ *www. mideastoffers.com* Ⓜ *Central.*

Outpost 186. This back-alley arts and performance space hosts experimental jazz and improvised music, film, multimedia, poetry, and graphic arts. But don't expect to order up a cocktail or snack; 186 doesn't serve anything besides music and chairs. Master guitarist Mick Goodrick accompanies figure drawing classes Sunday morning as "right brain sanctuary." Watch the online video to find your way to the space. All shows are at 8 pm unless otherwise noted. ⊠ *186½ Hampshire St., Inman Square* ⊕ *www.outpost186.com* ✉ *Suggested donation $10* Ⓜ *Central.*

Regattabar. Located inside Cambridge's Charles Hotel, Regattabar features regular favorites including leading men (Ron Carter, Joe Lovano, Lee Konitz), top guitarists (John Scofield, Mike Stern, Pat Martino), and local favorites. Tickets for shows run about $20–$40. The dimly lit 220-seat club with subtle nautical decor offers tasty fare and drinks. ⊠ *Charles Hotel, 1 Bennett St., Cambridge* ☎ *617/661–5000 calendar, 617/395–7757 tickets* ⊕ *www.regattabarjazz.com* Ⓜ *Harvard.*

Ryles Jazz Club. Soft lights, mirrors, and good barbecue set the mood for fine jazz on the ground-floor main stage, host to a steady showcase since the 1960s of new bands, favored locals, and national stars. Ryles's upstairs dance hall has earned its spurs as a sizzling Latin dancers' destination, especially on Noche Latina Tuesdays, when there's both lessons and dancing. There's world music, Brazilian, and open mike for jazz singers. Sunday jazz brunch requires reservations. Covers vary ($10–$20) and there is free parking for patrons. ⊠ *212 Hampshire St., Cambridge* ☎ *617/876–9330* ⊕ *www.ryles.com* Ⓜ *Bus 69, 83, or 91.*

The Sinclair. Bringing a long-awaited sophisticated rock music and dining venue to Harvard Square, The Sinclair's adventurous, near-nightly lineup of indie rock—with enticing flings into world, electronica, and jazz—often sells out. Its adjacent but quite separate restaurant and bar, with wanderlusty train and highway decor, serious beverage list, creative mixology, and cuisine inspired by regional Americana, is proving to be a winning formula. Accommodating 500, here's a party made to order for transient, academic, and streetwise grown-ups. ⊠ *52 Church St., Harvard Square* ☎ *617/547–5200* ⊕ *www.sinclaircambridge.com* Ⓜ *Harvard.*

SALSA CLUBS

Havana Club. At the Greek American Political Club overlooking Central Square, this 5,400-square-foot ballroom dance floor hosts a kaleidoscope of DJs and live bands, and often free burritos or nachos. Three hundred people may show up to dance salsa, creating a lively scene for dancers at any level. Open Monday is for bachata (sultry midtempo Dominican dance) and Friday and Saturday for salsa; with lessons at 9, the joint really gets hopping by 10 pm. ⊠ *288 Green St., Cambridge* ☎ *617/312–5550* ⊕ *www.havanaclubsalsa.com* Ⓜ *Central.*

Ryles. This jazz club's upstairs room hosts the city's friendliest Latin dance scenes. Noche Latina Tuesdays offer salsa lessons for newcomers with experts (lessons start 7 pm); then you can dance the night away. There's also merengue, bachata, and reggaeton. ⊠ *212 Hampshire St., Cambridge* ☎ *617/876–9330* ⊕ *www.ryles.com/dancing.cfm* ✉ *Cover $10–$15* Ⓜ *Bus 68 or 69.*

SOMERVILLE

Once marginal and blue-collar, crowded Somerville is now very cool. Look at Davis Square: a hub for the T and bike paths, the square's alive with cafés, clubs, a large theater, and ethnic eateries serving BBQ, sushi, wood-fired pizza, curry, bangers and mash, pad thai, and soba. It's a prime gathering spot for Tufts University students, vintage hippies, and young thinkers, and even hosts local festivals, like Davis ArtBeat and Honk! You can catch bands in storefront bars and cafés along Somerville Avenue and Washington Street.

BARS

Fodor's Choice ★ **The Burren.** Your true-emerald Irish music pub pulls in devoted locals and all fans of *craic* (enjoyable environment). Enthusiastic staff and professional bartenders expertly pour Guinness on tap and serve comfort food (fish-and-chips, bangers-and-mash, Irish stew, shepherd's pie). Pleasing decor, a sunny west-facing patio, an old-wood library bar, and slate specials add to the allure of live Irish music—acoustic groups—most nights in both the Front and Back Rooms. On weekends, check out the jazz brunch or the Beatles brunch. ⊠ *247 Elm St., Somerville* ☎ *617/776–6896* ⊕ *www.burren.com* Ⓜ *Davis.*

The Independent. In Somerville's Union Square, this comfortable neighborhood bar is a good spot to hit for a pint, martini, summertime gin-based cocktail with a quaint name ($10), and quality brews (36 drafts, 60 bottles). Brunch options include maple-bacon doughnuts and quinoa patties. ⊠ *75 Union Sq., Somerville* ☎ *617/440–6022* ⊕ *www.theindo. com* Ⓜ *Bus 86, 87, 91, CT2.*

Orleans. This American bar and restaurant opens floor-to-ceiling windows onto busy Holland Street and 15 all-sports screens onto diners and drinkers, excluding the patio. Nightly themes include trivia Wednesday and throwback Thursday with DJs for dancing, and there are weekend brunches. ⊠ *65 Holland St., Somerville* ☎ *617/591–2100* ⊕ *www. orleansrestaurant.com* Ⓜ *Davis.*

CAFÉS AND COFFEEHOUSES

Diesel Cafe. This bright, window-y corner spot with bold local artwork and spacious tables draws in Davis Square hipsters, Tufts students, and the LGBT sets. Luxuriate over crafted salads, soups, and wraps, house-made pastries, and gourmet coffee from Intelligentsia. Shoot pool, take selfies in a photo booth (!), or surf the Net. ⊠ *257 Elm St., Somerville* ☎ *617/629–8717* ⊕ *www.diesel-cafe.com* Ⓜ *Davis.*

MUSIC CLUBS

Fodor's Choice ★ **Somerville Theatre.** This keystone of Davis Square's growing culture presents films (five screens) and easily 40 concerts a year (The Boss, Adele, U2, and Louis CK have all played here). The 900-seat theater celebrates its centennial this year with special events and performances. In the coffered-ceiling, stone-tiled foyer you may buy beer, wine, popcorn, and ice cream to enjoy during the show. ⊠ *55 Davis Sq., Somerville* ☎ *617/625–5700* ⊕ *www.somervilletheatreonline.com* Ⓜ *Davis.*

PERFORMING ARTS

DANCE

Boston Dance Alliance. This group serves as a clearinghouse for an amazing array of local dance companies' classes, performances, and workshops. Visit the alliance's website for upcoming performances and venues. ⊠ *19 Clarendon St., South End* ☎ *617/456–6295* ⊕ *www.bostondancealliance.org* Ⓜ *Back Bay.*

BALLET

Boston Ballet. The city's premier dance company performs at the Boston Opera House. 2018 shows include *Romeo & Juliet*, Classic Balanchine, and *La Sylphide*. And of course, if you're visiting during the holidays, be sure to score seats to The *Nutcracker*. ⊠ *19 Clarendon St., South End* ☎ *617/695–6955* ⊕ *www.bostonballet.org* Ⓜ *Back Bay.*

José Mateo's Ballet Theatre. This troupe is building an exciting, contemporary repertory under Cuban-born José Mateo, the resident artistic director-choreographer. Performances, which include an original *Nutcracker,* take place October through April at the **Sanctuary Theatre,** a beautifully converted former church at Massachusetts Avenue and Harvard Street in Harvard Square. The vibe is intimate with cabaret-style seating. ⊠ *400 Harvard St., Cambridge* ☎ *617/354–7467* ⊕ *www.balletheatre.org* Ⓜ *Harvard.*

CONTEMPORARY

Dance Complex. Performances (and classes and workshops) by local and visiting choreographers take place at Odd Fellows Hall, an intimate space that draws a multicultural crowd. Styles range from classical ballet to contemporary and world dance. ⊠ *536 Massachusetts Ave., Central Sq., Cambridge* ☎ *617/547–9363* ⊕ *www.dancecomplex.org* Ⓜ *Central.*

FOLK/MULTICULTURAL

Multicultural Arts Center. The MAC in East Cambridge supports diversity through the performing arts. They put on jazz, dance, and visiting arts programs, and have two spacious galleries showcasing international visual arts. Galleries are open 10:30 am–6 pm and performances are usually Thursday and Saturday at 8 pm. ⊠ *41 2nd St., Cambridge* ☎ *617/577–1400* ⊕ *www.multiculturalartscenter.org* Ⓜ *Lechmere.*

World Music/CRASHarts. As the metro area's premier presenter of worldwide music and dance, World Music/CRASHarts has a truly global roster featuring exciting contemporary artists in their Boston debuts (like The Bad Plus and Freshlyground), as well as world music icons such as South Africa's Ladysmith Black Mambazo and Ireland's Mary Black. Its annual blockbuster Flamenco Festival packs the Cutler Majestic Theater. Performances unfold at many venues such as Somerville Theatre, Berklee Performance Center, Sinclair, Sanders Theatre, and the Paradise Rock Club. ⊠ *720 Massachusetts Ave., Central Sq., Cambridge* ☎ *617/876–4275* ⊕ *www.worldmusic.org* Ⓜ *Central.*

FILM

12

With its large population of academics and intellectuals, Boston has its share of discerning moviegoers and movie houses, especially in Brookline and Cambridge. Theaters at suburban malls and in Downtown may have better screens, if less adventurous fare. The *Boston Globe* has daily listings in the "Living/Arts" section; the *Boston Herald* Friday "Scene" section and the *Improper Bostonian* "Movies" section list films for the week. Movies cost $9–$13. Many theaters have half-price matinees, often rescinded during the opening run of a major film.

Brattle Theatre. A classic moviegoer's iconic den with 230 seats, Brattle Theatre shows classic movies, new foreign and indie films, theme series, and directors' cuts. Tickets sell out for its Valentine's Day screenings of *Casablanca*; the Bugs Bunny Film Festival in February; *Trailer Treats,* an annual fundraiser featuring classic and modern movie previews; and DocYard, a stunning series of documentaries. At Christmastime, expect seasonal movies like *It's a Wonderful Life* and *Holiday Inn.* Enjoy a rotating selection of local beers and wines. ⌧ *40 Brattle St., Harvard Sq., Cambridge* ☎ *617/876–6837* ⊕ *brattlefilm.org* Ⓜ *Harvard.*

Fodor's Choice
★
Coolidge Corner Theatre. This lovingly restored art deco theater presents an eclectic and exciting selection of world cinema: first-run art films, foreign films, documentaries, and classics. Two intimate screening rooms also offer occasional special programming highlighting experimental films and video. The independent nonprofit art house also holds book readings, private events, and popular midnight cult movies. One of Coolidge's signature programs is Science on Screen, a creative pairing of films with introductions by renowned science experts; the program has expanded to more than 50 independent theaters nationwide. ⌧ *290 Harvard St., Brookline* ☎ *617/734–2501, 617/734–2500 recorded info* ⊕ *www.coolidge.org* Ⓜ *Coolidge Corner.*

Harvard Film Archive. Screening independent, foreign, classic, and experimental films rarely seen in commercial cinemas, Harvard Film Archive is open to the public Friday through Monday. The 200-seat theater, with pristine film and digital projection, is located in the basement of the stunning brick-and-glass Carpenter Visual Arts Center, Le Corbusier's only American building. Tickets are $9; seniors and students, $7. ⌧ *Carpenter Center for the Visual Arts, 24 Quincy St., Cambridge* ☎ *617/495–4700* ⊕ *hcl.harvard.edu/hfa* Ⓜ *Harvard.*

Institute of Contemporary Art/Boston. Its stunning waterfront location and modern design are reason enough to visit the ICA/B, but its screening of edgy art flicks, award-winning foreign films, experimental visual media, and documentaries deserves a second look. ⌧ *100 Northern Ave., Waterfront* ☎ *617/478–3100* ⊕ *www.ica.org* Ⓜ *South Station, Courthouse, World Trade Center.*

Kendall Square Cinema. This cinema's nine screens are devoted to first-run independent and foreign films, and the concession stand offers hip goodies like coffee, empanadas, and homemade cookies. Note: 1 Kendall Square stands where Hampshire Street meets Broadway, a 10-minute walk from the Kendall Square T station. A free Galleria Mall shuttle runs from the T by the theater, Monday through

BIG-PICTURE BOSTON

Boston's ethnic enclaves, crooked cops, and love for the Red Sox have featured prominently in box-office hits. In addition to recent movies, like *Patriots Day, Ted 2, The Equalizer, Black Mass,* and *American Hustle,* here are some films with significant Boston cameos:

The Company Men (2010)

The Social Network (2010)

The Town (2010)

Gone Baby Gone (2007)

The Departed (2006)

Fever Pitch (2005)

Mystic River (2003)

Legally Blonde (2001)

Next Stop Wonderland (1998)

Good Will Hunting (1997)

Saturday from 9 to 7 and Sunday from noon to 7. Validated four-hour parking ($3) is available in an adjacent garage. ■TIP➔ If you're walking, be advised the area can get a bit desolate at night. ⊠ *1 Kendall Sq., Cambridge* ☎ *617/621–1202* ⊕ *www.landmarktheatres.com* Ⓜ *Kendall/MIT.*

Museum of Fine Arts. Recognized as one of the country's leading independent film showcases, MFA Film presents more than 500 screenings a year including foreign and classic films. They also host ten annual festivals including the Boston Jewish, French, Iranian, and Palestine film festivals. Theatergoers can grab snacks and drinks at the nearby Taste Café and Wine Bar, which is also a great spot for postfilm discussions. ⊠ *465 Huntington Ave.* ☎ *800/440–6975 box office,* 617/267–9300 ⊕ *www.mfa.org/programs/film* ⊠ *Tickets $11, though special screenings sometimes have a higher price* Ⓜ *Museum of Fine Arts, Ruggles.*

MUSIC

For its size, Boston has a great diversity and variety of live music choices. *(See also Music Clubs in Nightlife, above.)* Supplementing appearances by nationally known artists are performers from the area's many colleges and conservatories, which also provide music series, performing spaces, and audiences. Berklee College of Music has made itself especially visible, with student (and/or faculty) ensembles popping up at formal and informal venues far and wide, especially in summer months, playing mainly jazz, blues, rock, indie, pop, and world music.

Classical music aficionados love the Boston Symphony Orchestra, which performs at Symphony Hall October through early May and at Tanglewood Music Center in Lenox, Massachusetts, from late June through August. A favorite of TV audiences, the Boston Pops presents concerts of "lighter music" from May to July and during December. Throughout the year choose from an active roster of orchestral, chamber, and choral ensembles that enrich Boston's musical ambience.

Boston also has emerged as the nation's capital of early-music performance. Dozens of small groups, often made up of performers who have one foot in the university and another on the concert stage, play pre 18th century music on period instruments, often in small churches where the acoustics resemble the venues in which some of this music was first performed.

CHORAL GROUPS

It's hard to imagine another city with more active choral groups than Boston. Many outstanding choruses are associated with Boston schools and churches.

Boston Cecilia. Founded in 1876, this choral group is especially noted for period-instrument performances of Handel and Bach, and works by undersung contemporary composers. Its concerts are held regularly at Jordan Hall, Church of the Advent, and All Saints (Brookline). ☎ 617/232–4540 ⊕ www.bostoncecilia.org.

Cantata Singers. Cantata Singers perform choral music from many eras—renaissance (e.g., Claudio Monteverdi), Bach, and Mendelssohn to the present (e.g., John Harbison, Elena Ruehr). Concerts in Jordan Hall and First Church in Cambridge and Cary Hall in Lexington. ⊠ 729 Boylston St., Suite 305, Back Bay ☎ 617/868–5885 ⊕ www.cantatasingers.org Ⓜ Copley.

Chorus Pro Musica. This dynamic chorus, tackling classics (Bach, Vaughan Williams, Stravinsky) and modern works (Rautavaara, Poulenc, Pinkham) under the baton of young music director Jamie Kirsch, presents fall, holiday, and spring concerts at venues throughout Greater Boston. ⊠ Administrative office, 645 Boylston St. ☎ 617/267–7442 ⊕ www.choruspromusica.org.

CHURCH CONCERTS

Boston's churches have outstanding music programs. The Saturday Boston Globe and Boston Musical Intelligencer list performance schedules.

Emmanuel Music. At Emmanuel Church, known as "the Bach church" since 1970, the master's cantatas are sung during Holy Eucharist services on Sunday at 10 am, between September and May. The concerts, performed by a professional chamber orchestra and chorus, are among Boston's musical gems; tickets start at $30. Inquire about free Thursday noon concerts in Lindsey Chapel in February and March. ⊠ 15 Newbury St., Back Bay ☎ 617/536–3356 ⊕ www.emmanuelmusic.org Ⓜ Arlington.

Trinity Church. H.H. Richardson's 1877 neo-Romanesque masterwork is the centerpiece of Copley Square and a must-visit on any Back Bay tour. Trinity Boston Foundation presents free half-hour organ or choir recitals on Fridays at 12:15 pm, as well as seasonal choral concerts, in the magnificently textured and vaulted apse. The church is open daily from 9 to 5. Tours are self-guided ($7) or by group arranged through the church bookstore. Sunday services are at 7:45 am, 9 am, and 6 pm. ⊠ Trinity Church, 206 Clarendon St., Copley Sq., Back Bay ☎ 617/536–0944 ⊕ trinitychurchboston.org Ⓜ Back Bay/South End, Copley.

Frugal Fun

If you're feeling the pinch, you can be entertained at these locales without dropping a dime.

See a film, explore the galleries, or enjoy the courtyard café at the **Boston Public Library.**

Go baroque—but not broke—with classical and contemporary concerts performed by the Boston University Symphony Orchestra, Alea III, or College of Fine Arts faculty members at the **Tsai Performance Center.**

Head to **Trinity Church** for free Friday organ or choir recitals at 12:15 pm.

Get spirits up with jazz and blues at **Wally's Café** and **939**, where talented students from the Berklee College of Music perform.

Buy a coffee or smoothie, and surf the Web with free Wi-Fi at **Trident Booksellers & Café.**

See art in the making: check out one of the weekend **Boston Open Studios** events (⊕ *www.cityofboston. gov/arts/visual/openstudios.asp*) in neighborhoods throughout the city.

CONCERT HALLS

Berklee Performance Center. The main stage for the internationally renowned Berklee College of Music, the "BPC" is best known for its jazz and pop programs, but also hosts folk, world, and rock acts, and pop stars like Talking Heads, Aimee Mann, Snarky Puppy, and Melody Gardot. Bargain alert: BPC stages a wealth of excellent student and faculty shows, and showcases sets and clinics by visiting artists that cost next to nothing. ⊠ *136 Massachusetts Ave., Back Bay* ☎ *617/266–7455 box office, 617/747–2261 performance center* ⊕ *www.berklee.edu/BPC* Ⓜ *Hynes.*

Blue Hills Bank Pavilion. Up to 5,000 people gather on the waterfront in a huge white tent for breathtaking summertime concerts. National headliners—such as Florence & The Machine, Widespread Panic, Barenaked Ladies, Umphrey's McGee, Modest Mouse—play here from June through September. In chilly months, the scene turns to presenter Live Nation's Xfinity Center. Purchase tickets at Orpheum Theater or Ticketmaster. ⊠ *290 Northern Ave., South Boston* ☎ *617/728–1600* ⊕ *www. livenation.com/venues/14347/blue-hills-bank-pavilion* Ⓜ *South Station, World Trade Center.*

Boston Opera House. The glittering, regilded Boston Opera House hosts plays, musicals, and traveling Broadway shows (long runs for *Wicked, Once*) and has also booked performers as diverse as Sarah Brightman, Pat Metheny, and the late B.B. King. The magnificent building, constructed in 1926, also hosts Boston Ballet's iconic holiday sellout, Tchaikovsky's *Nutcracker.* ⊠ *539 Washington St., Downtown* ☎ *617/259–3400* ⊕ *www.bostonoperahouse.com* Ⓜ *Boylston, Chinatown, Downtown Crossing, Park St.*

Hatch Memorial Shell. On the bank of the Charles River, this wonderful acoustic shell, 100 feet wide and wood inlaid, is home to Boston Pops' famous Fourth of July concert and dozens of other free summer classical-orchestra concerts, zumba dance shows, and other events. Local radio stations air music shows and festivals here from April through October. Friday Flicks, often animated for children, are screened at sunset. ✉ *Off Storrow Dr. at embankment, Beacon Hill* ☎ *617/626–4970* Ⓜ *Charles/MGH, Arlington.*

Institute of Contemporary Art/Boston. This dazzling waterfront museum hosts experimental electronic, jazz, and world musicians, often in partnership with World Music/CRASHArts or Berklee College of Music. Expect the unexpected—concerts might contain a mix of disparate instruments, fusions of melody and spoken word, or DJs grooving electronica mashups. There are early evening concerts, and an open-air summertime series. ✉ *100 Northern Ave., Waterfront* ☎ *617/478–3100* ⊕ *www.icaboston. org* Ⓜ *South Station, Courthouse, World Trade Center.*

New England Conservatory's Jordan Hall. One of the world's acoustic treasures, New England Conservatory's Jordan Hall is ideal for solo and string quartet recitals yet spacious enough for chamber and full orchestras. The pin-drop intimacy of this all wood, 1,000 seat hall is in demand year-round for ensembles visiting and local. Boston Philharmonic and Boston Baroque perform here regularly. Dozens of free faculty and student concerts, jazz and classical, are a best-kept secret. ■TIP➔ The lobby box office is open 1½ hours before the start of any ticketed show, in addition to its normal daytime hours. ✉ *30 Gainsborough St., Back Bay* ☎ *617/585–1260 box office* ⊕ *necmusic.edu* Ⓜ *Symphony.*

Fodor'sChoice ★ **Sanders Theatre.** This gilt-wood jewel box of a stage is the preferred venue for many of Boston's classical orchestras and the home of Harvard University's many ensembles. The 180-degree stage design and superb acoustics afford intimacy and crystal projection. A favorite of folk, jazz, and world-music performers, the 1,000 seat Sanders hosts the holiday favorite, *Christmas Revels,* a traditional participatory Yule celebration. Winston Churchill, Martin Luther King, Wynton Marsalis, Leonard Bernstein, and Oprah Winfrey have lectured at this famed seat of oratory and music. ✉ *Harvard University, 45 Quincy St., Harvard Sq., Cambridge* ☎ *617/496–2222 box office* ⊕ *www.fas.harvard. edu/~memhall/sanders.html* Ⓜ *Harvard.*

Fodor'sChoice ★ **Symphony Hall.** One of the world's best acoustical concert halls—some say *the* best—has been home since 1900 to the Boston Symphony Orchestra (BSO) and the Boston Pops. Led by conductor Keith Lockhart, the Pops concerts take place in May and June and around the winter holidays. The hall is also used by visiting orchestras, chamber groups, soloists, and local ensembles. Rehearsals and daytime concerts for students are open to the public, with discounted tickets. ✉ *301 Massachusetts Ave., Back Bay* ☎ *617/266–1492* ⊕ *www.bso.org* Ⓜ *Symphony.*

TD Garden. New England's largest sports and entertainment arena, the TD Garden hosts concerts by big-name artists (Adele, Red Hot Chili Peppers, Katy Perry, Ed Sheeran, Imagine Dragons, and Kendrick Lamar to name a few) and special events (WWE, Disney On Ice, Harlem Globetrotters). The Garden is also home to NHL's Boston Bruins and NBA's Boston Celtics. ✉ *100 Legends Way, Old West End* ☎ *617/624–1000 event info line* ⊕ *www.tdgarden.com* Ⓜ *North Station.*

12

Tsai Performance Center. Boston University's Tsai Performance Center presents mostly free, mainly classical concerts by student, faculty, and professional groups. The Jeannette Neill Dance Studio, Alea III, JACK and Muir Quartets, and Boston Musica Viva are regular guests in this exquisitely proportioned and acoustically perfect 500-seat theater. ⊠ *685 Commonwealth Ave., Kenmore Square* ☎ *617/353–6467, 617/353–8725 box office* ⊕ *www.bu.edu/tsai* Ⓜ *Boston University East.*

CONCERT SERIES

FodorsChoice ★ **Boston Public Library.** Completed in 1895, the Central Library in Copley Square's McKim building is known for its classical serenity and elegance, and includes Bates Hall's majestic barrel-arched ceiling, John Singer Sargent murals, and an interior courtyard that plays host to the summer Concerts in the Courtyard series (June through August, Wednesday at 6 pm, Friday at 12:30 pm). There are also free daily Art and Architecture tours. The Central Library's Johnson building, reopened to the public in July 2016 after a multiyear renovation, is an open and vibrant space, while the new Newsfeed Cafe is home to a WGBH satellite radio and television studio that features live tapings of shows like Boston Public Radio, hosted by Jim Braude and Margery Eagan. ⊠ *700 Boylston St., Copley Sq., Back Bay* ☎ *617/536–5400* ⊕ *www.bpl.org* Ⓜ *Copley.*

Celebrity Series of Boston. This series presents about 50 signature events annually—renowned orchestras, chamber groups, jazz icons, international dance ensembles, and recitalists—at prestigious venues like Symphony Hall, Sanders Theatre, Jordan Hall, Pickman Hall, and Berklee Performance Center. In the prestigious mix you'll find cellist Yo-Yo Ma, Wynton Marsalis, author David Sedaris, pianist Emanuel Ax, *A Prarie Home Companion* host Chris Thile, and more. Top dance companies perform as well: Alvin Ailey American Dance Theater, Pilobolus, and more from around the globe. ⊠ *Administrative office, 20 Park Plaza, Suite 1032, Downtown* ☎ *617/482–6661* ⊕ *www.celebrityseries.org.*

FodorsChoice ★ **Isabella Stewart Gardner Museum.** Modeled after a Venetian palazzo, don't miss the unforgettable galleries that surround the museum's courtyard; it's home to masters such as Rembrandt, Raphael, Titian, Michelangelo, Whistler, and Sargent. The Renzo Piano wing provides a platform for contemporary artists, musicians, and scholars, and serves as an innovative venue where creativity is celebrated in all of its forms. The popular RISE Music Series features pop, rock, and hip-hop artists, while the STIR is an adventurous mix of contemporary art, music, and performance. ⊠ *25 Evans Way, The Fenway* ☎ *617/278–5156 box office, 617/566–1401 recorded info* ⊕ *www.gardnermuseum.org* 🎟 *$15; concert tickets extra* Ⓜ *Museum of Fine Arts, Fenway.*

Museum of Fine Arts. At the annual Concerts in the Courtyard series, enjoy jazz, blues, and folk concerts in the outdoor courtyard on Wednesday summer evenings. Otherwise, music happens at Remis Auditorium or the soaring glass Shapiro courtyard. First Fridays (free with admission, but secure advance tickets) draw young professionals who dance to DJ music. ⊠ *465 Huntington Ave., The Fenway* ☎ *800/440–6975 ticket sales, 617/369–3395 general number* ⊕ *www.mfa.org/programs/music* 🎟 *Free with admission* Ⓜ *Museum of Fine Arts.*

EARLY-MUSIC GROUPS

Boston Baroque. Founded by conductor Martin Pearlman as "Banchetto Musicale" in 1974, Boston Baroque showcases soloists and guest musicians in precision period-instrument performances of Bach, Handel, Vivaldi, Rameau, and Mozart operas. The holiday-season *Messiah* is a stunner; the 1992 CD version was the first of three Grammy nominations. Performances are held at Jordan Hall and Sanders Theatre in Cambridge. ☎ *617/484-9200* ⊕ *www.bostonbaroque.org.*

12

Boston Camerata. Founded in 1954, Boston Camerata has achieved international celebrity, thanks to its passionate commitment and popular recordings. Its loyal cadre of dedicated professional singers and early instrumentalists perform an extensive repertoire of exquisitely detailed medieval, renaissance, baroque, and American music—often themed and seasonal—in churches and concert halls worldwide. ☎ *617/262-2092* ⊕ *www.bostoncamerata.org.*

Boston Early Music Festival. Attune your ears to the rare sounds of theorbos, sackbuts, viols, rebecs, and shawms! Join the 15,000 dyed-in-the-wool early-music devotees who visit Boston each mid-June in odd-number years, when the biennial Boston Early Music Festival takes over the city for a week-long cavalcade of performances: opera, orchestra, chamber, solo recitals. Featured in 2017 were the operas Campra's *Le Carnaval de Venise* and Pergolesi's *La Serva Padrona & Livietta e Tracollo*, as well as many other concerts. The Festival also produces an annual concert series of medieval, renaissance, and baroque performances and master classes at the usual venues. ✉ *43 Thorndike St., Cambridge* ☎ *617/661-1812* ⊕ *www.bemf.org* Ⓜ *Lechmere.*

Handel & Haydn Society. Acclaimed for performances of baroque and classical music, the Handel & Haydn Society is one of the country's oldest performing arts organizations in America. The annual performances of Handel's *Messiah* have been a holiday favorite since 1854, and all concerts feature antique or replica instruments so the music is performed as it was the day it was written. Performances are held at Symphony Hall and other Boston venues. ☎ *617/266-3605 box office, 617/262-1815* ⊕ *www.handelandhaydn.org.*

ORCHESTRAS AND CHAMBER MUSIC

Boston Chamber Music Society. Under artistic directors Marcus Thompson and Ronald Thomas (emeritus), Boston Chamber Music Society performs the classical gamut from Mozart to Mahler to Britten at Harvard's Sanders Theatre or Cambridge Rindge and Latin's Fitzgerald Theatre. Starting in the 2017–18 season, the society began performing on Saturday morning at the Arlington Street Church in Back Bay. ☎ *617/349-0086* ⊕ *www.bostonchambermusic.org.*

Boston Philharmonic Orchestra. The charismatic Benjamin Zander—whose signature preconcert chats help audiences better understand the blockbuster symphonies they're about to hear—heads up Boston Philharmonic. Performances at Harvard's Sanders Theatre, New England Conservatory's Jordan Hall, Symphony Hall, and a variety of other locales often encompass symphonies by Beethoven, Mahler, Shostakovich, and Brahms, plus lots of concertos. ☎ *617/236-0999* ⊕ *www.bostonphil.org.*

Boston Pops. Under the agile baton of Keith Lockhart, Boston Pops (largely Boston Symphony musicians) perform a bracing blend of American standards, movie themes, and contemporary vocal numbers (with top-tier guests) during May and June at Symphony Hall, plus 40 festive holiday-season concerts. Outdoor concerts on July 3 and 4 at the Hatch Memorial Shell are followed by concerts at Boston Symphony Orchestra's summer home, Tanglewood in Lenox, Massachusetts, in July and August. The free outdoor concerts are packed; be sure to arrive early with blankets, folding chairs, and a picnic. ☎ *617/266–1492, 888/266–1200 box office* ⊕ *www.bso.org.*

Boston Symphony Orchestra. Founded in 1881, the Boston Symphony is one of America's oldest and most venerable orchestras, just two years under the baton of dynamic Latvian conductor Andris Nelsons. Its home season at Symphony Hall runs from September through April. In July and August the music migrates to Tanglewood, the orchestra's bucolic summer home in the Berkshire Mountains in Lenox, Massachusetts. Including tours to Carnegie Hall and China, and the Boston Pops concerts, the BSO performs more than 250 concerts annually. ⊠ *301 Massachusetts Ave., Back Bay* ☎ *617/266–1492, 888/266–1400 box office* ⊕ *www.bso.org* Ⓜ *Symphony.*

OPERA

Boston Lyric Opera. The critically acclaimed Boston Lyric Opera (BLO) stages four new operas each season that include traditional and updated versions of classics, as well as world premieres developed through its Opera Annex initiative. Recent productions include Puccini's *Tosca* ; the world premiere of *The Nefarious, Immoral but Highly Profitable Enterprise of Mr. Burke & Mr. Hare* by Julian Grant and Mark Campbell; Kurt Weill and Bertolt Brecht's pivotal *The Threepenny Opera*; and Leonard Bernstein's locally born 1954 one-act *Trouble in Tahiti*. ⊠ *11 Ave. de Lafayette, Downtown* ☎ *617/542–4912, 617/542–6772 audience services office* ⊕ *blo.org* ☜ *Tickets start at $25* Ⓜ *Boylston.*

Odyssey Opera of Boston. The former Boston Opera Company is under new management but with the same excellent conductor, Gil Rose. Odyssey Opera House presents classic and modern operas at various venues throughout the city including the Calderwood Pavilion at the Boston Center for the Arts, Jordan Hall, B.U. Theatre, and Suffolk University's Modern Theatre. ⊠ *Jordan Hall, 30 Gainsborough St.* ☎ *617/826–1626* ⊕ *www.odysseyopera.org* Ⓜ *Symphony.*

THEATER

In the 1930s Boston had no fewer than 50 performing-arts theaters; by the 1980s the city's Downtown Theater District had all but vanished. Happily, since the 1990s several historic theaters, extensively restored, have reopened to host pre-Broadway shows, visiting artists, comedy, jazz, and local troupes. The glorious renovation of the Opera House in 2004 added new light to the district. Established companies, such as the Huntington Theatre Company and the American Repertory

Theater in Cambridge, stage classic and modern repertory, premiere works by major writers like David Mamet, August Wilson, Tom Stoppard, and Don DeLillo, and pieces by new talents like Lydia Diamond and Diane Paulus.

MAJOR THEATERS

12

Fodor's Choice ★ **American Repertory Theater.** Founded by Robert Brustein and since 2009 under the helm of Tony Award–winning director Diane Paulus, the ART is one of America's most celebrated regional theaters, winning Tonys for Broadway originals *All the Way* and *Once* and revivals of *The Glass Menagerie, Pippin,* and *The Gershwins' Porgy and Bess.* The ART often premieres new works and seeks to expand the boundaries of theater through productions such as *Waitress, Finding Neverland,* and *Natasha, Pierre & The Great Comet of 1812* among others. The Loeb Drama Center, home of the ART, houses two theaters: the Mainstage and The Ex, a smaller black box often staging productions by the irreverent Harvard-Radcliffe Dramatic Club. OBERON, the ART's "club theater" with flexible stage design, engages young audiences in immersive theater (and has attracted national acclaim for its groundbreaking model), like Paulus's "disco-ball and hustle queen" extravaganza, *The Donkey Show,* every Saturday night. ⊠ *64 Brattle St., Harvard Sq., Cambridge* ☎ *617/547–8300* ⊕ *americanrepertory-theater.org* Ⓜ *Harvard.*

Fodor's Choice ★ **Boch Center.** Formerly the Citi Performing Arts Center, the recently renamed Boch Center is a performance-space complex dedicated to large-scale productions (at the former Wang Theater) and more intimate shows (at the Shubert and Colonial theaters). Expect big names (Steely Dan, Diana Ross, Radiolab, Brian Wilson), nationally touring Broadway shows, hot comedians, and occasional ballets. ⊠ *270 Tremont St., Theater District* ☎ *617/482–9393 general Boch Center, 866/348–9738 Shubert Theatre* ⊕ *www.bochcenter.org* Ⓜ *Boylston.*

Boston Opera House. The meticulously renovated 2,700-seat, beaux arts building has been lavished with $35 million worth of gold leaf, lush carpeting, and rococo ornamentation. It features lavish musical productions such as *Newsies, Kinky Boots,* and Boston Ballet's *The Nutcracker.* ⊠ *539 Washington St., Downtown* ☎ *617/259–3400* ⊕ *www.bostonoperahouse.com* Ⓜ *Boylston, Chinatown, Downtown Crossing, Park St.*

Charles Playhouse. The 1839 vintage Charles Playhouse—in its day a church, Prohibition-era speakeasy, and jazz club—has since 1995 hosted the inimitably indigo antics of *Blue Man Group,*and the zany whodunit *Shear Madness* since 1980. The Blue Men—a uniquely exhilarating trio of deadpan performance artists painted vivid cobalt—pound drums, share eureka moments, spray sloppy good will, and freely dispense toilet paper to clean up. (First-timer alert: dress casual, especially if you're seated down front.) ⊠ *74 Warrenton St., Theater District* ☎ *617/426–6912 general box office, 800/258–3626 Blue Man Group tickets nationwide, 617/426–5225 Shear Madness box office* Ⓜ *Boylston.*

Cutler Majestic Theatre at Emerson College. This handsome 1903 beaux arts–style theater, now linked to Emerson's adjacent communications college, has a tastefully restored and extravagantly gilt interior, where it hosts a dazzling array of professional and student productions including dance, drama, opera, comedy, and musicals. ⊠ *219 Tremont St., Theater District* ☏ *617/824–8000* ⊕ *cutlermajestic.org* Ⓜ *Boylston.*

Huntington Theatre Company. Boston's largest resident theater company consistently performs a high-quality mix of 21st-century plays and classics under the artistic direction of Peter DuBois, and commissions playwrights to produce original dramas. The Huntington performs at two locations: Boston University Theatre and the Calderwood Theatre Pavilion in the South End. ⊠ *Boston University Theatre, 264 Huntington Ave., Back Bay* ☏ *617/266–0800 box office* ⊕ *www.huntington-theatre.org* Ⓜ *Symphony.*

SMALL THEATERS AND COMPANIES

Boston Center for the Arts. Comprising more than a dozen quirky resident, emerging, and visiting troupes in six performance areas—two in the Calderwood Pavilion (Roberts, Wimberly), two black-box (Plaza) theaters, and two rehearsals halls—the massive circular brick Cyclorama, built in 1885 to house a 360-degree mural of the Battle of Gettysburg, today hosts concerts, trade events, and beer and wine festivals. The socially provocative and civically engaged Company One, the LGBTQ group Theatre Offensive, and the cutting-edge (off-off-Broadway) SpeakEasy Stage Company present shows here year-round. Forty resident visual artists work in studios above the spacious Mills Gallery, which presents six exhibits a year, and is home to the innovative Run of the Mills performance series. The eateries Banyan Bar + Refuge and the Beehive share this lively, diverse BCA enclave. ⊠ *539 Tremont St., South End* ☏ *617/426–5000* ⊕ *www.bcaonline.org* Ⓜ *Back Bay/South End, Copley.*

SPORTS AND
THE OUTDOORS

FENWAY PARK

For baseball fans a trip to Fenway Park is a religious pilgrimage. But even those who aren't fans will get a thrill at this historic field. The Boston Red Sox have played here since 1912. The oldest Major League Baseball ballpark is one of the last of its kind, a place where the scoreboard is hand-operated and fans endure uncomfortable seats.

(above) Take yourself out to a ball game at legendary Fenway Park. (lower right) Iconic Sox mark the park walls. (upper right) Flags adorn the epicenter of Red Sox Nation.

For much of the ballpark's history Babe Ruth's specter loomed large. The team won five titles by 1918 but endured an 86-year title drought after trading away the Sultan of Swat. The Sox "reversed the curse" in 2004, defeating the rival Yanks in the American League Championship Series after being down 3–0 in the series (an unheard of comeback in baseball) and sweeping the St. Louis Cardinals in the World Series. The Red Sox won it all again in 2007, against the Colorado Rockies, and yet again against the Cardinals in 2013, the first time since 1918 that the team cinched the series in its hometown. The curse is no more.

FUN FACT

A lone red seat in the right-field bleachers marks the spot where Ted Williams's 502-foot shot—the longest measurable home run hit inside Fenway Park—landed on June 9, 1946.

VACATION READING

For a glimpse into the psyche of a Red Sox fan read Bill Simmon's book *Now I can Die in Peace.*

THE NATION

The Red Sox have the most rabid fans in baseball. Knowledgeable and dedicated, they follow the team with religious-like intensity. Red Sox Nation has grown in recent years, much to the chagrin of diehards. You may hear the term "pink hat" used to derisively tag someone who is a bandwagon fan (i.e., anyone who didn't suffer with the rest of the "nation" during the title drought).

THE MONSTER

Fenway's most dominant feature is the 37-foot-high "Green Monster," the wall that looms over left field. It's just over 300 feet from home plate and in the field of play, so deep fly balls that would have been outs in other parks sometimes become home runs. The Monster also stops line drives that would have been over the walls of other stadiums, but runners can often leg these hits out into doubles (since balls are difficult to field after they ricochet off the wall).

THE MUSIC

Fans sing "Take Me Out to the Ballgame" during the seventh-inning stretch in every ballpark, but at Fenway they also sing Neil Diamond's "Sweet Caroline" at the bottom of the eighth. If the Sox win, the Standells' "Dirty Water" blasts over the loudspeakers at the end of the game.

THE CURSE

In 1920 the Red Sox traded pitcher Babe Ruth to the Yankees, where he became a home-run-hitting baseball legend. Some fans—most famously *Boston Globe* columnist Dan Shaughnessy, who wrote a book called *The Curse of the Bambino*—blamed this move for the team's 86-year title drought, but others will claim that "The Curse" was just a media-driven storyline used to explain the team's past woes. Still, fans who watched a ground ball roll between Bill Buckner's legs in the 1986 World Series or saw Aaron Boone's winning home run in the 2003 American League Division Series swear the curse was real.

VISIT THE NATION

13

Not lucky enough to nab tickets ahead of time? Try your luck at Gate E two hours before the game, when a handful of tickets are sold. There's a one-ticket limit, so everyone in your party must be in line.

If that doesn't yield results, you can still experience *the Nation*. Head down to the park and hang out on Yawkey Way, which borders the stadium. On game days it's closed to cars and filled with vendors, creating a street-fair atmosphere. Duck into a nearby sports bar and enjoy the game with other fans who weren't fortunate enough to secure seats. A favorite is the **Cask'n Flagon**, at Brookline Avenue and Lansdowne Street, across the street from Fenway.

The closest you can get to Fenway without buying a ticket is the **Bleacher Bar** (⊠ *82A Lansdowne St.*). There's a huge window in the center field wall overlooking the field. Get here early—it starts filling up a few hours before game time.

Updated by
Kim Foley
MacKinnon

Everything you've heard about the zeal of Boston fans is true; here you root for the home team. You cheer, and you pray, and you root some more. "Red Sox Nation" witnessed a miracle in 2004, with the reverse of the curse and the team's first World Series victory since 1918.

Then in 2007 the Sox proved it wasn't just a fluke with another series win, and yet again in 2013. In 2008 the Celtics ended its 18-year NBA championship drought with a thrilling victory over longtime rivals the LA Lakers. The six-time Stanley Cup Bruins and the five-time champion New England Patriots have proved that they are forces to be reckoned with.

Bostonians' long-standing fervor for sports is equally evident in their leisure-time activities. Harsh winters keep locals wrapped up for months, only to emerge at the earliest sign of oncoming spring. Once the mercury tops freezing and the snows begin to melt, Boston's extensive parks, paths, woods, and waterways teem with sun seekers and athletes—until the bitter winds bite again in November, and that energy becomes redirected toward white slopes, frozen rinks, and sheltered gyms and pools.

PLANNING

Department of Conservation & Recreation (*DCR*). Most public recreational facilities, including skating rinks and tennis courts, are operated by the Department of Conservation & Recreation. The DCR provides information about recreational activities in its facilities and promotes the conservation of Massachusetts parks and wilderness areas. ✉ *251 Causeway St., Suite 600, North End* ☏ *617/626–1250* ⊕ *www.mass.gov/dcr.*

SPORTS

Being a sports fan in Boston isn't like being a sports fan anywhere else. There's a sense of obligation to the home team, especially to the Red Sox. And while the offerings are spirited and plentiful for spectator sports, Boston also has many opportunities for participatory play as well, from skiing and ice-skating in winter to bicycling, boating, and golfing in warmer months.

13

BASEBALL

See the Fenway Park spotlight at the beginning of this chapter for information on the Boston Red Sox.

BASKETBALL

Boston Celtics. One of the most storied franchises in the National Basketball Association, the Boston Celtics have won the NBA championship 17 times since 1957, more than any other team in the league. The last title came in 2008, after a solid defeat of longtime rivals (the LA Lakers) ended an 18-year championship dry spell. Basketball season runs from late October to April, and playoffs last until mid-June. ⊠ *TD Garden, 100 Legends Way, Old West End* ☎ *866/423–5849* ⊕ *www.celtics.com* Ⓜ *North Station.*

BICYCLING

Department of Conservation & Recreation (*DCR*). For path locations, consult the Department of Conservation & Recreation website. ⊠ *251 Causeway St., Downtown* ⊕ *www.mass.gov/dcr* Ⓜ *North Station.*

BIKE PATHS
Dr. Paul Dudley White Bike Path. This 18-mile-long path follows both banks of the Charles River as it winds from Watertown Square to the Museum of Science. ⊠ *Watertown* ⊕ *www.mass.gov/eea/agencies/dcr/massparks/region-boston/recreation.html* Ⓜ *Science Park.*

RENTALS
Back Bay Bicycles. Road bikes rent here for $45 per day (weekly rates are also available)—cash only. City bikes rent for $35. ⊠ *362 Commonwealth Ave., Back Bay* ☎ *617/247–2336* ⊕ *www.papa-wheelies.com.*

Community Bicycle Supply. This South End place rents cycles from April through October. Their $25 daily rate also includes a helmet and lock. ⊠ *496 Tremont St., at E. Berkeley St., South End* ☎ *617/542–8623* ⊕ *www.communitybicycle.com* Ⓜ *Back Bay.*

TOURS
Fodor's Choice ★ **Urban AdvenTours.** A variety of themed excursions run throughout Boston and Cambridge, with most covering about 10 to 12 miles. They leave from Urban AdvenTours's Atlantic Avenue headquarters and are offered almost every day; in winter, the tours depend on the weather—call to confirm. The main tours start at $55 per person, and tickets are available for purchase through the website; bike, helmet, and water are

all included. A variety of rental bikes are also available. ⊠ *103 Atlantic Ave., Downtown* 🕾 *617/379–3590 for rentals and tours* ⊕ *www. urbanadventours.com* Ⓜ *Aquarium.*

See Massachusetts Bicycle Coalition, Back Bay Bicycles, and Community Bicycle Supply above for information on group rides.

BOATING

Except when frozen over, the waterways coursing through the city serve as a playground for boaters of all stripes. All types of pleasure craft, with the exception of inflatables, are allowed from the Charles River and Inner Harbor to North Washington Street on the waters of Boston Harbor, Dorchester inner and outer bays, and the Neponset River from the Granite Avenue Bridge to Dorchester Bay.

Boat Drop Sites. There are several boat drop sites along the Charles, including Clarendon Street, the Hatch Shell on Embankment Road, and Pinckney Street Landing (all in Back Bay); Brooks Street at Nonantum Road, and the Richard T. Artesani Playground, off Soldiers Field Road (both in Brighton); the Charles River Dam, at the Museum of Science in Cambridge; and Watertown Square, at Charles River Road in Watertown. ⊠ *Boston* ⊕ *www.mass.gov/eea/agencies/dcr/massparks/ recreational-activities/boat-ramps.html.*

Charles River Watershed Association. This association publishes detailed boating information on its website. ⊠ *Boston* 🕾 *781/788–0007* ⊕ *www. charlesriver.org.*

EVENTS

Fodor's Choice ★ **Head of the Charles Regatta.** In mid-October about 400,000 spectators turn out to cheer the more than 11,000 male and female athletes who come from all over the world to compete in the annual Head of the Charles Regatta, which in 2014 marked its 50th anniversary. Crowds line the banks of the Charles River with blankets and beer (although the police disapprove of the latter), cheering on their favorite teams and generally using the weekend as an excuse to party. Limited free parking is available, but the chances of finding an open space close to the race route are slim; take public transportation if you can. During the event, free shuttles run between the start and end point of the race route on both sides of the river. ⊠ *Banks of the Charles River, Harvard Square* 🕾 *617/868–6200* ⊕ *www.hocr.org* Ⓜ *Harvard, Central.*

LESSONS AND RENTALS

Boston University. From May to October, Boston University offers beginner to advanced rowing and sailing programs. ⊠ *Dewolfe Boathouse, 619 Memorial Dr., Harvard Square* 🕾 *617/353–9307 boathouse* ⊕ *www. bu.edu/fitrec* Ⓜ *Boston University Central, Boston University East.*

Charles River Canoe & Kayak Center. From May through mid-November you can rent a canoe, kayak, paddleboat, rowboat, or rowing shell from Charles River Canoe & Kayak Center. The center also offers a variety of canoeing and kayaking classes for all skill levels as well as organized group outings and tours. ⊠ *2401 Commonwealth Ave., Newton* 🕾 *617/965–5110* ⊕ *www.paddleboston.com.*

Community Boating. Near the Charles Street footbridge on the Esplanade, Community Boating is the host of America's oldest public sailing program. From April through October, $99 nets you a 30-day introductory membership, beginner-level classes, and use of sailboats and kayaks. Full memberships grant unlimited use of all facilities; splash around for 60 days for $245 or all season long for $315. Experienced sailors short on time can opt for a one-day sailboat rental for $85; kayaks and paddleboards rent for $45 per day. ✉ *21 David Mugar Way, Beacon Hill* ☎ *617/523–1038* ⊕ *www.community-boating.org* Ⓜ *Charles/MGH.*

13

Community Rowing. This organization teaches rowing courses from introductory to competitive adult and youth levels. Private lessons are also available. ✉ *Harry Parker Boathouse, 20 Nonantum Rd., Brighton* ☎ *617/779–8267* ⊕ *www.communityrowing.org.*

Jamaica Pond Boat House. From May to October, Courageous Sailing operates out of the Jamaica Pond Boat House and provides lessons and equipment for rowing and sailing on the pond, except when youth classes are in session; call ahead to confirm. One-hour kayak and sailboat rentals are $20 (rowboats are $15; $10 with a fishing license). Cash or check only. ✉ *Jamaica Way and Pond St., Jamaica Plain* ☎ *617/522–5061* ⊕ *courageoussailing.org/jamaica-pond* Ⓜ *Stony Brook, Green.*

FOOTBALL

COLLEGE

Boston College Eagles. With the only Division 1A football program in town, the Boston College Eagles play against some of the top teams in the country. ✉ *Alumni Stadium, Chestnut Hill* ☎ *617/552–4622* ⊕ *www.bceagles.com* Ⓜ *Boston College.*

Harvard University Crimson. Built in 1903, Harvard Stadium is the oldest concrete stadium in the country and the home of the Harvard University Crimson. The tongue-in-cheek halftime shows of the Harvard band make any game worth the trip. ✉ *Harvard Stadium, N. Harvard St. and Soldiers Field Rd., Allston* ☎ *617/495–2211* ⊕ *www.gocrimson. com* Ⓜ *Harvard.*

NFL

New England Patriots. Boston has been building a football dynasty over the past decade, starting with the New England Patriots' come-from-behind victory against the favored St. Louis Rams in the 2002 Super Bowl. Coach Bill Belichick and heartthrob quarterback Tom Brady then brought the team four more championship rings in 2004, 2005, 2014, and 2017, and have made Patriots fans as zealous as their baseball counterparts. Exhibition football games begin in August, and the season runs through the playoffs in January. The state-of-the-art Gillette Stadium is in Foxborough, 30 miles southwest of Boston. ✉ *Gillette Stadium, Rte. 1, off I–95 Exit 9, Foxborough* ☎ *508/543–1776 Ticketmaster* ⊕ *www. patriots.com* Ⓜ *Gillette Stadium.*

GOLF

Massachusetts Golf Association. This association represents 400 clubs in the state and has information on courses that are open to the public. ✉ *300 Arnold Palmer Blvd., Norton* ☎ *774/430–9100* ⊕ *www.mgalinks.org.*

COURSES

Boston is home to some of the best public courses in the country.

George Wright Golf Course. This hilly course is more challenging than the other Donald Ross–designed course at Franklin Park. It opens for the season starting in April each year. Tee times are necessary on weekends. ✉ *420 West St., Dorchester* ⊹ *From Forest Hills station, take the #50 bus, which goes right by the course* ☎ *617/364–2300* ⊕ *www.cityofbostongolf.com* ✉ *Weekends $50 ($45 for residents); weekdays $45 ($39 for residents)* 🏌 *18 holes, 6600 yards, par 70* Ⓜ *Forest Hills.*

William J. Devine Golf Course at Franklin Park. Donald Ross crafted this course in early 1896. It's open year-round, weather permitting. If you want to play 9 holes instead of 18, you can do so only after 1 pm on weekends. Charges for a golf cart tend to run about $11 to $20 extra per person. The course is part of delightful Franklin Park, which also has picnic facilities and jogging courses. Festivals and other outdoor activities take place all year. ✉ *1 Circuit Dr., Dorchester* ☎ *617/265–4084* ⊕ *www.cityofbostongolf.com* ✉ *Weekdays $40; weekends $45* 🏌 *18 holes, 6009 yards, par 70* Ⓜ *Forest Hills.*

HIKING

With the Appalachian Trail just two hours' drive from Downtown and thousands of acres of parkland and trails encircling the city, hikers will not have a lack of options in and around Boston.

FAMILY **Blue Hills Reservation.** A 20-minute drive south of Boston, the Blue Hills Reservation encompasses 7,000 acres of woodland with about 125 miles of trails, some ideal for cross-country skiing in winter, some designated for mountain biking the rest of the year. Although only 635 feet high, Great Blue Hill, the tallest hill in the reservation, has a spectacular view of the entire Boston metro area. It's open daily, and maps are available for purchase at the reservation headquarters or the Blue Hills Trailside Museum (1904 Canton Avenue, Milton). To get there, take Route 93 South to Exit 3, Houghton's Pond. ✉ *695 Hillside St., Milton* ☎ *617/698–1802* ⊕ *www.mass.gov/eea/agencies/dcr/massparks/region-south/blue-hills-reservation.html.*

Boston Harbor Islands National Park Area. Easily accessible from downtown Boston via ferry, the Boston Harbor Islands National Park Area is seldom crowded. The park maintains walking trails through diverse terrain and ecosystems. ✉ *Waterfront* ⊕ *www.bostonharborislands.org* Ⓜ *Aquarium.*

Middlesex Fells Reservation. Just a few miles north of Boston, the 2,575-acre Middlesex Fells Reservation has well-maintained hiking trails that pass over rocky hills, across meadows, and through wetland areas. Trails range from the quarter-mile Bear Hill Trail to the 6.9-mile Skyline

Trail. Mountain bikers can ride along the reservation's fire roads and on a designated loop trail. This sprawling reservation covers area in Malden, Medford, Stoneham, Melrose, and Winchester. To get to the western side of the reservation from Boston, take Route 93 North to Exit 33, and then take South Border Road off the rotary. ☎ 61///27-5380 ⊕ *www.mass.gov/eea/agencies/dcr/massparks/region-north/middlesex-fells-reservation.html.*

Stony Brook Reservation. Excellent hiking footpaths crisscross the 475-acre Stony Brook Reservation, which spans Hyde Park and West Roxbury. ⊠ *Turtle Pond Pkwy.* ☎ 617/333-7404 ⊕ *www.mass.gov/eea/agencies/dcr/massparks/region-boston/stony-brook-reservation.html.*

13

GROUP HIKES

FAMILY **Blue Hills Trailside Museum.** Managed by the Massachusetts Audubon Society, the Blue Hills Trailside Museum organizes hikes and nature walks. The museum has natural-history exhibits and live animals. The trails are open daily dawn to dusk and are free to explore; the museum is closed Monday. ⊠ *1904 Canton Ave., Milton ✢ Take Rte. 93 S to Exit 2B and Rte. 138 N* ☎ 617/333-0690 ⊕ *www.massaudubon.org/get-outdoors/wildlife-sanctuaries/blue-hills-trailside-museum* ⊠ *$5.*

HOCKEY

Boston hockey fans are informed, vocal, and extremely loyal. The stands are packed at Bruins games—especially since winning the Stanley Cup in 2011—despite high ticket prices. Local college hockey teams tend to give spectators plenty to celebrate at a much more reasonable price.

Beanpot Hockey Tournament. Boston College, Boston University, Harvard, and Northeastern teams face off every February in the Beanpot Hockey Tournament at the TD Garden. The colleges in this fiercely contested tournament traditionally yield some of the finest squads in the country. ⊠ *TD Garden, Old West End* ⊕ *www.beanpothockey.com* Ⓜ *North Station.*

Boston Bruins. Boston's hockey team is on the ice from September until April, frequently on Thursday and Saturday evenings. Playoffs last through early June. ⊠ *TD Garden, 100 Legends Way, Old West End* ☎ 617/624-2327 ⊕ *www.bostonbruins.com* Ⓜ *North Station.*

ICE-SKATING

FAMILY **Boston Common Frog Pond.** Thanks to a refrigerated surface, the Boston
Fodor's Choice Common Frog Pond transforms into a skating park from November
★ to mid-March, complete with a warming hut and concession stand. Admission is based on height: those 58 inches and over pay $6; those under 58 inches skate for free. Skate rentals cost $12 for adults and $6 for kids; lockers are $3. Frog Pond hours are Monday 10 to 4, Tuesday through Thursday and Sunday 10 to 9, and Friday and Saturday 10 to 10. With the gold dome of the State House in the background, it's a spectacular setting. ⊠ *Boston Common, enter near Beacon and Walnut Sts., Beacon Hill* ☎ 617/635-2120 ⊕ *www.bostonfrogpond.com* Ⓜ *Park St., Boylston.*

The Boston Marathon is the world's oldest annual marathon and perhaps the country's most loved road racing events.

Larz Anderson Park. Outside the city, try the skating rink in Larz Anderson Park, at the top of a wooded hill. Nonresidents pay $7 admission. Skate rentals are $6. The rink is open from December through early March. ⊠ *23 Newton St., Brookline ⊹ From Forest Hills T station, take 51 bus toward Cleveland Circle and get off at Clyde and Whitney Sts. The park is a 5-min walk* ☎ *617/739–7518* ⊕ *www.brooklinema.gov* Ⓜ *Forest Hills.*

Public Ice-skating Rinks. The Department of Conservation & Recreation operates more than 20 public ice-skating rinks; hours and season vary by location. Call for a complete list of rinks and their hours of operation. ⊠ *Boston* ☎ *617/626–1250* ⊕ *www.mass.gov/dcr.*

RUNNING AND JOGGING

Boston's parks and riverside pathways almost never lack for joggers, even in the worst weather. Paths on both sides of the Charles River are the most crowded and best maintained, particularly along the **Esplanade.** Watch out for in-line skaters and bikers. At **Castle Island** in South Boston, skaters and joggers zip past strolling lovebirds and parents pushing jogging strollers. The tranquil, wooded 1½-mile-long loop around idyllic **Jamaica Pond** is a slightly less crowded option.

EVENTS

Fodor'sChoice ★ **Boston Marathon.** Every Patriots' Day (the third Monday in April), fans gather along the Hopkinton-to-Boston route of the Boston Marathon to cheer on more than 25,000 runners from all over the world. The race ends near Copley Square in the Back Bay. ⊠ *Copley Sq., Back Bay* ⊕ *www.baa.org* Ⓜ *Copley, Arlington.*

The Boston Marathon

The Boston Marathon is held on the third Monday of April, which is also known as Patriots' Day in Massachusetts, a state holiday that commemorates the first battles of the Revolutionary War in 1775. Though it missed being the country's first marathon by a year (the first, in 1896, went from Stamford, Connecticut, to New York City), the Boston Marathon is arguably the nation's most prestigious. Why? It's the only marathon in the world for which runners have to qualify; it's the world's oldest continuously run marathon; and it's been run on the same course since it began.

The marathon passes through Hopkinton, Ashland, Framingham, Natick, Wellesley, Newton, Brookline, and Boston; only the last few miles are run in the city proper, which has a festival atmosphere. Throngs of supporters and fans come out to cheer on the racers and eat and drink at restaurants and bars along the route. Some spectators have returned to the same spot for generations, bringing their lawn chairs and barbecues.

In 2013, a horrific bombing near the race's finish line killed three people and injured scores of others. The tragic event shocked Boston and the nation, but runners and supporters have returned in even bigger numbers. Security, however, has gotten tighter during the race, especially in Boston proper. Driving is impossible anywhere near the route and the T is packed, so plan accordingly.

Tufts Health Plan 10K for Women. In October, women runners take the spotlight on Columbus Day for the Tufts Health Plan 10K for Women, which attracts about 7,000 participants and 20,000 spectators. Four American records have been set at this race since it began in 1977. There's also a Kids 1K fun run at Boston Common and other family-friendly activities. ⊠ *Boston Common, Back Bay* ☎ *888/767–7223 registration* ⊕ *tuftshealthplan.com/tufts-10k* Ⓜ *Park, Boylston.*

THE OUTDOORS

BEACHES

After more than 20 years of massive cleanup efforts, the water in Boston Harbor is safe for swimming, though many locals and visitors still prefer to head to more traditional beaches that are a short drive or train ride away. The rocky North Shore—about an hour away—is studded with New England beach towns, each with its favorite swimming spot. Alternatively, if the traffic isn't too awful (and during the summer, that's a big if), you can reach the southern tip of Cape Cod in about an hour. For information on the amazing beaches on the Cape and the nearby islands of Martha's Vineyard and Nantucket (which are reachable by ferry from Boston and several towns on the Cape), pick up a copy of *Fodor's Cape Cod, Nantucket, & Martha's Vineyard* or *Fodor's New England*.

NEAR TOWN

FAMILY **Nantasket Beach.** A 45-minute drive from downtown Boston, Nantasket Beach has warmer water than most local beaches. Kids love the tidal pools that form at low tide. A 1½-mile promenade makes for great people-watching. Take Route 3A South to Washington Boulevard, Hingham, and follow signs to Nantasket Avenue. **Amenities:** lifeguards; toilets. **Best for:** swimming; walking. ⊠ *Rte. 3A, Hull* ☎ *781/925–1777* ⊕ *www.mass.gov/eea/agencies/dcr/massparks/region-south/nantasket-state-park.html* ⌫ *$10 parking fee.*

FAMILY **Revere Beach.** Just north of the city, Revere Beach, the oldest public beach in America, has faded somewhat since its glory days in the early 20th century when it was a Coney Island–type playground, but it still remains a good spot to people-watch and catch some rays. The sand and water are less than pristine, but on hot summer days the waterfront is still packed with colorful local characters and Bostonians looking for an easy city escape. Most of the beach's former amusements are gone, but you can still catch concerts at the bandstand in summer. **Amenities:** food and drink; lifeguards; showers; toilets. **Best for:** swimming; walking. ⊠ *Revere Beach Blvd., Revere* ☎ *781/289–3020* Ⓜ *Revere Beach, Wonderland.*

BEACH FOOD

✕ **Kelly's Roast Beef.** The huge, juicy roast-beef sandwiches served at Kelly's Roast Beef, a local institution since 1951, are the sole reason some Bostonians make the trek to Revere. Other menu favorites include the fried clams and hand-breaded onion rings. It's open from 5 am to 2:30 am Sunday through Thursday, and until 3 am Friday and Saturday. ⊠ *410 Revere Beach Blvd., Revere* ☎ *781/284–9129* ⊕ *www.kellysroastbeef.com* Ⓜ *Revere Beach, Wonderland.*

NORTH OF TOWN

FAMILY
Fodor'sChoice
★
Crane Beach on the Crane Estate. The 1,200-acre Crane Beach on the Crane Estate, an hour's drive to the north of Boston in the 17th-century village of Ipswich, has 4 miles of sparkling white sand that serve as a nesting ground for the threatened piping plover, a small shorebird. It's one of the most stunning beaches in the state. From Route 128 North, take Exit 20A and follow Route 1A North for 8 miles. Turn right on Route 133 East and follow for 1½ miles. Turn left on Northgate Road and in ½ mile, turn right on Argilla Road and follow for 2½ miles to the entrance. Arrive early or come later in the afternoon as the parking lot does fill up and you could be turned away. Admission fees range from $2 to $30, depending on the time of year, day of the week, and whether you arrive on foot, by bike, or by car. **Amenities:** food and drink; lifeguards; parking (fee); showers; toilets. **Best for:** swimming; walking; sunset. ⊠ *Argilla Rd., Ipswich* ☎ *978/356–4354* ⊕ *www.thetrustees.org/places-to-visit/north-shore/crane-beach.html.*

FAMILY **Plum Island.** The well-groomed beaches of Plum Island, located in the Parker River National Wildlife Refuge, are worth the effort of the trek from Boston. The water is clear and blue, but quite cold. You can easily find a secluded spot to sunbathe or bird-watch, a popular activity, but make sure to call in advance in late summer to ask about greenhead flies; they can be vicious here. From I–95 follow Route 113 East (becomes Route 1A South) 3½ miles to Newbury. Then, take a left on Rolfe's Lane and a right onto the Plum Island Turnpike. **Amenities:** parking (fee); toilets. **Best for:** swimming; walking; solitude. ⊠ *Plum Island Blvd., Newburyport* ☎ *978/465–5753 including parking info* ⊕ *www.fws.gov/refuge/parker_river.*

FAMILY **Singing Beach.** In a quiet Cape Ann town 32 miles north of Boston, this beach gets its name from the musical squeaking sound its gold-color sand makes when you step on it. The beach is popular with both locals and out-of-towners in summer. It's also worth a visit in fall, when the crowds have gone home and you'll have the splendid shores all to yourself. There's a snack bar at the beach, but it's worth taking a 10-minute stroll up Beach Street into town to get a cone at Captain Dusty's Ice Cream (*60 Beach St., March–October*). The easiest, and cheapest, way to get here is by MBTA's Newburyport/Rockport commuter rail line from Boston's North Station to the Manchester stop, which is a 15-minute walk from the beach. From downtown Boston the train takes 45 minutes and costs $14.25 each way. **Amenities:** food and drink; lifeguards; showers; toilets. **Best for:** swimming; walking. ⊠ *Beach St., Manchester-by-the-Sea* ☎ *978/526–2019 summer phone* ⊕ *www.manchester.ma.us/Facilities/Facility/Details/Singing-Beach-11* 🅿 *Parking fee $25; walk-on fee $5.*

⇨ *For more information on North Shore beaches, see Chapter 15, Side Trips.*

PARKS

FAMILY
Fodor'sChoice
★
Arnold Arboretum. The sumptuously landscaped Arnold Arboretum is open all year to walkers, nature lovers, and joggers. Volunteer docents give free walking tours in spring, summer, and fall. ⊠ *125 Arborway, Jamaica Plain* ☎ *617/524–1718* ⊕ *www.arboretum.harvard.edu* Ⓜ *Forest Hills.*

Boston Harbor Cruises. Boston Harbor Cruises offers ferries to the Harbor Islands from Long Wharf (Downtown) with limited service in spring and fall. Service expands in June with additional departures from Hingham and Hull to six island destinations. High-speed catamarans run daily from May through mid-October and cost $17 round-trip. Other islands can be reached by the free interisland water shuttles that depart from Georges Island. ⊠ *Long Wharf, Waterfront* ☎ *617/227–4321* ⊕ *www.bostonharborcruises.com* Ⓜ *Aquarium.*

FAMILY
Fodor'sChoice
★
Boston Harbor Islands National Park Area. Comprising 34 islands and peninsulas, the Boston Harbor Islands National Park Area is something of a hidden gem for nature lovers and history buffs, with miles of lightly traveled trails and shoreline and several little-visited historic sites to explore. The focal point of the national park is 39-acre Georges Island, where you'll find the partially restored pre–Civil War Fort Warren that once held Confederate prisoners. Other islands worth visiting include Peddocks Island, which holds the remains of Fort Andrews, and Spectacle Island, a popular destination for swimming (with lifeguards). Lovells, Peddocks, Grape, and Bumpkin islands all allow camping with a permit from late June through Labor Day. Peddocks also has yurts available. Pets and alcohol are not allowed on the Harbor Islands. ⊠ *Visitor Pavilion, 191 W. Atlantic Ave., Downtown* ☎ *617/223–8666* ⊕ *www.bostonharborislands.org* Ⓜ *Aquarium.*

FAMILY   **Charles River Reservation.** Runners, bikers, and in-line skaters crowd the Charles River Reservation at the Esplanade along Storrow Drive, the Memorial Drive Embankment in Cambridge, or any of the smaller and less-busy parks farther upriver. Here you can cheer a crew race, rent a canoe or a kayak, or simply sit on the grass, sharing the shore with packs of hard-jogging university athletes, in-line skaters, moms with strollers, dreamily entwined couples, and intense academics, often talking to themselves as they sort out their intellectual—or perhaps personal—dilemmas. ⊠ *Back Bay* ☎ *617/626–1250* ⊕ *www.mass.gov/ eea/agencies/dcr/massparks/region-boston/charles-river-reservation. html* Ⓜ *Charles/MGH, Chinatown, Copley.*

FAMILY   **Emerald Necklace.** The six large public parks known as Boston's Emer-
Fodor's Choice   ald Necklace stretch 7 miles from the Back Bay Fens to Franklin Park
★   in Dorchester, and include Arnold Arboretum, Jamaica Pond, Olmsted Park, and the Riverway. The linear parks, designed by master landscape architect Frederick Law Olmsted more than 100 years ago, remain a well-groomed urban masterpiece. ⊠ *Boston* ⊕ *www.emeraldnecklace.org.*

Hatch Memorial Shell. On the Esplanade, the Hatch Memorial Shell hosts free concerts and outdoor events all summer. ⊠ *Esplanade, 47 David G. Mugar Way, Back Bay* ☎ *617/626–4970* Ⓜ *Charles/MGH.*

FAMILY   **Mt. Auburn Cemetery.** Cambridge's historic Mt. Auburn Cemetery is
Fodor's Choice   known as one of the best birding spots in the area and also has walk-
★   ing paths, gardens, and unique architecture. You can see the graves of such distinguished New Englanders as Oliver Wendell Holmes, Henry Wadsworth Longfellow, and Mary Baker Eddy. ⊠ *580 Mt. Auburn St., Mt. Auburn* ☎ *617/547–7105* ⊕ *mountauburn.org* Ⓜ *Harvard, then Bus 71 or 73 to Mount Auburn St. at Aberdeen Ave. stop.*

Rose Fitzgerald Kennedy Greenway. The Rose Fitzgerald Kennedy Greenway is a gorgeous 1½-mile-long ribbon of parks boasting fountains, organically maintained lawns and landscapes, hundreds of trees, and chairs, tables, and umbrellas for the public's use. It stretches from the North End (New Sudbury and Cross streets) to Chinatown (Kneeland and Hudson streets), curving through the heart of Downtown, just a few blocks from the harbor in most places. The Conservancy, a nonprofit foundation, operates, maintains, and programs the park with more than 350 events each year, including concerts, exercise classes, and farmers' and artisan markets. A mobile food program features more than 20 food trucks and carts operating seasonally in several locations on the Greenway, with the heart of the activity at Dewey Square Park. Kids will love the one-of-a-kind carousel with 36 seats featuring 14 characters native to the Boston area, including a lobster, rabbit, grasshopper, and falcon. ⊠ *Downtown* ☎ *617/292–0020* ⊕ *www.rosekennedygreenway. org* Ⓜ *South Station, North Station, Aquarium, Haymarket.*

SHOPPING

Updated by
Victoria Abbott
Riccardi

Shopping in Boston in many ways mirrors the city itself: a mix of classic and cutting-edge, the high-end and the hand-made, and international and local sensibilities. There is a strong network of idiosyncratic gift stores, handicrafts shops, galleries, and a growing number of savvy, independent fashion boutiques.

Boston's shops and department stores lie concentrated in the area bounded by Quincy Market, the Back Bay, and Downtown, with plenty of bargains in the Downtown Crossing area. The South End's gentrification creates its own kind of consumerist milieus, from housewares shops to avant-garde art galleries. In Cambridge you can find many shops around Harvard and Central squares, with independent boutiques migrating west along Massachusetts Avenue ("Mass Ave.") toward Porter Square and beyond.

There's no state sales tax on clothing. However, there's a 6.25% sales tax on clothes priced higher than $175 per item; the tax is levied on the amount in excess of $175.

BOSTON SHOPPING PLANNER

HOURS
Boston's shops are generally open Monday through Saturday from 10 or 11 am until 6 or 7 pm and Sunday from noon to 5. Many stay open until 8 pm one night a week, usually Thursday. Malls are open Monday through Saturday from 9 or 10 am until 8 or 9 pm and Sunday from noon to 6.

GETTING AROUND
Study the T map (*On the Go map*) before plunging into a shopping tour of Boston or Cambridge. You're almost always better off leaving your car behind than trying to navigate congested city streets and puzzle out parking arcana. Most major shopping neighborhoods are easily accessible on the T: Boston's Charles Street and Downtown Crossing and Cambridge's Harvard, Central, and Porter squares are on the Red Line; Copley Place, Faneuil Hall, and Newbury Street are on the Green Line; the South End is an easy trip on the Orange Line.

BOSTON

BEACON HILL

When the British occupied Boston in the 18th century, the Redcoats named Beacon Hill "Mount Whoredom" for the houses of ill-repute that lined Charles Street. In the 19th century Beacon Hill became home to the Boston Brahmins and eventually blossomed into an upper class neighborhood. Today the posh shops and homes lining the streets have become the most expensive pieces of real estate in the city.

Charles Street abounds with top-notch antiques stores such as Eugene Galleries and Devonia, as well as plenty of independently owned fashion boutiques and home-goods stores whose prices reflect their high Beacon Hill rents. River Street, parallel to Charles Street, is also an excellent source for antiques. Both are easy walks from the Charles Street T stop on the Red Line.

14

ANTIQUES

Devonia: Antiques for Dining. Feast your eyes on tens of thousands of pieces of tableware in this lovely shop, specializing in the Gilded Age (1880–1920). Some of the fabulous china sets here are fit for a queen some really were designed for royalty. The stunning selection of crystal even includes a custom-made set of Baccarat once owned by the Sultan of Brunei. ⊠ *15 Charles St., Beacon Hill* ☎ *617/523–8313* ⊕ *www. devonia-antiques.com* Ⓜ *Charles/MGH.*

E. R. Butler & Co. This museum-like store specializes in fine, American-made architectural fittings, but it's the jewelry and decorative accessories that stand out. Various designers fill the glass cases with one-of-a-kind pieces, like candy-color cabochon rings, fallen leaf silver pins, and pink pearl necklaces. European masters craft the paper-thin crystal coupes, porcelain birds, and silver serving spoons with decorative handles. ⊠ *38 Charles St., Beacon Hill* ☎ *617/722–0230* ⊕ *www.erbutler.com* ☉ *Closed Sun. and Mon.* Ⓜ *Charles/MGH.*

Eugene Galleries. Chockablock with prints, etchings, old maps, and books, this store has a generous selection of antique maps of Boston that date mainly from the 1850s to 1920s, which make for unique and lasting souvenirs. ⊠ *76 Charles St., Beacon Hill* ☎ *617/227–3062* ⊕ *eugenegalleries.com* Ⓜ *Charles/MGH.*

Marika's Antiques. This nearly 60-year-old store jam-packed with sterling serving wares, oil paintings, and furniture may appear a bit dusty and unpolished around the edges. It's what you don't see, however, that dazzles the eye: hundreds of pieces of estate and vintage jewelry locked in the shop's vault. Ranging from brilliant diamond necklaces and jeweled brooches for the flush set to affordable rings and antique cameos, the stash is yours to see (and buy) with a mere request. ⊠ *130 Charles St., Beacon Hill* ☎ *617/523–4520* ☉ *Closed Sun. and Mon.* Ⓜ *Charles/MGH.*

Persona. Using all precious metals and brightly colored stones, jeweler Gary Shteyman crafts gorgeous, unique pieces from his back-of-the-store workshop, such as a lacey-looking micropave white gold and diamond necklace and an edgy sterling cuff with a stingray inset. Approximately 10 other designers fill the rest of the cases with their chunky necklaces, earrings, bangles, and bold cocktail rings. A small selection of Miller leather totes and bags in rainbow colors also grace the store, which is the only U.S. retailer for this Paris-based brand. ✉ *62 Charles St., Beacon Hill* ☎ *617/266–3003* ⊕ *www.personastyle. com* Ⓜ *Charles/MGH.*

CLOTHING

Crush Boutique. Step down to this subterranean shop to find weekend casual outfits, jeans, silky shifts, and even party-girl attire. You'll also find affordable jewelry and handbags to dress up any ensemble. Crush's Newbury Street shop (between Fairfield and Gloucester streets) has a more LA vibe to it. ✉ *131 Charles St., Beacon Hill* ☎ *617/720–0010* ⊕ *www.shopcrushboutique.com* Ⓜ *Charles/MGH.*

Dress. True to its name, this shop owned by two young local women carries a number of great party dresses as well as flattering tees, pretty tops, pants, shoes, and accessories from emerging designers. ✉ *70 Charles St., Beacon Hill* ☎ *617/248–9910* ⊕ *www.dressboston.com* Ⓜ *Charles/MGH.*

Helen's Leather Shop. Channel your inner cowgirl (or -boy) at this family-owned shop specializing in Western wear, including hand-tooled boots embroidered, dyed, and crafted from leather and exotic skins. Choose from half a dozen brands of boots (Lucchese, Nocona, Dan Post, Tony Lama, Justin, and Frye); then browse through the leather sandals, jackets, briefcases, luggage, and accessories. ✉ *110 Charles St., Beacon Hill* ☎ *617/742–2077* ⊕ *www.helensleather.com* ☉ *Closed Wed.* Ⓜ *Charles/MGH.*

Holiday. A stockpile of flirty and feminine getups fill the fashionable racks of this pretty, pink shop along with a signature collection of handmade dresses, skirts, and tops that you can order in a dozen plus colors. Keep your eye out for the occasional vintage clutch. ✉ *53 Charles St., Beacon Hill* ☎ *617/973–9730* ⊕ *www.holidayboutique.net* Ⓜ *Charles/MGH.*

North River Outfitter. This shop is a preppy New Englander's heaven for adults, with racks of Vineyard Vines ties, men's needlepoint belts, Autumn Cashmere tops, and Saint James dresses. Next door (126 Charles Street) NRO Kids sells toys, books, and casual and dressy clothes for girls and boys. Farther down the block (39 Charles Street) you'll find NRO Sports, with running gear and tennis racquets along with the proper togs to match. ✉ *126 Charles St., Beacon Hill* ☎ *617/742–0089* ⊕ *www.northriveroutfitter.com* Ⓜ *Charles/MGH.*

FOOD

Savenor's. If you're hunting for exotic game meats, you've come to the right place. Savenor's food market, once Julia Child's favorite butcher, carries buffalo rump, alligator tail, even iguana. You'll find plenty of tamer choices, too, as well as outstanding cheeses, breads, and treats such as foie gras and smoked salmon. Another location operates in Cambridge. ✉ *160 Charles St., Beacon Hill* ☎ *617/723–6328* ⊕ *www. savenorsmarket.com* Ⓜ *Charles/MGH.*

GIFTS

Black Ink Boston. A wall full of rubber stamps stretches above unusual candles, cookie jars, and other home accessories and gift items. Need a rubber peanut eraser or polka-dot umbrella? You'll find it here (or in the sister store in Harvard Square, 5 Brattle Street). ⊠ *101 Charles St., Beacon Hill* ☎ *617/723–3883* ⊕ *www.blackinkboston.squarespace. com* Ⓜ *Charles/MGH.*

The Flat of the Hill. There's nothing flat about this fun, preppy collection of seasonal items, toiletries, toys, platters, and pillows, and whatever else catches the fancy of the shop's young owner. Her passion for color is evident—pick up a handbag in a rainbow assortment of leathers to add a pretty punch to your day. ⊠ *60 Charles St., Beacon Hill* ☎ *617/619– 9977* ⊕ *www.flatofthehill.com* ☼ *Closed Mon.* Ⓜ *Charles/MGH.*

Tibet Emporium. More upscale than your average imports store, Tibet Emporium goes beyond the usual masks and quilted wall hangings to offer beautifully delicate beaded silk pillowcases, pashmina wraps in every color imaginable, appliquéd and silk clothing, and finely wrought but affordable silver jewelry. ⊠ *103 Charles St., Beacon Hill* ☎ *617/723–8035* Ⓜ *Charles/MGH.*

JEWELRY

Twentieth Century Limited. You'll find every kind of rhinestone concoction imaginable for the bauble babe in your life here, as well as gently used 20th-century ladies' hats and pocketbooks. ⊠ *73 Charles St., Beacon Hill* ☎ *617/742–1031* ⊕ *www.boston-vintagejewelry.com* Ⓜ *Charles/MGH.*

GOVERNMENT CENTER AND THE NORTH END

GOVERNMENT CENTER

The heart of Government Center is the shops at Faneuil Hall Marketplace. Approximately 18 million people come here each year. There's been a marketplace on this spot since Faneuil Hall was built in 1742.

FOOD

Fodor's Choice ★ **Boston Public Market.** Opened in 2015, this indoor, year-round market houses nearly four-dozen vendors of locally sourced comestibles and goods that run the gamut from meats, cheeses, and eggs, to fresh-picked produce, prepared foods and New England–made wool and carved wooden bowls. Also here is The Boston Public Market Kitchen, which runs cooking demos, lectures, and educational programs. ⊠ *100 Hanover St., Government Center* ⊕ *bostonpublicmarket.org* Ⓜ *Hay-market/Government Center.*

SHOPPING CENTERS

Faneuil Hall Marketplace. This complex is both huge and hugely popular (drawing 18 million people a year), but not necessarily unique—most of its independent shops have given way to Banana Republic, Urban Outfitters, and other chains. Founded in 1742 as a market for crops and livestock, the place has plenty of history and offers one of the area's great à la carte casual dining experiences (Quincy Market). Pushcarts sell everything from apparel to jewelry to candy to Boston souvenirs, and buskers perform crowd-pleasing feats such as break dancing. ✉ *Bounded by Congress St., Atlantic Ave., the Waterfront, and Government Center, Government Center* ☎ *617/523–1300* ⊕ *www. faneuilhallmarketplace.com* Ⓜ *Government Center.*

THE NORTH END

This has to be one of Boston's best neighborhoods for shopping. Browse through the Italian greengrocers and butchers, inhaling the tantalizing aromas. Or get yourself a little bling at one of the stylish shops lining the crooked streets.

BOOKS

I Am Books. Once you've eaten your fill of pasta and cannoli, nourish your noggin at this independent, Italian American bookstore, where you'll find more than 1,200 titles in English and Italian. In addition to books written in Italian, including many children's books like Dr. Seuss, you'll find books devoted to Italian cooking, art, history, language, literature, and more, along with Italian comic books, magazines, ceramics, and fragrances. ✉ *189 North St., North End* ☎ *857/263–7665* ⊕ *www. iambooksboston.com.*

CLOTHING

Injeanius. The name says it all. Citizens of Humanity, JBrand, AG, Paige, and more denim cult favorites reside here along with casual sweaters, blouses, and T-shirts to top things off. ✉ *441 Hanover St., North End* ☎ *617/523–5326* ⊕ *www.injeanius.com* Ⓜ *Haymarket.*

Fodor's Choice ★ **Shake the Tree.** Irresistible defines this one-stop shop brimming with an eclectic array of strappy dresses and tops, unique body products, bags, fun jewelry, gifts, and home items that you never knew you needed. ✉ *67 Salem St., North End* ☎ *617/742–0484* ⊕ *www.shakethetreeboston.com* Ⓜ *Haymarket.*

DOWNTOWN BOSTON

Washington Street and Downtown Crossing are where to find bargains. Among the department and clothing stores here is Macy's.

BOOKS

Brattle Book Shop. The late George Gloss built this into Boston's best used- and rare-book shop. Today his son Kenneth fields queries from passionate book lovers. If the book you want is out of print, Brattle has it or can probably find it. The store has been in operation since 1825. ✉ *9 West St., Downtown* ☎ *617/542–0210, 800/447–9595* ⊕ *www. brattlebookshop.com* ☾ *Closed Sun.* Ⓜ *Downtown Crossing.*

SPECIALTY STORES

Bromfield Pen Shop. Dedicated to the fine art of writing since 1948, this small store carries more than 40 different brands of pens, ranging in price from $1.99 to $6,000. The friendly, knowledgeable staff will guide you through the selection of fountain, rollerball, and ballpoint pens, as well as pencils, in gold, silver, wood, and plastic from makers such as Cross, Visconti, and Faber-Castell. The store also stocks refills, inks, leather gifts, desk accessories, watches, and Swiss Army knives and offers on-site engraving within 24 hours. ✉ *5 Bromfield St., Downtown* ☎ *617/482–9053* ⊕ *www.bromfieldpenshop.com* ☾ *Closed Sun.* Ⓜ *Park St.*

Lannan Ship Model Gallery. The 6,000-square-foot space looks like the attic of a merchant seaman: in addition to finished 18th- and 19th-century ship models ($200 to $100,000-plus) and vintage pond yachts, among the treasures are lanterns, navigational instruments, and marine charts, prints, and oils. ⌂ *99 High St., Downtown* ☎ *617/451–2650* ⊕ *www.lannangallery.com* ⊗ *Closed Sun.* Ⓜ *South Station.*

Market Stalls at Boston Design Center. An eclectic mix of furniture from the 17th to the 20th centuries, as well as lighting, art, and decorative home goods, fill this 10,000-square foot boutique-like market that's open to the public; it's on the second floor of the Boston Design Center, which is normally accessible only to the trade. Peruse the 20-plus stalls, each owned by a different antique dealer, to score items like a Shaker-style sideboard, a gilded eagle-topped mirror, or antique etching. ⌂ *Boston Design Center, One Design Center Pl., Downtown* ☎ *617/439–6902* ⊕ *bostondesign.com* ⊗ *Closed weekends.*

14

BACK BAY AND THE SOUTH END

BACK BAY

This is the neighborhood of the elegant Mandarin Oriental Hotel—so need we say more about the shops you'll find here? Just in case: elegant, chic, modern, stylish. It's also home to Newbury Street, Boston's version of LA's Rodeo Drive. It's a shoppers' paradise, from high-end names such as Anne Fontaine to tiny specialty shops such as the Fish and Bone with up-to-the-minute art galleries and dazzling jewelers thrown into the mix.

Parallel to Newbury Street is Boylston Street, where you'll find a few standout shops such as Pompanoosuc Mills (hand-crafted furnishing) scattered among the other chains and restaurants.

ANTIQUES

Brodney Antiques & Jewelry. In addition to plenty of porcelain and silver, Brodney claims to have the biggest selection of estate jewelry in New England. ⌂ *145 Newbury St., Back Bay* ☎ *617/536–0500* ⊕ *www.brodney.com* ⊗ *Closed Sun.* Ⓜ *Copley.*

ART GALLERIES

Barbara Krakow Gallery. Emerging and established regional and international artists fill the walls here. Mediums include contemporary painting, photography, drawing, and sculpture. ⌂ *10 Newbury St., 5th fl., Back Bay* ☎ *617/262–4490* ⊕ *www.barbarakrakowgallery.com* ⊗ *Closed Sun. and Mon., and Sat. in July. Closed Aug.* Ⓜ *Arlington.*

Childs Gallery. The large selection of works for sale in this gallery, established in 1937, includes paintings, prints, drawings, watercolors, and sculpture from the 1500s to the present. For a special memento with more weight than a Red Sox hat, pick out a piece from the gallery's impressive collection of Boston expressionism and Boston School impressionism art. ⌂ *169 Newbury St., Back Bay* ☎ *617/266–1108* ⊕ *www.childsgallery.com* ⊗ *Closed Mon.* Ⓜ *Copley.*

Copley Society of Art. After more than a century, this nonprofit membership organization continues to present the works of well-known and aspiring New England artists, as well as out-of-town and foreign members. ✉ *158 Newbury St., Back Bay* ☎ *617/536–5049* ⊕ *www. copleysociety.org* ⊘ *Closed Mon. except by appointment* Ⓜ *Copley.*

Gallery NAGA. Specializing in contemporary paintings, primarily oil, watercolor, acrylic, and mixed media, this striking gallery in the neo-Gothic stone Church of the Covenant also displays sculpture, and furniture beyond your everyday tables and chairs. ✉ *67 Newbury St., Back Bay* ☎ *617/267–9060* ⊕ *www.gallerynaga.com* ⊘ *Closed Sun. and Mon. July and Aug.* Ⓜ *Arlington.*

Rolly-Michaux. You'll find only the highest-quality lithographs, etchings, contemporary arts, and photography here, including such masters as Moore, Calder, Picasso, Chagall, Miró, and Matisse. ✉ *290 Dartmouth St., Back Bay* ☎ *617/536–9898* ⊕ *www.rollymichaux.com* ⊘ *Closed Sun. and Mon.* Ⓜ *Copley.*

Vose Galleries. Established in 1841, Vose specializes in 19th- and 20th-century American art, including the Hudson River School, Boston School, and American impressionists. The addition of works of contemporary American realism recognizes an area that is often overlooked by the trendier set. ✉ *238 Newbury St., Back Bay* ☎ *617/536–6176* ⊕ *www.vosegalleries.com* ⊘ *Closed Sun. and Mon.* Ⓜ *Copley, Hynes.*

BEAUTY

Bella Santé. For top-notch facials, body scrubs, and massages, as well as medical-grade treatments and peels, head to this elegant, tranquil day spa. In addition to a well-trained staff, you'll find pristine facilities, including a locker room stocked with a bevy of tonics, lotions, and hair products. First-time guests receive a discount on select treatments. ✉ *38 Newbury St., Back Bay* ☎ *617/424–9930* ⊕ *www.bellasante.com* Ⓜ *Arlington.*

Exhale. This Zen-like sanctuary is deceptively large. The subterranean lower level houses a first-rate spa, selection of nourishing body and skin-care products, and a yoga studio. Upstairs, you'll find a core fusion studio and boutique offering soft clothing, candles, jewelry, and more. There's another location at the Battery Wharf Hotel. ✉ *28 Arlington St., Back Bay* ☎ *617/532–7000* ⊕ *www.exhalespa.com* Ⓜ *Arlington.*

Fresh. You won't know whether to wash with these body products or snack on them. Load up on shea butter–rich bars in such enticing scents as grapefruit, mangosteen, and sugar-lemon. The brown-sugar face polish with strawberry seeds will set your face aglow and leave you hungry. ✉ *121 Newbury St., Back Bay* ☎ *617/421–1212* ⊕ *www. fresh.com* Ⓜ *Copley.*

BOOKS

Trident Booksellers & Café. This two-story shop with windows overlooking Newbury Street is known as much for its eclectic collection of books and magazines as its all-day breakfast menu. Follow the pack and order either the lemon-ricotta-stuffed French toast or homemade corned beef hash and then settle in with a favorite read. Feel free to stay through lunch, dinner, and beyond, as the store's open until midnight daily, making it a popular spot with students. ⊠ *338 Newbury St., Back Bay* ☎ *617/267–8688* ⊕ *www.tridentbookscafe.com* Ⓜ *Hynes.*

CLOTHING

Alan Bilzerian. Satisfying the Euro crowd, this store sells luxe men's and women's clothing by such fashion darlings as Yohji Yamamoto and Ann Demeulemeester. ⊠ *34 Newbury St., Back Bay* ☎ *617/536–1001* ⊕ *www.alanbilzerian.com* ☾ *Closed Sun.* Ⓜ *Arlington.*

All Too Human. Boston native and Tufts graduate, Jessica Knez, a former buyer for Bergdorf Goodman, stocks laser-hot labels, like Proenza Schouler and Dries Van Noten, at her fashion-forward concept store for men and women. To entice an even broader audience, the store also displays edgy, rotating art installations. ⊠ *236 Clarendon St., Back Bay* ☎ *857/350–3951* ⊕ *www.alltoohumanboston.com* ☾ *Closed Sun.*

14

Anne Fontaine. You can never have too many white shirts—especially if they're designed by this Parisienne. The simple, sophisticated designs are mostly executed in cotton and priced at $295 and up. Complete your outfit with the store's selection of sleek skirts, slacks, and accessories; the store also carries dresses and outerwear. ⊠ *280 Boylston St., Back Bay* ☎ *617/423–0366* ⊕ *www.annefontaine.com* Ⓜ *Arlington, Boylston.*

Betsy Jenney. Ms. Jenney herself might easily wait on you in this small, personal store, where the well-made, comfortable lines cater to women who cannot walk into a fitted size-4 suit—in other words, most of the female population. The designers found here, such as Nicole Miller, are fashionable yet forgiving. ⊠ *114 Newbury St., Back Bay* ☎ *617/536–2610* ⊕ *www.betsyjenney.com* Ⓜ *Copley.*

Calypso St. Barth. The women's chic resort wear here bursts with bright colors, beautiful fabrics, and styles so fresh you might need a fashion editor to help you choose. Additionally, they have you covered from head to toe with strappy summer sandals, winter boots, scarves, belts, and various chapeaus. ⊠ *114 Newbury St., Back Bay* ☎ *617/421–1887* ⊕ *www.calypsostbarth.com* Ⓜ *Copley.*

Chanel. This spacious branch of the Parisian couture house carries suits, separates, bags, shoes, cosmetics, and, of course, a divine selection of little black dresses. ⊠ *6 Newbury St., Back Bay* ☎ *617/859–0055* ⊕ *www.chanel.com/en_US/fashion.html* Ⓜ *Arlington.*

Giorgio Armani. This top-of-the-line Italian couturier is known for his carefully shaped jackets, soft suits, and mostly neutral palette. Additionally, you'll find an A/X Armani Exchange store at 100 Huntington Avenue and 100 Cambridge Place inside the CambridgeSide Galleria. ⊠ *22 Newbury St., Back Bay* ☎ *617/267–3200* ⊕ *www.armani.com* Ⓜ *Arlington.*

Hello Caroline. Boston-bred Hilary Marino founded this airy, fresh boutique and filled it with fun and flirty frocks for the gal on the go—at work, on weekends, and date nights. The unusual, on-trend brands and modest prices make this a hot spot. The store has another branch in Brookline. ⊠ *252 Newbury St., Back Bay* ☎ *617/262–6800* ⊕ *www.hello-caroline.com.*

In the Pink. Don't be caught dead on Nantucket this year without your splashy pink, lime, yellow, and turquoise Lilly Pulitzer resort wear, available here along with shoes, home decor, and children's clothing. ⊠ *133 Newbury St., Back Bay* ☎ *617/536–6423* ⊕ *www.inthepinkonline.com* Ⓜ *Copley.*

Max & Riley. A mother-daughter team, both with retail backgrounds, opened this chic boutique that bursts with ruffled frocks, slim-waisted dresses, and plenty of jeans, tops, and jackets that appeal to both the working and party set. Celebrity fashionistas supply some of the labels, including Sarah Jessica Parker (shoes), Rachel Zoe, and Lauren Conrad. ⊠ *226 Newbury St., Back Bay* ☎ *617/236–1431* ⊕ *www.shopmaxandriley.com.*

Ministry of Supplyrgia. Inspired by the temperature-regulating materials used for NASA's astronaut clothes, three MIT students started this men and women's clothing store that features stretchy, moisture-wicking, wrinkle-free, machine-washable slacks, shirts, blouses, blazers, and jackets designed by a former Theory designer (think clean and elegant) in a simple palate of mainly white, black, gray, and blue. Interested in creating a bespoke blazer or top on-site? The store's 3-D print knitting machine can finish a garment in about two hours, with extra time needed to hand-finish various details. ⊠ *299 Newbury St., Back Bay* ☎ *617/236–4253* ⊕ *www.ministryofsupply.com.*

CRAFTS

Fodor'sChoice **Society of Arts & Crafts.** More than a century old, this is the country's oldest nonprofit crafts organization. In addition to selling a
★ fine assortment of ceramics, jewelry, glass, woodwork, and furniture from a rotating roster of more than 400 of the country's finest artists, the soaring space sponsors free art exhibits, and a featured artist in residence, who you can see working in the studio. ⊠ *100 Pier 4 , Suite 200, Back Bay* ⊹ *Above Ocean Prime restaurant on 2nd fl.* ☎ *617/266–1810* ⊕ *www.societyofcrafts.org* ⊘ *Closed Sun. and Mon.* Ⓜ *Silver Line MBTA to Court St. Station.*

GIFTS

Whitney + Winston. Looking for the perfect gift for that special baby, hostess, or doggie in your life? Founded by the owners of Crush women's clothing boutique, this cheerful shop has everything from picnic blankets and picture frames to cashmere wraps and ceramic tea sets. ⊠ *113 Charles St., Back Bay* ☎ *617/720–2600* ⊕ *www.whitneyandwinston.com.*

JEWELRY

Shreve, Crump & Low. Since 1796, Shreve has specialized in high-end treasures, including gems and handcrafted platinum rings, as well as men's and women's watches and high-quality antiques. But don't get the impression that you can't afford anything here: one of the store's best-selling items is a $99 ceramic pitcher called "The Gurgling Cod," in honor of the state fish. ⊠ *39 Newbury St., Back Bay* ☎ *617/267–9100* ⊕ *www.shrevecrumpandlow.com* ⊘ *Closed Sun.* Ⓜ *Arlington.*

Small Pleasures. From Victorian-era tourmaline cocktail rings to mint-condition pocket watches, vintage lovers should not miss the antique and estate jewelry that fills these cases. The staff is notably helpful and informed. ⊠ *Copley Pl.*, *142 Newbury St., Back Bay* ☎ *617/267–7371* ⊕ *www.small-pleasures.com* ⊘ *Closed Sun.* Ⓜ *Copley.*

MUSIC STORES

Newbury Comics. This outpost of the renowned pop-culture store carries vinyl, CDs, DVDs, quirky gifts, and an especially good lineup of independent pressings. You'll find three other locations on JFK Street in Cambridge, inside the CambridgeSide Galleria mall, and inside the Faneuil Hall Marketplace. ⊠ *332 Newbury St., Back Bay* ☎ *617/236–4930* ⊕ *www.newburycomics.com* Ⓜ *Hynes.*

SHOPPING CENTERS

Copley Place. An indoor shopping mall in the Back Bay, Copley Place includes such high-end shops as Christian Dior and Louis Vuitton. It is anchored by the pricey but dependable Neiman Marcus and the flashy, often overpriced Barneys. ⊠ *100 Huntington Ave., Back Bay* ☎ *617/262–6200* ⊕ *www.simon.com/mall/copley-place* Ⓜ *Copley, Back Bay.*

Downtown Crossing. This pedestrian mall has modestly priced stores like Macy's, H&M, TJ Maxx—and buzzes with local office folks dashing out for quick-serve lunches or after-work drinks. The nearby theater district, however, keeps the area bustling late into the evening. ⊠ *Washington St. from Amory St. to about Milk St., Downtown* Ⓜ *Downtown Crossing, Park St.*

Prudential Center. A skywalk connects Copley Place to the Prudential Center. The Pru, as it's often called, contains moderately priced chain stores such as Ann Taylor and Sephora and is anchored by Saks Fifth Avenue and Lord and Taylor. ⊠ *800 Boylston St., Back Bay* ☎ *800/746–7778* ⊕ *www.prudentialcenter.com* Ⓜ *Prudential.*

SPECIALTY STORES

The Fish and Bone. This boutique is dedicated to all things cat and dog. Choose from the enormous selection of collars, toys, and food. ⊠ *217 Newbury St., Back Bay* ☎ *857/753–4176* ⊕ *www.thefishandbone.com* Ⓜ *Arlington.*

THRIFT SHOPS

Castanet Designer Consignment. Chanel purses, Rick Owens jackets, and Hermès bracelets have all graced this jam-packed couture-quality consignment shop, which culls gently worn goods from fashion hounds across the country. Its picky choices are your gain. ⊠ *175 Newbury St., 2nd fl., Back Bay* ☎ *617/536–1919* ⊕ *www.shopcastanet.com* ⊘ *Closed Sun. and Mon.* Ⓜ *Arlington.*

Revolve. Come here to snag a vintage Chanel bag, some Manolo Blahnik heels, or the perfect designer dress to complete your outfit. The store receives designer booty every day, which they sell for about one-third of the retail price. Handbag hounds regularly stop in to peruse the store's generous selection. ⊠ *262 Newbury St., Back Bay* ☎ *617/262–0720* ⊕ *www.revolveboutiques.com.*

14

SOUTH END

The South End is not what it used to be and merchants are benefiting from the ongoing gentrification that has brought high real-estate prices and trendy restaurants to the area. Housed in what were at one time derelict buildings, chic home-furnishings, restaurants, bakeries, and gift shops line Tremont Street, starting at Berkeley Street. If you want to bring Fido or carry home a doggie treat, this is the neighborhood: there are oodles of chichi pet boutiques here, along with plenty of water bowls and dog biscuits. ■TIP➔ The MBTA's Silver Line bus runs through the South End.

ART GALLERIES

Alpha Gallery. This gallery specializes in paintings, drawings, watercolors, and mixed media works from contemporary American and foreign artists. It also has a fine selection of master prints and works from 20th-century American masters. ⊠ *460 C Harrison St., South End* ☎ *617/536–4465* ⊕ *www.alphagallery.com* ⊗ *Closed Sun. and Mon.* Ⓜ *Silver Line MBTA.*

Bromfield Art Gallery. Tucked among dozens of art studios in the artsy SOWA (South of Washington) area, this artist-run, members-only gallery mounts monthly shows featuring contemporary art in all forms, including printmaking, video, acrylic, ink drawing, and pastels. ⊠ *450 Harrison Ave., South End* ☎ *617/451–3605* ⊕ *www.bromfieldgallery. com* ⊗ *Closed Mon. and Tues.* Ⓜ *Tufts Medical Center.*

Samsøn Projects. A truly cross-cultural blend of exhibits, this gallery shows the experimental works of young contemporary and emerging artists. Head downstairs to the lower level to watch the current resident artist at work. ⊠ *29 Thayer St., South End* ☎ *617/357–7177* ⊕ *www. samsonprojects.com* ⊗ *Closed Sun.–Tues.* Ⓜ *Tufts Medical Center.*

BOOKS

Ars Libri Ltd. It's easy to be drawn into the rare and wonderful books on display here. The airy space is filled with tomes on photography and architecture, out-of-print art books, monographs, and exhibition catalogs. ⊠ *500 Harrison Ave., South End* ☎ *617/357–5212* ⊕ *www. arslibri.com* ⊗ *Closed Sat. in Aug.* Ⓜ *Back Bay.*

CHILDREN'S CLOTHING

CouCou. When you want your tot to standout sartorially, head to this globally sourced boutique packed with a thoughtfully curated selection of clothes; you'll also find toys and crafts, as well as a play room in the back of the store, a boon for frazzled parents with their little ones in tow. ⊠ *24 Union Park, South End* ☎ *617/936–4082* ⊕ *coucou-boston. myshopify.com* ⊗ *Closed Mon.*

Kodomo. With an emphasis on comfort, style, and fun, this flagship store stocks ethically made American and imported clothing for boys and girls that both genders can wear, like a zip hoodie printed with lions or rose-and-cream-striped leggings. There's also a nice selection of stuffed animals, dolls, and nursery swaddles, pillows, and blankets. Another location can be found in Beacon Hill. ⊠ *579 Tremont St., South End* ☎ *617/936–3808* ⊕ *kodomoboston.com.*

CLOTHING

Flock. This boho-chic boutique brims with cotton T-shirts, floral dresses, and vintage-inspired jewelry, along with whimsical gift items, like handmade keepsake boxes filled with colorful images and antique baubles. ⊠ *274 Shawmut Ave., South End* ☎ *617/391–0222* ⊕ *www.flockboston.com* ☉ *Closed Mon.* Ⓜ *Back Bay.*

Uniform. A casual menswear shop with an urban, classic feel. You'll find everything from jackets to socks to shaving needs. ⊠ *511 Tremont St., South End* ☎ *617/247–2360* ⊕ *www.uniformboston.com* ☉ *Closed Mon.* Ⓜ *Back Bay.*

Viola Lovely. Fashionistas flock to this sleek, white boutique to stock up on edgy tops, soft jackets, nipped waist dresses, and flattering slacks from established and emerging designers, like Protagonist, Rachel Comey, and Golden Goose. The cute satchels, jewelry, and footwear will complete your magazine-worthy look. ⊠ *1409 Washington St., South End* ☎ *857/277–0746* ⊕ *www.violalovely.com.*

HOME FURNISHINGS

Gifted. Enchanting homemade gifts from a rotating group of more than 60 artists (including the owner, Marie Corcoran) fill this dreamy boutique. Scoop up dainty charm and gemstone pendants, vegan handbags, men's ties and cufflinks, or a cute caterpillar wooden wall clock for that special little one in your life. This store has something for everyone, including you. ⊠ *2 Dartmouth St., South End* ☎ *617/716–9924* ⊕ *www.giftedboston.com* Ⓜ *Back Bay.*

Hudson. Specializing in custom furniture, this chic shop also carries casual, cool home goods, such as decorative throw pillows, marbleized pottery bowls, rugs, and luscious-smelling candles. ⊠ *12 Union Park St., South End* ☎ *617/292–0900* ⊕ *hudsonboston.com* Ⓜ *Back Bay, Prudential.*

Lekker. Dutch design with contemporary panache pervades South Washington Street's coolest furniture and home goods store. This is a great place to pick up a sleek dining set, the perfect accent table, some funky china, or a statement pendant light. ⊠ *1313 Washington St., South End* ☎ *617/542–6464* ⊕ *www.lekkerhome.com* Ⓜ *Back Bay.*

Olives & Grace. Brooklyn meets Boston at this indie boutique specializing in small-batch, handcrafted goods from artists, food makers, and gift producers across the country. From Bourbon marshmallows and goat's-milk soap to hand-stitched baby booties and wooden Boston coasters, the treasures in this shop are easy to browse and impossible to resist. ⊠ *623 Tremont St., South End* ☎ *617/236–4536* ⊕ *www.olivesandgrace.com* Ⓜ *Back Bay.*

THRIFT SHOPS

Fodor'sChoice ★ **Bobby from Boston.** For years this hidden gem was kept on the down low—but the word's out about this two-room space filled with one-of-a-kind finds. Although the items are mostly menswear, there are bargains for females, too. ⊠ *19 Thayer St., South End* ☎ *617/423–9299* ☉ *Closed Mon.* Ⓜ *Back Bay, Prudential.*

Fodor'sChoice ★ **Boomerangs–Special Edition.** Stepping into this cozy secondhand boutique feels like you could be in the salon of a very wealthy couple, who just happen to be unloading their cache of designer clothes

14

and housewares. Jade satin flats, beaded Armani tops, and vintage dresses and jewelry—all at a fraction of their original cost—are the sorts of treats you'll find sharing space with menswear, books, and silver-plated serving dishes. Area residents and businesses donate these treasures with all proceeds going to AIDS Action Committee. The branches in Cambridge, Jamaica Plain, and West Roxbury have much more downscale pickings. ✉ *1407 Washington St., South End* ☎ *617/456–0996* ⊕ *shopboomerangs.org* ☾ *Closed Mon.*

TOYS

Tadpole. This is a treasure trove of board games, dolls, trucks, blocks, books, and every other necessity for a kid's toy chest. Stock up on baby gear and essentials as well. ✉ *58 Clarendon St., South End* ☎ *617/778–1788* ⊕ *www.shoptadpole.com* Ⓜ *Back Bay.*

BOSTON OUTSKIRTS

BROOKLINE

Brookline, 4 miles west of Boston, lies on the Green Line of the MBTA. Centered around Coolidge Corner, the area brims with shops selling everything from Russian tchotchkes to ethnic foods. Book lovers should not miss Brookline Booksmith (✉ *279 Harvard St.*), an independent bookstore "dedicated to the fine art of browsing," with creaky wooden floors, a friendly staff, and a drool-worthy selection of hardcovers and paperbacks.

Fodor'sChoice
★

Brookline Booksmith. Since 1961 this independent bookseller has anchored Harvard Street, and enriched the Coolidge Corner community with poetry readings, book clubs, and author talks. Browse the well-edited selection of best sellers, hardcovers, and paperbacks, as well as the area toward the back packed with cards and fun gifts that range from cutting boards and tea towels to leather notebooks and printed scarves. ✉ *279 Harvard St., Brookline* ☎ *617/566–6660* ⊕ *www.brooklinebooksmith-shop.com* Ⓜ *Coolidge Corner.*

GIFTS

Boston General Store. This is the sort of shop every neighborhood should have—a warm, welcoming space filled with beautifully crafted, mainly locally sourced products. Bamboo pet brushes share space with handwoven French market baskets, fruit and flower cocktail syrups, vintage fabric neckties, and fragrances from a Boston-area perfumer, who uses only botanicals (no synthetics!) to create her scents. ✉ *305 Harvard St., Coolidge Corner* ☎ *617/232–0103* ⊕ *www.bostongeneralstore.com.*

SPECIALTY SHOPS

Uncommon Yarn. Whether you're a newbie or seasoned knitter, this store has everything you need to make that baby sweater or cap. There's a generous selection of domestic and imported yarns and fibers, along with a sun-drenched knitters lounge where you can stitch away the day. ✉ *1386a Beacon St., Brookline* ☎ *857/352–4281* ⊕ *www.uncommonyarn.com* ☾ *Closed Mon.*

CAMBRIDGE

Cross over the Charles River to Cambridge, just as historic as Boston and where Harvard University's famous campus provides a beautiful backdrop for a unique and charming shopping experience. Massachusetts Avenue, Brattle Street, and Mt. Auburn Street shape the area known as Harvard Square, the place to go in Cambridge for just about anything. A handful of chains and independent boutiques are clustered on Brattle Street.

At the junction of Massachusetts Avenue, Prospect Street, River Street, and Western Avenue, Central Square has an eclectic mix of furniture stores, used-record shops, ethnic restaurants, and small, hip performance venues. The best word to describe the ares is bohemian.

Porter Square, in north Cambridge, has distinctive clothing stores, as well as crafts shops, cafés, restaurants, and bars.

ANTIQUES

Cambridge Antique Market. Off the beaten track, this antiques hot spot has a selection bordering on overwhelming: five floors of goods from over 150 dealers ranging from 19th-century furniture to vintage clothing, much of it reasonably priced. Head to the basement for a large selection of secondhand bikes. For those with four wheels, a parking lot sits next to the building. ⊠ *201 Monsignor O'Brien Hwy., Cambridge* ☎ *617/868–9655* ⊕ *www.marketantique.com* ⊗ *Closed Mon.* Ⓜ *Lechmere.*

BOOKS

Grolier Poetry Bookshop. A beloved hangout for T.S. Eliot and E.E. Cummings when they attended Harvard, this tiny shop founded in 1927 carries classic, modern, and contemporary in-print poetry from all over the world. ⊠ *6 Plympton St., Cambridge* ☎ *617/547–4648* ⊕ *www.grolierpoetrybookshop.org* ⊗ *Closed Sun. and Mon.* Ⓜ *Harvard.*

Harvard Book Store. Time disappears as you browse the tables and shelves of this always-busy bookstore packed with new titles upstairs and used and remaindered books downstairs. The collection's diversity has made the store a favored destination for academics. ⊠ *1256 Massachusetts Ave., Cambridge* ☎ *617/661–1515* ⊕ *www.harvard.com* Ⓜ *Harvard.*

Fodor'sChoice ★ **Harvard Coop Society.** Begun in 1882 as a nonprofit service for students and faculty, the Coop is now managed by Barnes & Noble College, a separate entity that manages college campus bookstores. In addition to books and textbooks (many discounted), school supplies, clothes, and accessories plastered with the Harvard emblem are sold here, as well as basic housewares geared toward dorm dwellers. If you're looking for a public restroom, you'll find it here. ⊠ *1400 Massachusetts Ave., Cambridge* ☎ *617/499–2000* ⊕ *store.thecoop.com* Ⓜ *Harvard.*

Raven Used Books. Looking for a stash of scholarly used books? Raven's attracts local students eager to unload their university press titles. The store stocks approximately 16,000 carefully used books on topics ranging from social and political theory to art and architecture and buys more than 1,000 books weekly with discounts ranging from 50% to 80% off the cover price. ⊠ *23 Church St., Harvard Square* ☎ *617/441–6999* ⊕ *www.ravencambridge.com* Ⓜ *Harvard.*

CLOTHING

Mint Julep. Cute dresses, playful skirts, and form-fitting tops make up the selection here. The Cambridge location is a little larger and easier to navigate, but Brookline houses the original. ⊠ *6 Church St., Cambridge* ☎ *617/576–6468* ⊕ *www.shopmintjulep.com* Ⓜ *Harvard.*

CRAFTS

Cambridge Artists' Cooperative. Unique, handcrafted ceramics, weavings, jewelry, wood- and leatherwork fill this two-level store, with more than 200 global artists represented—more than half of whom hail from New England. ⊠ *59A Church St., Cambridge* ☎ *617/868–4434* ⊕ *www.cambridgeartistscoop.com* Ⓜ *Harvard.*

GIFTS

Nomad. Low prices and an enthusiastic staff greet you at this globally inspired store carrying fair-trade crafts, folk art, fashion, accessories, and home decor from around the corner and around the world. In addition to cute dresses, tunics, and tops, you'll find Indian good-luck *torans* (wall hangings), Mexican *milagros* (charms), mirrors to keep away the evil eye, silver jewelry, and recycled cloth tote bags from Cambodia. In the basement you'll find kilims, hand-painted tiles, and wooden artifacts. ⊠ *1741 Massachusetts Ave., Cambridge* ☎ *617/497–6677* ⊕ *www.nomadcambridge.com* Ⓜ *Porter.*

Tokai Japanese Gifts. Located in the Porter Exchange building, this quaint corner of Japan has a lovely assortment of Japanese tableware—bowls, serving dishes, trays, and chopstick rests—along with lots of other little treasures like origami paper, *yukata* (cotton robes), incense, and high-end kimonos. ∎TIP➜ Savor delicious Japanese food at any of the small restaurants and noodle shops in the same building just a few steps away. ⊠ *1815 Massachusetts Ave., Cambridge* ☎ *617/864–5922* ⊕ *www.tokaijapanesegifts.com* Ⓜ *Porter.*

FOOD

Cardullo's. This snug, nearly 70-year-old, family-owned and -operated shop in Harvard Square purveys exotic imports, including cheeses, chocolates, biscuits, jams, olive oils, and mustards, along with sandwiches to go. You'll also find a generous assortment of champagnes and domestic caviar, fine wines, and assorted beers. ⊠ *6 Brattle St., Cambridge* ☎ *617/491–8888, 800/491–8288* ⊕ *www.cardullos.com* Ⓜ *Harvard.*

HOME FURNISHINGS

Abodeon. New York decorators come to town just to shop this incredible collection of 20th- and 21st-century modern housewares, both newly produced classic designs and pristine-condition vintage. You might come across an Eames lounge chair, a complete set of modern Scandinavian dinnerware, or a Lucite dining set from the early 1970s. But that's not all: tucked among the furniture and housewares, you'll find a fun and quirky collection of items for the office, bath, and beyond, like a Seven Year Pen and snowball candle. ⊠ *1731 Massachusetts Ave., Cambridge* ☎ *617/497–0137* ⊕ *www.abodeon.com* ☉ *Closed Mon. and Tues.* Ⓜ *Porter.*

SHOES

Concepts. Sneaker collectors love having what other people can't find and this store features exclusives by Nike, New Balance, Vans, Adidas, and others. Fanatics line up around the block when a limited-edition shoe debuts. ✉ *37 Brattle St., Cambridge* ☎ ⊕ *www.cncpts. com* Ⓜ *Harvard.*

Marathon Sports. Known for its personalized service, Marathon gives advice for choosing the perfect shoe, whether you're a beginning walker or a serious sprinter. With numerous branches, including one in Boston (671 Boylston Street) and another in Brookline (1638 Beacon Street), this flagship store sees many a marathoner stopping in to buy shoes before the Boston race each spring. ✉ *1654 Massachusetts Ave., Cambridge* ☎ *617/354–4161* ⊕ *www.marathonsports.com* Ⓜ *Harvard.*

SHOPPING CENTERS

CambridgeSide Galleria. Macy's and Sears anchor this basic three-story mall with a food court; it's a big draw for local high-school kids and an easy walk from the Museum of Science. ✉ *100 CambridgeSide Pl., Kendall Square* ☎ *617/621–8666* ⊕ *www.cambridgesidegalleria.com* Ⓜ *Lechmere, Kendall/MIT via free shuttle.*

Galleria at Harvard Square. Not to be confused with CambridgeSide Galleria, this Harvard Square emporium houses a few decent, independently owned restaurants and a collection of boutique shops. ✉ *57 JFK St., Cambridge* Ⓜ *Harvard.*

SPECIALTY STORES

Curio Spice Co. Working on a saffron farm in Greece helped jump-start owner Claire Cheney's foray into the world of spices. She now sells more than 100 in her pretty apothecary-like store, alongside vintage tins of her creative spice blends—check out the flower-filled one with pink pepper, hibiscus, rose, mint, and ylang-ylang. Cheney sources her mainly organic and fair-trade spices from New England and international farms and she's knowledgeable about scents, origins, and use for every spice she carries. ✉ *2265 Massachusetts Ave., Cambridge* ☎ *617/945–1888* ⊕ *www.curiospice.com.*

Fodor's Choice ★ **Leavitt & Peirce.** A throwback to another era, this storied tobacco shop has been in the same location since 1883, when it served as a clubby gathering spot for young Harvard men, who puffed away while playing pool on the back billiard tables. While Harvard oars, hockey sticks, and photos still adorn the ivy-green walls, the store now caters to a broader clientele in search of quality smoking items, toiletries, chess and checker sets, and small gift items, such as beer steins. Don't miss the four chess tables on the second level, where you can rent pieces for $2 an hour (checkers and backgammon are available, too). ✉ *1316 Massachusetts Ave., Harvard Square* ☎ *617/547–0576* ⊕ *www.leavittpeirce.com* Ⓜ *Harvard.*

Out-of-Town News. Smack in the middle of Harvard Square, this landmark kiosk sells a staggering selection of the world's newspapers and magazines. ✉ *0 Harvard Sq., Cambridge* ☎ *617/354–1441* Ⓜ *Harvard.*

14

THRIFT SHOPS

The Garment District. Step into this warehouse-like building and head to the second level to find a massive selection of vintage, used, and new clothing and accessories. Boston Costume, the sister business on the first floor, draws thrift pickers to the back room to paw through an 850-pound bale of clothes that's dumped on the floor each day; items are sold for $2 per pound ($1 on Friday). Students crowd the entire store year-round, and everyone comes at Halloween for that perfect costume. ⊠ *200 Broadway, Cambridge* ☎ *617/876–5230* ⊕ *www.garmentdistrict.com* Ⓜ *Kendall/MIT.*

Keezer's Classic Clothing. In the late 19th century when young Harvard men needed spending money for dates and vintage Port, they sold their handmade suits to the original owners of this men's store founded in 1895. JFK, in fact, used to send his valet to Keezer's each spring to unload unwanted duds. Now, this shop is many a man's secret weapon for dress and formal wear at an informal price. Pick up new or used suits, tuxedos, ties, shirts, and pants, or stop by to rent all the necessities for a black tie event. ⊠ *140 River St., Cambridge* ☎ *617/547–2455* ⊕ *www.keezers.com* ☯ *Closed Sun.* Ⓜ *Central.*

Oona's. Crowded racks of vintage and eclectic modern dresses, coats, tops, and lingerie are reason enough to stop by this unique boutique. But, the helpful staff and cheerful vibe just make doing so that much more fun. ⊠ *1210 Massachusetts Ave., Cambridge* ☎ *617/491–2654* ⊕ *www.oonasboston.com* Ⓜ *Harvard.*

TOYS

FAMILY **Henry Bear's Park.** This charming neighborhood store with multiple branches, including one in Brookline (19 Harvard Street), specializes in huggable bears and collectible dolls; it also sells books, toys, and games. ⊠ *Porter Sq. Shopping Center, 17 White St., Cambridge* ☎ *617/547–8424* ⊕ *www.henrybear.com* Ⓜ *Porter.*

FAMILY **The World's Only Curious George Store.** Decorated with tropical plants, a fake hut, and tot-size chairs, and equipped with puzzles, toys, activity sets, and books of all kinds for all ages, this store is a wonderland for kids and a parent's salvation on a rainy day. ⊠ *Harvard Square, 1 JFK St., Cambridge* ☎ *617/547–4500* ⊕ *thecuriousgeorgestore.com* Ⓜ *Harvard.*

SIDE TRIPS
FROM BOSTON

WELCOME TO SIDE TRIPS FROM BOSTON

TOP REASONS TO GO

★ **Early American history:** From Plimoth Plantation to Salem, Concord, and Lexington, you can visit colonial-reenactment museums, Revolutionary War battle sites, historic homes, and inns.

★ **Seafaring communities:** Set off on a whale watch from Gloucester, warm yourself after a windy coastal walk in Rockport with clam chowder, and admire the dedicated routine of local fishermen.

★ **Revisit your reading:** Nathaniel Hawthorne's House of Seven Gables still stands in Salem. Liberate yourself with a swim in Thoreau's Walden Pond. In Concord, see where both Louisa May Alcott and Ralph Waldo Emerson penned their works.

★ **Cranberry bogs:** The bogs' red, green, gold, and blue colors dot Cape Cod and the Plymouth area.

★ **The Mayflower II:** The story of the Pilgrims' Atlantic crossing comes alive in Plymouth.

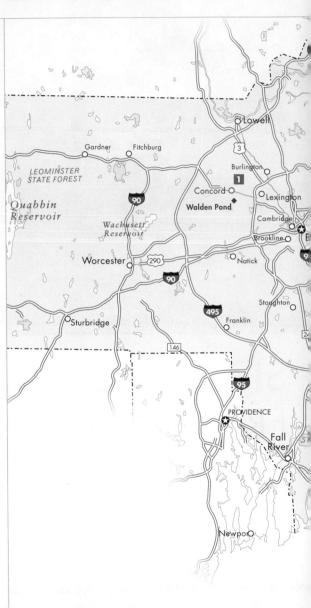

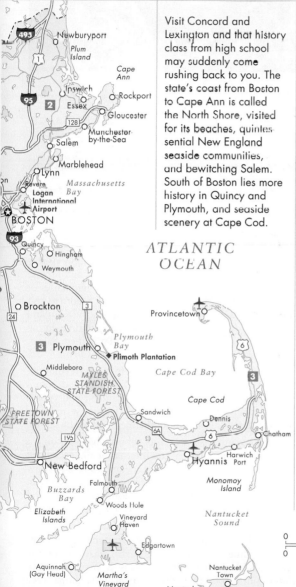

Visit Concord and Lexington and that history class from high school may suddenly come rushing back to you. The state's coast from Boston to Cape Ann is called the North Shore, visited for its beaches, quintessential New England seaside communities, and bewitching Salem. South of Boston lies more history in Quincy and Plymouth, and seaside scenery at Cape Cod.

1 Northwest of Boston.
This region brims with the markers of American history. Names like Thoreau, Emerson, and Hawthorne take on fresh meaning after you've visited their homes and haunts, and Revolutionary War battle sights highlight both Lexington and Concord.

2 The North Shore.
Classic New England waterfront towns dot the Atlantic Coast northeast of Boston. Highlights include seafaring history-steeped communities such as Marblehead, Gloucester, and Essex; bewitching Salem; and family-friendly beaches.

3 South of Boston. Gain insights here into what the earliest American settlers experienced. In Plymouth and Plimoth Plantation, learn how the Pilgrims raised food, built their homes, and survived under harsh conditions. New Bedford's whaling culture and Portuguese heritage come alive on the cobblestone streets along the docks. And don't forget vacation-central Cape Cod!

15

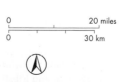

Updated
by Megan
Johnson

History lies thick on the ground in the towns surrounding Boston—from Pilgrims to pirates, witches to whalers, the American Revolution to the Industrial Revolution. The sights outside the city are at least as interesting as those on Boston's Freedom Trail. When you're ready to trade history lessons for beach fun, Cape Cod to the south and the North Shore to the northeast entice sand-and-sun seekers.

Rich in more than history, the areas surrounding Boston also allow visitors to retrace the steps of famous writers, bask in the outdoors, and browse shops in funky artist communities. The haunts of literary luminaries of every generation lurk throughout Massachusetts. Head to Concord to visit the place where Henry David Thoreau wrote his prophetic *Walden* and where Louisa May Alcott's *Little Women* brightened a grim time during the Civil War. Relive Nathaniel Hawthorne's vision of Puritan-era Salem. Stop in Lowell to see where Jack Kerouac lived before going *On the Road*.

The seaside towns of Massachusetts were built before the Revolution, during the heyday of American shipping. Ipswich's First Period homes (there are more here than anywhere else in the nation) and Newburyport's majestic Federal Style mansions, grand old houses, and bustling waterfronts evoke a bygone world of clipper ships, robust fishermen, and sturdy sailors.

In a more contemporary vein, Boston and its suburbs have become a major destination for food and wine lovers. Internationally acclaimed chefs, including Barbara Lynch, Frank McClelland, and Ming Tsai, draw thousands of devoted, discerning foodies to their restaurants each year. The state's extensive system of parks, protected forests, beaches, and nature preserves satisfies everyone from the avid hiker to the beach bum.

WHEN TO GO
The dazzling foliage and cool temperatures make fall the best time to visit Massachusetts. Summer, especially late in the season when the water is a bit warmer, is ideal for beach vacations. Many towns save their best for winter—inns open their doors to carolers, shops serve eggnog, and lobster boats parade around Gloucester Harbor.

BUDGETING YOUR TIME

Though Massachusetts is small, you can easily spend several weeks exploring it. If you have a few days, head to a town or two north and south of Boston, such as Concord, Plymouth, and Salem. With a week you may want to add on the Berkshires or spend the entire time relaxing on Cape Cod.

GETTING HERE AND AROUND

AIR TRAVEL

Boston's Logan International Airport is the state's major airport. Trains, ferries, and small commuter flights take you to points around the state. If you're driving to Cape Cod, avoid the Friday late-afternoon-to-early-evening summer rush.

BOAT TRAVEL

Though not covered in this chapter, Martha's Vineyard, Nantucket, and Cape Cod are popular getaway destinations from Boston. High-speed ferries provide transportation to Martha's Vineyard and Nantucket. The Bay State Cruise Co. and Boston Harbor Cruises run 90-minute ferry rides between Boston and Cape Cod's Provincetown from May through October; reservations are strongly recommended. For details on what to see and do in these destinations, see *Fodor's Cape Cod, Nantucket, and Martha's Vineyard*.

Contact Bay State Cruise Co. ☎ *877/783–3779* ⊕ *www.baystatecruisecompany.com.*

CAR TRAVEL

Outside Boston you need a car to explore the state. Expect heavy traffic heading in and out of the city at rush hour, generally from 6 am to 9 am and 4 pm to 7 pm.

From Boston to Lexington, pick up Route 2 West in Cambridge. Exit at Routes 4/225. Turn left on Massachusetts Avenue for the National Heritage Museum. For Lexington's town center, take the Waltham Street–Lexington exit from Route 2. Follow Waltham Street just under 2 miles to Massachusetts Avenue; you'll be just east of the Battle Green. The drive takes about 30 minutes. To continue to Concord, head farther west on Route 2. Or take Interstate 90 (the Massachusetts Turnpike) to Interstate 95 North, and then exit at Route 2, heading west. Driving time is 40–45 minutes from Boston.

The primary link between Boston and the North Shore is Route 128, which follows the coast northeast to Gloucester. To pick up Route 128 from Boston, take Interstate 93 North to Interstate 95 North to Route 128. If you stay on Interstate 95, you'll reach Newburyport. From Boston to Salem or Marblehead, follow Route 128 to Route 114 into Salem or continue to Marblehead. Driving from Boston to Salem takes about 35–40 minutes; to Gloucester or to Newburyport, about 50–60 minutes.

To get to Plymouth, take the Southeast Expressway Interstate 93 South to Route 3 (toward Cape Cod); Exits 6 and 4 lead to downtown Plymouth and Plimoth Plantation, respectively. Allow about one hour.

15

TRAIN TRAVEL

The MBTA's commuter rail offers service to Newburyport, Ipswich, Rockport, Salem, and Gloucester. Travel times are usually 70 minutes or less.

Massachusetts Bay Transportation Authority. ☎ *800/392–6100, 617/222–3200 ⊕ www.mbta.com.*

RESTAURANTS

Massachusetts invented the fried clam, and it's served in many North Shore restaurants. Creamy clam chowder is another specialty. Eating seafood in the rough—from paper plates in seaside shacks—is a revered local custom. At country inns you'll find traditional New England dinners: double-cut pork chops, rack of lamb, game, Boston baked beans, Indian pudding, and the dubiously glorified New England boiled dinner (corned beef and cabbage with potatoes, carrots, turnips, and other vegetables).

HOTELS

Although Boston has everything from luxury hotels to charming bed-and-breakfasts, the signature accommodation outside Boston is the country inn; less extravagant and less expensive are B&B establishments, many of them in private homes. Make reservations well in advance if traveling in the summer. Smoking has been banned in all Massachusetts hotels.

WHAT IT COSTS			
$	**$$**	**$$$**	**$$$$**
Restaurants	under $15	$15–$24	$25–$32	over $32
Hotels	under $150	$150–$225	$226–$325	over $325

For restaurants, prices are per person, for a main course at dinner. For hotels, prices are for two people in a standard double room in high season, excluding 11.95% in hotel and sales tax and service charges. Local taxes may also apply.

TOURS

Concord Chamber of Commerce. April through November, Concord Chamber of Commerce runs walking tours focusing on the Revolutionary War or the area's rich literary history. Each tour lasts about 1½ hours and departs from the Concord Visitor Center on Sunday, Monday, and holidays at noon; Friday at 1; and Saturday at 11 and 1. Private tours are also available. ⊠ *58 Main St. (visitor center address), Concord* ☎ *978/369–3120 ⊕ www.concordchamberofcommerce.org.*

Essex River Cruises & Charters. From May to October, Essex River Cruises & Charters organizes narrated cruises of nearby salt marshes and rivers. They also offer private charters for all occasions, including New England–style clambakes served on tidal beaches. Book online or call ahead for schedules and reservations. ☎ *978/768–6981 ⊕ www.essexcruises.com.*

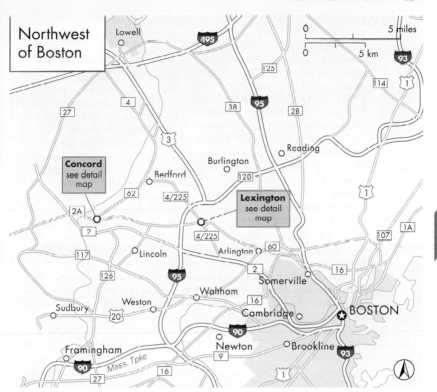

Northwest of Boston

Lowell

Concord
see detail
map

Lexington
see detail
map

Reading

Burlington

Bedford

Arlington

Lincoln

Somerville

Waltham

Sudbury   Weston   Cambridge   ☆ BOSTON

Framingham   Mass. Tpke.   Newton   Brookline

0   5 miles
0   5 km

Gray Line of Boston & Cape Cod. Daily June through October and on weekends in May, Gray Line Boston & Cape Cod offers motor-coach tours from Boston to Lexington's Battle Green and Concord's Old North Bridge area. Seasonal trips to Salem, Marblehead, Newport, Cape Cod, Martha's Vineyard, and Plymouth, and city tours of Boston are also available. ☎ *781/986–6100, 617/720–6342, 781/986–6100* ⊕ *www.graylineboston.com.*

NORTHWEST OF BOSTON

Northwest of the city, Lexington and Concord embody the spirit of the American Revolution. Sites of the first skirmishes of the Revolutionary War, these two quintessential New England towns were also cradles of American literature; several historic homes and small museums here are dedicated to some of the country's first substantial writers—Ralph Waldo Emerson, Nathaniel Hawthorne, Louisa May Alcott, and Henry David Thoreau.

LEXINGTON

16 miles northwest of Boston.

Incensed against the British, American colonials burst into action in Lexington in April 1775. On April 18, patriot leader Paul Revere alerted the town that British soldiers were approaching. The next day, as the British advance troops arrived in Lexington on their march toward Concord, the Minutemen were waiting to confront the redcoats in what became the first skirmish of the Revolutionary War.

These first military encounters of the American Revolution are very much a part of present-day Lexington, a modern suburban town that sprawls out from the historic sites near its center. Although the downtown area is generally lively, with ice-cream and coffee shops, boutiques, and a great little movie theater, the town becomes especially animated each Patriots' Day (April 19 but celebrated on the third Monday in April), when costume-clad groups re-create the Minutemen's battle maneuvers and Paul Revere rides again.

To learn more about the city and the 1775 clash, stop by the **Lexington Visitors Center.**

TAKE A TOUR

Liberty Ride. Ride along the historic Battle Road while your costumed guide recounts the exciting events of April 19, 1775, and the literary legacy that defined American identity and culture. This 90-minute trolley tour begins and ends at the Lexington Visitors Center. Purchase tickets online in advance at ⊕ *libertyride. us.* ✉ *1875 Massachusetts Ave.* ☎ *339/223–5623* ⊕ *libertyride. us* 🎫 *$28.*

GETTING HERE AND AROUND

Massachusetts Bay Transportation Authority (MBTA) operates bus service in the greater Boston area and serves Lexington.

Bus Contact MBTA. ☎ *617/222–3200, 800/392–6100* ⊕ *www.mbta.com.*

ESSENTIALS

Visitor Information Lexington Visitors Center. ✉ *1875 Massachusetts Ave.* ☎ *781/862–1450* ⊕ *www.lexingtonchamber.org.*

EXPLORING

Battle Green. It was on this 2-acre triangle of land, on April 19, 1775, that the first confrontation between British soldiers, who were marching from Boston toward Concord, and the Colonial militia known as the Minutemen took place. The Minutemen—so called because they were able to prepare themselves at a moment's notice—were led by Captain John Parker, whose role in the American Revolution is commemorated in Henry Hudson Kitson's renowned 1900 *Minuteman* statue. Facing downtown Lexington at the tip of Battle Green, the statue's in a traffic island, and therefore makes for a difficult photo op. ✉ *Junction of Massachusetts Ave. and Bedford St.* 🎫 *Free.*

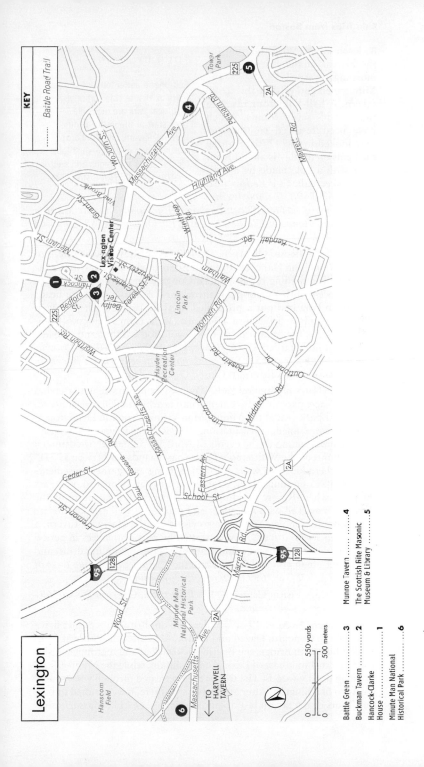

Lexington

Battle Green **3**
Buckman Tavern **2**
Hancock-Clarke House **1**
Minute Man National Historical Park **6**
Munroe Tavern **4**
The Scottish Rite Masonic Museum & Library **5**

KEY

...... Battle Road Trail

Lexington Visitor Center

Hanscom Field

Minute Man National Historical Park

Lincoln Park

Hayden Recreation Center

TO HARTWELL TAVERN

0   550 yards
0   500 meters

Buckman Tavern. While waiting for the arrival of the British on the morning of April 19, 1775, the Minutemen gathered at this 1690 tavern. A half-hour tour takes in the tavern's seven rooms, which have been restored to the way they looked in the 1770s. Among the items on display is an old front door with a hole made by a British musket ball. ⊠ *1 Bedford St.* ☎ *781/862–5598* ⊕ *www.lexingtonhistory.org* ✍ *First Shot! Package (Buckman Tavern, Munroe Tavern, and Hancock-Clarke House): $15. One house: $8* ☉ *Closed Oct. 31–Apr.*

> **TOUR BY PHONE**
>
> Cell-phone audio tours of various parts of Minute Man National Historical Park are available. They start at the visitor center, Hartwell Tavern, and Concord's North Bridge entrance—just look for the audio-tour signs and call ☎ 978/224–4905 for instructions.

Hancock-Clarke House. On April 18, 1775, Paul Revere came here to warn patriots John Hancock and Sam Adams (who were staying at the house while attending the Provincial Congress in nearby Concord) of the advance of British troops. Hancock and Adams, on whose heads the British king had put a price, fled to avoid capture. The house, a parsonage built in 1698, is a 10-minute walk from Lexington Common. Inside is the Treasures of the Revolution exhibit, and outside, a Colonial herb garden. ⊠ *36 Hancock St.* ☎ *781/861–0928* ⊕ *www.lexingtonhistory.org* ✍ *$8; $15 combination ticket includes Buckman Tavern and Munroe Tavern* ☉ *Closed Oct. 31–Apr.*

FAMILY **Minute Man National Historical Park.** West of Lexington's center stretches this 1,000-acre park that also extends into nearby Lincoln and Concord. Begin your park visit at the **Minute Man Visitor Center** in Lexington to see the free multimedia presentation, "The Road to Revolution," a captivating introduction to the events of April 1775. Staffed by costumed park volunteers, the Whittemore House has a hands-on "Try on 1775!" exhibit where kids can wear colonial clothing and gather ingredients for a meal. Continuing along Highway 2A toward Concord, you pass the point where Revere's midnight ride ended with his capture by the British; it's marked with a boulder and plaque, as well as an enclosure with wayside exhibits. You can also visit the 1732 **Hartwell Tavern,** a restored drover's (driver's) tavern staffed by park employees in period costume; they frequently demonstrate musket firing, militia drills, and talk about life in colonial Massachusetts. ⊠ *Hwy. 2A, ¼ mile west of Hwy. 128* ☎ *978/369–6993* ⊕ *www.nps.gov/mima.*

North Bridge Visitor Center. ⊠ *174 Liberty St., Concord* ☎ *978/369–6993* ⊕ *www.nps.gov/mima.*

Munroe Tavern. As April 19, 1775, dragged on, British forces met fierce resistance in Concord. Dazed and demoralized after the battle at Concord's Old North Bridge, the British backtracked and regrouped at this 1695 tavern 1 mile east of Lexington Common, while the Munroe family hid in nearby woods. The troops then retreated through what is now the town of Arlington. After a bloody battle there, they returned to Boston. Tours of the tavern last about 30 minutes. ⊠ *1332 Massachusetts*

Ave. ☎ 781/862–0295 ⊕ www.lexingtonhistory.org ☜ $8; $15 combi-nation ticket includes Hancock-Clarke House and Buckman Tavern ⊙ Closed weekdays Apr. and May.

The Scottish Rite Masonic Museum & Library. View artifacts from all facets of American life, put in social and political context. Specializing in the history of American Freemasonry and Fraternalism, the changing exhibits and lectures also focus on local events leading up to April 1775 and illustrate Revolutionary-era life through everyday objects such as blacksmithing tools, bloodletting paraphernalia, and dental instruments, including a "tooth key" used to extract teeth. ✉ *33 Marrett Rd., Hwy. 2A at Massachusetts Ave.* ☎ *781/861–6559* ⊕ *www.srmml.org* ☜ *Donations accepted.*

CONCORD

About 10 miles west of Lexington, 21 miles northwest of Boston.

The Concord of today is a modern suburb with a busy center filled with arty shops, places to eat, and (recalling the literary history made here) old bookstores. Autumn lovers, take note: Concord is a great place to start a fall foliage tour. From Boston, head west along Route 2 to Concord, and then continue on to find harvest stands and apple picking around Harvard and Stow.

15

GETTING HERE AND AROUND
The MBTA runs buses to Concord. On the MBTA Commuter Rail, Concord is a 40-minute ride on the Fitchburg Line, which departs from Boston's North Station.

Bus and Train Contact MBTA. ☎ *617/222–3200, 800/392–6100* ⊕ *www.mbta.com.*

ESSENTIALS
Visitor Information Concord Visitor Center. ✉ *58 Main St.* ☎ *978/369–3120* ⊕ *www.concordchamberofcommerce.org.*

EXPLORING
FAMILY **Concord Museum.** The original contents of Emerson's private study, as well as the world's largest collection of Thoreau artifacts, reside in this 1930 Colonial Revival building just east of the town center. The museum provides a good overview of the town's history, from its original American Indian settlement to the present. Highlights include American Indian artifacts, furnishings from Thoreau's Walden Pond cabin (there's a replica of the cabin itself on the museum's lawn), and one of the two lanterns hung at Boston's Old North Church to signal that the British were coming by sea. If you've brought children, ask for a free family activity pack. ✉ *200 Lexington Rd., GPS address is 53 Cambridge Tpke.* ☎ *978/369–9763* ⊕ *www.concordmuseum.org* ☜ *$10.*

Old Manse. The Reverend William Emerson, grandfather of Ralph Waldo Emerson, watched rebels and Redcoats battle from behind his home, which was within sight of the Old North Bridge. The house, built in 1770, was occupied continuously by the Emerson family for almost two centuries, except for a 3½-year period during which Nathaniel Hawthorne rented it. Furnishings date from the late 18th century. Tours run

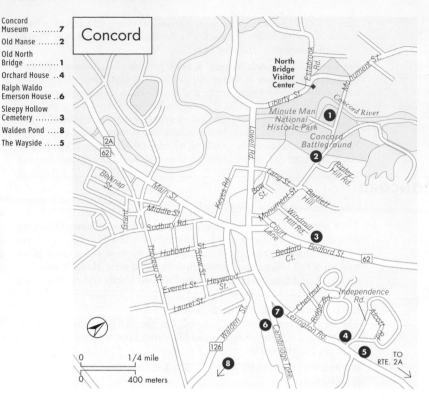

Concord
Museum 7

Old Manse 2

Old North
Bridge 1

Orchard House ..4

Ralph Waldo
Emerson House ..6

Sleepy Hollow
Cemetery 3

Walden Pond 8

The Wayside 5

Concord

North
Bridge
Visitor
Center

Minute Man
National
Historic Park

Concord
Battleground

0   1/4 mile

0   400 meters

TO
RTE. 2A

throughout the day and last 45 minutes, but call ahead to check. Don't whip out your camera, however: photography is prohibited inside the house. ✉ *269 Monument St.* 📞 *978/369–3909* ⊕ *www.thetrustees.org/ places-to-visit/greater-boston/old-manse.html* ✉ *Grounds free; house tours $10* ☞ *Grounds are open yr-round sunrise–sunset.*

Old North Bridge. A half mile from Concord center, at this bridge, the Concord Minutemen turned the tables on the British on the morning of April 19, 1775. The Americans didn't fire first, but when two of their own fell dead from a Redcoat volley, Major John Buttrick of Concord roared, "Fire, fellow soldiers, for God's sake, fire." The Minutemen released volley after volley, and the Redcoats fled. Daniel Chester French's famous statue *The Minuteman* (1875) honors the country's first freedom fighters. The lovely wooded surroundings give a sense of what the landscape was like in more rural times. Guests who take the Liberty Ride trolley tour from Lexington Center will be treated to a quick stop at the bridge. ✉ *Concord* ⊕ *www.nps.gov/mima.*

Orchard House. The dark brown exterior of Louisa May Alcott's family home sharply contrasts with the light, wit, and energy so much in evidence within. Named for the apple orchard that once surrounded it, Orchard House was the Alcott family home from 1857 to 1877. Here Louisa wrote *Little Women*, based in part on her life with her three

Literary Concord

The first wholly American literary movement was born in Concord, the tiny town west of Boston that, quite coincidentally, also witnessed the beginning of the American Revolution.

Under the influence of essayist and poet Ralph Waldo Emerson, a group eventually known as the Transcendental Club (but called the Hedges Club at the time) assembled regularly in Emerson's Concord home. Henry David Thoreau, a fellow townsman and famous proponent of self-reliance, was an integral club member, along with such others as pioneering feminist Margaret Fuller and poet Ellery Channing, both drawn to Concord simply because of Emerson's presence.

These are the names that have become indelible bylines in high-school anthologies and college syllabi, but Concord also produced beloved authors outside the Transcendentalist movement. These writers include Louisa May Alcott of *Little Women* fame and children's book author Harriet Lothrop, pseudonymously known as Margaret Sydney. Even Nathaniel Hawthorne, whose various temporary homes around Massachusetts constitute a literary trail all their own, resided in Concord during the early and later portions of his career.

The cumulative inkwells of these authors have bestowed upon Concord a literary legacy unique in the United States, both for its influence on literature in general and for the quantity of related sights packed within such a small radius. From Alcott's Orchard House to Hawthorne's Old Manse, nearly all their houses remain standing, well preserved and open for tours.

The Thoreau Institute, within walking distance of a reconstruction of Thoreau's famous cabin in the woods at Walden Pond, is a repository of his papers and original editions. Emerson's study sits in the Concord Museum, across the street from his house. Even their final resting places are here, on Authors Ridge in Sleepy Hollow Cemetery, a few short blocks from the town common.

15

sisters; and her father, Bronson, founded the Concord School of Philosophy—the building remains behind the house. Because Orchard House had just one owner after the Alcotts left, and because it became a museum in 1911, more than 80% of the original furnishings remain, including the semicircular shelf-desk where Louisa wrote *Little Women*. ⊠ *399 Lexington Rd.* ☎ *978/369–4118* ⊕ *www.louisamayalcott.org* ⌨ *$10.*

Ralph Waldo Emerson House. The 19th-century essayist and poet Ralph Waldo Emerson lived briefly in the Old Manse in 1834–35, then moved to this home, where he lived until his death in 1882. Here he wrote the *Essays*. Except for artifacts from Emerson's study, now at the nearby Concord Museum, the Emerson House furnishings have been preserved as the writer left them, down to his hat resting on the newel post. You must join one of the half-hour-long tours to see the interior. ⊠ *28 Cambridge Tpke., at Lexington Rd.* ☎ *978/369–2236* ⊕ *www.nps.gov/nr/ travel/massachusetts_conservation/ralph_waldo_emerson_house.html* ⌨ *$8* ⊙ *Mid-Apr.–Oct., closed Mon.–Wed. Closed Nov.–mid-Apr.* ☞ *Call ahead for tour scheduling information.*

Sleepy Hollow Cemetery. This garden cemetery on the National Registry of Historic Places served as a place of inspiration and a final resting place for American literary greats like Louisa May Alcott, Ralph Waldo Emerson, Henry David Thoreau, and Nathaniel Hawthorne. Each Memorial Day Alcott's grave is decorated in commemoration of her death. ⊠ *Bedford St. (Hwy. 62), 24 Court La. and Bedford St.* ✛ *1 block east of Monument Sq. in Concord* ☎ *978/318–3233.*

Fodor'sChoice   **Walden Pond.** For lovers of Early American literature, a trip to Concord
★   isn't complete without a pilgrimage to Henry David Thoreau's most famous residence. Here, in 1845, at age 28, Thoreau moved into a one-room cabin—built for $28.12—on the shore of this 100-foot-deep kettle hole formed by the retreat of an ancient glacier. Living alone for the next two years, Thoreau discovered the benefits of solitude and the beauties of nature. *Walden,* published in 1854, is a mixture of philosophy, nature writing, and proto-ecology. The site of the original house is staked out in stone. A full-size, authentically furnished replica of the cabin stands about ½ mile from the original site, near the Walden Pond State Reservation parking lot. During the summer, don't be shocked if you aren't allowed entrance: Walden Pond has a visitor capacity. ⊠ *915 Walden St. (Hwy. 126)* ✛ *To get to Walden Pond State Reservation from the center of Concord—a trip of only 1½ miles—take Concord's Main St. a block west from Monument Sq., turn left onto Walden St., and head for the intersection of highways 2 and 126. Cross over Hwy. 2 onto Hwy. 126, heading south for ½ mile* ☎ *978/369–3254* ⊕ *www.mass.gov/dcr/ parks/walden* ⊡ *Free, $8 for vehicles with Massachusetts plates, $10 for vehicles with non-Massachusetts plates* ↻ *No dogs allowed.*

The Wayside. Nathaniel Hawthorne lived at the Old Manse in 1842–45, working on stories and sketches; he then moved to Salem (where he wrote *The Scarlet Letter*) and later to Lenox (*The House of the Seven Gables*). In 1852 he returned to Concord, bought this rambling structure called The Wayside, and lived here until his death in 1864. The home certainly appealed to literary types: the subsequent owner of The Wayside, Margaret Sidney, wrote the children's book *Five Little Peppers and How They Grew* (1881), and before Hawthorne moved in, the Alcotts lived here, from 1845 to 1848. An exhibit center, in the former barn, provides information about the Wayside authors and links them to major events in American history. Hawthorne's tower-study, with his stand-up writing desk, is substantially as he left it. ⊠ *455 Lexington Rd.* ☎ *978/318–7863* ⊕ *www.nps.gov/nr/travel/pwwmh/ma47.htm* ⊡ *$7* ☉ *Closed Tues., Wed., and in winter.*

SPORTS AND THE OUTDOORS

South Bridge Boat House. You can reach the North Bridge section of the Minute Man National Historical Park by water if you rent a canoe or kayak at the South Bridge Boat House and paddle along the Sudbury and Concord rivers. You can even paddle all the way to Sudbury or up to Billerica. ⊠ *496 Main St.* ☎ *978/369–9438* ⊕ *www.southbridgeboat-house.com* ⊡ *Canoes $16/hr weekdays, $18/hr weekends and holidays; kayaks $16/hr single, $17/hr double on weekdays, $17/hr single, $18 double on weekends and holidays* ↻ *Closed Nov. 1–Apr. 1.*

WHERE TO EAT

$$
AMERICAN
✕ **Main Streets Market & Cafe.** Cyclists, families, and sightseers pack into this brick building, which was used to store munitions during the Revolutionary War. Wood floors and blackboard menus add a touch of nostalgia, but the extensive menu includes many modern hits. $ *Average main: $18* ✉ *42 Main St.* ☎ *978/369-9948* ⊕ *www.mainstreetsmarketandcafe.com* ☰ *No credit cards.*

THE NORTH SHORE

The slice of Massachusetts's Atlantic Coast known as the North Shore extends past Boston to the picturesque Cape Ann region just shy of the New Hampshire border. In addition to miles of woods and beaches, the North Shore's highlights include Marblehead, a stunningly classic New England sea town; Salem, which thrives on a history of witches, writers, and maritime trades; Gloucester, the oldest seaport in America; Rockport, rich with crafts shops and artists' studios; and Newburyport, with its redbrick center and clapboard mansions, and a handful of typical New England towns in between. Bustling during the short summer season and breathtaking during the autumn foliage, the North Shore is calmer (and colder) between November and June. Since many restaurants, inns, and attractions operate on reduced hours, it's worth calling ahead off-season.

15

MARBLEHEAD

17 miles north of Boston.

Marblehead, with its narrow and winding streets, beautifully preserved clapboard homes, sea captains' mansions, and harbor, looks much as it must have when it was founded in 1629 by fishermen from Cornwall and the Channel Islands. One of New England's premier sailing capitals, Marblehead continues to attract boats from along the Eastern seaboard each July during Race Week—first held in 1889. Parking in town can be difficult; lots at the end of Front Street or on State Street by the Landing restaurant are the best options.

ESSENTIALS

Visitor Information Marblehead Chamber of Commerce Information Booth. ✉ *131 Essex St.* ☎ *781/631-2868* ⊕ *www.marbleheadchamber.org.*

EXPLORING

Abbot Hall. The town's Victorian-era municipal building, built in 1876, displays Archibald Willard's painting *The Spirit of '76.* Many visitors, familiar since childhood with this image of the three Revolutionary veterans with fife, drum, and flag, are surprised to find the original in an otherwise unassuming town hall. Also on-site is a small naval museum exploring Marblehead's maritime past. ✉ *188 Washington St.* ☎ *781/631-0528 town clerk* 🔁 *Free.*

Fort Sewall. Magnificent views of Marblehead, of the harbor, the Misery Islands, and the Atlantic are best enjoyed from this fort built in 1644 atop the rocky cliffs of the harbor. Used as a defense against the French in 1742 as well as during the War of 1812, Fort Sewall is today open to

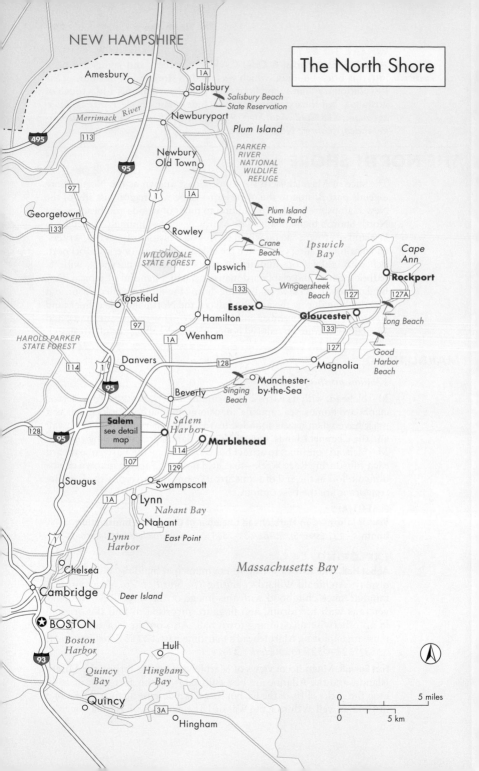

The North Shore

NEW HAMPSHIRE

Amesbury

Salisbury

Salisbury Beach
State Reservation

Merrimack River

Newburyport

495

113

Plum Island

95

Newbury
Old Town

PARKER
RIVER
NATIONAL
WILDLIFE
REFUGE

1A

97

1

1A

Plum Island
State Park

Georgetown

133

Rowley

Crane
Beach

Ipswich
Bay

Cape
Ann

WILLOWDALE
STATE FOREST

Ipswich

Rockport

Topsfield

133

Wingaersheek
Beach

127

127A

97

Hamilton

Essex

Gloucester

Long Beach

HAROLD PARKER
STATE FOREST

1A

Wenham

133

114

1

Danvers

128

127

Magnolia

Good
Harbor
Beach

95

Beverly

Singing
Beach

Manchester-
by-the-Sea

128

95

Salem
see detail
map

Salem
Harbor

107

114

Marblehead

Saugus

129

Swampscott

1A

Lynn

Nahant Bay

Nahant

Lynn
Harbor

East Point

Chelsea

Massachusetts Bay

Cambridge

Deer Island

BOSTON

93

Boston
Harbor

Hull

Quincy
Bay

Hingham
Bay

Quincy

3A

Hingham

0   5 miles

0   5 km

TAKE A SEAFARING TOUR

Essex River Cruises & Charters.
Essex River Cruises & Charters organizes narrated cruises of nearby salt marshes and rivers. They also offer private charters for all occasions, including New England-style clambakes served on tidal beaches. Book online or call for reservations. ⊠ *Essex Marina, 35 Dodge St., Essex* ☎ *978/768–6981, 800/748–3706* ⊕ *www.essexcruises.com.*

Yankee Fleet Deep Sea Fishing.
Yankee Fleet Deep Sea Fishing exposes guests to 60 years of experience finding the best fishing spots in Gloucester. Whether you're a beginner, a world-traveling adventurer, or somewhere in between, the crew at Yankee will show you a good time on a variety of trips, including half-day/all-day/overnight fishing, tuna, overnight cod and haddock, and overnight snapper and grouper trips. Call for reservations. ⊠ *1 Parker St., Gloucester* ☎ *855/546–3474, 800/943–5464* ⊕ *www.yankeefleet.com* 🅿 *Prices vary* ☞ *Free parking is available right before ticket shack.*

the public as community parkland. Barracks and underground quarters can still be seen, and Revolutionary War reenactments by members of the modern day Glover's Marblehead Regiment are staged at the fort annually. ⊠ *End of Front St.* ☎ *781/631–0000 town hall* 🄯 *Free.*

The 1768 Jeremiah Lee Mansion. Marblehead's 18th-century high society is exemplified in this mansion run by the Marblehead Museum. Colonel Lee was the wealthiest merchant and ship owner in Massachusetts in 1768, and although few original furnishings remain, the unique hand-painted wallpaper and fine collection of traditional North Shore furniture provide clues to the life of an American gentleman. Across the street at the main museum (open year-round), the J.O.J. Frost Gallery & Carolyn Lynch Education Center pays tribute to the town's talented 19th-century native son. ⊠ *161 Washington St.* ☎ *781/631–1768* ⊕ *www.marbleheadmuseum.org/properties/lee-mansion* 🄯 *$10.*

WHERE TO EAT AND STAY
For expanded hotel reviews, visit Fodors.com.

$
SEAFOOD
✕ **The Landing.** Decorated in nautical blues and whites, this pleasant restaurant sits right on Marblehead harbor, with a deck that's nearly in the water. The restaurant offers classic New England fare like clam chowder and broiled scrod, and serves brunch on Sunday. **Known for:** waterside dining; classic New England menu; local feel. 🟡 *Average main: $12* ⊠ *81 Front St.* ☎ *781/639–1266* ⊕ *www.thelandingrestaurant.com* ▬ *No credit cards.*

$$
B&B/INN
Fodor's Choice
★
🏨 **Harbor Light Inn.** Housed in a pair of adjoining 18th-century mansions in the heart of Old Town Marblehead, this elegant inn, which is now honored as one of the Distinguished Inns of New England, features many rooms with canopy beds, brick fireplaces, and Jacuzzis. **Pros:** beautiful location; tavern with pub grub; outdoor swimming pool. **Cons:** confusing town to navigate; Jacuzzis are loud; two-night minimum stay on weekends during high season; prices spike in high season. 🟡 *Rooms from: $169* ⊠ *58 Washington St.* ☎ *781/631–2186* ⊕ *www.harborlightinn.com* 🛏 *23 rooms* 🍴 *Breakfast.*

15

The House of the Seven Gables inspired Nathaniel Hawthorne's book of the same name.

SALEM

16 miles northeast of Boston, 4 miles west of Marblehead.

Known for years as the Witch City, Salem is redefining itself. Though numerous witch-related attractions and shops still draw tourists, there's much more to the city. But first, a bit on its bewitched past...

The witchcraft hysteria emerged from the trials of 1692, when several Salem-area girls fell ill and accused some of the townspeople of casting spells on them. More than 150 men and women were charged with practicing witchcraft, a crime punishable by death. After the trials later that year, 19 people were hanged and one man was crushed to death.

Though the witch trials might have built Salem's infamy, it'd be a mistake to ignore the town's rich maritime and creative traditions, which played integral roles in the country's evolution. Frigates out of Salem opened the Far East trade routes and generated the wealth that created America's first millionaires. Among its native talents are writer Nathaniel Hawthorne, the intellectual Peabody sisters, navigator Nathaniel Bowditch, and architect Samuel McIntire. This creative spirit is today celebrated in Salem's internationally recognized museums, waterfront shops and restaurants, galleries, and wide common.

To learn more on the area, stop by the **Regional Visitor's Center.** Innovatively designed in the Old Salem Armory, the center has exhibits, a 27-minute film, maps, and a gift shop.

House of the
Seven Gables **1**

Peabody Essex
Museum **2**

Salem Maritime
National
Historic Site **3**

Salem Witch
Museum **4**

Salem
Witch Trials
Memorial **5**

15

ESSENTIALS

Visitor Information Destination Salem. ⊠ *81 Washington St., Suite 204* ☎ *978/744–3663, 877/725–3662* ⊕ *www.salem.org.* **Regional Visitor Center.** ⊠ *2 New Liberty St.* ☎ *978/740–1650* ⊕ *www.nps.gov/ner/sama.*

EXPLORING

House of the Seven Gables. Immortalized in Nathaniel Hawthorne's classic novel, this site is itself a historic treasure. Built in 1668 and also known as the Turner-Ingersoll Mansion, the house includes the famous secret staircase, a re-creation of Hepzibah's cent shop from *The House of Seven Gables*, and some of the finest Georgian interiors in the country. Also on the property is the small house where Hawthorne was born in 1804; built in 1750, it was moved from its original location a few blocks away. ⊠ *115 Derby St.* ☎ *978/744–0991* ⊕ *www.7gables.org* 🎟 *$14.*

Fodor's Choice   **Peabody Essex Museum.** Salem's world class museum celebrates superla-
★   tive works from around the globe and across time, including American art and architecture, Asian export art, photography, maritime art and history, as well as Native American, Oceanic, and African art. Its 30 galleries, housed in a contemplative blend of modern design, represent a diverse range of styles; exhibits include pieces ranging from American decorative and seamen's art to an interactive Art & Nature Center and photography. While there be sure to tour the Yin Yu Tang house. This

Landlubbers can go to sea at Salem's Peabody Essex Museum.

fabulous 200-year-old house dates to the Qing Dynasty (1644–1911) of China. The museum brought it over from China in sections and reassembled it here. ⊠ *East India Sq.* ☎ *978/745–9500, 866/745–1876* ⊕ *www.pem.org* ✉ *$20.*

Salem Maritime National Historic Site. Near Derby Wharf, this 9¼-acre site focuses on Salem's heritage as a major seaport with a thriving overseas trade. It includes the 1762 home of Elias Derby, America's first millionaire; the 1819 Custom House, made famous in Nathaniel Hawthorne's *The Scarlet Letter*; and a replica of the *Friendship*, a 171-foot, three-masted 1797 merchant vessel. There's also an active lighthouse dating from 1871, as well as the nation's last surviving 18th-century wharves. Newer to the site is the 1770 Pedrick Store House, moved from nearby Marblehead and reassembled right on Derby Wharf; the two-story structure once played a vital role in the lucrative merchant seaside trade. ⊠ *193 Derby St.* ☎ *978/740–1650 visitor center* ⊕ *www.nps.gov/sama* ✉ *Free with the exception of the film "Salem Witch Hunt.".*

Salem Witch Museum. An informative and fun introduction to the 1692 witchcraft hysteria, this museum has a 15-minute guided tour through their exhibit, "Witches: Evolving Perceptions," that describes witch hunts through the years. ⊠ *19½ Washington Sq. N* ☎ *978/744–1692* ⊕ *www.salemwitchmuseum.com* ✉ *$12.*

Salem Witch Trials Memorial. Dedicated by Nobel Laureate Elie Wiesel in 1992, this quiet, contemplative space—an antidote to the relentless marketing of the merry-witches motif—honors those who died because they refused to confess that they were witches. A stone wall is studded

CLOSE UP

The First Witch Trial

It was in Danvers, not Salem, that the first witch trial was held, originating with the family of Samuel Parris, a minister who moved to the area in 1680 from Barbados, bringing with him two slaves, including one named Tituba. In 1691 Samuel's daughter, Betty, and niece, Abigail, began having fits. Tituba, who had told Betty and Abigail stories of magic and witchcraft from her homeland, baked a witch cake to identify the witches who were harming the girls. The girls in turn accused Tituba of witchcraft. After three days of questioning, which included beatings from Samuel and a promise from him to free her if she cooperated, Tituba confessed to meeting the devil (in the form of a black hog or dog). She also claimed there were other witches in the village, confirming the girls' accusations against Sarah Good and Sarah Osborne, but she refused to name any others. Tituba's trial prompted the frenzy that led to the deaths of 20 accused witches.

15

with 20 stone benches, each inscribed with a victim's name, and sits next to Salem's oldest burying ground. ⊠ *Liberty St.* ✢ *Between Charter and Derby Sts.* ⊕ *salem.org/listing/witch-trials-memorial.*

ARTS AND ENTERTAINMENT
THEATER
Cry Innocent: The People versus Bridget Bishop. This show, the longest continuously running play north of Boston, transports audience members to Bridget Bishop's witchcraft hearing of 1692. After hearing historical testimonies, the audience cross-examines the witnesses and decides whether to send Bridget to trial or not. Actors respond in character revealing much about the Puritan frame of mind. Each show is different and allows audience members to play their "part" in history. ⊠ *Old Town Hall, 32 Derby Sq.* ☎ *978/810-2588* ⊕ *www.cryinnocentsalem.com* ⤢ *$13–$25.*

WHERE TO EAT AND STAY
For expanded hotel reviews, visit Fodors.com.

$$
SEAFOOD
✕ **Finz Seafood & Grill.** This contemporary seafood restaurant on Salem Harbor treats patrons to prime canal views. Seafood potpie and lobster rolls highlight the lunch menu, while sesame-crusted tuna or steamed lobster are dinner favorites. **Known for:** outdoor seating; classic New England seafood; canal-side views. ⑤ *Average main: $21* ⊠ *76 Wharf St.* ☎ *978/744-8485* ⊕ *www.hipfinz.com.*

$$$
AMERICAN
✕ **Ledger Restaurant and Bar.** Housed in a 200-year-old building that until recently was the second longest continuously operating bank in the entire country, Ledger takes its name from the massive amount of banking ledgers the owners found in the building. Enjoy a modern-day spin on traditional 19th-century dishes and cocktails while checking out the multitude of original features incorporated into the restaurant, including deposit boxes and a huge safe that serves as the restaurant's walk-in refrigerator. **Known for:** historic digs; modern take on 19th-century cuisine; cleverly repurposed decor. ⑤ *Average main: $26* ⊠ *125 Washington St.* ☎ *978/594-1908* ⊕ *www.ledgersalem.com.*

$$ **Amelia Payson House.** Built in 1845, this Greek Revival house is a
B&B/INN comfortable bed-and-breakfast near all the historic attractions. **Pros:**
Fodor'sChoice fireplaces in each room; outdoor lounge with a fire pit; on-site parking.
★ **Cons:** no children under 12; hard to get reservations. ⑤ *Rooms from:
$195* ✉ *16 Winter St.* ☎ *978/744–8304* ⊕ *www.ameliapaysonhouse.
com* ➳ *3 rooms* ⦿ *Breakfast.*

$$ **The Hawthorne Hotel.** Elegantly restored, this full-service landmark
HOTEL hotel celebrates the town's most famous writer and is within walk-
ing distance from the town common, museums, and waterfront. **Pros:**
lovely, historic lobby; free parking available behind hotel; free Wi-Fi.
Cons: many rooms are small; no swimming pool; no spa. ⑤ *Rooms
from: $159* ✉ *18 Washington Sq. W* ☎ *978/744–4080, 800/729–7829*
⊕ *www.hawthornehotel.com* ➳ *93 rooms (89 in main building, and 4
in guesthouse)* ⦿ *No meals* ☞ *$25 charge per room per night for pets.*

$$ **The Merchant.** The 11-room Merchant is an intimate, design-forward
HOTEL hotel in the heart of Salem's historic district. **Pros:** complimentary off-site
parking at Riley Plaza; free Wi-Fi; downstairs lounge with fully stocked
"BYOB Mixer Bar". **Cons:** no elevator; no in-room fridge; books up
quickly. ⑤ *Rooms from: $159* ✉ *148 Washington St.* ☎ *978/745–8100*
⊕ *www.themerchantsalem.com* ➳ *11 rooms* ⦿ *No meals.*

GLOUCESTER

37 miles northeast of Boston, 8 miles northeast of Manchester-by-the-Sea.

On Gloucester's fine seaside promenade is a famous statue of a man
steering a ship's wheel, his eyes searching the horizon. The statue,
which honors those who go down to the sea in ships, was commis-
sioned by the town citizens in celebration of Gloucester's 300th anni-
versary in 1923. The oldest seaport in the nation (with some of the
North Shore's best beaches) is still a major fishing port. Sebastian
Junger's 1997 book *A Perfect Storm* was an account of the fate of
the *Andrea Gail,* a Gloucester fishing boat caught in the storm of the
century in October 1991. In 2000 the book was made into a movie,
filmed on location in Gloucester.

ESSENTIALS

Visitor Information Cape Ann Chamber of Commerce. ✉ *33 Commercial
St.* ☎ *978/283–1601* ⊕ *www.capeannchamber.com.* **Cape Ann Chamber of
Commerce, Rockport Visitor Center.** ✉ *170 Main St., (Rte. 127), Rockport*
☎ *978/546–9372* ⊕ *www.rockportusa.com.*

EXPLORING

Cape Ann Museum. The recently renovated Cape Ann Museum celebrates
the art, history, and culture of Cape Ann. The museum's collections
include fine art from the 19th century to the present, artifacts from the
fishing, maritime, and granite-quarrying industries, as well as textiles,
furniture, a library archives, and two historic houses. ✉ *27 Pleasant St.*
☎ *978/283–0455* ⊕ *www.capeannmuseum.org* 🖺 *$12.*

Hammond Castle Museum. Inventor John Hays Hammond Jr. built this
structure in 1926 to resemble a "medieval" stone castle. Hammond is
credited with more than 500 patents, including remote control via radio

waves. The museum contains medieval-style furnishings and paintings, and the Great Hall houses an impressive 8,200-pipe organ. From the castle you can see Norman's Woe Rock, made famous by Longfellow in his poem "The Wreck of the Hesperus." ⊠ *80 Hesperus Ave., south side of Gloucester off Rte. 12 /* ☎ *978/283-2080, 978/283-7673* ⊕ *www. hammondcastle.org* ☜ *$10* ☞ *Closed in winter.*

Rocky Neck. Situated on a peninsula within Gloucester's working harbor, the town's creative side thrives in this neighborhood, one of the oldest continuously working artists' colonies in the United States. Its alumni include Winslow Homer, Maurice Prendergast, Jane Peter, and Cecilia Beaux. Call for winter hours. ⊠ *6 Wonson St.* ☎ *978/515-7005* ⊕ *www. rockyneckartcolony.org.*

SPORTS AND THE OUTDOORS
BEACHES
Gloucester has the best beaches on the North Shore. From Memorial Day through mid-September parking costs $20 on weekdays and $25 on weekends, when the lots often fill by 10 am.

Good Harbor Beach. This beach has calm, waveless waters and soft sand, and is surrounded by grassy dunes, making it perfect any time of year. In summer (June, July, and August), it is lifeguard patrolled, handicap accessible, and there is a snack bar if you don't feel like packing in food. The restrooms and showers are wheelchair accessible, and you can pick up beach toys at the concessions. On weekdays parking is plentiful, but the lot fills by 10 am on weekends. In June, green flies can be bothersome. **Amenities:** food and drink; lifeguards; parking (fee); showers; toilets. **Best for:** swimming; walking. ⊠ *Clearly signposted from Rte. 127A* ☜ *Parking $25 per car; $30 on weekends and holidays.*

Long Beach. Just as its name implies, this soft-sand beach that is half in Rockport, half in Gloucester is long, and it's also broad. It draws crowds from the houses that border it, particularly on weekends. Pay attention to the tide schedule, or you may find there's no beach to sit on. Cape Ann Motor Inn is nearby. Parking is very limited. Don't even think of parking on neighborhood streets if you don't have a town parking sticker—you will be towed. However, there is a lot on the Gloucester side. **Amenities:** none. **Best for:** swimming; walking. ⊠ *Off Rte. 127A on Gloucester-Rockport town line, off Rockport Rd.*

Wingaersheek Beach. With white sand and dunes, Wingaersheek Beach is a well-protected cove with both a beach side and a boat side. The white Annisquam lighthouse is in the bay. The beach is known for its miles of white sand and calm waters. On weekends arrive early. The parking lot generally fills up by midmorning. It's handicap accessible and beach wheelchairs are available on request. **Amenities:** food and drink; parking (fee); toilets. **Best for:** swimming; walking. ⊠ *232 Atlantic St.* ✛ *Take Rte. 128 N to Exit 13* ☜ *Limited parking, $25 per car; $30 on weekends and holidays.*

15

WHERE TO EAT AND STAY

For expanded hotel reviews, visit Fodors.com.

$$
\text{AMERICAN}
$$

$$ ✕ **The Franklin Cafe.** This contemporary nightspot offers bistro-style
AMERICAN chicken, roast cod, and steak frites, perfect for the late-night crowd (it's
open until midnight during the summer). Live jazz is on tap every other
Tuesday and every Friday evening. **Known for:** open late; friendly vibe;
moderate prices. ⑤ *Average main: $20 ⊠ 118 Main St.* ☎ *978/283–7888*
⊕ *www.franklincafe.com* ⊘ *No lunch.*

$$ ✕ **Passports.** In the heart of Downtown Gloucester, Passports serves up
ECLECTIC a modern take on classic New England seafood. The fried oysters and
FAMILY house haddock are favorites here, and there's always local art hanging
on the walls for patrons to buy. ⑤ *Average main: $15 ⊠ 110 Main St.*
☎ *978/281–3680.*

$ 🏨 **Cape Ann's Marina Resort & Spa.** This year-round hotel less than a mile
RESORT from downtown Gloucester comes alive in summer. **Pros:** free Wi-Fi;
FAMILY full marina; indoor pool and Jacuzzi with poolside bar. **Cons:** hotel surrounded by parking lots; price hike during summer; bar area can be loud
in summer. ⑤ *Rooms from: $145 ⊠ 75 Essex Ave.* ☎ *978/283–2116,*
800/626–7660 ⊕ *www.capeannmarina.com* ⤳ *31 rooms* ⦿ *No meals.*

$ 🏨 **Cape Ann Motor Inn.** On the sands of Long Beach, this three-story,
HOTEL shingled motel has no-frills rooms except for the balconies and ocean
views. **Pros:** exceptional view from every room; kids under five stay
free; free Wi-Fi. **Cons:** thin walls; motel quality; summer season can
be loud and crowded. ⑤ *Rooms from: $100 ⊠ 33 Rockport Rd.*
☎ *978/281–2900, 800/464–8439* ⊕ *www.capeannmotorinn.com*
⤳ *31 rooms* ⦿ *Breakfast.*

$$ 🏨 **Castle Manor Inn.** With original woodwork and cozy fireplaces, this
B&B/INN restored 1900 Victorian inn perfectly captures the Cape Ann aesthetic.
Fodor'sChoice **Pros:** discount parking passes to the local beaches; historic; close to
★ Gloucester's beaches. **Cons:** closes for the winter; roads in the area
can be windy and confusing; may be too intimate for some travel-
ers. ⑤ *Rooms from: $150 ⊠ 141 Essex Ave.* ☎ *978/515–7386* ⊕ *www.*
castlemanorinn.com ⤳ *26 rooms.*

ROCKPORT

41 miles northeast of Boston, 4 miles northeast of Gloucester on Rte. 127.

Rockport, at the very tip of Cape Ann, derives its name from the local
granite formations. Many Boston-area structures are made of stone cut
from its long-gone quarries. Today the town is a tourist center with a
well-marked, centralized downtown that is easy to navigate and access
on foot. Unlike typical tourist-trap landmarks, Rockport's shops sell
quality arts, clothing, and gifts, and its restaurants serve seafood or
home-baked cookies rather than fast food. Walk past shops and colorful
clapboard houses to the end of Bearskin Neck for an impressive view of
the Atlantic Ocean and the old, weather-beaten lobster shack known as
Motif No. 1, a popular subject for amateur painters and photographers.

ESSENTIALS

Visitor Information Rockport Visitor Center. ⊠ *170 Main St.* ☎ *978/283–*
1601 ⊕ *www.rockportusa.com.*

WHERE TO EAT AND STAY

For expanded hotel reviews, visit Fodors.com.

$$
SEAFOOD

✕ **Brackett's Ocean View.** A big bay window in this quiet, homey restaurant provides an excellent view across Sandy Bay. The menu includes chowders, fish cakes, and other seafood dishes. **Known for:** seafood. $ *Average main: $18* ✉ *25 Main St.* ☎ *978/546-2797* ⊕ *www.bracketts.com* ☾ *Closed Columbus Day–mid-Apr.*

$$
B&B/INN

Addison Choate Inn. Just a minute's walk from both the center of Rockport and the train station, this 1851 inn sits in a prime location. **Pros:** free parking; comfortable, spacious porch for relaxing; free Wi-Fi. **Cons:** only one bedroom on the first floor; most rooms require taking the stairs; may be too intimate a setting for some. $ *Rooms from: $189* ✉ *49 Broadway* ☎ *978/546-7543, 800/245-7543* ⊕ *www.addisonchoateinn.com* ⇄ *6 rooms* ❛❍❜ *Breakfast.*

$
HOTEL
FAMILY

Bearskin Neck Motor Lodge. Near the end of Bearskin Neck, this small brick-and-shingle motel offers guests the best of both worlds: beautiful, ocean-front rooms, as well as easy access to shopping and restaurants. **Pros:** all rooms have balconies and unobstructed ocean views; central location; mini-refrigerators in rooms. **Cons:** lots of summertime tourists; heavy "classic motel" vibe; high prices in summer. $ *Rooms from: $135* ✉ *64 Bearskin Neck* ☎ *978/546-6677, 877/507 6272* ⊕ *www.bearskinneckmotorlodge.com* ☾ *Closed early Dec.–Mar.* ⇄ *8 rooms* ❛❍❜ *No meals.*

ESSEX

35 miles northeast of Boston, 12 miles west of Rockport.

The small seafaring town of Essex, once an important shipbuilding center, is surrounded by salt marshes and is filled with antiques stores and seafood restaurants.

GETTING HERE AND AROUND

Head west out of Cape Ann on Route 128, turning north on Route 133.

ESSENTIALS

Visitor Information Escape to Essex. ⊕ *www.visitessexma.com.*

EXPLORING

FAMILY **Essex Shipbuilding Museum.** At what is still an active shipyard, this museum chronicles over 300 years of wooden shipbuilding. Essex launched approximately 4,000 vessels, most of them two-masted fishing schooners for the Gloucester fleet. The museum offers shipbuilding demonstrations, events, and self- and fully guided tours. The collection includes ship models on loan from the Smithsonian, as well as the 83-foot *Evelina M. Goulart*—one of only seven remaining Essex-built schooners. ✉ *66 Main St. (Rte. 133)* ☎ *978/768-7541* ⊕ *www.essexshipbuildingmuseum.org* ⌖ *Self-guided tour $7; guided tour $10.*

SHOPPING

David Neligan Antiques. For the discerning collector, this shop specializes in high-quality European and English furniture, accessories, art, and more. ✉ *38 Main St.* ☎ *978/768-3910.*

15

Main Street Antiques. Anything and everything from the 18th to the 20th centuries seems to be here—furniture, diamond jewelry, prints—all on four floors of treasure-hunting glory. ⊠ *44 Main St.* ☎ *978/768–7039.*

WHERE TO EAT

$$
SEAFOOD
FAMILY
Fodor'sChoice
★

✕ **Woodman's of Essex.** According to local legend, this is where Lawrence "Chubby" Woodman invented the first fried clam back in 1916. Today this sprawling wooden shack with indoor booths and outdoor picnic tables is *the* place for seafood in the rough. **Known for:** fried clams. ⑤ *Average main: $18* ⊠ *121 Main St. (Rte. 133)* ☎ *978/768–2559, 800/649–1773* ⊕ *www.woodmans.com.*

SOUTH OF BOSTON

People from all over the world travel south of Boston to visit Plymouth for a glimpse into the country's earliest beginnings. The two main stops are the Plimoth Plantation, which re-creates the everyday life of the Pilgrims; and the *Mayflower II,* which gives you an idea of how frightening the journey across the Atlantic must have been. As you may guess, November in Plymouth brings special events focused on Thanksgiving. Farther south, New Bedford recalls the world of whaling.

EN
ROUTE

Adams National Historic Park. Take a guided tour of the birthplace and homes of Presidents John Adams and his son John Quincy Adams, as well as the Stone Library and Adams Crypt, where the Adams presidents and their wives are buried in Quincy's Church of the Presidents. Tours begin at the NPS Visitor Center and Bookstore at 1250 Hancock Street, with trolley transportation to all sites. Get your parking validated adjacent to the visitor center on Saville Road. ⊠ *135 Adams St., Quincy* ☎ *617/770–1175, 617/773–1177 park headquarters* ⊕ *www.nps.gov/ adam* ☒ *$10* ⊙ *Closed Dec.–Mar.*

PLYMOUTH

40 miles south of Boston.

On December 26, 1620, 102 weary men, women, and children disembarked from the *Mayflower* to found the first permanent European settlement north of Virginia (they had found their earlier landing in Provincetown to be unsuitable). Today Plymouth is characterized by narrow streets, clapboard mansions, shops, antiques stores, and a scenic waterfront. To mark Thanksgiving, the town holds activities including historic-house tours and a parade. Historic statues dot the town, including depictions of William Bradford, Pilgrim leader and governor of Plymouth Colony for more than 30 years, on Water Street; a Pilgrim maiden in Brewster Gardens; and Massasoit, the Wampanoag chief who helped the Pilgrims survive, on Carver Street.

ESSENTIALS

Visitor Information Plymouth Visitor Information Center. ⊠ *130 Water St., at Hwy. 44* ☎ *508/747–7525, 800/872–1620* ⊕ *www.seeplymouth.com.*

Continued on page 278

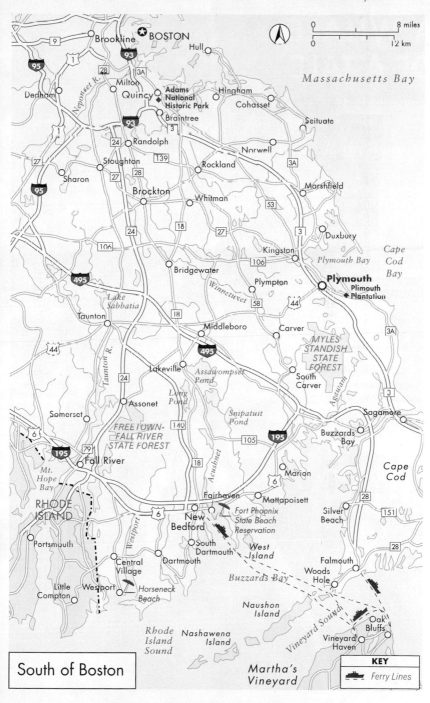

15

South of Boston

KEY
Ferry Lines

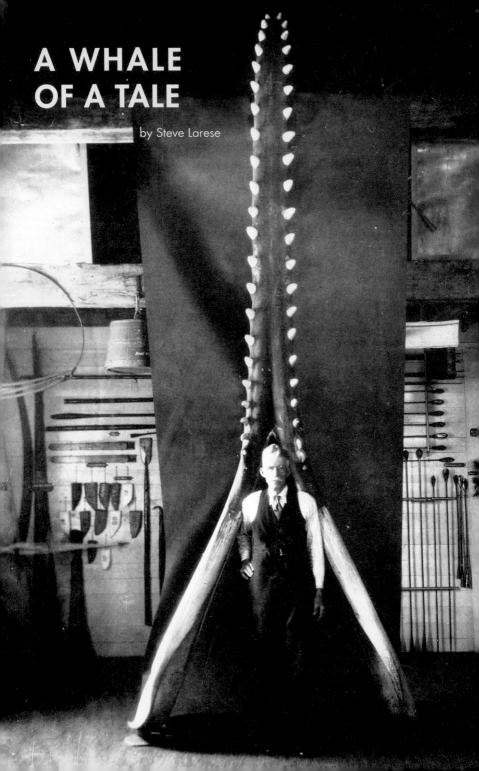

A WHALE OF A TALE

by Steve Larese

WHALING IN NEW ENGLAND TIMELINE

mid-1600s	America enters whaling industry
1690	Nantucket enters whaling industry
1820	*Essex* ship sunk by sperm whale
1840s	American whaling peaked
1851	*Moby-Dick* published
1927	The last U.S. whaler sails from New Bedford
1970s	Cape Cod whale-watching trips begin
1986	Ban on whaling by the International Whaling Commission
1992	Stellwagen Bank National Marine Sanctuary established

Cameras have replaced harpoons in the waters north of Cape Cod. While you can learn about New England's whaling history and perhaps see whales in the distance from shore, a whale-watching excursion is the best way to connect with these magnificent creatures—who may be just as curious about you as you are about them.

Once relentlessly hunted around the world by New Englanders, whales today are celebrated as intelligent, friendly, and curious creatures. Whales are still important to the region's economy and culture, but now in the form of ecotourism. Easily accessible from several ports in Massachusetts, the 842-square-mile Stellwagen Bank National Marine Sanctuary attracts finback, humpback, minke, and right whales who feed and frolic here twice a year during their migration. The same conditions that made the Stellwagen Bank area of the mouth of Massachusetts Bay a good hunting ground make it a good viewing area. Temperature, currents, and nutrients combine to produce plankton, krill, and fish to feed marine mammals.

(opposite) Whaling museum custodian and a sperm whale jaw in the 1930s. (top) Hunted to near extinction, humpbacks today number about 60,000, and are found in oceans worldwide.

ON LAND: MARINE AND MARITIME MUSEUMS

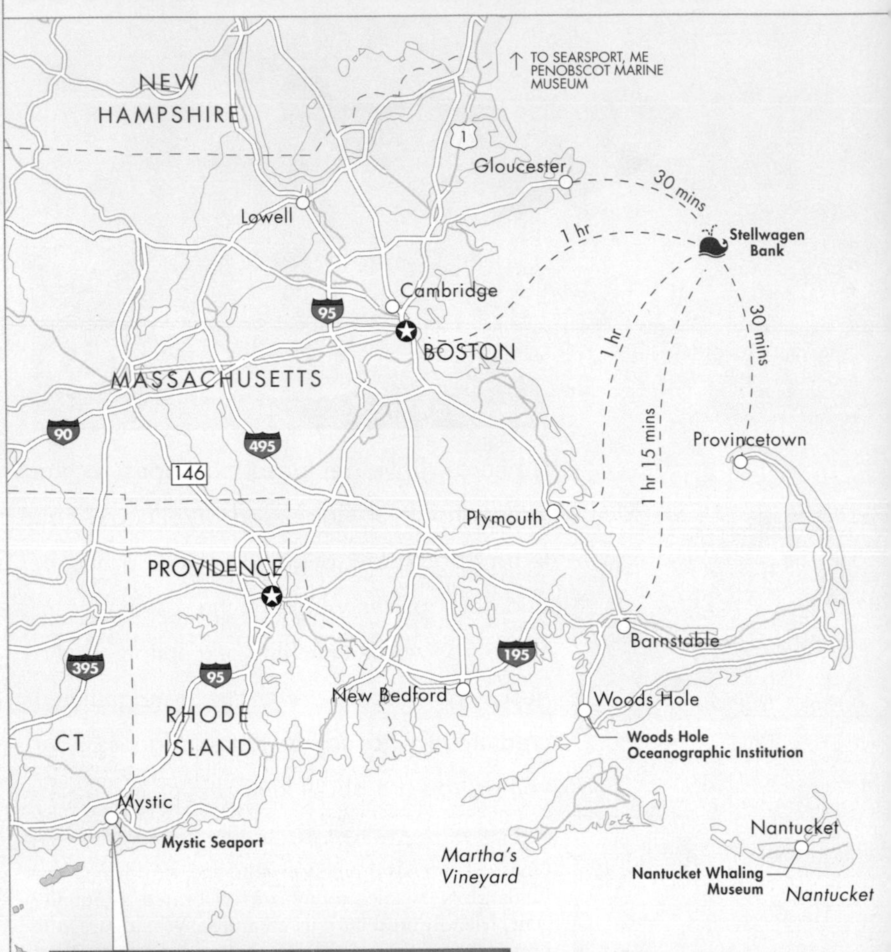

↑ TO SEARSPORT, ME
PENOBSCOT MARINE
MUSEUM

NEW
HAMPSHIRE

Gloucester

1

Lowell

30 mins

1 hr

Stellwagen
Bank

Cambridge

95

BOSTON

MASSACHUSETTS

1 hr

30 mins

90

495

Provincetown

146

1 hr 15 mins

Plymouth

PROVIDENCE

395

95

Barnstable

RHODE
ISLAND

New Bedford

Woods Hole

CT

Woods Hole
Oceanographic Institution

Mystic

Mystic Seaport

Nantucket

Martha's
Vineyard

Nantucket Whaling
Museum

Nantucket

0   20 miles

0   20 km

Whaling ships, like the *Charles W.
Morgan* at Mystic Seaport, hunted
whales for their baleen and oil.

Even landlubbers can learn about whales and whaling at these top New England institutions.

Nantucket Whaling Museum. This former whale-processing center and candle factory was converted into a museum in 1929. See art made by sailors, including masterful scrimshaw—intricate nautical scenes carved into whale bone or teeth and filled in with ink ⌧ *Nantucket, Massachusetts* ☎ *508/228–1894* ⊕ *www.nha.org.*

★ **New Bedford Whaling Museum.** More than 200,000 artifacts are collected here, from ships' logbooks to harpoons. A must-see is the 89-foot, half-scale model of the 1826 whaling ship *Lagoda* ⌧ *New Bedford, Massachusetts* ☎ *508/997–0046* ⊕ *www.whalingmuseum.org.*

New Bedford Whaling National Historical Park. The visitor center for this 13-block waterfront park provides maps and information about whaling-related sites, including a sea captain's mansion and restored whaling schooner. ⌧ *New Bedford, Massachusetts* ☎ *508/996–4095* ⊕ *www.nps.gov/nebe.*

★ **Mystic Seaport.** Actors portray life in a 19th-century seafaring village at this 19-acre living-history museum. Don't miss the 1841 *Charles W. Morgan*, the world's only surviving wooden whaling ship ⌧ *Mystic, Connecticut* ☎ *860/572–0711* ⊕ *www.mysticseaport.org.*

Penobscot Marine Museum. Maine's seafaring history and mostly shore-whaling industry is detailed inside 13 historic buildings ⌧ *Searsport, Maine* ☎ *207/548–2529* ⊕ *www.penobscot marinemuseum.org.*

THE GREAT WHITE WHALE

Herman Melville based his 1851 classic *Moby-Dick: or, The Whale* on the true story of the *Essex*, which was sunk in 1821 by huge whale; an albino sperm whale called Mocha Dick; and his time aboard the whaling ship *Acushnet*.

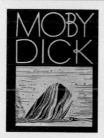

Nantucket Whaling Museum

New Bedford Whaling Museum

Mystic Seaport

15

IN FOCUS A WHALE OF A TALE

AT SEA: WHALE-WATCHING TOURS

COMMON NORTH ATLANTIC SPECIES

0   10   20   30   40   50   60   70 (ft)

Atlantic white-sided dolphin. These playful marine mammals can grow to 7 feet. Note the distinct yellow-to-white patches on their sides. Highly social, dolphins group in pods of up to 60 and hunt fish and squid.

Minke whale. Named for a Norwegian whaler, this smallest of baleen whales grows to 30 feet and 10 tons. It is a solitary creature, streamlined compared to other whales, and has a curved dorsal fin on its back.

Humpback whale. These 40-ton baleen whales are known for their acrobatics and communicative songs. Curious animals, they often approach boats. By blowing bubbles, humpbacks entrap krill and fish for food.

North Atlantic right whale. Called the "right" whales to hunt, this species travels close to shore and is the rarest of all whales—there are only around 300. Note the callosities (rough skin) on their large heads.

Finback whale. The second-largest animal on Earth (after the blue whale, which is rarely seen here), these baleen whales can weigh 50 tons and eat 4,000 lbs of food a day. Look for the distinctive dorsal fin near their fluke (tail).

SEAWORTHY TRIP TIPS

When to Go: Tours operate April through October; May through September are the most active months in the Stellwagen Bank area.

Ports of Departure: Boats leave from Barnstable and Provincetown on Cape Cod, and Plymouth, Boston, and Gloucester, cutting across Cape Cod Bay to the Stellwagen area. Book tours at least a day ahead in the height of the summer season. Hyannis Whale Watcher in Barnstable, the Dolphin Fleet, Portuguese Princess, Captain John's Whale Watch in Plymouth, the New England Aquarium and Boston Harbor Cruises in Boston are just a few of your options. *See Thar She Blows box in this chapter for more information.*

Cost: Around $40. Check company Web sites for coupons.

What to Expect: All companies abide by guidelines so as not to harass whales. Tours last 3 to 4 hours and almost always encounter whales; if not, vouchers are often given for another tour. Passengers are encouraged to watch the horizon for water spouts, which indicate a surfaced whale clearing its blowhole to breathe air. Upon spotting an animal, the boat slows and approaches the whale to a safe distance; often, whales will approach an idling boat and even swim underneath it.

What to Bring: Plastic bags protect binoculars and cameras from damp spray. Most boats have a concession stand, but pack bottled water and snacks. ■TIP➜ Kids (and adults) will appreciate games or other items to pass the time in between whale sightings.

What to Wear: Wear rubber-soled footwear for slick decks. A waterproof outer layer and layers of clothing will help in

Hyannis Whale Watcher Cruises, Cape Cod Bay

varied conditions, as will sunscreen, sunglasses, and a hat that can be secured. Most boats have cabins where you can warm up and get out of the wind.

Comforting Advice: Small seat cushions like those used at sporting events may be appreciated. Consider taking motion-sickness medication before setting out. Ginger candy and acupressure wristbands can also help. If you feel queasy, get some fresh air and focus your eyes on a stable feature on the shore or horizon.

Photo Hints: Use a fast shutter speed, or sport mode, to avoid blurry photographs. Most whales will be a distance from the boat; have a telephoto lens ready. To avoid shutter delay on your point-and-shoot camera, lock the focus at infinity so you don't miss that breaching whale shot.

DID YOU KNOW?

Most boats have a naturalist aboard to discuss the whales and their environment. Many companies contribute to population studies by reporting the individual whales they spot. Whale tails, called flukes, are distinct and used like fingerprints for identification.

EXPLORING

National Monument to the Forefathers. The largest freestanding granite statue in the United States, this allegorical monument stands high on an 11-acre hilltop site. Designed by Hammet Billings of Boston in 1854 and dedicated in 1889, it depicts Faith, surrounded by Liberty, Morality, Justice, Law, and Education, and includes scenes from the Pilgrims' early days in Plymouth. ⊠ *Allerton St.* ⊕ *www.seeplymouth.com.*

FAMILY **Pilgrim Hall Museum.** From the waterfront sights, it's a short walk to one of the country's oldest public museums. Established in 1824, Pilgrim Hall Museum transports you back to the time of the Pilgrims' landing with objects carried by those weary travelers to the New World. Historic items on display include a carved chest, a remarkably well-preserved wicker cradle, Myles Standish's sword, and John Alden's Bible. ⊠ *75 Court St. (Rte. 3A)* ☎ *508/746–1620* ⊕ *www.pilgrimhall. org* ⊠ *$8* ⊘ *Closed Jan.*

FAMILY
Fodor'sChoice
★ **Plimoth Plantation.** Against the backdrop of the Atlantic Ocean, and 3 miles south of downtown Plymouth, this living museum shares the rich, interwoven story of the Plymouth Colony and the Wampanoag homeland through engaging daily programs and special events. A 1620s Pilgrim village has been carefully re-created, from the thatch roofs, cramped quarters, and open fireplaces to the long-horned livestock. Throw away your preconception of white collars and funny hats; through ongoing research, the Plimoth staff has developed a portrait of the Pilgrims that's more complex than the dour folk in school textbooks. Listen to the accents of the "residents," who never break out of character. Feel free to engage them in conversation about their life. Don't worry, 21st-century museum educators are on hand to help answer any questions you have as well. On the Wampanoag homesite meet native people speaking from a modern perspective of the traditions, lifeways, and culture of Eastern Woodlands Indiginous people. Note that there's not a lot of shade here in summer. ⊠ *137 Warren Ave. (Hwy. 3A)* ☎ *508/746–1622* ⊕ *www. plimoth.org* ⊠ *$28* ⊘ *Closed mid-Nov.–mid-Mar.*

FAMILY **Plymouth Rock.** This landmark rock, just a few dozen yards from the *Mayflower II,* is popularly believed to have been the Pilgrims' stepping-stone when they left the ship. Given the stone's unimpressive appearance—it's little more than a boulder—and dubious authenticity (as explained on a nearby plaque), the grand canopy overhead seems a trifle ostentatious. Still, more than a million people a year come to visit this world-famous symbol of courage and faith. ⊠ *Water St.*

WHERE TO EAT

$$
SEAFOOD
FAMILY ✕**Blue-eyed Crab Grille & Raw Bar.** Grab a seat on the outside deck overlooking the water at this friendly, somewhat funky (plastic fish dangling from the ceiling), fresh-fish shack. Enjoy Caribbean cocktails on the patio, or hang out in the colorful dining room. **Known for:** views of the water; funky decor; tropical cocktails. ⑤ *Average main: $22* ⊠ *170 Water St.* ☎ *508/747–6776* ⊕ *www.blue-eyedcrab.com* ▭ No credit cards.

TRAVEL SMART
BOSTON

GETTING HERE AND AROUND

Boston's maze of old and new fuses together remarkably well with a little patience. Follow its endless array of narrow, twisting one-way streets radiating from Boston Harbor in the east, and you'll reach the bustle of the Italian-flavored North End. Go west and hit Faneuil Hall, the quaintly named streets of Downtown, and the bricky expanse of Government Center; head southwest toward the Old West End, the "Gahden"—home of the Celtics and Bruins—and the historic Beacon Hill. The Back Bay's orderly (and alphabetical) grid of streets runs southwest from the base of Beacon Hill, where you'll discover the retail wonderland near patrician Copley Square, Prudential Center, and artsy, boutique-filled Newbury Street. Beyond that the Fenway opens onto many art museums, the Emerald Necklace's skein of parkland and ponds, and Fenway Park, baseball field of the much-loved yet oft-reviled Red Sox. To the south spreads the eclectic, trendy South End.

The wide and handsome Charles River serves as a natural dividing line between Boston and its northern neighborhoods and suburbs, including Charlestown and the cities of Cambridge and Somerville. (The Charles is edged with paths to jog, bike, stroll, and gaze at scullers, skylines, and sailing dinghies.) The Fort Point Channel and its picturesque waterside Harbor Walk beneath the spectacularly suspended Zakim Bridge links Downtown with the lively Seaport and Fan Pier districts and South Boston.

Walking is by far the best way to go in this compact, finely detailed city. In good weather, bicycling is also an option (*see Bike Travel*), as are pedicabs. But the next-best transport within Boston or its near environs is the MBTA system, called "the T" for short. Five "subway" lines—comprising underground trains and aboveground trolleys/light rail, as well as buses—run through the entire city and outlying suburbs, with additional bus networks filling in some of the gaps. You can ride the T to nearly all major points of interest in the city; you'll probably only need a car to get out of town.

■TIP→ Ask the local tourist board about hotel and transportation packages that include tickets to major museum exhibits or other special events.

■ AIR TRAVEL

More than 40 airlines operate at Logan International Airport (BOS), offering nonstop flights to 120 cities. Flying (actual air) times to Boston from New York average 1 hour; it's 1½ hours from Washington, D.C., 2¼ hours from Chicago, 3 hours from Miami, 3½ hours from Dallas, 5½ hours from Los Angeles, 6½ hours from London, 13 hours from Tokyo, and 20 hours from Sydney. Delta, American Airlines, and JetBlue run daily shuttle flights from New York and Washington, D.C.

■TIP→ The Boston Convention and Visitor Bureau's website (www.bostonusa.com, 1-888-733-2678) has direct links to worldwide airlines and national bus lines that service the city. You can book flights here, too.

AIRPORTS

Boston's major airport, Logan International (BOS), is across the harbor, barely 2 miles from Downtown, and can be easily reached by taxi, water taxi, or bus/subway via MBTA's Silver or Blue line. Logan's four passenger terminals are identified by the letters A, B, C, and E. Free airport shuttle buses run between the terminals and airport hotels. Some airlines use different terminals for international and domestic flights; most international flights arrive at Terminal E. A visitor center is in Terminal C. Worcester Regional Airport (ORH), T.F. Green

Airport (PVD) in Providence, Rhode Island, and Manchester Boston Regional Airport (MHT) in New Hampshire are about an hour's drive from Boston.

Airport Information Logan Airport Customer Information Hotline. ☎ 800/235–6426. **Logan International Airport (Boston).** ✉ I–90 east to Ted Williams Tunnel ☎ 800/235–6426 ⊕ www.massport. com/logan Ⓜ Airport. **Manchester Boston Regional Airport.** ✉ Off I–293/Rte. 101, Exit 2, Manchester ☎ 603/624–6539 ⊕ www. flymanchester.com. **T.F. Green Airport.** ✉ 2000 Post Rd., Off I–95, Exit 13, Warwick ☎ 888/268–7222, 401/737–4000 ⊕ www. pvdairport.com.

GROUND TRANSPORTATION
BUSES OR SHUTTLE VANS

Several companies offer shared-van service to many Boston-area destinations. Most provide door-to-door service to several major Back Bay and Downtown hotels. Reservations are not required, because vans swing by all the terminals every 15 minutes. One-way fares are $17 (less for each additional person). Easy Transportation runs sizeable vans from the airport to the Back Bay Hilton, Radisson, and Lenox hotels from 6 am to 9 pm. Star Shuttle operates shared vans from the airport to the Marriott Copley Place and Sheraton Copley, every hour on the half hour, from 7:30 am to 2 am. The best deal is Logan Express, with buses from the airport to the suburbs of Braintree, Framingham, Peabody, Woburn, and Back Bay. One-way fares are $12 to the suburbs and $7.50 to Back Bay; accompanied children under 10 ride free.

Contacts Easy Transportation. ☎ 617/869–7760 ⊕ www.easytransportationinc.com. **Logan Express.** ☎ 800/235–6426 ⊕ www. massport.com/logan-airport/To%20and%20 From%20Logan/LoganExpress.aspx. **Star Shuttle.** ☎ 617/230–6005 ⊕ www.starshut-tleboston.com.

CAR

For recorded information about traveling to and from Logan Airport, as well as details about parking, contact the airport's ground-transportation hotline. Traffic in the city can be maddening; it's a good idea to take public transportation to and from the airport.

When driving from Logan to Downtown Boston, the most direct route is by way of the Sumner Tunnel ($2.05 each way). On weekends, holidays, and after 10 pm weekdays, you can get around Sumner Tunnel backups by using the Ted Williams Tunnel ($2.05 each way), which will steer you onto the Southeast Expressway south of Downtown Boston. Follow the signs to I–93 northbound to head back into the Downtown area.

▌ BICYCLE TRAVEL

Bicycling has finally come of age in Boston. It's common today to see both locals and tourists biking along inner-city streets as well as pedestrian malls and other auto-free zones. Car drivers are becoming more used to sharing the road with bicycles, and an increasing number of designated bike lanes are helping make things safer for everyone. Note that helmets are required for anyone 16 or younger.

The city has a growing number of stands for locking your bike. Bicycles can be hitched to racks on the front of most buses or carried onto subway cars (with the exception of the Green Line) during nonpeak hours, with "peak" defined as 7 am to 10 am and 4 pm to 7 pm. "Pedal and Park" bike cages are available to cyclists at major transit hubs like Alewife and Forest Hills Stations.

BIKE RENTAL

The typical fee for a hybrid bike (with helmet and lock) is $40 per eight-hour day. Centrally located bike rental and repair shops include Back Bay Bicycles, Landry's Bikes, and Urban AdvenTours; some bike shops offer guided tours. State law requires that all rental companies have helmets available to renters.

HUBWAY

Boston's short-term bike rental program is primarily commuter-oriented, but it can also be a handy and fun way for travelers to cover relatively short distances. Members are able to unlock a bike from a Hubway dock, ride it for up to 30 minutes, and then return it to any other dock. There's no additional charge for any ride that lasts less than 30 minutes, and the docks are in dozens of strategic locations throughout the metro area.

Short-term memberships are available for 24 hours ($8), 3 days ($15), and by the month ($20), and you must be 18 or over to join. Sign up online or via one of the kiosks at each dock. Note that the prices don't include a helmet, which isn't mandatory but which is a good idea, or a lock, which isn't necessary if you're taking the bike directly to another dock.

Before taking a bike out, plan your route to the next dock—the Hubway's website and the free Spotcycle app (downloadable for iOS and Android) show docks' locations, and how many bikes and empty spaces are available at each. If you don't manage to return a bike within 30 minutes, an overtime fee will be charged to your credit card. Such fees can be stiff, especially if you've kept the bike longer than an hour.

TRAILS

The advocacy group MassBike has a website with general info for cyclists. Visit the city's ⊕ *boston.gov* website for links to maps of bike lanes and bike-friendly trails in Greater Boston and beyond. There are more than 100 car-free miles of largely interconnected waterfront pathways now open to bikes, from Charlestown and the Waterfront to Dorchester and Quincy. Both banks of the Charles River have scenic paths heading westward to Watertown and Newton. Other dedicated bicycle paths, some made from repurposed former rail lines, connect the hub with outer suburbs; the Minuteman Trail, for instance, heads westward from Cambridge for 15 miles, linking Arlington, Lexington, Concord, and Bedford.

Bicycle Information Back Bay Bicycles. ⊠ *362 Commonwealth Ave., Back Bay* ☎ *617/247–2336* ⊕ *papa-wheelies.com.* **Hubway.** ☎ *855/948–2929* ⊕ *www.thehubway.com.* **Landry's Bicycles.** ⊠ *890 Commonwealth Ave., Allston* ☎ *617/232–0446, 617/783–5804* ⊕ *www.landrys.com.* **MassBike** (*Massachusets Bicycle Coalition*). ⊠ *50 Milk St., 16th Fl., Downtown* ☎ *617/542–2453* ⊕ *massbike.org.* **Urban AdvenTours.** ⊠ *103 Atlantic Ave., Waterfront* ☎ *617/670–0637 shop, 617/379–3590 tours and rentals* ⊕ *www.urbanadventours.com.*

▌ BOAT TRAVEL

ARRIVING BY BOAT

Several boat companies make runs between the airport and Downtown destinations. Take the free Shuttle Bus 66 from any terminal to the airport's ferry dock to catch Boston's water taxis.

Rowes Wharf Water Taxi goes from Logan Airport to Rowes Wharf, Downtown, or other stops, for $12 per person ($20 round-trip). It operates daily year-round.

Harbor Express water taxis (part of the MBTA system) take passengers from Logan Airport to Long Wharf, Downtown ($10), and to Quincy and Hull on the South Shore ($12). Boats leave approximately every 40–45 minutes from 6:20 am to 10:30 pm on weekdays, and from 8:20 am to 10:30 pm on weekends.

Boston Harbor Cruises has an on-call boat service between the airport and several Downtown locations that operates year-round from 6:30 am to 10 pm Monday through Saturday and 6:30 am to 8 pm on Sunday. One-way fares to or from the airport are $12, and round-trip tickets are $20. One-way service to Charlestown or North Station is $20, and $18 to the Black Falcon Cruise Ship Terminal.

GETTING AROUND BY BOAT

MBTA commuter boat service operates weekdays between several Downtown harbor destinations, Charlestown, and quite a few locations on the South Shore. One-way fares range from $3.25 to $17 depending on the destination; seniors and students ride half-price, children under 11 are free. Schedules change seasonally, so call ahead.

Information Boston Harbor Cruises. ☎ 617/422-0392 ⊕ www.bostonharborcruises. com. **Harbor Express.** ☎ 617/222-6999. **Rowes Wharf Water Taxi.** ☎ 617/406-0504 pick-up line, 774/766-2471 reservations or cruises ⊕ www.roweswharfwatertaxi.com.

▌ BUS TRAVEL

ARRIVING BY BUS

Greyhound has buses to Boston from all major cities in North America. Besides its main location at South Station, Greyhound has suburban terminals in Newton and Framingham. Peter Pan Bus Lines connects Boston with cities elsewhere in Southern New England, New Jersey, New York, and Maryland.

Concord Coach runs buses between Boston and several cities in New Hampshire and Maine. C&J sends buses up the New Hampshire coast to Newburyport, Massachusetts; Dover, New Hampshire; Durham, New Hampshire; and Portsmouth, New Hampshire. Concord and C&J both leave from South Station (which is connected to the Amtrak station) and Logan Airport. BoltBus offers cheap fares in well-kept buses between Boston, New York City, Philadelphia, and Washington, D.C. (express service between Boston and New York City is also available). Megabus also offers low fares, and serves New York City and points south along the East Coast. Both companies leave from South Station.

If you want to travel in style, the Limo-Liner provides luxury bus service (with television, movies, high-speed Internet, and food-and-drink service) between

Boston's Hilton Back Bay and Manhattan's Hilton New York for $89–$99 each way. This service is open to the general public, not just guests of the Hilton. Reservations are a good idea.

Fares and schedules for all buses except LimoLiner are posted at South Station, at many of the tourist kiosks, and online. Major bus lines now offer Wi-Fi service at no charge. You can usually purchase your tickets online, and major credit cards are accepted for all buses.

Bus Information BoltBus. ☎ 877/265-8287 ⊕ www.boltbus.com. **C&J.** ☎ 800/258-7111 ⊕ www.ridecj.com. **Concord Coach.** ☎ 800/639-3317 ⊕ www.concordcoachlines. com. **Greyhound.** ☎ 800/231-2222 nationwide, 617/526-1801 South Station ⊕ www. greyhound.com. **LimoLiner.** ☎ 844/405-4637 ⊕ www.limoliner.com. **Megabus.** ☎ 877/462-6342 ⊕ www.megabus.com. **Peter Pan Bus Lines.** ☎ 800/343-9999 ⊕ www.peterpanbus.com.

Station Information South Station. ✉ 2 S. Station, Atlantic Ave. and Summer St., Downtown Ⓜ South Station.

GETTING AROUND BY BUS

Buses of the Massachusetts Bay Transportation Authority (MBTA) crisscross the metropolitan area and travel farther into suburbia than the subway and trolley lines. Most bus routes run from 5:30 am to 12:30 am.

CharlieCards (reloadable stored-value fare cards) are available for free at many subway terminals from ticket agents, who are generally there from 7 am to 7 pm. The hard-plastic cards can be loaded at fare kiosks with cash or with debit or credit cards. To pay the bus fare, tap your pass on the fare plate when you enter.

Fares within the city are $2.75 if paying in cash, or $2.25 if paying with a prepurchased CharlieCard; fares are higher for longer suburban lines. Fare machines accept paper currency but do not return change.

Bus Information MBTA. ☎ *800/392–6100, 617/222–5146 TTY* ⊕ *www.mbta.com.*

▌CAR TRAVEL

Having a car in Boston may be convenient if you're planning day trips outside the city limits, but driving within the city should be avoided, as it's often confusing and stressful. Roads are congested, traffic makes maneuvering difficult, and signage is cryptic (or nonexistent). Parking spaces are often hard to come by, especially during major events like the Boston Marathon and Red Sox games, or even large conventions.

If you must drive and you're unfamiliar with the city, it's important to plan your route in advance. Traveling with a GPS unit or smartphone, or renting one from your car-rental agency, can be a real help.

Boston motorists are notorious for driving aggressively. Pay extra attention to other drivers, and watch out for those using the emergency breakdown lanes (illegal unless posted otherwise), passing on the right, failing to yield, or turning from the wrong lane.

Unlike most of the USA, Greater Boston uses many traffic circles, also known as rotaries. The law states that cars entering traffic circles must yield to cars already in the circle, but don't expect all drivers to obey this rule.

GAS STATIONS

There are few gas stations in Downtown. Try Cambridge Street (behind Beacon Hill, near Massachusetts General Hospital), near Logan Airport in East Boston, along Commonwealth Avenue or Cambridge Street in Allston/Brighton, or off the Southeast Expressway just south of Downtown Boston.

Cambridge service stations are along Memorial Drive, Massachusetts Avenue, and Broadway. In Brookline, try Commonwealth Avenue or Boylston Street. Gas stations with 24-hour service can be found at many exits off Route 3 to Cape Cod, suburban ring roads Route 128 and Interstate 95, and at service plazas on the Massachusetts Turnpike (Interstate 90). Most offer both full- and self-service.

PARKING

Parking on Boston streets is tricky. Some neighborhoods have strictly enforced residents-only rules, with just a handful of two-hour visitors' spaces; others have meters, which cost 25¢ for 12 minutes, with a two-hour limit. On-street parking is free before 8 am and after 8 pm, and all day Sunday. Keep $5 in quarters handy, as some city meters take nothing else. Newer meters accept credit cards and issue receipts that you leave on your dashboard, on the street side. You may also be able to pay with the ParkBoston app on your smartphone.

The parking police are watchful and ruthless—it's not unusual to find a ticket on your windshield five minutes after your meter expires. Repeat offenders who don't pay fines may find the "boot" (an immovable steel clamp) secured to a wheel.

Major public lots are at Government Center, Quincy Market, beneath Boston Common (entrance on Charles Street), beneath Post Office Square, at Prudential Center, at Copley Place, and off Clarendon Street near the John Hancock Tower. Smaller lots and garages are scattered throughout Downtown, especially around the Theater District and off Atlantic Avenue in the North End. Most are expensive; expect to pay up to $12 an hour or $40 to park all day. The few city garages are a comparative bargain, such as the large one beneath Boston Common. Theaters, restaurants, stores, and tourist attractions often provide patrons with some free parking; ask your establishment to validate your receipt. Most Downtown restaurants offer valet parking, $10–$20.

ROAD CONDITIONS

Bostonians are notorious for driving erratically and aggressively. These habits, coupled with inconsistent street and traffic signs, one-way streets, and heavy congestion, make it a nerve-wracking city to navigate. Many urban roadways are under constant reconstruction or are roughly surfaced. Potholes and aboveground manhole covers are common hazards. Better to err on the side of caution: give yourself extra time to arrive at your destination.

ROADSIDE EMERGENCIES

Dial 911 in an emergency to reach police, fire, or ambulance services. If you're a member of the AAA auto club, call its 24-hour help bureau.

RENTAL CARS

Rates in Boston begin at about $40 a day on a weekly rate for an economy car with air-conditioning, automatic transmission, and unlimited mileage. This doesn't include gas, insurance charges, or the 6.25% tax and $10 surcharge. All major agencies have branches at Logan International Airport, even Zipcar.

▮ PEDICAB TRAVEL

Pedicabs, human-powered three-wheeled bicycle rickshaws, are popular modes of transport in spring and summer around Boston and Cambridge. These vehicles, which hold two adults easily and three with difficulty, are manned (some womaned) by trained cyclists who wear eye-catching shirts, exude good nature and stamina, and have the gift of gab. You can hail one of these three-wheelers on the street, or phone for one, with an average wait of 10 minutes. Boston patrons most often use them to get from point A to a not-too-distant point B; on Red Sox game days, pedicabs swarm towards Fenway Park, usually arriving ahead of auto traffic.

There are no fixed fares, since the bikers work for tips; pay your biker (cash only) what you think the ride was worth, though be ready for a sour look if you pay much less than $10 a mile or so. Try to agree on a fee ahead of time. Most pedicabs also offer tours, with minimum fixed fees.

Pedicab Information Boston Pedicab.
☏ 617/266–2005 ⊕ www.bostonpedicab.com. **Boston Rickshaw.** ☏ 857/997–6315.
Cambridge Pedicab. ☏ 617/370–3707 ⊕ cambridge-pedicab.com.

▮ SUBWAY TRAVEL

The Massachusetts Bay Transportation Authority (MBTA)—known as "the T"—operates subways, buses, and trolleys along five connecting lines, as well as many bus and several rail commuter lines that reach nearby suburbs and cities. Subways and buses operate from about 5:30 am to about 1 am, with limited late-night service. A 24-hour hotline and the MBTA website have specific information on routes, schedules, fares, wheelchair access, and other matters. Free maps are available at the MBTA's Park Street Station information stand, open daily from 7 am to 10 pm. The MBTA website has a useful trip planner tool.

GETTING AROUND ON THE SUBWAY

"Inbound" trains head into the city center (Park Street Station) and "outbound" trains head away from it. If you get on the Red Line at South Station, the train heading toward Alewife (Cambridge) is inbound. But once you reach Park Street, the train becomes outbound. Similarly, the Green Line to Fenway Park would be the Boston College or Cleveland Circle train. Large maps prominently posted at each station show the line(s) that serve it, with each stop marked; small maps are overhead in each car. Free 24-hour shuttle buses connect Airport Blue Line Station with all airline terminals. Shuttle Bus 22 runs between the subway and Terminals A and B, and Shuttle Bus 33 runs between the subway and Terminals C and E.

The Red Line originates at Braintree and Quincy Center to the south; the routes join near South Boston at the JFK/UMass stop and continue to Alewife, the northwest corner of Cambridge by suburban Arlington. (The Mattapan high-speed line, or M-line, is considered part of the overall Red Line. Originating in Ashmont Station, it transports passengers via vintage yellow trolleys to Mattapan Square.)

The Green Line operates elevated trolleys that dip underground in the city center. The line originates at Cambridge's Lechmere, heads south, and divides into four westward routes: B ends at Boston College (Commonwealth Avenue); C ends at Cleveland Circle (Beacon Street, in Brighton); D ends at Riverside (Newton at Route 128); and E ends at Heath Street (Huntington Avenue in Jamaica Plain).

The Blue Line runs weekdays from Bowdoin Square (and weeknights and weekends from Government Center) to the Wonderland Racetrack in Revere, north of Boston. The Blue Line is best if you're heading to North Station, Faneuil Hall, North End/Waterfront, or Back Bay (the Hynes Convention Center, Prudential Center area). The Orange Line runs from Oak Grove in north suburban Malden southwesterly to Forest Hills near the Arnold Arboretum in Jamaica Plain.

The Silver Line (a bus line with its own dedicated lanes) has four routes. SL1 connects South Station to Logan Airport; SL2 runs between South Station and the Design Center; SL4 connects Dudley Square and South Station; and SL5 runs between Downtown Crossing and Dudley Square, also stopping in Boylston.

FARES AND PASSES

T fares are $2.75 for adults paying in cash or $2.25 with a reloadable CharlieCard. Bus fares are $2 ($1.70 with a CharlieCard). The SL1 and SL2 bus lines are priced as if they were part of the subway. Children ages 11 and under ride free. Senior citizens and students with proper ID pay $1.10. Fares on the commuter rail—the Purple Line—vary

from $2.25 to $12.50, depending on distance, but are much more expensive if you pay cash on-board.

Getting a CharlieCard makes it easier to transfer between the subway and the bus, because such transfers are free and you don't need to keep track of individual tickets. Get your CharlieCard from a ticket agent at subway terminals during business hours (7 am to 7 pm); from a machine at the T stations at North Station, South Station, or Back Bay; the CharlieCard office at Downtown Crossing; or online or from some retailers. Check the T's website for detailed information.

One-day ($12) and seven-day ($21.25) passes are available for unlimited travel on subways, city buses, and inner-harbor ferries. Buy passes at any full-service MBTA stations. Passes are also sold at the Boston Common Visitor Information Center *(see Visitor Information)* and at some hotels.

Contact MBTA. ☎ *800/392–6100, 617/222–3200, 617/222–5146 TTY* ⊕ *www.mbta.com.*

▌TAXI TRAVEL

Cabs are available around the clock. You can find them outside most hotels and at designated cabstands around the city. Taxis generally line up around South Station, near Faneuil Hall Marketplace, at Long Wharf, near Massachusetts General Hospital, in the Theater District, and in Harvard Square. You can also call or use smartphone apps, such as Lyft or Uber to get a taxi or other hired car.

A taxi ride within the city of Boston costs $2.60 at entry for the first 1/7 mile, and 40¢ for each 1/7 mile thereafter. Licensed cabs have meters and provide receipts. An illuminated rooftop sign indicates an available cab. If you're going to or from the airport or to the suburbs, ask about flat rates. Cab drivers may charge extra for multiple stops. One-way streets, and major traffic jams, make circuitous routes necessary, but also add to the fare.

Trying to hail a cab at 2 am, when most bars close, can prove difficult, and there will often be a 20- to 30-minute wait if you phone for one. Using Uber or Lyft, or heading to a cabstand, may be your most efficient late-night choice. Avoid "rogue taxis." These sleek black town cars (legitimate Boston taxis are white) aggressively offer rides on the street or at airports; their drivers often charge more than the agreed-upon rate, and may even be dangerous. Always check for a valid taxi medallion plate and a posted photo ID of the driver.

Taxis can be hired outside each terminal at Logan Airport. Fares to and from Downtown should be about $20, including tip. Taxis must pay an extra toll of $5.25 and a $2.75 airport fee when leaving the airport, which will be tacked onto your bill at the end of the trip. On the way back to the airport, you'll pay the $2.75 fee again, but not the $5.25 toll.

Taxi Companies Boston Metro Cab.
☎ *617/782–5500* ⊕ *www.boston-cab.com.*
Independent Taxi Operators Association (ITOA). ☎ *617/426–8700 taxi dispatch, 617/268–1313* ⊕ *www.itoataxi.com.* **Top Cab.**
☎ *617/266–4800* ⊕ *topcab.us.* **Town Taxi Dispatch of New England.** ☎ *617/536–5000* ⊕ *www.towntaxiboston.com.*

▌ TRAIN TRAVEL

Boston is served by Amtrak at North Station, South Station, and Back Bay Station. North Station is the terminus for Amtrak's *Downeaster* service from Boston to New Hampshire and Maine. South Station and Back Bay Station, nearby, accommodate frequent Northeast Corridor departures to and arrivals from New York, Philadelphia, and Washington, D.C. Amtrak's *Acela* train cuts the travel time between Boston and New York to 3½ hours. South Station and Back Bay Station are the two stops in Boston for Amtrak's *Lake Shore Limited,* which travels daily between Boston and Chicago by way of Albany, Rochester,

Buffalo, and Cleveland. Amtrak tickets, schedules, and reservations are available at Amtrak stations, online, by telephone, and through travel agents. Free maps are available at the MBTA's Park Street Station information stand.

Amtrak ticket offices accept all major credit cards, cash, traveler's checks, and personal checks when accompanied by a valid photo ID and a major credit card. You may pay on board with cash or a major credit card, but a surcharge will apply. Amtrak has both reserved and unreserved trains. During peak times, such as Friday night, get a reservation and a ticket in advance (you may also save money by buying in advance). Trains at nonpeak times are unreserved, with seats assigned on a first-come, first-served basis.

The MBTA runs commuter trains to nearby points south, west, and north. Trains bound for Worcester, Needham, Forge Park, Providence (Rhode Island), and Stoughton leave from South Station and Back Bay Station; those to Fitchburg, Lowell, Haverhill, Newburyport, and Rockport operate out of North Station; those to Middleboro/Lakeville, Kingston/Route 3, Plymouth, and Greenbush depart from South Station.

MBTA commuter-rail stations generally accept only cash. Buy your ticket in advance, or be ready to pay a $1–$2 surcharge in cash when you're on board.

Train Information Amtrak. ☎ *800/872–7245* ⊕ *www.amtrak.com.* **Back Bay Station.** ✉ *145 Dartmouth St., Back Bay.* **North Station.** ✉ *100 Legends Way, Causeway and Friend Sts., North End.* **South Station.** ✉ *700 Atlantic Ave., at Summer St., Downtown* Ⓜ *South Station.*

ESSENTIALS

■ COMMUNICATIONS

INTERNET

Most Downtown hotels offer free or fee-based Wi-Fi in their rooms or at least in common areas. Check with your hotel before arriving to confirm.

You'll find that many Internet cafés on Newbury Street and throughout the city offer free Wi-Fi. Most coffee shops, including branches of Pavement, Peets, Starbucks, and Espresso Royale, have free Wi-Fi available to customers. Others may charge a small fee (from $2 and up) depending on the minutes of usage.

■ DAY TOURS AND GUIDES

Traveling to Boston on a package tour makes it quite convenient for those interested only in hitting the highlights or major historic sites such as the Freedom Trail, Faneuil Hall, the Bunker Hill Memorial, Quincy Market, and Harvard Square. If you're interested in exploring more neighborhoods, a tour will likely not give you time to visit them.

BOAT TOURS

Boston has many waterways that offer stunning views of the city skyline. Narrated sightseeing water tours generally run from spring through early fall, usually until Columbus Day weekend. These trips normally last ¾–1½ hours and cost upward of $25. Many companies offer whale watches, and sunset or evening cruises with entertainment.

Fees and Schedules Boston Duck Tours. ☎ 617/267-3825 ⊕ www.bostonducktours. com. **Boston Harbor Cruises.** ⊠ 1 Long Wharf ☎ 877/733-9425, 617/227-4321 ⊕ www.bostonharborcruises.com. **Charles Riverboat Company.** ⊠ 100 Cambridge Pl., Suite 320, Cambridge ☎ 617/621-3001 ⊕ www.charlesriverboat.com. **Liberty Clipper.** ⊠ 67 Long Wharf ☎ 617/742-0333 ⊕ www.libertyfleet.com. **Massachusetts**

Bay Lines. ⊠ 60 Rowes Wharf ☎ 617/542-8000, 617/934-2610 tickets ⊕ www. massbaylines.com.

BUS TOURS

Bus tours, which cost around $25 and run daily from mid-March to early November, cover the main historic neighborhoods in less than four hours. Reserve bus tours at least a day in advance.

Fees and Schedules Boston Private Tours. ⊠ 707 Main St. ☎ 978/771-4471 ⊕ www. bostonprivatetours.com. **Brush Hill Tours.** ⊠ Transportation Bldg., 16 Charles St. S ☎ 800/343-1328 ⊕ www.graylineboston.com.

THEME TOURS

See how the beer's made, get the deep dope on literary Boston and its architectural marvels, or stroll through the gorgeous greenspace of Boston's parks with one of these themed tours. Some organizations have special restrictions, such as an age minimum for children. Many tours are free, but require a reservation at least a few days in advance. It's always a good idea to call ahead to confirm schedules.

BEER TOURS

Boston Brew Tours. Suds enthusiasts may opt for a true micro-brewery crawl with Boston Brew Tours. ☎ 617/453-8687 ⊕ bostonbrewtours.com ⊠ From $65.

Harpoon Brewery. Get the behind-the-scenes scoop on Harpoon's brewing process with a tour; be sure to stop in the beer hall for an expertly poured pint and a fresh pretzel. ⊠ 306 Northern Ave., Waterfront ☎ 617/456-2322 ⊕ www. harpoonbrewery.com ⊠ $5.

Samuel Adams Brewery. Explore the beer-making process in depth at Samuel Adams and enjoy a few samples along the way. ⊠ Boston Beer Company, 30 Germania St., Jamaica Plain ☎ 617/368-5080 tours ⊕ www.samueladams.com ⊠ Free with $2 donation to local charity.

CHILDREN'S TOURS

Boston by Little Feet. Specifically designed for children ages 6–12, this tour explains the history of Boston's Freedom Trail from a child's perspective. Kids must be accompanied by an adult. ✉ *Meet at Samuel Adams statue in front of Faneuil Hall* ☎ *617/367–2345* ⊕ *www.bostonbyfoot.com/tours/Boston_By_Little_Feet* 💲 *$12 on-site ($10 online), free for children 6 and under.*

GARDEN, PARKS, AND ARCHITECTURE TOURS

Boston Athenaeum. To capture the true flavor of Boston's intelligentsia, make a reservation for an art and architecture tour of the Boston Athenæum, the grande dame of Boston's private libraries. ✉ *10½ Beacon St., Beacon Hill* ☎ *617/227–0270* ⊕ *www.bostonathenaeum.org* 💲 *Free.*

Boston Park Tours. Stop by the kiosk in Boston Common for information on walking tours of the Freedom Trail, parks, and more. ✉ *Parks and Recreation Dept. kiosk in Boston Common, 148 Tremont St.* ☎ *617/635–4505* ⊕ *www.cityofboston.gov/parks.*

TROLLEY TOURS

Narrated trolley tours, which usually cost $38 or so, don't require reservations and are more flexible than bus tours; you can hop on and hop off as often as you want. A full trip, with narrated historical details, normally lasts 1½ to 2 hours. All trolleys run daily, though less frequently off-season. Because they're open vehicles, be sure to dress appropriately for the weather.

Beantown Trolley. This two-hour narrated tour, with two photo stops, takes visitors past major sights in town such as Fanueil Hall, Boston Common, and Fenway Park. Ticket also includes a harbor cruise or ticket to the Mapparium at the Mary Baker Eddy Library. ☎ *781/985–6100* ⊕ *www.graylineboston.com* 💲 *From $40.*

Old Town Trolley. This trolley has popular one-, two-, and three-day hop-on, hop-off tours that cover all the city highlights. ✉ *380 Dorchester Ave., South Boston* ☎ *855/396–7433 general* ⊕ *www.trolleytours.com/boston* 💲 *From $38.*

WALKING TOURS

Boston is the perfect city for walking tours, to explore history, literature, the city's ethnic neighborhoods, and other subjects. Most tours cost about $20 and last one to two hours. Guides prefer to keep groups at fewer than 20 people, so always reserve ahead. Several organizations give tours once or twice a day spring through fall and by appointment (if at all) in winter. Others run tours a few days a week, spring through fall. If you'd rather not take a tour using your own two legs, there's also a tour that lets you see the sights on a Segway.

Fees and Schedules Black Heritage Trail. ✉ *44 Joy St., Beacon Hill* ☎ *617/742–5415* ⊕ *www.maah.org.* **Boston by Foot.** ✉ *290 Congress St., Suite 100* ☎ *617/367–2345* ⊕ *www.bostonbyfoot.com.* **Boston Center for Adult Education.** ✉ *122 Arlington St.* ☎ *617/267–4430* ⊕ *www.bcae.org.* **Boston Common Visitor Information Center.** ☎ *888/733–2678* ⊕ *www.bostonusa.com.* **Boston Segway Tours.** ✉ *199 State St., Government Center* ☎ *617/421–1234* ⊕ *www.bostonsegwaytoursinc.com.* **Cambridge Center for Adult Education.** ✉ *42 Brattle St., Cambridge* ☎ *617/547–6789* ⊕ *www.ccae.org.* **Freedom Trail.** ☎ *617/357–8300* ⊕ *www.thefreedomtrail.org.* **Harvard Campus Tours.** ✉ *Harvard Information Center, 1350 Massachusetts Ave., Cambridge* ☎ *617/495–1573* ⊕ *www.harvard.edu/visitors.* **Historic New England.** ✉ *141 Cambridge St.* ☎ *617/227–3956* ⊕ *www.historicnewengland.org.* **National Parks Service Visitor Center.** ☎ *617/242–5642* ⊕ *www.nps.gov/bost.* **North End Market Tour.** ✉ *6 Charter St.* ☎ *617/523–6032* ⊕ *bostonfoodtours.com.* **Women's Heritage Trail.** ☎ *617/945–5639* ⊕ *www.bwht.org.*

WHALE-WATCHING TOURS

Ships depart regularly for whale-watching excursions from April or May through October, from coastal towns all along the bay. Humpbacks, finbacks, and minkes feed locally in season, so you're sure to see a few—and on a good day you may see dozens. Bring warm clothing, as the ocean breezes can be brisk; rubber-soled shoes are also a good idea.

Boston Harbor Cruises. The high-speed catamarans of Boston Harbor Cruises glide to the whaling banks in half the time of some other cruises, allowing nearly as much whale time in only a three-hour tour. Tours are operated from March to November; call for schedule and reservations. Discounted and validated parking is available in two locations: The Harbor Garage and the Rowes Wharf Garage. Be sure to check the website for specific instructions. ⊠ *1 Long Wharf, next to aquarium* ☎ *617/227–4321, 877/733–9425* ⊕ *www.bostonharborcruises.com* ↻ *Can last more than 3 hrs* Ⓜ *Aquarium.*

Cape Ann Whale Watch. Board the *Hurricane 2,* the largest and fastest whalewatch vessel in northern Massachusetts, for a guaranteed whale sighting. Be sure to make a reservation first. Another bonus: free parking. ⊠ *Rose's Wharf, 415 Main St., Gloucester* ☎ *800/877–5110* ⊕ *www.seethewhales.com* ✉ *$48* ☾ *Closed Nov.–Apr.*

Captain Bill's Deep Sea Fishing/Whale Watch. Hop aboard the *Miss Cape Ann* for a tour with Captain Bill's Deep Sea Fishing/Whale Watch team, staffed with knowledgeable naturalists from the Whale Center of New England. Tours run May to October, and sightings are guaranteed. ⊠ *24 Harbor Loop, Gloucester* ☎ *978/283–6995, 800/339–4253* ⊕ *www.captbillandsons.com.*

Capt. John Boats. Several daily whalewatch cruises leave from Plymouth Town Wharf, and head into Cape Cod Bay and Stellwagen Bank. ⊠ *10 Town Wharf, Plymouth* ☎ *508/746–2643* ⊕ *www.captjohn.com* ✉ *$49.*

▌ GEAR

The first rule of Boston weather: no rules! A chilly, overcast morning can become a sunny, warm afternoon—and vice versa. Try to layer your clothing so that you can remove or add garments as needed for comfort. Rain may appear with little warning, so pack a raincoat and umbrella if you have the room. Boston is a great walking city—despite picturesque but bumpy cobblestone streets, brick walkways, and uneven asphalt—so be sure to bring comfortable shoes. In all seasons, it's often breezier (and colder) along the coast; carry a windbreaker, fleece jacket, or sweatshirt or hoodie when touring the beach or harbor areas.

▌ HOURS OF OPERATION

Banks are generally open weekdays 9 am to 4 or 5 pm, plus Saturday 9 am to noon or 1 pm at some branches. Public buildings are open weekdays 9 to 5.

Although hours vary quite a bit, most museums are open Monday through Saturday 9 or 10 am to 5 or 6 pm and Sunday noon to 5 pm. Some are closed one day a week, usually Monday.

Major pharmacy chains—CVS, Rite-Aid, and Walgreens—are generally open daily between 7 or 9:30 am and 8 or 10 pm; independently owned pharmacies tend to close earlier. Some are open 24/7.

Boston stores are generally open Monday through Saturday 10 or 11 am to 6 or 7 pm, closing later during the holiday-shopping season. Mall shops often stay open until 9 or 10 pm; malls and some tourist areas may also be open Sunday noon to 5 or 6 pm.

▮ MONEY

Prices are generally higher in Beacon Hill, the Back Bay, and Harvard Square than other parts of town. You're more likely to find bargains in the North End, Kenmore Square, Downtown Crossing, and Cambridge's Central Square. Many museums offer free admission on one weekday evening, and reduced admissions at all times for children, students, and senior citizens.

ITEM	AVERAGE COST
Cup of Coffee	$2–$3
Glass of Wine	$8 and up
Glass / Bottle of Beer	$4.50 and up
Slice of Pizza	$2–$3
One-Mile Taxi Ride	$7
Museum Admission (adult)	$15–$30

▮ RESTROOMS

Public restrooms outside of restaurants, hotel lobbies, and tourist attractions are rare in Boston, but you'll find clean, well-lighted facilities at South Station, Faneuil Hall Marketplace, and the Visitor Information Center on Boston Common. A candid assessment of Boston's classier "watering holes" is found at ⊕ *www.universalhub.com/restrooms*.

▮ SAFETY

Violent crime in Boston is rare but do be wary of pickpockets, scam artists, and car thieves. As in any large city, use common sense, especially after dark. Stay with the crowds and walk on well-lighted, busy streets. Take cabs or park in well-lighted lots or garages.

Subways and trolleys are safe, but stay on your guard. Don't take unmarked taxis or any taxi that lacks a posted photo ID of the driver. The MBTA has its own police officers (who patrol stations and monitor them via video); don't hesitate to ask them for help.

▮ TAXES

Hotel room charges in Boston and Cambridge are subject to state and local taxes of up to 14.45%. A sales tax of 7% is added to restaurant and take-out meals, and a sales tax of 6.25% is added to all other goods except non-restaurant food and clothing valued at less than $175.

▮ TIME

Boston is in the Eastern time zone, 3 hours ahead of Los Angeles, 1 hour ahead of Chicago, 5 hours behind London, and 15 hours behind Sydney. Daylight Savings Time (DST) is observed. DST begins the second Sunday in March, when clocks are set ahead one hour, and ends the first Sunday in November, when clocks are set back an hour (tip for remembrance: "Spring forward, and Fall behind").

▮ TIPPING

In restaurants the standard gratuity is 15% to 20% of your bill. Many restaurants automatically add a 15% to 20% gratuity for groups of six or more.

Tip taxi drivers 10%–15% of the fare, and airport and hotel porters $1–$2 per bag. It's also usual to tip chambermaids $2 to $3 daily. Hotel room-service tips vary and may be included in the meal charge. Masseuses and masseurs, hairstylists, manicurists, and others performing personal services generally get a 15% tip. Tour guides may be tipped a few dollars for good service. Concierges may be tipped anywhere from $5 to $20 for exceptional service, such as securing a difficult dinner reservation or helping plan a personal sightseeing itinerary. Theater ushers, museum guides, and gas-station attendants generally do not receive tips.

TIPPING GUIDELINES FOR BOSTON	
Bartender	$1 to $2 per drink
Bellhop	$1 to $5 per bag, depending on the level of the hotel
Hotel Concierge	$5 or more, if he or she performs a service for you
Hotel Doorman	$1 to $2 if he helps you get a cab
Hotel Maid	$2 to $3 a day (daily or at the end of your stay, in cash)
Hotel Room-Service Waiter	$1 to $2 per delivery, even if a service charge has been added
Porter at Airport or Train Station	$1 to $2 per bag
Skycap at Airport	$1 to $3 per bag checked (in addition to any airline-imposed fees)
Taxi Driver	10% to 15%, but round up the fare to the next dollar amount
Tour Guide	10% of the cost of the tour
Valet Parking Attendant	$1 to $2, only when you get your car
Waiter	15% to 20%, with 20% being the norm at high-end restaurants; nothing additional if a service charge is added to the bill
Other	Restroom attendants in expensive restaurants expect small change or $1. Tip coat-check personnel at least $1 to $2 per item checked; if there's a fee, then nothing

▌ VISITOR INFORMATION

Contact the city and state tourism offices for general information, details about seasonal events, discount passes, trip planning, and attraction information. The National Park Service office screens an entertaining and informative eight-minute slide show on Boston's historic sites and supplies you with maps and directions. The Welcome Center, Boston Common Visitor Information Center, and the Cambridge Tourism Office cheerfully offer general information.

Contacts Boston Common Visitor Information Center. ⊠ *139 Tremont St., On the Common, Downtown* ☎ *617/536–4100* ⊕ *www.bostonusa.com/visit/planyourtrip/resources/vic.* **Cambridge Tourism Office.** ⊠ *4 Brattle St., Harvard Square* ☎ *800/862–5678, 617/441–2884* ⊕ *www.cambridge-usa.org.* **Greater Boston Convention and Visitors Bureau.** ⊠ *2 Copley Pl., Suite 105, Back Bay* ☎ *888/733–2678, 617/536–4100* ⊕ *www.bostonusa.com.* **Massachusetts Office of Travel and Tourism.** ⊠ *State Transportation Bldg., 10 Park Plaza, Suite 4510, Back Bay* ☎ *800/227–6277, 617/973–8500* ⊕ *www.massvacation.com.* **National Parks Service Visitor Center.** ⊠ *Faneuil Hall, Downtown* ☎ *617/242–5642* ⊕ *www.nps.gov/bost.*

ONLINE RESOURCES

Boston.com, home of the *Boston Globe* online, has news and feature articles, ample travel information, and links to towns throughout Massachusetts. *The Improper Bostonian* has nightlife, movie, restaurant, and arts listings. The Bostonian Society answers frequently asked questions about Beantown history on its website. The iBoston page posts wonderful photographs of buildings of architectural and historical importance. *WickedLocal* provides a more relaxed (and somewhat irreverent) take on Boston and suburban news and information.

All About Boston Boston.com. ⊕ *www.boston.com.* **Bostonian Society.** ⊕ *boston-history.org.* **iBoston.** ⊕ *www.iboston.org.* **The Improper Bostonian.** ⊕ *www.improper.com.* **Wicked Local.** ⊕ *www.wickedlocal.com.*

INDEX

A

A Cambridge House Inn ⊤,
177
Abbott Hall, 259
Abe & Louie's ✕, 138
Abiel Smith School, 45
Acorn Street, 11
Adams National Historic Park,
270
Addison Choate Inn ⊤, 269
African Meeting House, 45
African Methodist Episcopal
Church, 45
Air travel, 249, 280–281
Alden & Harlow ✕, 149
Algiers Coffee House ✕, 122
All Star Sandwich Bar ✕, 149
Alley (bar), 188
Allston, 193–194
Amelia Payson House ⊤, 266
American Repertory Theatre,
211
Ames Boston Hotel ⊤, 168
Ancient & Honorable Artillery
Company of Massachusetts,
56
Antico Forno ✕, 132
Antiques, shopping for,
229–230, 233, 241, 269–270
Appleton Bakery + Cafe ✕, 87
Aquariums, 75, 78
Arboretums, 111, 225
Architecture tours, 28, 92, 125,
289
Area Four ✕, 149
Arlington Street Church, 93
Arnold Arboretum of Harvard
University, 111, 225
Art galleries and museums.
⇨See Museums and art
galleries
Arts, 180–182, 265
Atlantic Beer Garden ✕, 107
Atlantic Fish Co. ✕, 138–139
Audio tours, 254
Average costs, 291.⇨See also
Price categories

B

B & G Oysters ✕, 142
Babbo Pizzeria ✕, 134–135
Back Bay, The, 20, 28–29,
87–98, 138–145, 172–175,
188–190, 233–237
Back Bay Bicycles, 217
Back Bay mansions, 92

Baker House, 126
Ballet, 202
Barking Crab Restaurant ✕,
137
Bars, 182–184, 185–187,
188–189, 190–191, 192, 193,
194, 195–196, 201, 215
Baseball, 214–215, 217
Basketball, 217
Battery Wharf Hotel ⊤, 168
Battle Green, 252
Bay Village, 98
Beaches, 223–225, 267
Beacon Hill, 18, 39–48,
130 131, 167, 182–183,
229–231
Beacon Hill Hotel & Bistro ⊤,
167
Beacon Street, 43
Beanpot Hockey Tournament,
221
Beantown Pub, 185–186
Beantown Trolley, 289
Bearskin Neck Motor Lodge
⊤, 269
Beat Brasserie (music club), 199
Beauty supplies, shopping for,
234
Beehive (jazz club), 191
Beer, 107, 194, 288
Bell in Hand Tavern, 183–184
Bella Luna & The Milky Way
✕, 146
Benedetto ✕, 149
Benjamin Franklin Statue, 75,
78–79
Berklee Performance Center,
206
Bicycling, 217–218, 281–282
Black Heritage Trail, 27, 43, 45
Black Rose ✕, 58, 184
Blackstone Block, 55–56
Bleacher Bar ✕, 101
Blue Dragon ✕, 135
Blue-eyed Crab Grille & Raw
Bar ✕, 278
Blue Hills Bank Pavilion, 206
Blue Hills Reservation, 220
Blue Hills Trailside Museum,
221
Boat and ferry travel, 249,
282–283
Boat drop sites, 218
Boat tours, 48, 78, 250, 261,
276–277, 288
Boating and sailing, 218–219,
258

Bobby from Boston (shop), 239
Boch Center, 211
Bond Restaurant and Lounge,
186
Bookstores, 232, 234–235,
238, 241
Boomerangs-Special Edition
(shop), 239–240
Boston Athenaeum, 44, 289
Boston Ballet, 202
Boston Baroque (early music
group), 209
Boston Beer Company, 194
Boston Beer Works (bar),
182–183, 192
Boston Bowl, 198
Boston Brew Tours, 288
Boston Bruins, 221
Boston Camerata (early music
group), 209
Boston Cecilia (choral group),
205
Boston Celtics, 217
Boston Center for the Arts,
98, 212
Boston Chamber Music Society,
209
Boston College Eagles, 219
Boston Common, 18, 27, 39–48,
130–131, 167
Boston Common Frog Pond,
221
Boston Common Visitor Infor-
mation Center, 41
Boston Dance Alliance, 202
Boston Duck Tours, 48
Boston Early Music Festival,
209
Boston Film Festival, 22
Boston Harbor Cruises, 225,
290
Boston Harbor Hotel at Rowes
Wharf ⊤, 168
Boston Harbor Islands National
Park Area, 220, 225
Boston Latin School, 78–79
Boston Lyric Opera, 210
Boston Marathon, 22, 222, 223
Boston Marriott Cambridge
⊤, 177
Boston Marriott Copley Place
⊤, 172
Boston Marriott Long Wharf
⊤, 168
Boston Massacre Memorial, 41
Boston Massacre Site, 79
Boston Open Studio, 206

Boston Opera House, *79, 206,*
211
Boston Outskirts, *21, 106–112,*
146–148, 176, 193–194, 240
Boston Park Plaza ⌐, *172*
Boston Park Tours, *289*
Boston Philharmonic, *209*
Boston Pops, *210*
Boston Pops Concert and Fire-
works Display, *22*
Boston Public Garden, *27, 28,*
90–91
Boston Public Library, *27, 91,*
206, 208
Boston Public Market, *58, 231*
Boston Red Sox, *214–215*
Boston Symphony Orchestra,
210
Boston Tea Party Ships &
Museum, *77*
Boston University, *218*
Boston Women's Heritage
Trail, *27*
Boston Women's Memorial, *94*
Bova's Bakery ✕, *64*
Bowling alleys, *192, 196–197,*
198
Boxer Boston Hotel ⌐, *168*
Boylston Street, *93*
Brackett's Ocean View ✕, *269*
Brattle House, *122*
Brattle Street, *115, 122–125*
Brattle Theatre, *123, 203*
Bricco ✕, *132*
Brighton Music Hall, *193*
Brimstone Corner, *47*
Bristol Bar, *188*
Brookline, *111–112, 147–148,*
176, 240
Brookline Booksmith (shop),
240
Buckman Tavern, *254*
Bukowski Tavern, *188–189*
Bunker Hill Monument, *67,*
68–69, 71
Burren, The (bar), *201*
Bus tours, *25, 251, 288*
Bus travel, *23, 252, 281,*
283–284
Business hours, *129, 181, 290*
Butcher Shop, The ✕, *143*

C

Café Algiers, *197*
Café ArtScience ✕, *150*
Cafés and coffeehouses, *87,*
122, 133, 185, 189, 197, 201
Caffe dello Sport ✕, *133*
Caffé Paradiso ✕, *133*

Caffe Vittoria ✕, *61, 133, 185*
Cambridge, *21, 114–126,*
149–152, 177–178, 195,
241–244
Cambridge Brewing Co. (bar),
195
Cambridge Common, *119*
Cantab Lounge (club), *199*
Cantata Singers (choral group),
205
Cape Ann Motor Inn ⌐, *268*
Cape Ann Museum, *266*
Cape Ann Whale Watch, *290*
Cape Ann's Marina Resort &
Spa ⌐, *268*
Capital Grille, The ✕, *139*
Captain Bill's Deep Sea Fish-
ing/Whale Watch, *290*
Capt. John Boats (whale watch-
ing), *290*
Car rental, *285*
Car travel, *23, 249, 281,*
284–285
Cardullo's Gourmet Shop ✕,
115
Castle Island Park, *109, 222*
Castle Manor Inn ⌐, *268*
Celebrity Series of Boston, *208*
Central Burying Ground, *42*
Centre Street Café ✕, *146*
Chamber music, *209–210*
Champions Sports Bar, *189*
Chandler Inn ⌐, *175*
Chandler Studios ⌐, *175*
Charles Hotel ⌐, *177*
Charles Playhouse, *211*
Charles River Canoe & Kayak
Center, *218*
Charles River Reservation, *226*
Charles River Watershed Asso-
ciation, *218*
Charles Street, *44*
Charles Street Meeting House,
45
Charlesmark Hotel ⌐, *172*
Charlestown, *19, 66–72, 134,*
185
Charlestown Navy Yard, *71–72*
Charlestown Navy Yard Visitors
Information Center, *72*
Charliepass and Charliecard,
23
Cheers (bars), *183, 184*
Chestnut Street, *44, 46*
Children, attractions for, *41,*
44, 47–48, 49, 50, 56, 57, 58,
61, 62, 65, 70–71, 72, 77–78,
82–83, 90–91, 94–95, 97,
104, 109–110, 111, 118–119

dining with, *130, 134–135,*
137, 141–142, 143, 146, 148,
150, 151
lodging with, *168, 169, 170,*
171, 172, 173, 174, 176,
177, 178
shopping, *238*
tours, *289*
Children's Museum, *75, 77–78*
Chinatown, *79, 137*
Choral groups, *205*
Chorus Pro Musica, *205*
Christ Church, *121*
Christopher Columbus Park,
79–80
Church concerts, *205*
Church of the Covenant, *93*
Churches, *28, 39, 47, 50, 61,*
64, 92–93, 94, 95, 96, 119,
120, 121, 205
concerts in, *205*
City Hall, *58–59*
Clery's (bar), *190*
Climate, *22*
Clothing stores, *230, 232,*
235–236, 238–239, 242
Club Café, *191*
Club Passim (café), *197*
Coffeehouses and cafés, *87,*
122, 133, 185, 189, 197, 201
Colleges and universities,
119–122, 123, 125–126, 218
Colonnade Hotel ⌐, *172*
Comedy clubs, *187, 197, 199*
Comedy Connection (club), *187*
Comedy Studio (club), *197*
Commonwealth Avenue Mall,
94
Communications, *288*
Community Bicycle Supply, *217*
Community Boating, *219*
Community Rowing, *219*
Concert halls, *206–208*
Concert series, *208*
Concord, *255–259*
Concord Museum, *255*
Contemporary dance, *202*
Coolidge Corner Theatre, *107,*
203
Copley Place, *94*
Copley Square, *28, 94*
Copley Square Hotel ⌐, *173*
Copp's Hill Burying Ground,
42, 53, 60
Costs, *13, 291.* ⇨*See also* Price
categories
Courtyard ✕, *92*
Courtyard by Marriott Boston
Brookline ⌐, *176*
Crafts, shopping for, *236, 242*

Craigie on Main ✕, 150
Crane Beach, 224
Credit cards, 13
Cutler Majestic Theatre at
  Emerson College, 212
Cutty's ✕, 147

D

Dance, 202
Dance clubs, 187–188
Dance Complex, 202
Dante ✕, 150
Darryl's Corner Bar & Kitchen,
  190
David Neligan Antiques, 269
Davio's ✕, 139
Delux Café, 190
Department of Conservation &
  Recreation, 216
Deuxave ✕, 139
Dexter Pratt House, 124
Diesel Café, 201
Dining. ⇨See Restaurants
Dr. Paul Dudley White Bike
  Path, 217
Dorchester, 109–111
Dorchester Heights Monument
  and National Historic Site,
  111
Downtown Boston, 19, 75–84,
  134–138, 167–172, 185–188,
  232–233
Doyle's Café, 194
Drink (bar), 186
Driving. ⇨See Car travel
Druid (bar), 195
Dumpling Cafe ✕, 137
Durgin-Park Market Dining
  Room ✕, 131, 184

E

Early music groups, 209
Eastern Standard Kitchen and
  Drinks ✕, 115
Ebenezer Clough House, 62
Edward M. Kennedy Institute
  for the United States Senate,
  109–110
El Oriental de Cuba ✕, 146
Eldo Cake House ✕, 79
Eliot Hotel 📷, 173
Elmwood, 124
Emerald Necklace, 27, 226
Emergencies, 285
Emerson, Ralph Waldo, 257
Emmanuel Church, 94
Emmanuel Music (church con-
  certs), 205
Encore 📷, 175

Envoy Hotel 📷, 168–169
Esplanade, 94–95, 222
Essex, 269–270
Essex Shipbuilding Museum,
  269
Estragon Tapas ✕, 143
Ether Monument, 91
Exeter Street Theater, 95

F

Fairmont Copley Plaza Hotel
  📷, 94, 173
Faneuil Hall, 53, 56
Faneuil Hall Marketplace,
  231–232
Federal Reserve Tower, 80
Felipe's Taqueria ✕, 115
Fenway, 20, 101–104, 145–146,
  175–176, 192–193
Fenway Park, 101, 103,
  214–216
Festivals and seasonal events,
  22–23, 27, 203, 204, 209,
  218, 222, 223
Film, 22, 203–204
Finz Seafood & Grill ✕, 265
First Baptist Church, 95
First Church of Christ, Scientist,
  95
First Parish in Cambridge and
  the Old Burying Ground, 121
Fishing, 261
Flat Top Johnny's (pool hall),
  196–197
Flour Bakery + Café ✕, 98, 143
Fodor, Eugene, 13
Folk dance, 202
Food, shopping for, 230, 231,
  242
Football, 219
Fort Sewall, 259, 261
Four Seasons Hotel Boston
  📷, 173
Fours, The (bar), 183
Franklin Café, The ✕, 143, 190
Franklin Café (Gloucester) ✕,
  268
Franklin Park Zoo, 110
Frederick Law Olmstead
  National Historic Site,
  111–112
Free attractions and events, 27
Freedom Trail, 27, 31, 32
Freepoint Hotel 📷, 177
FuGaKyu ✕, 147
Full Moon ✕, 150

G

Garden tours, 289
Gay and lesbian clubs, 188,
  191, 193, 194
George Middleton House, 45
George Washington statue, 91
George Wright Golf Course,
  220
Gibson House, 95–96
Gift shops, 231, 236, 240, 242
Giulia ✕, 150
Gloucester, 266–268
Godfrey Hotel 📷, 169
Golf, 220
Good Harbor Beach, 267
Good Life (bar), 186
Government Center, 18–19,
  53–64, 131–132, 183–185,
  231–232
Granary Burying Ground, 42
Great Dome, 126
Great Scott (rock club), 193
Greater Boston Convention &
  Visitors Bureau, 22
Green Dragon Tavern, 184
Green Street ✕, 151
Grendel's Den (bar), 195
Grill 23 & Bar ✕, 139
Gryphon House 📷, 175

H

Hammond Castle Museum, 266
Hancock-Clarke House, 254
Handel & Haydn Society, 209
Hanover Street, 61
Harbor Light Inn 📷, 261
Harborfest, 22
Harborside Inn 📷, 169
HarborWalk, 27
Hard Rock Cafe (club), 184–185
Harp (bar), 183
Harrison Gray Otis Houses, 46
Harvard Art Museums, 118
Harvard Coop Society (shop),
  241
Harvard Film Archive, 203
Harvard Gardens ✕, 50
Harvard Information Center,
  120–121
Harvard Museum of Natural
  History, 118
Harvard Square, 116, 118–122
Harvard Square Hotel 📷, 177
Harvard University, 119–122
Harvard University Crimson,
  219
Harvard Yard, 119–121
Harvest ✕, 151

Hatch Memorial Shell, 206–207
Haunted Happenings, 23
Havana Club (salsa club), 200
Hawthorne Hotel, The ☷, 266
Haymarket, 59
Head of the Charles Regatta, 22, 218
Helmand, The ✕, 151
Hennessy's (bar), 184
Henrietta's Table ✕, 151
Henry Vassall House, 124–125
Hiking, 220–221
Hilton Boston Back Bay ☷, 173
Hilton Boston Downtown/ Faneuil Hall ☷, 169
Hilton Boston Logan Airport ☷, 176
Hockey, 221
Holden Chapel, 119
Holocaust Memorial, 57
Home furnishings, shopping for, 239, 242
Hooper-Lee-Nichols House, 125
Hotel Commonwealth ☷, 175–176
Hotels. ⇨See also Lodging
price categories, 165, 250
House of Blues (bar), 192
House of the Seven Gables, 263
Howl at the Moon (bar), 186
Hubway, 282
Huntington Theatre Company, 212
Hyatt Boston Harbor ☷, 176
Hyatt Regency Boston ☷, 169
Hynes Convention Center, 97

I

Ice-skating, 221–222
Icon (dance club), 187
Improv Asylum (comedy club), 197
ImprovBoston (comedy club), 197, 199
Independent, The (bar), 201
Inn @ St. Botolph ☷, 174
Institute of Contemporary Art, 27, 109
Institute of Contemporary Art/ Boston, 203, 207
InterContinental Boston ☷, 169
Internet, 288
Irish Heritage Trail, 27
Irving House ☷, 178
Isabella Stewart Gardner Museum, 27, 101, 103–104, 208
Island Creek Oyster Bar ✕, 145
Itineraries, 24–26

J

Jacque's Cabaret, 188
Jamaica Plain, 111, 146–147, 194
Jamaica Pond, 222
Jamaica Pond Boat House, 219
Jewelry stores, 231, 236–237
Jillian's Boston (entertainment complex), 192
JJ Foley's Cafe, 191
Joe's American Bar & Grill ✕, 139–140
Jogging, 222–223
John F. Kennedy Federal Office Building, 59
John F. Kennedy Library and Museum, 110
John F. Kennedy National Historic Site, 112
John Hancock Tower, 28, 96
John Harvard's Brewery & Ale House, 195
John J. Smith House, 45
José Mateo's Ballet Theatre, 202

K

Kava ✕, 143–144
Kelly's Roast Beef ✕, 224
Kendall Hotel ☷, 178
Kendall Square, 125–126
Kendall Square Cinema, 203–204
Kenmore Square, 104, 145–146, 175–176
Kimpton Hotel Marloew ☷, 178
Kimpton Nine Zero ☷, 169
Kimpton Onyx Hotel ☷, 170
King's Chapel, 75, 80
King's Chapel Burying Ground, 75, 80–81
Kinsale (bar), 186
Kresge Auditorium, 126

L

L. A. Burdick Chocolates ✕, 124
Lala Rokh ✕, 130
Landing, The ✕, 261
Langham Hotel ☷, 170
Larz Anderson Park, 222
Last Hurrah (bar), 186
Laugh Boston (comedy club), 199
Le Meridien Cambridge ☷, 178
Leather District, 81
Leavitt & Peirce (shop), 243

Ledger Restaurant and Bar ✕, 265
Legal Oysteria ✕, 66
Legal Sea Foods ✕, 75, 135
Lenox Hotel ☷, 174
Leonard P. Zakim Bunker Hill Memorial Bridge, 50
Le's ✕, 151
Les Sablons ✕, 151–152
Les Zygomates ✕, 135
L'Espalier ✕, 140
Lewis and Harriet Hayden House, 45
Lexington, 252, 254–255
Lexington Visitor Center, 252
Liberty Hotel Boston ☷, 167
Libraries, 27, 91, 206, 208, 255
Limelight Stage + Studios (bar), 186–187
Lion's Tail (bar), 191
List Visual Arts Center, 125, 126
Little Donkey ✕, 152
Lizard Lounge (rock club), 199
Lodging, 13, 164–178, 250, 261, 266, 268, 269
atlas, 153–162
children, 168, 169, 170, 171, 172, 173, 174, 176, 177, 178
neighborhoods, 166
price categories, 165, 250
reservations, 165
taxes, 129
tipping, 129, 291–292
Loew's Boston Hotel ☷, 174
Long Beach, 267
Longfellow House–Washington's Headquarters, 123
Louisburg Square, 42–43
Lucky's Lounge, 187

M

Machine (bar), 193
Main Street Antiques, 270
Main Street Market & Cafe ✕, 259
Mamma Maria ✕, 132
Mandarin Oriental Boston ☷, 174
Marblehead, 259, 261
Massachusetts Golf Association, 220
Massachusetts Institute of Technology (MIT), 125–126
Massachusetts State House, 27
Mei Mei Restaurant ✕, 147–148
Memorial Church, 120
Memorial Hall, 120

Memorial to the Irish Famine, 81
Menton ✕, 135
Merchant, The ⊠, 266
Meritage Restaurant + Wine Bar ✕, 138
Middle East & ZuZu Restaurant & Nightclub, 199
Middlesex Fells Reservation, 220 221
Middlesex Lounge, 196
Millennium Bostonian Hotel ⊠, 170
Minute Man National Historical Park, 254
Mr. Bartley's Burger Cottage ✕, 115
Mistral ✕, 144
MIT Chapel, 126
Money, 13, 291
Mooo ✕, 131
Mount Auburn Cemetery, 123, 226
Mt. Vernon Street, 46
Multicultural Arts Center, 202
Multicultural Dance, 202
Munroe Tavern, 254–255
Museum of African American History, 43, 45
Museum of Fine Arts, 27, 104, 204, 208
Museum of Science, 49
Museums and art galleries, 5, 6, 7, 8, 27, 39, 43, 45, 46, 47–48, 49, 50, 62, 72, 77–78, 83, 95–96, 103–104, 109–110, 115, 118, 121, 122, 123, 124–125, 204, 208, 221, 233–234, 238, 255, 263–264, 266–267, 269, 275, 278
Music, 204–210
Music clubs, 184–185, 190, 191–192, 193–194, 199–200, 201
Music shops, 237
Myers + Chang ✕, 144
Mystic Seaport, 275

N

Nantasket Beach, 224
Nantucket Whaling Museum, 275
National Monument to the Forefathers, 278
National Park Service Tour, 27
Navy Yard Bistro and Wine Bar ✕, 66
Needham Bowlaway, 198
Neptune Oyster ✕, 133

New Bedford Whaling Museum, 275
New Bedford Whaling National Historical Park, 275
New England Aquarium, 75, 78
New England Conservatory's Jordan Hall, 207
New England Historic Genealogical Society, 96
New England Patriots, 219
Newbury Guest House ⊠, 174
Newbury Street, 87, 96
Nichols House, 46
Nick's Comedy Stop, 187
Nightlife and the arts, 265
No. 9 Park ✕, 131
Noir (bar), 196
North Bridge Visitor Center, 254
North End, The, 18–19, 59–64, 132–134, 185, 232
North Shore, 259–270
Northwest of Boston, 251–259

O

O ya ✕, 135–136
Oak Long Bar + Kitchen, 189
Odyssey Opera of Boston, 210
Oishii Boston ✕, 144
Old City Hall, 81
Old Corner Bookstore Site, 75, 81
Old Manse, 255–256
Old North Bridge, 256
Old North Church, 53, 61
Old South Church, 96
Old South Meeting House, 75, 82–83
Old State House, 53, 83
Old Town Trolley, 289
Old West Church, 50
Old West End, The, 18, 39, 49–50
Oleana ✕, 152
Omni Parker House ⊠, 170
Opening Our Doors Day, 27
Opera, 210
Orchard House, 256–257
Orchestras, 209–210
Orinoco ✕, 152
Orleans (bar), 201
Ostra ✕, 140
Out of Town News (newsstands), 121, 243
Outdoor activities. ⇨See Sports and outdoor activities
Outpost 186 (music club), 200

P

Paradise Rock Club, 193
Park Street Church, 47, 75
Parking, 27, 284
Parks and gardens, 27, 28, 55, 61, 79–80, 90–91, 98, 109, 110, 111, 112, 220, 222, 225–226, 254, 270, 275, 290
Passports ✕, 268
Paul Revere House, 53, 62
Paul Revere Mall, 61, 62
Paul Revere statue, 62
Paul Revere's ride, 63
Pavement Coffeehouse ✕, 87
Peabody Essex Museum, 263–264
Peabody Museum of Archeology & Ethnology, 121
Pedicab travel, 285
Penobscot Marine Museum, 275
Performing arts, 202–212
Phillips School, 45
Pier 6 ✕, 69
Pilgrim Hall Museum, 278
Plimoth Plantation, 23, 278
Plough & Stars, The (bar), 196
Plum Island, 224–225
Plymouth, 270, 278
Plymouth Rock, 278
Plymouth Visitor Information Center, 270
Polcari's Coffee ✕, 133
Pool halls, 192, 196–197, 198
Porto ✕, 140
Post 390 ✕, 140
Prezza ✕, 133
Price categories, 13
average costs, 291
for dining, 129, 250
for lodging, 165, 250
Prudential Center, 97
Prudential Center Skywalk Observatory, 97
Public Garden, 27
Public Ice-skating Rinks, 222
Publick House, The ✕, 148

Q

Q Restaurant ✕, 137
Quincy Market, 53, 56, 57–68

R

Radcliffe Institute for Advanced Study, 123
Ralph Waldo Emerson House, 257
Rani Bistro ✕, 148
Ray & Maria Stata Center, 126

Red Room @ Café 939 (music club), 190, 206
Red Sox, 214–215
Regattabar (jazz club), 200
Regina Pizzeria ✕, 133
Renaissance Boston Waterfront Hotel 🖳, 170–171
Restaurants, 13, 39, 50, 53, 58, 61, 64, 66, 69, 71, 75, 79, 87, 92, 96, 98, 101, 107, 115, 122, 124, 127–152, 250, 259, 261, 265, 268, 269, 270, 278
American, 259, 265
atlas, 153–162
brunch, 144
cafés and coffeehouses, 87, 133, 185, 189, 197, 201
children, 130, 134–135, 137, 141–142, 143, 146, 148, 150, 151
dress code, 129
hours, 129
price categories, 129
reservations, 129
seafood, 261, 265
smoking, 130
taxes, 129, 291
tipping, 129, 291–292
tours, 129
Restrooms, 291
Revere, Paul, 53, 61, 62, 63
Revere Beach, 224
Revere Hotel 🖳, 171
Ristorante Euno ✕, 134
Ritz-Carlton Boston Common 🖳, 171
Robert Gould Shaw 54th Regiment Memorial, 41, 45
Rockport, 268–269
Rocky Neck, 267
Rogers Building, 126
Rose Fitzgerald Kennedy Greenway, 64, 226
Row 34 ✕, 136
Rowes Wharf, 83
Royal Sonesta Boston 🖳, 178
Royale (music club), 188
RumBa (bar), 187
Running, 222–223
Rutland Square, 98
Ryles Jazz Club, 200

S
Sacco's Bowl Haven, 198
Safety, 39, 66, 74, 101, 291
St. Paul's Episcopal Cathedral, 47
St. Stephen's, 64
Salem, 262–266

Salem Maritime National Historic Site, 264
Salem Street, 64
Salem Witch Museum, 264
Salem Witch Trials, 265
Salem Witch Trials Memorial, 264–265
Salsa clubs, 200
Saltie Girl ✕, 141
Samuel Adams Brewery, 107, 288
Sanders Theatre, 207
Scampo ✕, 131
Scottish Rite Masonic Museum & Library, 255
Scullers Jazz Club, 194
Seaport Boston Hotel 🖳, 171
Select Oyster Bar ✕, 141
Semitic Museum, 122
Sevens Ale House (bar), 183
1768 Jeremiah Lee Mansion, The, 261
Sever Hall, 119–120
Shake the Tree (shop), 232
Shoe stores, 243
Shopping, 228–244, 269–270
Side trips from Boston, 246–278
Sightseeing tours, 25, 27, 28, 32, 78, 80, 83, 101, 114, 115, 120–121, 125, 126, 130, 203, 204, 217–218, 250–251, 252, 257, 276–277, 288–290
Silvertone ✕, 136
Sinclair (music club), 200
Singing Beach, 225
Sleepy Hollow Cemetery, 258
Smith Court, 45
Society of Arts & Crafts, 230
Soldiers and Sailors Monument, 41
Somerville, 201
Somerville Theater, 201
Sonsie ✕, 141, 189
Sorellina ✕, 141
South Boston, 109, 185–188
South Bridge Boat House, 258
South End, The, 20, 97–98, 142–145, 175, 190–193, 238–240
South of Boston, 270–271, 278
South Station, 84
Specialty stores, 232–233, 237, 240, 243
Sportello ✕, 136
Sports and outdoor activities, 214–226, 258, 267
Sports Museum of New England, 50

SRV ✕, 144–145
State House, 47–48
State Street, 84
Stony Brook Reservation, 221
Subways, 23, 285–286
Summer Shack ✕, 141–142
Sunset Grill & Tap (bar), 193
Swan Boats, 90
Sweet Cheeks ✕, 145
Symbols, 13
Symphony Hall, 27, 97, 101, 207

T
Taberna de Haro ✕, 148
Taj Boston Hotel 🖳, 174
Tangierino ✕, 134
Taxes, 129, 291
Taxis, 286–287
TD Garden, 207
Ten Tables ✕, 147
Terramia Ristorante ✕, 134
Thanksgiving Parade, 23
Theater, 210–210, 265
Theme tours, 288
Thrift shops, 237, 239–240, 244
1369 Coffeehouse, 197
Tickets, 181–182
Tiger Mama ✕, 146
Time, 291
Timing the visit, 22–23, 248, 277
Tipping, 129, 291–292
Toad (bar), 196
Top of the Hub (bar), 189
Topsfield Fair, 23
Toro ✕, 145
Tory Row, 122–125
Tours, 25, 27, 28, 32, 78, 80, 83, 101, 114, 115, 120–121, 125, 126, 130, 203. 204, 217–218, 250–251, 252, 257, 276–277, 288–290
Toy stores, 240, 244
Trade ✕, 138
Train travel, 23, 250, 287
Transportation, 23, 39, 53, 67, 74, 87, 101, 114, 228, 249–250, 280–287
Trident Booksellers & Café ✕, 96, 189, 206
Trinity Church, 28, 92–93, 205, 206
Trolleys, 252, 289
Trophy Room, The (bar), 191
Troquet ✕, 142
Tsai Performance Center, 206, 208

Tufts Health Plan *10K for
Women, 223*
21st Amendment (bar), *183*
2 Phillips Street, *45*

U

U. S. Custom House, *84*
Uni ✕, *142*
Union Boat Club Boathouse, *95*
Union Oyster House ✕, *132*
Union Park, *55, 98*
Urban AdvenTours, *217–218*
USS *Cassin Young, 72*
USS *Constitution, 67, 69, 71*
USS *Constitution* Museum, *27,
71, 72*

V

Vendome Monument, *94*
Venu (dance club), *187*
Verb Hotel, The , *176*
Vilna Shul, *48*
Visitor information, *22, 115,
181, 216, 223, 252, 254, 255,*

*259, 262, 263, 266, 268,
278, 292*

W

W Boston , *171*
Walden Pond, *258*
Walk to the Sea, *27*
Walking tours, *115, 250, 289*
Wally's Café (jazz club),
191–192, 206
Warren Tavern, *67, 71, 185*
Washington Memorial Garden,
61
Waterfront, *137–138*
Wayside, The, *258*
Weather, *22*
Web sites, *292*
Westin Boston Waterfront ,
171
Westin Copley Place Boston ,
174–175
Whale watching and whaling,
272–277, 290

Whiskey Saigon (dance club),
188
Wiesner Building, *126*
William J. Devine Golf Course
at Franklin Park, *220*
Wingaersheek Beach, *267*
Woodman's of Essex ✕, *270*
Working Waterfront Festival,
23
World Music/CRASHarts (the-
ater), *202*

X

XV Beacon , *167*

Y

Yotel , *172*
Yvonne's ✕, *136*

Z

Zaftigs ✕, *148*
Zoos, *110*

PHOTO CREDITS

NOTES

NOTES

ABOUT OUR WRITERS

Megan Johnson has spent her entire life in New England, and the last fifteen years in Boston. A graduate of Simmons College, she previously worked at the Boston Herald's *Inside Track* before going freelance in 2013. She is a regular contributor to *People Magazine,* the *Boston Metro, Architectural Digest,* and a variety of other publications. A resident of East Boston, Megan swears that it's the best neighborhood in the entire city. This year, Megan tackled the Experience, Nightlife, Where to Stay, and Side Trips chapters.

Kim Foley MacKinnon is an award-winning Boston-based editor, journalist and travel writer. Her work has appeared in the *Boston Globe, AAA Horizons, Travel + Leisure, USA Today* and *U.S. News & World Report,* among others. Travel is her passion, with food a close second. She has also written and contributed to a number of guidebooks. For this edition, Kim updated all of the neighborhood chapters, as well as Sports and Outdoors and Travel Smart.

Victoria Abbott Riccardi is a food, wine, and travel writer for such publications as *Bon Appetit, Food & Wine,* and the *New York Times.* She is author of the *New York Times* 2003 Notable Book *Untangling My Chopsticks: A Culinary Sojourn in Kyoto* (Broadway) and a contributing writer for *Japanese Women Don't Get Old or Fat* (Delacorte Press); *Culinary Biographies* (Yes Press Inc.); and *The Story of Tea: A Cultural History and Drinking Guide* (Ten Speed Press). She now lives in Newton, MA, having resided in Kyoto, Japan where she studied tea kaiseki and Paris, France, where she attended Le Cordon Bleu, worked in a restaurant called Le Potiron (The Pumpkin), and sold chocolate chip cookies to homesick Americans. Victoria updated the Where to Eat and Shopping chapters of this guide.

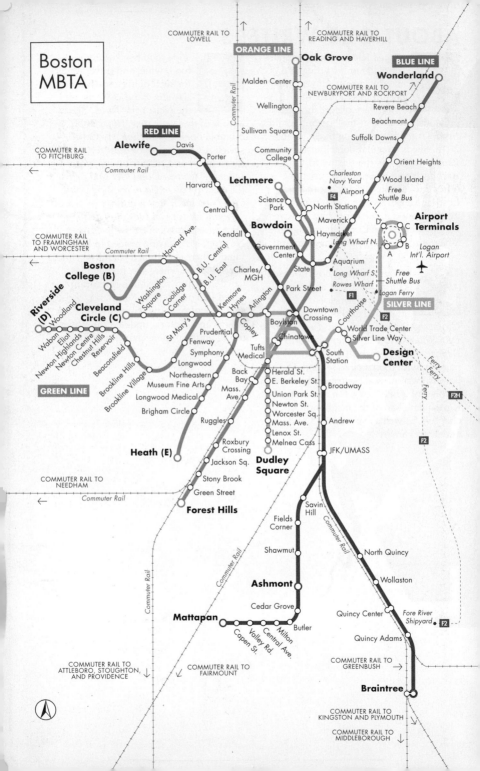